INSIDERS AND

# THE LITTMAN LIBRARY OF
# JEWISH CIVILIZATION

# INSIDERS AND OUTSIDERS

◆

## *Dilemmas of East European Jewry*

◆

*Edited by*
RICHARD I. COHEN
JONATHAN FRANKEL
*and*
STEFANI HOFFMAN

Oxford · Portland, Oregon
**The Littman Library of Jewish Civilization**
2010

The Littman Library of Jewish Civilization
Chief Executive Officer: Ludo Craddock
Managing Editor: Connie Webber

PO Box 645, Oxford OX2 OUJ, UK
www.littman.co.uk

———

Published in the United States and Canada by
The Littman Library of Jewish Civilization
c/o ISBS, 920 N.E. 58th Avenue, Suite 300
Portland, Oregon 97213-3786

A catalogue record for this book is available from the British Library

Library of Congress Cataloging-in-Publication Data
Insiders and outsiders : dilemmas of East European Jewry / edited by Richard I. Cohen,
Jonathan Frankel, and Stefani Hoffman.
p. cm.
Includes bibliographical references and index.
ISBN 978-1-906764-00-5
1. Jews—Europe, Eastern—Intellectual life.
2. Jews—Cultural assimilation—Europe, Eastern.
3. Jews—Europe, Eastern—Identity.
4. Jews—Europe, Eastern—Politics and government—20th century.
5. Jews—Lithuania—Vilnius.   6. Jews—Ukraine—Chernivtsi.
7. Europe, Eastern—Ethnic relations.
I. Cohen, Richard I.   II. Frankel, Jonathan.   III. Hoffman, Stefani.
DS135.E83I45 2010
305.892'4047—dc22                                        2009027046

Publishing co-ordinator: Janet Moth
Production: John Saunders
Design: Pete Russell, Faringdon, Oxon.
Proof-reading: Agnes Erdos
Index: Samuel Barnai
Typeset by Hope Services (Abingdon) Ltd
Printed in Great Britain on acid-free paper by the
MPG Books Group, Bodmin and King's Lynn

*To*

Ezra Mendelsohn, איש אשכולות

*from his colleagues, students, and friends*

# *Acknowledgements*

THIS book developed out of a conference on 'Insiders, Outsiders and Modern East European Jewry', held at the Hebrew University of Jerusalem in January 2006, that honoured the seminal work of Ezra Mendelsohn in this field. Mendelsohn's oeuvre draws on his vast knowledge of social, political, and cultural movements in the modern period. Skilfully situating the dilemmas of east European Jews within the changing terrain of east European and American society, he has won recognition as one of the leading historians of modern Jewish history. His dedication and integrity have earned him the respect of students and colleagues not only at the Hebrew University but also in numerous institutions where he has served as visiting professor, including the University of Michigan, the École des Hautes Études en Sciences Sociales, Paris, New York University, Columbia University, Duke University, and Boston University. It is our pleasure to dedicate this book to our esteemed colleague Ezra.

Three editors collaborated on this volume. While the editing tasks were shared by all three, Stefani Hoffman was chiefly responsible for seeing the material through from start to finish. As the editing process was coming to its end, our dear friend and colleague Jonathan Frankel passed away in May 2008. Jonathan had been involved in the original formulation of the book's contents, read and commented on all the articles, and continued to work with acuity and dedication even as his illness progressed. We deeply mourn his loss.

\*

We would like to thank various institutions and individuals for their invaluable help on this project. The Avraham Harman Institute of Contemporary Jewry and the Leonid Nevzlin Research Center for Russian and East European Jewry, both of the Hebrew University, organized and helped fund the conference. Other Hebrew University sponsors of the conference were the Conference Committee, the Faculty of Humanities, the Tamara and Saveli Grinberg Chair, and the European Forum. Additional help was provided by the Posen Foundation of Lucerne, Switzerland, and the Polish Institute. Special thanks go to Nitza Genuth, administrative director, Samuel Barnai, conference assistant, and Rachel Natan, director of finances, of the Institute of Contemporary Jewry, and to Jonathan Dekel-Chen, director, and Avital Dubinsky, administrative director, of the Nevzlin Center for their role in ensuring the successful running of the conference.

We are additionally grateful to Dalia Ofer, head of the Institute of Contemporary Jewry from 2004 to 2006 and the current head, Eli Lederhendler, for their personal support and the support of the Institute for seeing this publication through to a successful completion. Dalia Ofer also chaired the conference planning committee, which consisted of Steven Aschheim, Israel Bartal, Richard Cohen, and Jonathan Frankel.

*Jerusalem, October 2008*                                RICHARD I. COHEN
                                                         STEFANI HOFFMAN

# Contents

## PART I
## INSIDER/OUTSIDER: THE CULTURAL
## CONUNDRUM

PART II

## ACCULTURATION, ASSIMILATION, AND IDENTITY

PART III

## INCLUSION/EXCLUSION:
## SOCIETY AND POLITICS

**PART IV**

TWO CITIES AND TALES OF BELONGING

# Plates

*between pages 50 and 51*

1.  Mark Antokolsky, *Jesus before the People's Court*, 1876

2.  Maurycy Gottlieb, *Christ Preaching at Capernaum*, 1878/9

3.  Reuven Rubin, *Temptation in the Desert*, 1921

4.  Reuven Rubin, *Self-Portrait*, 1921

5.  Reuven Rubin, *The Encounter (Jesus and the Jew)*, c.1922

6.  Ephraim Moses Lilien, preparatory drawing for a postcard produced for the Fifth Zionist Congress, 1901

7.  Reuven Rubin, *Jesus and the Last Apostle*, 1922

8.  Reuven Rubin, *Meal of the Poor*, 1922

9.  Reuven Rubin, *The Madonna of the Homeless*, 1922

10. Reuven Rubin, *Self-Portrait with a Flower*, 1923(?)

11. Albrecht Dürer, *Self-Portrait as Man of Sorrows with Birch and Scourge*, 1522

12. Reuven Rubin, *The Prophet in the Desert*, 1923

13. Reuven Rubin, *First Seder in Jerusalem*, 1950

# Note on Transliteration

THE transliteration of Hebrew in this book reflects consideration of the type of book it is, in terms of its content, purpose, and readership. The system adopted therefore reflects a broad approach to transcription, rather than the narrower approaches found in the *Encyclopaedia Judaica* or other systems developed for text-based or linguistic studies. The aim has been to reflect the pronunciation prescribed for modern Hebrew, rather than the spelling or Hebrew word structure, and to do so using conventions that are generally familiar to the English-speaking reader.

In accordance with this approach, no attempt is made to indicate the distinctions between *alef* and *ayin*, *tet* and *taf*, *kaf* and *kuf*, *sin* and *samekh*, since these are not relevant to pronunciation; likewise, the *dagesh* is not indicated except where it affects pronunciation. Following the principle of using conventions familiar to the majority of readers, however, transcriptions that are well established have been retained even when they are not fully consistent with the transliteration system adopted. On similar grounds, the *tsadi* is rendered by 'tz' in such familiar words as barmitzvah. Likewise, the distinction between *ḥet* and *khaf* has been retained, using *ḥ* for the former and *kh* for the latter; the associated forms are generally familiar to readers, even if the distinction is not actually borne out in pronunciation, and for the same reason the final *heh* is indicated too. As in Hebrew, no capital letters are used, except that an initial capital has been retained in transliterating titles of published works (for example, *Shulḥan arukh*).

Since no distinction is made between *alef* and *ayin*, they are indicated by an apostrophe only in intervocalic positions where a failure to do so could lead an English-speaking reader to pronounce the vowel-cluster as a diphthong—as, for example, in *ha'ir*—or otherwise mispronounce the word.

The *sheva na* is indicated by an *e*—*perikat ol*, *reshut*—except, again, when established convention dictates otherwise.

The *yod* is represented by *i* when it occurs as a vowel (*bereshit*), by *y* when it occurs as a consonant (*yesodot*), and by *yi* when it occurs as both (*yisra'el*). Names have generally been left in their familiar forms, even when this is inconsistent with the overall system.

# REFLECTIONS ON INSIDERS AND OUTSIDERS

## A General Introduction

### STEVEN E. ASCHHEIM

THIS VOLUME is dedicated to an exploration of 'insiders' and 'outsiders' in modern east European Jewish history. Each author has probed various aspects of this theme within a wide range of social, cultural, and political contexts and local, urban, and national settings. The task of this introduction is not to summarize their work and findings—what would be the point of reading them if one knows in advance what they have to say?—but rather to provide some kind of general conceptual and historical framework for thinking about the categories themselves and rendering explicit some of the assumptions and problems regarding notions of 'insiders' and 'outsiders' that usually remain implicit in treatments of this subject.

This is no easy assignment. For notions of 'insiders' and 'outsiders', it would appear, are universal organizing categories. Societies, cultures, and individual as well as collective identities are constituted and function by dint of the fluid dynamics of inclusion and exclusion, by defining the conditions and content of 'normalcy' and 'abnormalcy', by openly or tacitly invoking conditions of belonging and non-belonging, and through the setting up of— often ironically unstable and permeable—exits and entrances.[1] For every in-group there will be those who are without, excluded. One could, conceivably, write not just the whole of Jewish, but perhaps even human, history in terms of the putative insider/outsider binary and its various refining permutations. In their different ways, anthropology and psychology—the social sciences in general—seek to provide us with maps and perspectives of these processes. Thus, an entire discipline, 'the sociology of deviance', represents an attempt to systemically capture the phenomenon. Outsiders, they tell us, are simply those groups and individuals who, for one reason or another, deviate from the normative rules that govern social and cultural systems. Their nature, given identities, and location are to be understood as standing

---

[1] The classic work by Mary Douglas, *Purity and Danger: An Analysis of Concepts of Pollution and Taboo* (London, 1966), remains one of the most insightful general approaches to the question.

in dialectical relationship to, and tension with, these power structures and meaning-endowing norms.

There are many such kinds of theories, but their very generality does not provide much succour for historians whose interests inevitably focus upon the context-bound nature of phenomena and the dynamics and nuances of particular cases and situations. To be sure, general questions and problems still arise. Who defines 'insiders' and 'outsiders' and how are these constituted? Are 'modern' variants to be differentiated from their pre-modern predecessors? Do we employ objective and structural or subjective and psychological criteria of 'outsiderdom' or some combination of both? Viewed from the perspective of the 'insider', historically outsiders have typically been despised and stigmatized (which, in turn, may often have strengthened their internal cohesiveness) but they may also be relatively ignored or tolerated and, in some cases, even valorized. Indeed, in our own times, as William Ian Miller has pointed out, we have witnessed a shift in emotional economy, resulting in a certain ambiguity towards outsiders. A widening of empathic capacities, not merely in traditional terms of class and rank, is being extended to groups of outsiders—racial, ethnic, the mentally and physically handicapped, and so on—in which the classical indifference, fear, contempt, or mistrust of outsiders becomes mingled with a certain liberal guilt, anxiety, and self-doubt.[2] This certainly would apply to the most literal and visible 'outsiders' of our time—the homeless.

There is a similarly wide spectrum regarding the possible personal and collective self-image of outsiders themselves. One may variously attempt to eradicate, blur, minimize, or simply put up with one's outsider status and identity. Yet at times it may be affirmed and become a matter of positive choice (this will certainly be true in different gradations and inflections when considering the modern Jewish case). To be sure, that condition, its freedom of manoeuvre and action, and its self-image will also depend upon the ways in which the normative 'inside' defines it. There are too many variations and interactions to allow any simple or clear-cut a priori answers.

But we are already running ahead of ourselves. Given the ubiquitous nature of the insider/outsider divide, when it comes to thinking about the Jewish outsider we need to establish a distinction between life in traditional or feudal corporate society and more centralized modern states. In the former, Jews as a self-defined exilic community were clearly 'outside' the normative and religious structures of Christian society. Jews were not Christians, and both parties elaborated a series of rituals and social practices that ensured separation and prevented mixing. To be sure, this does not mean that Jews were entirely cut off from wider contexts—they were,

---

[2] See William Ian Miller, *The Anatomy of Disgust* (Cambridge, Mass., 1997), 235.

indeed, engaged in various aspects of economic and political life and, like the Jews of Ashkenaz, even forged identities that ensued from, and were identified with, their particular local environments. For all that, life lived within one's own identificatory framework provided a self-definitional security and value sustenance absent from later times. Under those conditions, there could be no consciousness of being an 'outsider' in the modern sense. Being Jewish was a datum that simply constituted the given in everyday life (unless one converted into the Christian or Muslim religious community).

This was a context that allowed for little or no intermediate space: only exceedingly exceptional individuals, such as Baruch Spinoza, removed themselves from identification with any of these communities. But in the modern secular world apostasy hardly represents the touchstone of being an outsider. In the new order of centralized (and, later, nationalized) states—characterized increasingly by principles of individual (rather than corporate) membership, aspirations to equal rights and citizenship, and ever greater normative and cultural homogeneity—the production, structure, and very meaning of outsiderdom undergoes transformation. The novel possibility of full societal membership renders 'outsiderdom' itself a structurally problematic datum of consciousness, psychologized and questioned, a matter of potential identity strain and discomfort. At the same time it can also become dialectically transfigured into a source and space of separate, positive self-assertion and pride.

Minorities, as Shulamit Volkov has perceptively pointed out, did not exist in feudal society and the world of estates. The notion of minorities, of numerical relevance and superiority, could emerge only in social structures characterized by categories of, and aspirations to, unity and equality. Volkov defines minorities thus: 'a group permanently residing within a more or less homogenous society, normally rendered distinct by more than one objective characteristic, possessing a particular consciousness of itself as a group and ideologically committed to full equality and integration without abandoning its uniqueness'.[3] This definition is astute but requires qualification. It may apply more precisely to Jewish than to some other modern minorities. Thus it is not certain that Europe's Roma and Sinti have, either historically or contemporaneously, aspired to integration, nor does it apply to religious groups such as the Amish in the United States.

What is certain, however, is that modern 'outsiderdom' cannot be grasped outside this emergent majority/minority context. Yet, both conceptually and socio-psychologically, we need to distinguish between the two. Minorities possess, and are defined by, fairly clear-cut objective characteristics. 'Outsiderdom' is above all marked by its subjective, existential, and

---

[3] See Shulamit Volkov, 'Excursus on Minorities in the Nation-State', in her *Germans, Jews, and Antisemites: Trials in Emancipation* (New York, 2006), ch. 8.

psychological dimensions. *This is because all the variations of self-consciousness, the dilemmas, discontents, and achievements of the modern (Jewish or non-Jewish) outsider arise out of the (possibly frustrated) potential for integration, the dynamics of partial connectedness, and a degree of presumed entitlement quite absent from traditional societies.*

Like Simmel's stranger, the 'outsider' is not entirely alien and external, not totally foreign, as, say, the barbarians were to the Greeks. In order to qualify as 'outsiders' there must, in some way, be a salient connection to the 'inside'. The outsider, in this sense, possesses a certain relevance, and can make claims that—no matter how disputed—have a certain standing. There are no centres without margins, insides without outsides; the inside is constituted by constructing the outside.[4] But this is a relationship that is always fluid, and in modern (and certainly postmodern) societies all 'essentialized' centres and identities come increasingly under question.[5] For, as David Rechter argues in his contribution to this volume in Chapter 12 (although he refers to the case of Czernowitz, his observation has a more general application):

the insider/outsider dualism proves to be something of a false dichotomy, perhaps better conceived, as noted at the outset, as two shifting poles of a continuum. An insider/outsider framework implies an at least somewhat stable centre around which an individual or a collective situates itself. . . . But if the centre itself shifts, how to fix its boundaries? As a consequence, determining the relative status and meaning of insider/outsider is fraught with difficulty, and these sometimes useful descriptors should be applied selectively and with due caution.

This permeability will obviously affect the subjective psychodynamics of modern Jewish outsiderdom, whose self-definitions cover a wide and dynamic spectrum of positions, ranging from the extreme of Benjamin Disraeli, who flaunted his outsider, 'exotic' Jewish origins as a mark of superiority, to Otto Weininger's tortured ruminations on Jewish being. Dilemmas of personal and collective self-constitution will be newly defined and heightened when boundaries are most fluid and blurred. This, paradoxically, may apply not only to the (more familiar) situations where invisible barriers to integration still operate and where the power play of insider/outsider dynamics creates any number of tensions, ambiguities, and misunderstandings. (Leon Volovici's account in Chapter 4 of the Jewish writer

[4] This is a recognition that is shared both by formal classical sociology and, in different form, by contemporary deconstruction. As Edward Shils formulates it: 'Society has a center. There is a central zone in the structure of society. . . . Membership . . . is constituted by relationship to this central zone.' See his 'Center and Periphery', in *Center and Periphery: Essays in Microsociology* (Chicago, 1975), 3.

[5] For a provocative discussion of these issues in general, and with regard to matters Jewish in particular, see Michael P. Steinberg's impassioned plea against essentializing conceptions in his *Judaism Musical and Unmusical* (Chicago, 2007).

Mihail Sebastian (whose real name was Iosef Hechter) and his relationship with his antisemitic Romanian mentor Nae Ionescu constitutes a fine example of this.) But discomfort may apply, too, when one's particularity is threatened by too 'successful' an absorption, too much 'assimilation'. Many west European and American Jews regard themselves as trapped within a kind of double bind: the integrative ease that comes with the narrative of an inclusive 'Judaeo-Christian' civilization—and the concern of being swallowed by it. It would not be an exaggeration to say that the balance between full integration ('insiderdom') and the maintenance of a distinctive, separate identity ('outsiderdom') is an exceedingly fine one and that, ironically, Jews were, and still are, not entirely comfortable with either condition.[6] This may account for the fact that, as David Biale has observed, Jews possess a consciousness of 'occupying an anomalous status. They represent the boundary case whose very lack of belonging to a recognizable category creates a sense of unease.'[7]

In related fashion, much of the elaborate and ambivalent discourse—in praise, condemnation, and fear—surrounding the modern outsider is tied to divergent perceptions of the simultaneously putatively emancipatory, dissolutive, and corrupting influences of that most powerful modernizing and shared institution: the city. At the same time as cities are portrayed as the source of newfound opportunity, integration, and freedom for previously disenfranchised groups, a persistent counternarrative holds such urban centres as precisely the breeding grounds of corruption, internal subversion, decadence, crime, and degeneration, places of refuge and succour to any number of invidious outsiders: criminals, radicals, homosexuals, Jews, and so on.

All these themes converge in George L. Mosse's suggestive thesis as to the connection between the making of the modern outsider and the overall development of middle-class society and what he calls its accompanying 'bourgeois morality'. In this schema, not just Jews but also all purported outsiders are endowed with similar negative characteristics, stereotyped as antithetical to middle-class moral, aesthetic, sexual, and economic criteria of 'respectability' and 'normality'. The 'normal' (and ideal) bourgeois male is held to be manly, self-controlled, honest, healthy, clean, and handsome; outsiders are abnormal, effeminate, nervous, sickly, wily, dirty, and ugly. Such constructions of 'normality' and 'abnormality', the fundamental yardsticks of respectability, act essentially as mechanisms of social control, the means by which all can be assigned their designated place: normal and abnormal, healthy and sick, rooted and restless, native and foreigner, the productive and the profligate.

---

[6] For an interesting analysis of this tension see Rael Meyerowitz, *Transferring to America: Jewish Interpretations of American Dreams* (Albany, NY, 1995), esp. 262–3.

[7] See the introduction to David Biale, Michael Galchinsky, and Susan Heschel (eds.), *Insider/Outsider: American Jews and Multiculturalism* (Berkeley, 1998), 5.

Most radically, Mosse has argued that, in this sense, Nazism represents the most extreme expression of bourgeois morality: its classical victims— Gypsies, homosexuals, asocials, the mentally and physically handicapped— correspond exactly with constructions of the bourgeois 'outsider'.[8] But what of Nazism's ultimate victim, the Jew? For, after all, within nineteenth- and twentieth-century western and central Europe, Jews had resolutely under-gone a process of cultural, political, and social embourgeoisement; their aspirations, comportment, and self-definition were decidedly bourgeois. In order to deal with this dilemma, Mosse demonstrates the manifold ways in which antisemites and those opposed to Jewish emancipation and integra-tion determinedly read the Jews out of the middle class by repeatedly attributing to them the 'non-bourgeois' traits of typical outsiders. Jews were effeminate, nervous, peripatetic, sickly, schemingly parasitic, and so on.

Mosse's insights, linking the nature and content of modern 'outsiderdom' to the specific dynamics of bourgeois morality, are intriguing. Moreover, his insistence that all outsiders, non-Jews as well as Jews, are endowed with similar characteristics provides us with a salutary reminder that post-emancipation Jewish history inevitably operates within wider, rather than self-enclosed, contexts. Yet, for the purposes of this volume, the applicability of his ideas may be somewhat limited. They do not really provide space for an autonomous (or relatively autonomous) consciousness; in this view the 'outsider' is almost exclusively the Sartrean creation of normative fears and prejudices. Nor does this perspective allow us to follow the contestational dynamics that determine who shall be 'insiders' and 'outsiders' *within* Jewish communities themselves. Perhaps most importantly, Mosse's work applies most directly to developments centred around western and central Europe rather than the somewhat different east European Jewish experience that is the subject of this volume. To be sure, the 'east'/'west' divide is both problem-atic and to some extent artificial, yet in overall terms more traditional, pre-bourgeois and pre-emancipation patterns prevailed on the eastern side of the divide—even if we grant that Mosse's model understates a continuing, specifically Christian, anti-Judaic animus running through emergent secular bourgeois society, and even if we grant that within various areas of late nine-teenth- and early twentieth-century eastern Europe 'modern' bourgeois pat-terns of integration and dilemmas of identity became increasingly apparent.

These more general theories apart, there is a vast literature on intellectu-als and their creative role as outsiders (who sometimes are able to influence, and even penetrate, the centre). This is the burden of Peter Gay's analysis of the greatness, anxiety, and excitement of Weimar culture: 'the creation of outsiders, propelled by history into the inside, for a short, dizzying, fragile

---

[8] See especially George Mosse, *Nationalism and Sexuality: Respectability and Abnormal Sexuality in Modern Europe* (New York, 1985).

moment'.[9] Gay's portrait did not single out Jews in his rather dazzling list of intellectuals and artists. But, clearly, special attention has been given to estranged Jewish intellectuals. As double social 'outsiders' they are presumed to possess a kind of privileged perspective unavailable to those locked into the conventional prejudices and presuppositions of the inside.[10] Paul Mendes-Flohr has portrayed the modern Jewish intellectual as a cultural and cognitive insider but a social outsider;[11] Georg Simmel's 'stranger' has very similar characteristics. The stranger 'is an element of the group itself. His position as a full-fledged member involves both being outside it and confronting it' (he cites the history of European Jews as the classical example of this type, and in many ways his portrait may be autobiographical).[12] While, typically, most of these analyses refer to the central European experience,[13] they clearly have a far more general application.

Thus, most famously, Isaac Deutscher (born in Chrzanów, Poland) includes the Polish-born Rosa Luxemburg and Russian Leon Trotsky in his list of admired 'non-Jewish Jews' (together with Baruch Spinoza, Heinrich Heine, Karl Marx, and Sigmund Freud). 'You may, if you wish to', he writes,

place them within a Jewish tradition. They all went beyond the boundaries of Jewry. They all found Jewry too narrow, too archaic, and too constricting. They all looked for ideals and fulfillment beyond it, and they represent the sum and substance of much that is greatest in modern thought. . . . Did they have anything in common with one another? . . . in some ways they were very Jewish indeed. They had in themselves something of the quintessence of Jewish life and of the Jewish intellect. They were a priori exceptional in that as Jews they lived on the borderlines of various civilizations, religions, and national cultures. They were born and brought up on the borderlines of various epochs. Their mind matured where the most diverse cultural influences crossed and fertilized each other. They lived on the margins or in the nooks and crannies of their respective nations. Each of them was in society and yet not of it. It was this that enabled them to rise in thought

[9] Peter Gay, *Weimar Culture: The Outsider as Insider* (New York, 1970), p. xiv.

[10] Many of George Steiner's writings point in this direction. For one example, see 'A Kind of Survivor', in his *Language and Silence: Essays on Language, Literature, and the Inhuman* (New York, 1977). See, too, Isaiah Berlin's rather surprising essay, 'Jewish Slavery and Emancipation', in Alexander Manor (ed.), *The Jews and the National Question* (Tel Aviv, n.d.), 127–56.

[11] See Paul Mendes-Flohr, 'The Study of the Jewish Intellectual: A Methodological Prolegomenon', in his *Divided Passions: Jewish Intellectuals and the Experience of Modernity* (Detroit, 1991), esp. 37.

[12] 'The Stranger' appears in Kurt H. Wolff (ed.), *The Sociology of Georg Simmel* (New York, 1950), 402–8 (the quote appears on p. 402). On the Jews as the quintessential strangers, see p. 403.

[13] See, most prominently, George L. Mosse's *German Jews Beyond Judaism* (Bloomington, Ind., 1985). For a more popular treatment see Frederic V. Grunfeld, *Prophets without Honour: A Background to Freud, Kafka, Einstein and their World* (New York, 1979).

above their societies, above their nations, above their times and generations, and to strike out mentally into wide new horizons and far into the future.[14]

It is worth pointing out, parenthetically, that for those with a more positive 'internal' Jewish commitment, this question of detached estrangement is seen as neither an inevitable nor a desirable response to modernity. Leo Strauss, perhaps the most articulate expositor of this viewpoint, explicitly inveighed against one of Deutscher's models in this regard. Spinoza is upbraided for taking for granted 'the philosophic detachment or freedom from the tradition of his own people; that detachment is "unnatural", not primary, but the outcome of a liberation from the primary attachment, of an alienation, a break, a betrayal. The primary is fidelity, and the sympathy and love that go with fidelity.'[15]

In many ways this narrative—of the privileged intellectual perspective of the outsider—is a highly consolatory, self-validating point of view. 'Because I was a Jew', declared Freud, 'I found myself free from many prejudices which limited others in the employment of their intellects and as a Jew I was prepared to go into opposition and to do without the agreement of the "compact majority".'[16] This functions both as an explanation of, and a kind of triumphalist justification for, secular Jewish achievement. To be fair, this is not merely an exclusively Jewish perception. The Polish Catholic philosopher Leszek Kołakowski has put the case most eloquently:

It was only by, as it were, exiling themselves from their collective exile that they [the Jews] became exiles in the modern sense. However hard they may have tried, they failed (at least, most of them) to lose entirely their identity of old and to be unreservedly assimilated; they were looked upon as alien bodies by the indigenous tribes, and it was probably this uncertain status, the lack of a well-defined identity, which enabled them to see more and to question more than those who were satisfied with their inherited and natural sense of belonging . . . precisely because by barring to them the path to the moral and intellectual safety of the tribal life— whether French, Polish, Russian, or German—they left them in the privileged position of outsiders.[17]

In many ways this fits into a larger existentialist cult—a species of male rite of passage from painful adolescence into manhood—popular during the 1950s, in which the outsider was defined by a kind of ruthless honesty, an

---

[14]  See the essay 'The Non-Jewish Jew' in Isaac Deutscher's collection bearing the same title, *The Non-Jewish Jew and Other Essays* (London, 1968). The quote appears on pp. 26–7.

[15]  See Leo Strauss's preface to the English translation of his *Spinoza's Critique of Religion* (New York, 1965), 24.

[16]  Thus Freud to members of the Viennese B'nai B'rith, 6 May 1926, quoted in Peter Gay, *A Godless Jew: Freud, Atheism, and the Making of Psychoanalysis* (New Haven, 1987), 137.

[17]  Leszek Kołakowski, 'In Praise of Exile', in his *Modernity on Endless Trial* (Chicago, 1990), 56–7.

authenticity marked by its self-celebrating radical nonconformity. Albert Camus described his (by now classic) outsider simply as someone who refused to lie (to himself as well as to others)![18] In related fashion, the modern outsider in general, but the Jewish one in particular, is held to be above all characterized by a kind of cosmopolitan borderlessness, a scepticism concerning conventional and epistemological boundaries, a viewpoint in which all versions of essentialized and fixed identities are questioned and refused. 'Freud's view of Moses as both insider and outsider', Edward Said tells us, 'is extraordinarily interesting and challenging.' His most profound insight, stemming from his claim that the founder of Jewish identity was himself a non-European Egyptian, according to Said, posits the limits of the most tightly knit communities. For Freud, Said concludes, 'identity cannot be thought or worked through itself alone; it cannot constitute or even imagine itself without that radical originary break or flaw which will not be repressed, because Moses was Egyptian, and therefore always stood outside the identity inside which so many have stood, and suffered—and later, perhaps, even triumphed'.[19]

But there are clearly problems that arise from this notion of a privileged 'unhoused', outsider perspective (in a diasporic age of mobility and globalization, immigration, population movements, refugees, and exiles there exists a current tendency to universalize what was previously an essentially Jewish narrative). As Michael Walzer has pointed out, the achievement of critical distance and intellectual detachment should by no means be confused with the marginality of outsiders. Indeed, he argues, marginality may equally act as a thoroughly distorting factor undercutting the capacity for

[18]  Camus explicitly argued this in the 1955 afterword to his novel *L'Étranger* (*The Outsider*, or *The Stranger*). On the male aspect of this phenomenon, see Marcel Berlins, 'What is it about Albert Camus' *The Outsider* that makes it such an enduring favourite with men?', *Guardian*, 12 Apr. 2006. (I have gleaned this from <http://www.guardian.co.uk/commentisfree/2006/apr/12/books.comment>). Colin Wilson's self-indulgent 1954 work *The Outsider* was also part of this cult. James Thurber's satirical question is apt here: 'Why do you have to be a nonconformist like everybody else?'

[19]  See Edward W. Said, *Freud and the Non-European* (London, 2003). The quotes are from pp. 16 and 54 respectively. I am fully aware of the highly ideological and political charge contained in Said's book. I am using this piece agnostically and as yet another example of the ways in which Jewish intellectuality, dual outsiderdom, and a certain cosmopolitanism have been linked. In critiquing Said's advocacy of the non-Jewish Jew, a rather outraged Leon Wieseltier asks, 'then why not the non-Palestinian Palestinian?' See his piece entitled 'The Ego and the Yid', *The New Republic*, 7 Apr. 2003, p. 38. Said and Wieseltier represent diametrical opposites. The former insists upon denying and opposing 'essentialized' identity while Wieseltier writes: 'The Jews are not Europeans and they are not non-Europeans. They are Jews, an autonomous people with an autonomous history that had directed them, in different times and in different places, against their will and according to their will, toward certain peoples and away from certain peoples.' But for 'outsiders' both 'non-essentialist' *and* 'autonomist' assumptions may be problematic and their choices in practice more grey and less stark.

critical judgement (similar to the related, but opposite, danger of over-identification with the normative centres of power). 'Detachment', he writes, 'stands to the marginal and the central in exactly the same way: free of the tensions that bind the two together'.[20]

Given the peculiarly complex and fluid, and remarkably creative, inside/outside relationship of Jews to modern culture, these notions must surely possess some validity.[21] But identifying the role that their 'Jewishness' or Judaism plays in these creative moments remains an enormously subtle and complex task in which both blanket denial of its relevance (in effect, the refusal of any autonomy to the dimensions of Jewish existence) and wilful assertions of its overwhelming significance (which overlook the thick influence of the tempting blandishments and, by now, quite 'natural' internalization of cultures outside that tradition) need to be scrupulously and sceptically analysed. No wonder the definitive history of the modern Jewish intellectual has not yet been written, although, as Richard I. Cohen's essay (Chapter 1) makes clear, much of the work done by Ezra Mendelsohn serves as an excellent prolegomenon.

The field is rife with any number of temptingly attractive propositions linking modes of outsidership with Jewish intellectual insight and creativity. They are usually as problematic as they are suggestive. Take, as just one amongst many instances, the notion that modern theorists and historiographers of nationalism have typically been a species of double outsider, enunciated by Jews (not necessarily identified with Judaism) who left their formerly multinational imperial homelands and migrated into different civilizations (thus Hans Kohn, Karl Deutsch, Ernst Gellner, and Eric Hobsbawm hailed from Austro-Habsburg lands and travelled respectively to Palestine, the US, and England, while Elie Kedourie left his Iraqi birthplace and the former Ottoman empire for the British Isles). Their location on the borders of richly textured, multicultural societies at a time when national tensions were becoming increasingly apparent (and their subsequent emigration), clearly rendered them sensitive to, and critical of, the structures, constructions, inclusions, and exclusions of nationalism. These are, to be sure, telling examples (although in each case the nature and role of Jewishness would have to be somehow validated); yet one would want to be wary of too easy, self-congratulatory generalizations. One should keep in mind that none of the earlier great thinkers and theorists of nationalism, such as Herder, Renan, Michelet, Lord Acton, Fichte, and so on, or even many of its

---

[20] See Michael Walzer, *Interpretation and Social Criticism* (Cambridge, Mass., 1987), ch. 2, 'The Practice of Social Criticism', esp. 35–40.

[21] I have tried to address some of these aspects in *Beyond the Border: The German-Jewish Legacy Abroad* (Princeton, 2007), a work that could have profited from some of the more critical observations made in the present essay.

prominent contemporary theorists and historians such as Benedict Anderson, Rogers Brubaker, Adrian Hastings, John Breuilly, can be said to be 'outsiders' in any significant sense, or even Jewish.

Posed in this way, the issue now seems to be rather overworked, if not sterile, and it is one of the central achievements of Jonathan Frankel's brave piece, 'The "Non-Jewish Jews" Revisited: Solzhenitsyn and the Issue of National Guilt' (Chapter 10), that he has taken the discussion of Isaac Deutscher's secular and universalist 'non-Jewish Jews'—outsiders to both normative and Jewish society—in a new and provocative direction. In what sense, Frankel asks, can radicals such as Marx, Trotsky, and Rosa Luxemburg—who all dismissed any meaningful relationship to their Jewish origins—be regarded as Jews, part of the parameters of Jewish history? In what ways, despite everything, were they not merely self-proclaimed 'outsiders' to the Jewish world but also 'insiders'? Frankel addresses himself to the highly sensitive charge that committed Jewish communists played a central role in the horrors of the 1917 revolution, the implementation of Bolshevik rule, and the running of the Gulags. Taking up Solzhenitsyn's moral question and challenge, Frankel poses the question thus: if all the Bolsheviks, Russians and Jews alike, were outsiders to their communities, schismatics in his terms, at what point do their numbers become statistically significant? Can peoples and communities disavow their own schismatics? Was there not an obligation to remember their own progeny? Frankel's contribution sensitively and acutely engages the relevant distinctions and nuances such an obligation may or may not entail (and renders it superfluous for me to rehearse here). Invoking Karl Jaspers's important distinction between guilt and shame, his conclusions, for a Jewish historian, are remarkably frank, refreshingly unapologetic. We cannot with any degree of consistency, Frankel argues, praise the Jewish 'outsiders' whom we admire and disclaim those who may reflect poorly upon us:

Solzhenitsyn's insistence that the Jewish people cannot simply shrug off the Trotskys, Uritskys, and Yagodas as 'non-Jewish', as outsiders, is certainly persuasive. If Jews take pride in Heinrich Heine, Felix Mendelssohn, Benjamin Disraeli, and Boris Pasternak, who were Jews by birth but were baptized into the Christian faith, can it be logical—as distinct from comfortable—to disown the 'non-Jewish Jews' who as Bolsheviks participated in destroying Russia's emergent democracy in 1917; in establishing a brutal (albeit 'proletarian') dictatorship; and in provoking a ferocious civil war across the length and breadth of that vast country? [22]

If Frankel's reflections on these Jewish outsiders bring with them a measure of discomfort, Ruth R. Wisse's treatment of a different kind of outsider—

---

[22] For a sensitive philosophical and historical treatment of these questions in general see Jerzy Jedlicki, 'Heritage and Collective Responsibility', in Ian Maclean, Alan Montefiore, and Peter Winch (eds.), *The Political Responsibility of Intellectuals* (Cambridge, 1990).

one who decidedly belonged to, yet worked against, the Jewish community—
is not likely to create a greater sense of ease. Her examination, in Chapter 11,
of the Jewish *moser* or *malshin*, the informer and denunciator (the negative
counterpart of the traditional *shtadlan*, the intercessor who works on behalf of
community interests), elucidates perhaps the most morally problematic and
extreme form of internal rupture. Betrayal or treason is, by definition, a matter of insiders turning against their own (although what constitutes betrayal
or treason and who defines it will always be a matter of contestation). Wisse's
analysis of these Jewish 'defectors'—be they well-intentioned reformist
maskilim, idealists, or simply unscrupulous opportunists, extortionists—illuminates, as she puts it, not the usual corruptions of power but those of powerlessness and the temptations that accompany vulnerable minority status.

   Clearly, however, Wisse does not believe that this is purely a by-product
of the lack of sovereignty and majority status, for she argues that with the
creation of the State of Israel similar arguments continue to apply. Israel, she
insists,

is not only besieged by enemies but also subjected to the kind of delegitimization
that Christianity and Marxism, in their time, applied to Judaism and the Jewish
people. The contemporary pressure against Israel on many fronts encourages
Jewish defection and 'tale-bearing', which will probably rise in proportion to the
vehemence of the attacks . . . enemies exploit divisions for their own hostile ends,
by conscripting allies from within the polity to help destroy its democratic unity.
The Jews and Israel have never been without enemies at the gate, enemies many
times their political and demographic strength. The latitude enjoyed by Israelis in
blaming their government and one another is subject to exploitation for anti-
Jewish ends.

This is not the only, and certainly not the most central, insider/outsider
irony that Zionism has produced. The attainment of statehood, of course,
did successfully transform the Jews from a vulnerable minority into a sovereign majority, thus creating a new centre, a new 'inside'. But this also
inevitably produced its own framework and system of inclusions and exclusions. Zionism does not abolish the insider/outsider condition but inverts
and reinscribes it.[23] If the Jewish outsider now becomes the insider, this
entails a dual act of both Jewish diasporic and Palestinian displacement and
the creation of a new set of outsiders.

---

[23] Hannah Arendt put it thus: 'After the war it turned out that the Jewish Question, which
was considered the only insoluble one, was indeed solved—namely, by means of a colonized
and then conquered territory—but this solved neither the problem of the minorities nor the
stateless. On the contrary, like virtually all other events of our century, the solution of
the Jewish question merely produced a new category of refugees, the Arabs, thereby increasing the number of the stateless and rightless by another 700,000 to 800,000 people.' See
Arendt, *The Origins of Totalitarianism* (Cleveland, 1958), 290.

This issue is reflected in Zvi Jagendorf's nuanced contribution to this volume (Chapter 2), which acutely demonstrates how both these themes respectively permeate the poetry of Itzik Manger and Avot Yeshurun (Yehiel Perlmutter). In different ways, their work confronts, and is haunted by, the refugee status of both Jews and Palestinians and their yearnings for 'home'— and the impossibilities and ironies implicit in that search. To be sure, Zionism for Itzik Manger was never really an option or a goal. Indeed, as Jagendorf demonstrates, in his world outsidership is a kind of existential given, home as much a burden as a comfort, an unresolved longing shared by all uprooted people. Manger, that 'chameleon poet' working both inside and outside Jewish nostalgia, ultimately does find home in Canaan, but it is demystified, 'just dry earth as we are all'.

For Avot Yeshurun, who came to find home in Palestine, the pain of abandoning his parents' house in Poland and the discovery that Palestine was a 'home' to another people became thoroughly intertwined. 'Yeshurun', Jagendorf writes,

believed he was coming home when he was ferried off the boat at Bat Galim in 1925 by an Arab porter. Home, for this young man from Przedmieście/Krasnystaw in Poland, was Erets Yisrael. But throughout his work he is haunted by the guilt of being an accomplice in the ruin of homes, first that of his parents in the shtetl and then the homes of the Palestinian Arabs, whose villages and traditional way of life seemed to him to mirror his parents' world. This guilt constitutes the burden of much of his poetry.

The fact that Yeshurun uses the Arabic word *ḥirbet* (an abandoned ruined house) in his advocacy of the instability of language, Jagendorf tells us, is a key to 'a man torn between languages, places, and ruins. His language, he is telling us, should be read as evidence of ghostly presences that we might hurry to ignore. The ruin demands to be examined, it blurs distinctions between inside and outside, it reveals traces of lives lived, homes abandoned, and languages once spoken.'

Obviously, Zionism represents a diametrically different paradigm from, indeed a quite deliberate revolt against, the more general, modern 'exilic' experience of Jewish outsiderdom. The essays in this volume cover both dimensions of that history and probe the manifold collective and personal permutations of the insider/outsider conundrum and the dilemmas (and attempted resolutions) of inclusion and exclusion in the context of modern east European Jewish history. There is a clear unity of theme here but also an obvious and refreshing multiplicity of contexts, approaches, and attitudes. To be sure, the individual and collective mediations between universality and particularity, the constitution, fluidity, interconnections, reinforcements, blurrings, and erasures of identities, and the formation, contestation, breakdown, and reconfiguration of physical, mental, social, and geographical borders, of belonging and non-belonging are general human issues. They do, however, acquire a special sharpness and urgency within Jewish history in both its internal dimensions and its relations with the wider world. Many of these tensions, paradoxes, and ironies characterize and animate Ezra Mendelsohn's remarkably creative oeuvre. I can think of no more fitting celebration of his work.

# PART I

# INSIDER/OUTSIDER
## *The Cultural Conundrum*

# ONE

# THE PROJECT OF JEWISH CULTURE AND ITS BOUNDARIES
## *Insiders and Outsiders*

### RICHARD I. COHEN

JEWISH CULTURAL HISTORY, an enigmatic category, seems to be having a moment of glory, valiantly asserting its existence against more sacred and iconic historiographical traditions. Music, theatre, literature, and the visual arts are engaging historians (and others) for their own sake or as part and parcel of an integrative approach to the study of history. Inevitably this turn brings into focus fundamental issues, and most specifically the question of how to situate works with a Jewish theme, apparent or hidden. Should the boundaries enclosing 'Jewish culture' be narrowly or broadly drawn? A spate of recently published books and articles with at least some ostensible claim to fall within these boundaries take up such varied themes as idolatry, iconoclasm, art criticism and collecting, museology, monuments, synagogue architecture, and ceremonies, ranging from antiquity to the present, while monographs and exhibitions have featured artists of Jewish origin—Marc Chagall, Maurycy Gottlieb, R. B. Kitaj, Jozef Israëls, Ephraim Moses Lilien, Moritz Oppenheim, Ben Shahn, Arthur Szyk, and others. Authored by anthropologists, art historians, philosophers, historians, literary scholars, and others, these works emerge from diverse concerns and premises, illuminating the attraction visual culture presently exerts and the convergence of disciplines.[1]

Profiting from this upsurge of interest, and somewhat responsible for it, Jewish museums have proliferated in the last two decades, becoming an integral part of the public space in many European and American cities, portraying historical developments, culture, and religion, and often playing up the 'contribution of Jewish artists to civilization'. Clearly, the museological tendency has heightened the notion that Jewish visual culture is a formative part of Jewish life, and it has often staked a claim, consciously or unconsciously,

[1] See Barbara Kirshenblatt-Gimblett and Jonathan Karp (eds.), *The Art of Being Jewish in Modern Times* (Philadelphia, 2007), introduction and the extensive biographical references.

that works whose creators were of Jewish origin necessarily reflected in some form or fashion an expression of their Jewishness. (Various exhibitions of artists of Jewish origin, from those held at the beginning of the twentieth century to those in recent years, are indicative of such an orientation.) Indeed, from its inception Jewish museology has tended to underplay the tension between insider and outsider, so central to the core of art by minority artists, in order to highlight the aesthetic achievements of the Jews.

Francis Haskell's book *History and its Images* provides a thought-provoking framework for any reflections on this nexus and the cultural currents that shaped the production of Jewish art. Haskell, a distinguished English art historian, goes to great lengths to show that over several centuries art critics have made inadequate efforts to see works of art as a reflection of a period or a state of mind. Reading Haskell's critique of some of the giants of the Western historical tradition such as Gibbon, Michelet, Burckhardt, and Huizinga is a humbling experience for anyone attempting to bridge the worlds of art and society. Applying exacting criteria, he wisely cautions against leaps of interpretation—for example, intimating that a particular work of art is inspired by a prophetic genius—and he recommends a much less arbitrary approach that gives due credit and concern to the specific 'language' of art, 'which can be understood only by those who seek to fathom its varying purposes, conventions, styles and techniques'.[2] His more positivistic approach to art history stands at loggerheads with such cultural historians as Peter Burke, Carlo Ginzburg, Simon Schama, and Theodor Rabb, to name but a few, who, while sharing some of Haskell's misgivings and cautions, continue to explore the artistic terrain with much imagination. Their efforts have been supplemented by new schools of cultural studies and art history that have questioned the basic premises of formerly accepted disciplinary criteria.

This essay will look at the way a distinguished scholar of Jewish history, Ezra Mendelsohn, has incorporated visual culture and other forms of cultural creativity into his oeuvre and how he has dealt with the challenges and pitfalls of interdisciplinary research that Haskell paraded before the non-art historian. A historian of east European Jewry, Mendelsohn was attracted from the outset of his career to the political struggles of Jews in Russia and Poland in the late nineteenth and the twentieth centuries. He was particularly concerned with the ways in which Jews organized themselves in a multinational situation and how they constructed their identity vis-à-vis the state and other minorities in times of dramatic change. In these works the tension between insiders and outsiders was a central factor in his understanding of politics and society. The same is true of the way he has shaped cultural history.

---

[2] Francis Haskell, *History and its Images: Art and the Interpretation of the Past* (New Haven, 1993), 8–9.

Even in his political studies, Mendelsohn has been sensitive to the way politics and culture overlap. Already in his first monograph, *Class Struggle in the Pale*,[3] he explored the efforts of the Jewish labour movement in its earliest years (until the revolution of 1905) to expand the literature available to workers in Yiddish and noted the crucial role that illegal and legal libraries played in disseminating general knowledge and literature. In this book, Mendelsohn examined the cultural efforts initiated by the workers' movement to mobilize support for the cause.

Several years later, when he embarked on his remarkable comparative study, *The Jews of East Central Europe between the World Wars*,[4] Mendelsohn provided an overview of the cultural developments in each country of the region, usually in an astute comparative manner, to sharpen the question why (and how) minority Jewish culture flourished better in some political contexts than in others. He shows how political developments contributed to the cultural choices Jews adopted. Recognizing the crucial importance of their minority status in these countries, he is constantly aware of the wider comparative context, taking into account other minority groups in each country or, looking across borders, other Jews. In the section devoted to aspects of Jewish cultural life, based on his seminal work *Zionism in Poland*,[5] Mendelsohn remarks: 'Moreover, the unification of Congress Poland with Galicia and the eastern borderlands, while causing serious problems for Jewish politics, was a blessing for Jewish culture. Indeed, the role of Litvaks in Yiddish cultural life in the capital was so great as to cause some grumbling in Polish Jewish circles with regard to the "foreign invasion" from the Lithuanian-Belorussian lands.'[6]

Having established the political context, Mendelsohn then proceeds to highlight the role played by the press, theatre, literature, and education. Alluding to prominent Jewish creative writers working in Polish in the interwar period, he concludes with a surprising, but not atypical, remark: 'The presence of a small but important Polish Jewish cultural elite demonstrates the heterogeneous character of Polish Jewry and belies any meaningful comparison with other oppressed groups such as the American blacks, whose contribution to the high culture of the majority was much less striking.'[7] Years later, he would cite American blacks' success as performers of high musical culture as an example of how minorities can become 'insiders' via the world of music. Mendelsohn assimilates into the narrative, here and in many other instances, his deep personal interest in and concern with the

---

[3] Ezra Mendelsohn, *Class Struggle in the Pale: The Formative Years of the Jewish Workers' Movement in Tsarist Russia* (Cambridge, 1970).

[4] Ezra Mendelsohn, *The Jews of East Central Europe between the World Wars* (Bloomington, Ind., 1983).

[5] Ezra Mendelsohn, *Zionism in Poland: The Formative Years, 1915–1926* (New Haven, 1981).

[6] *The Jews of East Central Europe*, 63.        [7] Ibid. 68.

evolution of American blacks, part of his personal background and rearing in a strongly leftist political milieu and his historical sensitivity to how other minorities have fared in different countries.[8]

The constant interplay of the historian who on the one hand relishes comparative analysis while on the other hand penetrating deeply into the circumstances of Jewish life prevents Jewish history from being either marginalized or reified. The minority paradigm—the insider/outsider predicament—is used to subtly enlarge while also sharply distinguishing the particular situation in which the Jews functioned.

Mendelsohn never fails to situate the particular cultural development within its historical context—be it Latvian Jewish culture in the inter-war period, the music of the nineteenth-century Viennese cantor Solomon Sulzer and of other cantors from the period, the writings of the Galician author Joseph Roth, or, of course, the art of Maurycy Gottlieb. Unravelling the context in all its ramifications—cultural, political, sociological, religious, or psychological, or a combination of them—becomes a central process in Mendelsohn's method of interpreting and understanding the evolution of the Jewish minority's cultural development, and in treating specific works of art and literature. Thus, as he wrote of the dearth of Jewish literary creativity in Lithuania between the two world wars:

Interwar Lithuania, however, cut off as it was from the Polish kresy [eastern bor-derlands] and from the Soviet Union, the home of a poor, small, and isolated Jewish community, was not an important center of Jewish literature or theater. The major Jewish writers of the interwar years were attracted to the great Jewish communities of Poland, the Soviet Union, and, to a lesser extent, Romania.[9]

Does Mendelsohn imply that cultural creativity is *determined* by the context? That would be stretching the point; but in his *On Modern Jewish Politics* he does argue that certain contexts are more amenable to Jewish cultural creativity than others as they enable the minority status of Jews to emerge more clearly.[10]

Had Mendelsohn been invited to participate in the *Representations* sympo-sium of 1985 on 'Art or Society: Must We Choose?', where historians and art historians were asked to respond, I assume that he would have opted for a different direction than that of the editor, Svetlana Alpers, the art historian, who claimed that she turns first to consider visual creativity before bringing social-cultural evidence to bear. Mendelsohn would probably have main-tained that his analysis of various cultural phenomena originated from his understanding of the social and political situation from which they emerged.

---

[8] These tendencies are also apparent from various volumes that he edited: see *Jews and Other Ethnic Groups in a Multi-Ethnic World* (= *Studies in Contemporary Jewry*, 3) (1987) and *Essential Papers on Jews and the Left* (New York, 1997).

[9] *The Jews of East Central Europe*, 233.

[10] Ezra Mendelsohn, *On Modern Jewish Politics* (Oxford, 1993).

That is, he had already made a choice—his understanding of society significantly determined his interpretation of cultural developments. He and others have argued that the development of ever new political and cultural currents has complicated the implications of identity, making the essentialist approach adopted by Martin Buber in the early years of the twentieth century and often pursued by Jewish museums untenable. They often made a statement about Jewish creativity, in some instances as a response to accepted antisemitic arguments like those of Richard Wagner, and believed that 'Jewish artists' necessarily expressed in their oeuvre aspects of their Jewishness. Mendelsohn rejects this approach categorically.

In trying to distinguish the social and cultural processes in artistic work, Mendelsohn would side, however, with two of Haskell's central arguments—the need to relinquish the fallacies that historians and art historians share the same approach and that they share the same research orientation. The premise of a cultural historian such as Mendelsohn is that the terrain of 'Jewish culture' changed dramatically in the nineteenth and twentieth centuries through the Jews' encounter with wider political and social developments, and that those currents, along with other biographical and artistic developments, shaped the world of the artistic creator. Inevitably an enquiry born of this approach will overstep (to some extent) the boundary Haskell established with regard to a specific 'language' of art, 'which can be understood only by those who seek to fathom its varying purposes, conventions, styles and techniques'.[11]

But, as intimated above, context has another facet in Mendelsohn's writings. It looms as an important safeguard against parading Jewish essentialism or uniqueness, although *malgré lui* they are not absent even from his writings—for with all his attentiveness and attraction to the universal mode, he is profoundly bound to a Jewish Zionist vision. However, when he identifies the 'uniqueness' of a historiographical claim, he pounces on it with little patience. For it is too simple, or, as he wrote of another author, 'downright silly', to attribute *carte blanche* Jewish characteristics to an acculturated figure of Jewish origin before the nature of that person's belonging and attachment to a Jewish context (what Mendelsohn calls in one instance 'Jewish layers', and in others 'Jewish subplots' or 'angles') is clearly determined. Quoting the old Yiddish saying that may have a medieval precursor, 'As the gentiles go, so go the Jews', he argues that Jews are no different from others, and the forces that influenced non-Jews influenced Jews no less. He thus derides those who fall back into the non-contextual perspective and resort to a discourse about the 'Jewish contribution to civilization'—a concept that grew by leaps and bounds during the twentieth century, fostered greatly by the apologetic drive to reject antisemitic claims to the contrary. This discourse

[11] Haskell, *History and its Images*, 9–10.

has produced a myriad of books, encyclopedias, and compendia that have an overriding concern: to celebrate Jewish creativity in a variety of professions, from science to sports.[12]

Mendelsohn constantly bewails this uncritical approach (or to put it in his more vivid language, these 'ridiculous practices') and warns of its pitfalls and handicaps. Modern Jewish history cannot avoid the unclear zones of identity and belonging', the more ambiguous terrain of cultural creativity, and it needs to find the appropriate balance between the nature of the artist's creativity and the question of the extent, if any, of the Jewish influence on his or her output. In this spirit, and recognizing that many Jews in modern times, in both the East and the West, have assertively disassociated or disconnected themselves from their Jewish origins, Mendelsohn argued in a noteworthy essay, 'Should We Take Notice of Berthe Weil?', for an inclusive approach to Jewish history.[13] Such an effort would entail treating, for example, Felix Mendelssohn-Bartholdy's life (or, for that matter, the twentieth-century artists Louis Lozowick (1892–1973) or William Gropper (1897–1977)) as an integral part of Jewish history, while cautioning against misinterpreting their work by simply classifying them as 'Jewish music' (in the way certain critics would like to see Mendelssohn, Meyerbeer, or Anton Rubinstein) or as 'Jewish art'. Defining boundaries demands methodological subtlety that can be validated only in the context of a serious exploration of the individual's belonging and attachment that allows for contradictory currents in his or her behaviour and life's work.

In the last two decades, cultural allusions, which had appeared in all of Mendelsohn's major studies in the 1970s and 1980s, invariably attracting and surprising with their literary, musical, and artistic references, have moved to the foreground of his research. The historian thus treats 'artists of Jewish origin' from eastern Europe and America as no different from political activists, for example. They, too, lived in a complex multinational setting, and their life predicaments and their attraction/accommodation to or rejection/dissociation from their Jewish roots figure prominently in Mendelsohn's interpretation of their oeuvre. The artists' lives and works need to be contextualized no less than those of non-cultural figures and movements. For even as the artists maintained different levels of engagement with Jewish culture and civilization, their work was seldom grounded within that thematic realm alone and was clearly in dialogue in one manner or another with artistic styles and trends, and with languages and cultural phenomena, in the surrounding culture, thus inevitably complicating the definition of a 'Jewish artist'.

[12] See Jeremy Cohen and Richard I. Cohen (eds.), *Jewish Contribution to Civilization: Reassessing an Idea* (Oxford, 2008).
[13] Ezra Mendelsohn, 'Should We Take Notice of Berthe Weil? Reflections on the Domain of Jewish History', *Jewish Social Studies*, NS 1/1 (1994), 22–39.

Mendelsohn introduced this important yardstick and understanding in his article on the Jewish presence in nineteenth-century music; in his work on the theme of universalism among Jewish artists; in his enquiry into left-wing Jewish artists in America; in his many book reviews on cultural themes; and, of course, in his essays on Gottlieb and ultimately in *Painting a People*. The pattern of these cultural-historical contributions emerged in Mendelsohn's study, with Milly Heyd, of the art of the Soyer brothers, where outsiders and insiders converged dramatically.[14]

Though Raphael, Moses, and Isaac Soyer adamantly rejected being identified as 'Jewish artists', the in-depth study of their background uncovered profound traces of the 'Jewish context' of their art and the ways in which it informed the interpretation of their work. Mendelsohn and Heyd vividly evoke the trials and tribulations of Jewish working-class immigrants in the 1930s, the brothers' active engagement in left-wing politics, their concern for the plight of American blacks, and, in the case of Raphael Soyer, his complex relationship with his father. Scrutinizing the interplay between the art and its historical and artistic context enables us, through Mendelsohn and Heyd's interpretation, to arrive at a singular view of Jewish acculturation in America and the cultural problematics of the immigration process.[15] The Soyers' art becomes integrated into the 'domain' of Jewish history, regardless of whether Raphael should be categorized as a Jewish, American, or east European artist.

For Mendelsohn this was also a moment of personal reflection. The Soyers were his uncles, some of the illustrations in the article are in his possession, and the circle of east European immigrants in New York with strong left-wing political leanings was his family setting. Traces of this vibrant immigrant context also appeared in sections of *On Modern Jewish Politics*, another work with a strong personal angle to it, and later in Mendelsohn's study of left-wing Jewish artists and communism in inter-war America.[16]

In the latter study one sees the attempt to integrate a school of artists into the canon of Jewish history, not as clearly self-declared Jews, but as artists of Jewish origin whose work is informed by different agendas, or 'subplots'. By unveiling them Mendelsohn asserts that artists such as Gropper and Lozowick had made, in some ways, a 'Jewish choice' by throwing in their lot with the universal visions of communism. Turning again to Jews on the margins of American society and Jewish concerns, engaged in universalistic

[14] Milly Heyd and Ezra Mendelsohn, '"Jewish" Art? The Case of the Soyer Brothers', *Jewish Art*, 19–20 (1993–4), 194–211.

[15] For a recent full-length study of Raphael Soyer, see Samantha Baskind, *Raphael Soyer and the Search for Modern Jewish Art* (Chapel Hill, NC, 2004).

[16] Ezra Mendelsohn, 'Jews, Communism, and Art in Interwar America', in Jonathan Frankel and Dan Diner (eds.), *Dark Times, Dire Decisions: Jews and Communism* (= *Studies in Contemporary Jewry*, 20) (2004), 99–132.

struggles, and outsiders in both contexts, Mendelsohn detects in their bio-
graphies and artistic work a certain recognition of Jewishness that on some
level fuelled their universalistic utopia. The Jewish 'outsider' needs to be
recast as at least a partial 'insider'.

However, at this juncture it can be asked whether the socio-historical context has not determined too neatly the cultural conclusion. Is Mendelsohn
leading us to an a priori assumption that 'Jewish layers' can always be
revealed? Here, perhaps, one would have wanted a comparative study of
artists of Jewish origin where such forms of Jewish self-expression simply
cannot be found.

Mendelsohn delights in shedding light on the figures and tendencies that
exemplify the paradoxical process of Jewish integration into the mainstreams
of American and European society in the last two hundred years.[17] They
speak to his own personal background, cultural affinities, and, I daresay, personal paradoxes. These figures include individuals for whom the interaction
with the majority culture—and the insider/outside divide—has been, as it
has been for Mendelsohn himself, a creative process. Thus, *contra* Haskell,
only a historian would leap across countries and chronology in order to
group together artists of Jewish origin and assert that they shared a common
attitude—a vision of universalism—in at least some of their artwork.[18]

In his essay 'Jewish Universalism', Mendelsohn asserted that universalism
was a goal shared, inter alia, by such diverse figures as the Polish Jewish artist
Samuel Hirshenberg (1865–1908) in his iconizing the figure of Spinoza, and
by the contemporary comic artist Art Spiegelman. Spiegelman created a cultural storm when he imaginatively placed a hasidic Jew kissing an Afro-
American woman on the cover of the Valentine's Day issue of the *New Yorker*
(1993) following the violent tension between hasidim and Afro-Americans in
Crown Heights, New York. Mendelsohn's essay juxtaposes various American
and east European artists in order to advance the claim that modern Jewish
artists were disproportionately drawn to the ideal of a world that would
overcome apparently unbridgeable hostilities.

Clearly an essay that focuses on a historical theme in totally distant situations and not on the language of the art itself goes against the grain of
Haskell's forewarnings. Mendelsohn is not affirming the need to interpret all
the work of R. B. Kitaj, Raphael Soyer, or Maurycy Gottlieb, for example, in
this manner. However, the universalist vision that they and others articu-

[17] Ezra Mendelsohn, 'On the Jewish Presence in Nineteenth-Century European Musical
Life', in id. (ed.), *Modern Jews and their Musical Agendas* (= *Studies in Contemporary Jewry*, 9)
(1993), 3–16.
[18] Ezra Mendelsohn, 'Jewish Universalism: Some Visual Texts and Subtexts', in Jack
Kugelmass (ed.), *Key Texts in American Jewish Culture* (New Brunswick, 2003), 163–84. This
essay builds on his postscript in *Painting a People: Maurycy Gottlieb and Jewish Art* (Hanover,
NH, 2002), which he entitled 'Gottlieb's Children—The Universalistic Impulse in Jewish Art'.

lated visually at some point suggests to the historian a 'problem' worthy of interpretation—especially to a historian such as Mendelsohn, who regards the universalist impulse as a recurrent issue in modern Jewish history and part of the paradox of the 'insiders'/'outsiders' divide.

In contradistinction, Mendelsohn seldom employs antisemitism as the determining contextual framework for understanding the mindset or self-image of these artists, even though it impinged prominently on the lives of some of them; similarly, in his research into the inter-war period Mendelsohn rarely uses the persistent rise in antisemitism and the impending shadows presaging the Second World War as the overriding prism through which he analyses that period. Certainly only a highly qualified historian is able to write about a period engulfed in antisemitism without sinking into a one-dimensional approach; yet Mendelsohn's attraction to the universalistic theme never blinds him from seeing the dark years of Jewish history or recognizing that some artists of Jewish origin (for example, Arthur Szyk) harboured both universalist messages and their opposite at different times in their lives.

Maurycy Gottlieb, the Galician Jewish artist of the late nineteenth century who suffered from antisemitism but also provocatively struggled with the figure of Jesus, was thus a felicitous choice by Mendelsohn for the in-depth monograph, *Painting a People*. Here was a precocious artist whose work brilliantly assimilated regnant artistic styles, engaged the contemporary predicaments of Jews and Poles, and touched during his lifetime and posthumously many individuals of different persuasions and beliefs. Gottlieb, too, was a marginal figure in terms of Jewish historical studies but, unlike Meyerbeer or Franz Boas, or Lozowick, his life and work left no doubt that they had to be situated in some manner within a Jewish framework, notwithstanding Polish claims to his Polish roots.

Indeed, Mendelsohn turns the issue of Gottlieb's identity as viewed by Poles and Jews, and his historical affiliation (Gottlieb's reception by Poles and Jews after his death), into a significant instance of *Rezeptionsgeschichte*, describing the extraordinary variety of interpretations that have been applied to Gottlieb's oeuvre. Thus, paradoxically, the artist's appropriation into the Polish national canon has to a significant extent lent him 'insider' status within a specifically Polish milieu. A striking example can be found in the present-day exhibition of Gottlieb's *Jesus Preaching at Capernaum* in a special gallery in the National Museum in Warsaw devoted to Jan Matejko, the foremost Polish history painter of the nineteenth century and Gottlieb's dedicated mentor.[19] *Jesus Preaching at Capernaum* hangs opposite Matejko's

[19] On this painting see Ezra Mendelsohn, 'Art and Jewish–Polish Relations: Matejko and Gottlieb at the National Museum in Warsaw', in András Kovács (ed.), *Jewish Studies at the Central European University* (Budapest, 2000), 171–80.

towering work, *The Battle at Grunwald*, completed in 1878, a remarkable jux-taposition.

Matejko's painting, as Mendelsohn shows, deals with a major victory of Polish forces in 1410 against the Order of the Teutonic Knights, a dramatic moment in the national history of the Poles, who at the time of its composi-tion in the 1870s were living under Habsburg, German, and Russian rule and bereft of national sovereignty. Considering that in that same period Germany had attained unification under Bismarck while the Poles had been defeated in their revolt in 1863, Matejko's painting was a clarion call to maintain the Polish nationalist spirit. In Mendelsohn's words: 'The gallery in which it is exhibited remains a place of pilgrimage, where visitors are inspired by its vision of Polish bravery and take to heart, no doubt, the need for eternal vigilance against Poland's rapacious neighbours.'[20]

In this holy of holies of Polish nationalism, amidst other works by Matejko and contemporary Polish artists, Gottlieb's *Jesus Preaching at Capernaum* is displayed. Mendelsohn speculates about the presence of both works in the same gallery, wondering how Gottlieb's painting speaks to Matejko's. His intertextual commentary is intriguing. *Jesus Preaching at Capernaum* represents, in his view, 'the hope for a society based on universal-ism and love, in which Jews and Poles, both connected to the figure of Christ, will live in peace and harmony'.[21] It thus provides an additional ele-ment—universalism—to the nationalist call addressed in Matejko's work. Though the exact date when the painting was hung in this fashion is not clear, one can certainly claim that this positioning of the work of Gottlieb, an admired student of Matejko's, drafts the Jewish painter into the realm of 'Polish artists'. Gottlieb has not been forgotten by the Poles, who—albeit only at certain junctures—have evoked his memory since his death in 1879.

But Gottlieb has also been appropriated by Jews who want to claim him for their own. Martin Buber, who in 1901 sensitively addressed the artist's 'melancholy and struggle', saw in Gottlieb's work a precursor of the 'new Judaism' (that is, of Zionism) 'a herald who . . . is not blessed to behold the promised land himself'.[22] Yet, as Mendelsohn has shown, other Jews did not ascribe a national orientation to Gottlieb. Those whom he identifies as integrationists, for example, claimed that Gottlieb's art originated from and confirmed their world-view and championed the acculturation of Jews into Polish society. The struggle over the legacy of this artist and his identity—as insider or outsider—did not, however, end there. Critics divided along

[20] See Mendelsohn, 'Art and Jewish–Polish Relations', 173.
[21] Ibid. 180; see also Mendelsohn, 'Art and Jewish History: Gottlieb's *Jesus Preaching at Capernaum*' (Heb.), *Tsiyon*, 62 (1997), 173–91.
[22] *The Early Buber. Youthful Zionist Writings of Martin Buber*, ed. and trans. Gilya G. Schmid (Syracuse, 1999), 56.

ideological lines in their interpretations of individual works. Thus, the eminent Polish Zionist leader Osias Thon, while drafting Gottlieb into the nationalist arena at a major exhibition of Gottlieb's work in Kraków in 1932, rejected *Jesus Preaching at Capernaum* for failing to convey the artist's national instinct.[23] This was, however, at a time that mounting antisemitism threatened to thwart the aspirations of those who trusted in some form of alliance with the Poles. The war years and their difficult aftermath sealed that option for years to come. Ultimately, Mendelsohn concluded that Gottlieb was 'all things to all men', though he, not surprisingly, sees Gottlieb as 'the artist of Jewish universalism above all'.[24]

Certainly, Gottlieb found in Mendelsohn a dedicated and imaginative interpreter who devoted several years of exhaustive study and research to exploring the Jewish and Polish layers within his outlook and oeuvre, the subplots and angles of his life. Few Jewish artists of the nineteenth century have received such intense and careful scrutiny. The monograph joins studies of other Jewish artists in the East and West who, as noted earlier in this essay, have recently preoccupied the world of scholarship. Among nineteenth-century artists Moritz Oppenheim has clearly attracted the most wide-ranging attention and, interestingly, in his case, too, it was a mainstream historian, Ismar Schorsch, who opened up new avenues in the approach to his art. The comparison is instructive. Schorsch's single article on Oppenheim concentrated on his famous series *Scenes from Traditional Jewish Family Life*, which preoccupied the artist in the last period of his life. Schorsch's goal was similar to Mendelsohn's—he encouraged the art to talk history, to provide another text to reconstruct the German Jewish history of the nineteenth century. He even boldly claimed that Oppenheim's political message 'is best deciphered by the historian of German Jewry and not the historian of Jewish art'.[25] Schorsch's insights into Oppenheim's paintings were many but his ultimate synthesis is what is important in our context:

The paintings of Oppenheim . . . reflect how far German Jewry had come since . . . the French Sanhedrin. The issue was no longer the need to relinquish but the right to retain. Self-respect had begun to replace fear. A protracted struggle for admission and equality had crystallized a vision of emancipation that not only provided a framework for Jewish survival but also made a contribution to the political theory of the modern state.[26]

---

[23] Mendelsohn, 'Art and Jewish History' (Heb.), 190.    [24] Id., *Painting a People*, 195.
[25] Ismar Schorsch, 'Art as Social History: Moritz Oppenheim and the German Jewish Vision of Emancipation', in id., *From Text to Context: The Turn to History in Modern Judaism* (Hanover, NH, 1994), 94. The essay first appeared in Elisheva Cohen (ed.), *Moritz Oppenheim: The First Jewish Painter*, Israel Museum catalogue (Jerusalem, 1983).
[26] Schorsch, 'Art as Social History', 110.

To return to the 1985 *Representations* symposium, Oppenheim's paintings *confirmed* Schorsch's original social understanding of German Jewry—his perspective on German Jewry in the nineteenth century strongly determined his reading of the artwork.

How does Mendelsohn approach Gottlieb? As can be expected from a historian who, as we have seen, prides himself on context and comparative history, he commences with a brief but dazzling portrait of Galicia and Galician Jewry during the second half of the nineteenth century—probably more than was required to situate Gottlieb and his work, but it provides the interface between the artist and his time:

As Maurycy Gottlieb's biography demonstrates, the 1860s and 1870s were not the worst of times in the history of Polish-Jewish relations, but neither were they the best of times. His life, work, and reception bear witness to the complex web of prejudices, occasional admiration, and profound ambiguity that has characterized the attitudes of Polish non-Jews towards their Jewish neighbors in modern times.[27]

Even though at times Mendelsohn may pay all too brief attention to the paintings and offers interpretations that can be seen as excessively contextual and perhaps not sufficiently derived from the language of the paintings themselves, one cannot but be impressed by the range and depth of this study. Tracing Gottlieb's styles and themes, Mendelsohn pursues him to study Orientalist painting, Polish representations of Jews in the nineteenth century, Polish historical painting, the place of Jesus in Jewish thought and painting, and the world of seventeenth-century Amsterdam Jewry, not to speak of Gottlieb's more private and self-reflective paintings. In each situation, Mendelsohn enters into a new world of associations and problems and widens the scope of the discussion in an engaging and intriguing manner. Whether discussing Gottlieb's *Shylock and Jessica* or *Jews Praying in the Synagogue*, or *Da Costa in the Synagogue*, Mendelsohn weaves a wide web of associations and excursuses by delving deeply into the cultural world he has created for himself. These artistic portrayals, part of what Mendelsohn calls Gottlieb's 'Jewish pantheon of people, real and fictional', constitute for the author the artist's 'ideals of universalism',[28] a tradition among Jewish artists that he already began to elaborate upon in the monograph.

*Painting a People* takes nothing for granted, mines and scrutinizes every piece of evidence, and leaves the reader with a sense of clairvoyance. One last brief example: Mendelsohn subtly treats Gottlieb's relationship with his famous teacher Jan Matejko, particularly in the wonderful exploration of Gottlieb's 'revelatory' encounter in Vienna in 1872 with Matejko's painting *Rejtan: The Fall of Poland* (1866). Sifting through the various sources depicting

---

[27] Mendelsohn, *Painting a People*, 18–19.      [28] Ibid. 138.

this seminal moment in Gottlieb's life, Mendelsohn tries to determine why it so engaged his subject. He offers two explanations: one, that the artist, 'like many other young Jews of his and subsequent generations, found the dramatic, tragic, and romantic history of Poland, so eloquently depicted in this canvas, highly attractive, even irresistible'. Second: 'Perhaps, too, the seed was sown, at this early date, of Gottlieb's later conviction that Poles and Jews were linked by a common heritage of suffering, since both were once great nations brought low by their unscrupulous enemies.'[29] In interpreting Gottlieb's response in the context of the Galician predicament that he knows so well, Mendelsohn views him as a not untypical figure of his age: Oppenheim's Galician counterpart?

*Painting a People* is a remarkable achievement that considerably advances our way of studying Jewish visual culture. Clearly, Mendelsohn is a classic historian with a modernist, personalized bent. He believes that he can get to the bottom of a phenomenon by digging further and further. This is for him the essence of history. One can find answers, even build hypotheses, especially if one thinks comparatively and contextually. For the postmodernist, deconstructionist historian, Mendelsohn is not the answer. He simply does not belong. Not a man of jargon, Mendelsohn spends little time developing abstract theoretical constructs, refrains from name-dropping references to luminary thinkers to impress, but he is a good old-time believer in hard facts, carefully sifted, engagingly displayed, and elegantly crafted. Though Haskell would still possibly remain unconvinced he, too, would be hard pressed to deny the contribution of this cultural historian to the understanding of Maurycy Gottlieb and other cultural figures of the last century and a half.

[29] Ibid. 30.

# TWO

# GOTT FUN AVROHOM
## *Itzik Manger and Avot Yeshurun Look Homewards*

ZVI JAGENDORF

ITZIK MANGER AND AVOT YESHURUN (born Yehiel Perlmutter) were near-contemporaries and almost *landsmen*. They confront, in idiosyncratic, colourful language, one directly the other indirectly, the cataclysmic events of a time that propelled Avot Yeshurun from the shtetl to the shores of Palestine in 1925 and sent Manger wandering from Warsaw through Europe and North Africa, fleeing Hitler's advance. For Avot Yeshurun, who went to Palestine to find 'home', the pain of abandoning his parents' house in Poland and the discovery that Palestine was 'home' to another people became intertwined and a focus of his poetry and polemics.

For Manger, born in Czernowitz, homecoming, let alone Zionism, was never a real option or a goal. He was a Yiddish troubadour, balladeer, drunkard, and scribbler of poems on the back of unpaid bills. He was a vagabond as a literary persona but also in life, imagining himself a Gypsy, singing for a living in tenement courtyards. Home, to this mindset, is as much a burden as a comfort. We can hear this in the last stanzas of his best-known ballad 'Oyfn veg shtet a boym' ('By the Wayside Stands a Tree'), in which the little bird who wants to fly is loaded down by the clothes his worried mother piles on him:

> I stretch my wings, but, oh, the weight
> The crush of heavy clothing
> That my mother piled upon
> A weak and tender fledgling.
>
> I take a sad and mournful look
> Where mamma's eyes are crying
> Her love it was that stopped her son
> Spreading wings and flying.[1]

Manger the poet did fly away, and even in the midst of his chaotic escape from Hitler continued his work of creating an ahistorical folk history, a kind

---

[1] Itzik Manger, *Lid un balade* (Tel Aviv, n.d.), 369–70. All translations of Manger are my own.

of *Canterbury Tales* of Jewish life set in a rapidly disappearing landscape of the Yiddish imagination. In this folk history the chapter on homecoming is called 'Rus', or Ruth, one of a series of dramatic ballads that set biblical stories and characters firmly in the landscape of Poland and the Ukraine in a time that could be modern or biblical, or indeed both simultaneously. It is a poem about refugees yearning for home, and in its revealing epigraph Manger tells us of his own parallel state in 1940 when he was writing it: 'Two-thirds of this poem, along with other manuscripts, got lost during the time of my roaming and wandering.'[2] 'Rus', then, is the saved fragment, a poem written by a refugee in North Africa, imagining Naomi, Ruth, and Orpah in the Ukraine or Moab, each dreaming of coming home, one back to Canaan and the God of Abraham, another to her father's Polish village and Pan Jezus.

Manger is a dramatic poet. He speaks through character and dialogue and, like the anonymous creators of the medieval mystery plays, he lets his characters, local people caught up in the biblical drama, speak like contemporaries, with all the humour and irony that this implies. In 'Rus' Manger doesn't follow the focus of received interpretations on Naomi and Ruth and the founding of the House of David in Bethlehem. We could call that the insider's approach, a mostly Jewish story about *them* joining *us*. Manger's version is a Jewish/*goyish* story about the separation of a Jewish mother and her *shikse* (non-Jewish) daughter-in-law, each drawn to her distant home: Canaan for Naomi, and for Orpah a Catholic village in Ukraine. No journey home has priority in this humane presentation of parting from one life to return to an earlier one. *Heimweh* is universal.

'Gott fun Avrohom' is how the sequence starts in the dark of a Saturday night in a village house. The old lady Naomi is mumbling the familiar Yiddish *tkhine*, or Saturday-night prayer of women asking God for protection as the sabbath departs. This is a liminal prayer, poised between the sabbath and the everyday, rest and work, the sacred time inside and the dangerous week outside. It is an iconic text of motherhood in the Jewish home, like the blessing of the sabbath candles, and it is spoken conversationally to God in an intimate Yiddish idiom mixed with Hebrew phrases: 'God of Abraham and of Isaac and of Jacob. Protect your beloved people Yisroel from all bad things, for your praise, as the beloved holy shabes goes away.'[3] A *heymish* prayer, but the familiar in Manger's poem is framed by strangeness:

> Old Naomi stands in the dark of the room
> Murmuring Gott fun Avrohom
> The blonde wives of her sons sit by her side
> And listen, respectful and numb.

[2] Itzik Manger, *Medresh itsik* [Itzik's Midrash] (Jerusalem, 1969), 108.
[3] My translation from a prayer-book text.

'Gott fun Avrohom, almighty God
The holy shabes goes by
And just like shabes in a stranger's place
My joy has slipped away.'[4]

There are two *shikses* in the room, nice girls but blonde, and Naomi's shabes is isolated, separate from the goyish village where she has found refuge in Moab/Ukraine. Home, *real* home, is the mythical land of the Bible, which will also be the land of her death:

(*Naomi resolves*)
Step by step, she'll make her own way
Till she sets down her foot in Canaan
Where the angel of death stands waiting for her
To become her second man.[5]

But this resolve is not a simple one. Naomi struggles between the pull of an idealized, far-away home, Canaan, and the real earth she has lived on for years with her husband and sons, where their graves, the old mill, and their fields demand she stay. But the pull of Canaan is greater. It is:

The land where the fathers lived long ago
The land where the almond grows
Where the wind and the eagle are pious and good
And a holy melody blows.

There over fields and forests and hills
Over meadows and woodlands and streams,
The place where God is really at home
And not just a voice in your dream.[6]

That is Naomi's way, familiar to us from the Jewish folk imagination. But Manger's scene is not an exclusively Jewish one. Other people have homes, too, even *goyim* and peasants. The humaneness of the 'Rus' sequence lies in the analogy between Naomi and Orpah, an analogy that illuminates their *parting* of ways rather than their joining.

Manger shows us Orpah longing for her childhood home as she reads a letter from her father the peasant:

Orpassia, little daughter, come home
Your mother's old and in pain
Krassa the cow has had her calf
And everything's right as rain.

---

⁴ Manger, *Lid un balade*, 263.     ⁵ Ibid. 264.     ⁶ Ibid. 274.

Stashek the miller with his bloody axe
Cut his wife up in her bed
Now he's in jail, praise the Lord
We earn our daily bread

.        .        .        .

Innkeeper Itzik, the Yid around here,
Has had all his windows smashed
And Itzik himself and his household all
Got themselves beaten and bashed

O Antek the scrivener who works in the court
Came over to me yesterday
'I heard Orpassia's man is dead
And her life is drifting away.

Tell her she should come home to us
Write her I'm ready and game
Even if she once married a Yid
I'll take her just the same.'[7]

Writing in Yiddish in North Africa, Manger doesn't know whether he has any readers or where they are, but supposing there are some somewhere, he invites them to enter into the ordinary, everyday, violent and peaceful life of Orpassia's father and to feel her longing for this home watched over by Pan Jezus. Manger's plight, his loneliness, only opened him up to a home-longing shared by all uprooted people. What arouses his interest here is not the traditional unifying 'your people is my people' of Ruth but the splitting of the ways and the parallel, separate paths of Jew and non-Jew returning to separate homes. One inspires the other, as Orpah says to Naomi:

'That, old Naomi, is my village and home
To that place through the clouds am I drawn
Forgive me then, it's your own return
Reminds me of where I was born.'[8]

'Rus', which begins with Naomi's 'Gott fun Avrohom', ends with her prayer where the roads part:

Happy is he who makes his way home
After so many years far away.[9]

Naomi's prayer is an optimistic one, fair to all the homes longed for, and very touching if we think of Manger writing it on scraps of torn paper on a suitcase somewhere. He was never a homebody but he was a chameleon

---

[7] Ibid. 269–70.        [8] Ibid. 278.        [9] Ibid.

poet, inside and outside Jewish nostalgia, a juggler of opposites. Even at the end of his wandering life when, a sick man, he came, like Naomi, to die in Canaan, now known as Israel, he wrote about homecoming with humour and irony. Alluding to Judah Halevi's memorable lines:

אפול לאפי עלי ארצך וארצה אבניך מאוד ואחונן את עפריך

I'd fling myself down on the ground and treasure your stone and favour your dust.

Itzik chooses *not* to be a pilgrim in the Holy Land:

> I won't kiss your dust like that singer of old
> Though my heart is heavy with song and with tears
> What's kiss your dust? *I am your dust*
> And kissing yourself, folks, is weird.[10]

Manger's Canaan is not the distant place where 'God is really at home'; it is an intimate part of Itzik the Gypsy. It mingles with his humanity. It may be, finally, home but it's just dry earth, as are we all.

Paradoxically, the vagabond Manger is far more at ease and tolerant in his imagination of homecoming than Avot Yeshurun. As a dramatic poet, Manger speaks through his characters, whereas Avot Yeshurun's voice is lyrical and obsessively his own. He believed he was coming home when he was ferried off the boat at Bat Galim in 1925 by an Arab porter. Home, for this young man from Przedmieście/Krasnystaw in Poland, was Erets Yisrael. But throughout his work he is haunted by the guilt of being an accomplice in the ruin of homes, first that of his parents in the shtetl and then the homes of the Palestinian Arabs, whose villages and traditional way of life seemed to him to mirror his parents' world. This guilt constitutes the burden of much of his poetry.

Avot Yeshurun's world is radically split. He is a creature of two landscapes and at least two languages, which fight in his sensibility like Jacob and Esau in their mother's womb. Poland and Erets Yisrael, meadow and desert, Yiddish and Hebrew, Yehiel Perlmutter and Avot Yeshurun. These are the apparently irreconcilable landmarks by which he must navigate. In an interview towards the end of his life he said:

When I was in Europe I was that landscape. I was Krasnystaw, the chestnut grove in my town, that was me . . . there's a term *erets gezerah*. The dictionary says 'a deserted land, a land of punishment'. My sense is different: it is . . . a cutting land that slices you in two. Part here and part there. I belong to both landscapes.[11]

[10] Manger, *Lid un balade*, 486.
[11] Interview with Avot Yeshurun by Helit Yeshurun (Heb.), *Ḥadarim* (Winter 1982/3), 92–109: 97. All translations of Avot Yeshurun's works are my own.

He was supposed to have resolved this conflict by a heroic act of home-building, but instead he finds himself sucked deeper and deeper into contradictions. Revolutionary and shocking parallels suggest themselves. The Arab village and the shtetl resemble each other. They appear to be backward but the ruin of their traditional ways—in which he is implicated—impoverishes him. Equally, the ruin of the little huts of the *ḥalutsim* in Tel Aviv, victims of developers, reminds him of the deserted shacks on the streets of Krasnystaw.

The abandoning of home, his parents, and their language—Yiddish—is the major trauma that defines Avot Yeshurun's work. Unlike Manger's Naomi, there's no going back for him except in painful memory. Instead, the modernist, rebellious poet of the contemporary chaos of Tel Aviv has to make do with what there is—cacophony, urban mess, the secular confusion of a modern city with which he struggles to make peace in the light of his memories:

The places where we were, the houses we saw, the people we knew follow us around secretly. So, in Tel Aviv, the shtetl I came from follows me around. Tel Aviv doesn't mind, she understands that you love in her, streets and corners that remind you of the past. . . . So when they knock down an old house—oy, that's no good. Tel Aviv the Holy City.[12]

Tel Aviv is for him a palimpsest of the shtetl, holy in so far as its remaining shabby sheds and sandy byways remind him of home. But even that trace of the lost home is being erased by the developers.

Breaking and splitting are images that lie at the heart of Avot Yeshurun's struggle with the two landscapes and the two languages to which he is bound:

> How can I get up in the morning with one town in my heart
> And another in my eyes
> How can I get cured of this break?[13]

When the editors of a literary journal ask him for a poem, he echoes the Psalmist on singing by the rivers of Babylon:

> But how can I make you a new poem?
> I'm on the crossroads between Krasnystaw and Przedmieście.[14]

He's not in Tel Aviv. He's in his exilic home between the two ghosts of a shtetl and he will never arrive at his destination.

The contrast between what the poet sees and what he remembers is also at the heart of his continuing engagement with the expulsion of the Palestinians in the war of 1948 and the disappearance of their old culture

---

[12] Avot Yeshurun, *Collected Poems* [Kol shirav], 4 vols. (Tel Aviv, 1995–2001), ii. 33.
[13] Ibid. iv. 15.                                                    [14] Ibid. 61.

from the landscape. He can't forget that it was Arab peasants who welcomed the motherless lad from Poland, and whose sturdy arms and innate generosity in offering food and warm, simple words in a mixture of Arabic and Ladino helped him find his way. He learns to call the land 'mother' not from a Hebrew song of the *ḥalutsim* but from an Arab peasant woman selling food by the roadside.

The iconic image of the Arab woman squatting on the earth and offering food (transposed into the refugees fleeing from villages and towns and seeking shelter in miserable shacks and holes) appears in early poems such as 'Pass Over the Hovels' ('Pesaḥ al kukhim'; 1952),[15] which is about the expulsion and its banishment from the Israeli consciousness. The image reappears in a later collection *The Syrian–African Rift* (*Hashever hasuri afrikani*, 1974) as a memory of a vanished world:

> On the dirt path between Goldberg grove and Tel Aviv
> At the parting of the ways
> A woman in a small tent cooking lentils for Ramadan
> Hawaja, she said,
> Night, Hawaja, the night hour of darkness
> Is here.
> On my right Tel Aviv, ahead of me Jaffa and from the minaret
>     of *Jamma Yaffi* Ahmad Shar'a calls verses
> Of Ramadan
> I walk along the dirt path
> Thinking of the parting of the ways.[16]

Again the poet finds himself in between, at a place where roads lead in different directions. This time he is not between two shtetls but between Tel Aviv and Jaffa—*Yaffi*. The two towns are still separate in the scene of memory, and the landscape is still that of Palestine, Goldberg orange grove and a dirt path rather than apartment blocks and a highway. But the reader of this 1974 collection knows that the old town with its sounds and smells has been enveloped by Tel Aviv, and little remains of its Arab character. The poet remembers and returns in his mind to a scene of serenity that is also a scene of parting. Just as he left his parents' home, abandoning the music and language of its religious ways, so he walks along the path away from Yaffi and the woman cooking a dish for Ramadan. Yaffi is a ghost town now, and Goldberg grove is a name remembered by few. Avot Yeshurun, at the parting of the ways, in Poland and in Palestine, takes upon himself a double burden of guilt, one for the abandonment of his parents and the other for the disappearance of Arab Jaffa.

---

[15] Literally, 'Passover on the Hovels', with a punning reference to contemporary indifference to the fate of the Arab refugees.     [16] *Collected Poems* (Heb.), ii. 141.

This in-betweenness of Avot Yeshurun is reflected strongly in his poetics. He broke with his mother tongue to write Hebrew, but the old language won't leave him alone. At first it is a dream language, and we might think of him as a *ḥaluts* in the 1930s living a spartan life of physical labour and beginning to write poetry. He gets letters in Yiddish from home but he won't speak the language with anyone. Nor does he answer the letters. So the unspoken/unwritten language finds him at night.

In an interview he has described the violence he did to this language and the turmoil this caused: 'I broke my father and mother . . . I broke their festivals and their Shabbat . . . I broke their power of speech. I broke their language. I couldn't stand their Yiddish.'[17]

He changes his name from Yehiel Perlmutter to Avot Yeshurun, and tries to flee like Jonah from the inner call, but the Yiddish refuses to be silenced and becomes the dream language: 'And should you dream or speak in Yiddish, out of your sleep quick you had to translate it all into Hebrew and only then could you go back to bed.'[18] Torn between the two languages, writing in one, dreaming in the other, he cannot resolve the tension. Translation is a bad bargain, a desperate measure to buy a night's sleep, and not a resolution of the struggle.

Yeshurun's poetics, however, moves towards a way of healing the wound of his split consciousness. The healing medicine is in the Tel Aviv street. Taking his cue from the babble of languages spoken in the city of immigrants, he creates an evocative hybrid language out of the ruins of Yiddish, traces of the past, bits of *golus*, combined with the ungrammatical, lawless Hebrew of the street. 'From the breaking up of Polish to speak Hebrew, from driving Hungarian crazy, from German and Yiddish. That's our language today. There are words in Hebrew that got rich when they emigrated.'[19]

To use the analogy of old and new in Tel Aviv, the destruction of the shanty quarters of the pioneering days doesn't have to result in sterile commercial centres. The new city should be an idiosyncratic mix, a creative mess of bits from all over.

Such a mess is not easy to live with or an intelligible idiom to write in, and one Saturday night in Dizengoff Square, in a poem called 'A Poem About' ('Shir bekesher'), Avot Yeshurun calls on his mother and her 'Gott fun Avrohom' to help him find his way:

> 'God of Abraham, you know languages,
> You talked to my mother in an old language in Yiddish
> When you walked out on shabbat
> Among the stars.
> My Hebrew isn't pure

[17] Ibid. ii. 124.    [18] Ibid. i. 279.    [19] Ibid. ii. 128.

My Hebrew is *chaplap* and speaks *chaplapish* and nonsense
It isn't *satisfactorish*
Here I am walking out at night to the park, to the square, to Dizengoff
In a fog of words
So it's impossible.'[20]

'Gott fun Avrohom' is both a tender memory of Saturday night at home and a medicine for healing the language split that he experiences in Tel Aviv. He goes into the cacophonous city ashamed of his clownish, ungrammatical, mongrel Hebrew. It's not pure. But neither is 'Gott fun Avrohom'. The old lady talked with God, not just in Yiddish but also in a mixture of Yiddish and Hebrew:

דו ביסט דאך הנותן ליעף כוח. גיב דיינע ליבע יידישע קינדערלך אויך כוח . . .

You are *the giver of strength to the weary*. Give your beloved Jewish children strength also . . .

And God listens approvingly. He doesn't belong to the Union for the Suppression of Yiddish. The poet borrows his mother's multilingual God for the evening and takes him to Dizengoff to listen to the chat on the park benches:

> 'You (God), who hear talk in seventy translations
> At night in the park and in Dizengoff Square
> Look: "So what did you buy?" "Naftalin for the cupboards"
> "Me too I want that"
> That's our language today.
> And whaddya know. That's what we've got.'[21]

Avot Yeshurun feels for this language because it is the mongrel speech of immigrants and bears traces of languages no longer spoken and homes abandoned and destroyed. But it's alive here, unapologetic, and because it's *sha'atnez*,[22] an unlawful mixture, it is all the more resilient.

In the interview from which I have already quoted, Avot Yeshurun defended his strange grammar and orthography in which he breaks with the conventional arrangement of letters and diacritical marks, for example, by spelling the Hebrew pronoun *hu* as הא (*heh–kubuts–alef*) rather than הוא. He wants the word incorrectly spelled to indicate the instability of language, which he terms 'the ruin of the language [*ḥirbet shel hasafah*]'[23]—using for 'ruin' the Arabic word that denotes the ruin of an abandoned house, a familiar sight in the landscape of the Sharon and Galilee.

---

[20] *Collected Poems* (Heb.), ii. 182; I have tried in my translation here to do justice to his neologisms, or mongrel language.      [21] Ibid.
[22] He uses the term designating a religiously proscribed mixture of fibres.
[23] *Ḥadarim* (Winter 1982/3), 99.

*Ḥirbet* is a key word to our understanding of this unusual poet as a man torn between languages, places, and ruins. His language, he is telling us, should be read as evidence of ghostly presences that we might hurry to ignore. The ruin demands to be examined, it blurs distinctions between inside and outside, it reveals traces of lives lived, homes abandoned, and languages once spoken. The word as ruin is much more than the orthographic whim of a rebellious poet. It is evidence of the catastrophe that destroyed old worlds in Europe and in the Middle East, but also of the poet's struggle to hold together experiences that would fragment into incomprehension but for the heroic imagination that labours to hold them together.

# THREE

# AGONY AND RESURRECTION
## *The Figure of Jesus in the Work of Reuven Rubin*

### AMITAI MENDELSOHN

I T IS HARD TO THINK of any one historical figure in the Jewish context whom the title 'Insider/Outsider', with all its complex and contradictory features, suits more aptly than Jesus of Nazareth. For two thousand years Jews have had to contend with his presence. He has been considered a false messiah, a sorcerer who attempted to lead God's chosen people astray, or alternatively, in modern scholarship, as an authentic Jew who had no intention of creating a new religion and whose words were twisted by some of his followers, especially Paul. Whatever view one adopts, he was, and in many ways still is, an inseparable part of Jewish life.

In this essay I will discuss the representation of Jesus in the early work of one of Israel's most famous artists—Reuven Rubin (1893–1974). I will focus on the works he painted in the early 1920s, in his homeland Romania, and in his first year in Palestine, 1923. His work in those years drew its inspiration from the surrounding world of Jewish thought, poetry, literature, and art; yet the impact of both symbolism and expressionism on his oeuvre is no less apparent. The mixture of influences on Rubin's work, and his open-mindedness in this period, prove him to be a complex and thought-provoking artist and make his engagement with the image of Jesus all the more challenging.

The end of the eighteenth century saw a change in the perception of Jesus among Christian and Jewish scholars. The traditional Jewish perception of Jesus prior to the modern era was characterized by attitudes of ridicule, hatred, or, at best, indifference. Yet there were also more moderate Jewish views, the most important being that of Maimonides, who stated that although Jesus was a false messiah he did play an important role in the spread

This essay is based on a chapter in my MA thesis: 'Religious Themes in Reuven Rubin's Early Works: 1914–1923', directed by Professor Gannit Ankori and submitted to the Department of Art History of the Hebrew University of Jerusalem (2005). In 2006 it was published as the text for the catalogue of the exhibition in the Israel Museum, Jerusalem: Amitai Mendelsohn, *Prophets and Visionaries: Reuven Rubin's Early Years, 1914–23* (Jerusalem, 2006).

of monotheism among the pagans.[1] Some six hundred years later, at the end of the famous Lavater affair in which the Swiss theologian Johann Caspar Lavater tried to persuade the philosopher Moses Mendelssohn to accept Jesus as saviour, Mendelssohn wrote that he respected Jesus as a moral person but did not accept his divinity or the fact that he wished to create a new religion. Mendelssohn's assertion was directed against Christians who tried to convert Jews, and it was meant to provide support to Jews who chose to remain loyal to their faith.[2]

Similar ideas about the figure of Jesus emerged in the works of two Jewish historians: Heinrich Graetz, who, in his monumental *History of the Jews* (1853–76), claimed that Jesus was a Jew who had no intention of abandoning his faith, and Abraham Geiger, who, in *Judaism and its History* redefined Jesus as a Pharisee and early Christianity as pagan and a betrayal of Jesus's Jewish mission.[3] Such sympathetic attitudes towards Jesus infuriated many within the Jewish world. Several major Zionist figures debated the role of Jesus[4]—Joseph Hayim Brenner showed a sympathetic attitude towards him, as did poets Uri Zvi Greenberg and Abraham Shlonsky.[5] In 1922 Joseph Klausner published the book *Jesus of Nazareth—His Life, Times, and Teaching*, in which he stated that although Jesus was not a messiah or a prophet he was a model of righteousness, and should therefore be honoured and respected. Klausner's book was widely disseminated and, for the most part, well received in the Yishuv, and went through some eight editions in Israel (not counting translations and editions abroad); the most recent one was published in 1999.[6]

Interestingly, a number of distinguished Jewish artists adopted the figure of Jesus as a Jew who preached the ideals of love and virtue and as someone who could not but have deplored the cruel Christian treatment of the Jewish people over so many centuries. In his sculpture *Jesus before the People's Court* (1876), the Russian artist of Jewish origin Mark Antokolsky depicted Jesus bound in ropes, wearing a skullcap and sidelocks, with clear Semitic features

---

[1] Avigdor Shinan (ed.), *Jesus through Jewish Eyes* [Oto ha'ish: yehudim mesaperim al yeshu] (Tel Aviv, 1999), 39–46, 62–91.

[2] Alexander Altmann, *Moses Mendelssohn: A Biographical Study* (London, 1973), 204–5, 261–3. On this issue see also Moses Mendelssohn, *Jerusalem and other Jewish Writings*, trans. Alfred Jospe (New York, 1969), 133.

[3] Heinrich Graetz, *History of the Jews*, ed. Bella Löwy, 6 vols. (Philadelphia, 1941), ii. 145–66; Abraham Geiger, *Judaism and its History*, trans. Maurice Mayer (New York, 1865), 214–45; Susannah Heschel, *Abraham Geiger and the Jewish Jesus* (Chicago, 1998).

[4] See Tsvi Sadan, *Flesh of our Flesh: Jesus of Nazareth in Zionist Thought* [Basar mibsarenu: yeshua minatseret bahagut hatsiyonit] (Jerusalem, 2008).

[5] For the most recent discussion of Jesus in Hebrew literature see Neta Stahl, *Jewish Cross: Representations of Jesus in Twentieth-Century Hebrew Literature* [Tselem yehudi: yitsugav shel yeshu basifrut ha'ivrit beme'ah ha'esrim] (Tel Aviv, 2008).

[6] Sadan, *Flesh of our Flesh* (Heb.), ch. 6.

(Plate 1); Maurycy Gottlieb, the Polish Jewish artist, also depicted Jesus with a head covering, wearing a *talit* (a Jewish prayer shawl), in a dramatic scene facing his judges (1877/9). In another important painting by Gottlieb (1878/9; Plate 2), Jesus is wearing a *talit* and a head covering while preaching at Capernaum. Other Jewish artists in the twentieth century, such as Wilhelm Wachtel and, most famously, Marc Chagall, painted Jesus as a Jew in the context of wrongs done to the Jews by Christians. In these works Jesus is depicted as bearing the burden of the Jews' suffering no less than the sins of the Christian perpetrators.[7] Rubin may or may not have been aware of his predecessors' treatment of Jesus, but it appears that his own depiction of him was unique and even revolutionary for his time.

Reuven Rubin was born in the town of Galatz in south-eastern Romania in 1893. In 1912 he travelled to Palestine to enrol in the new Bezalel art school that had opened in 1906. But a year later he left, disappointed, and moved on to Paris, where he stayed until the outbreak of the First World War, when he returned to Romania. After the war, in 1919, he moved to Czernowitz, the capital of Bukovina (annexed to Romania as a result of the war), and there he created some of his most important early works. In 1921 he travelled to New York, where he was to exhibit with his fellow artist Arthur Kolnik in the Anderson Galleries, under the auspices of the famous photographer and champion of modern art, Alfred Stieglitz.[8] Rubin returned to Romania in the following year, this time making his temporary home in Bucharest. He was involved in Zionist activities all through his years in Romania, particularly during his final stay in Bucharest, and in April 1923 he left the country of his birth and returned to Palestine for good. Arriving in the port of Jaffa at the age of 29, already an accomplished artist, Rubin gradually modified his palette and his subject matter, eventually creating his well-known Land of Israel style.

It was in the early post-war period (1921–3), prior to his emigration to Palestine, that Rubin created some of his most interesting paintings, which treat the figure of Jesus in an intriguing manner. *Temptation in the Desert* (1921; Plate 3), a key work in his early output, is of central importance in terms of his identification with Jesus. Incorporating various artistic influences, the painting presents an original synthesis of scenes from the New Testament. It also contains a deeply felt personal dimension as it was in part a response to the death of Rubin's brother during the First World War. The style is expressive, resembling particularly that of Egon Schiele.

[7] For a detailed discussion on this topic see Ziva Amishai-Maisels, 'The Jewish Jesus', *Journal of Jewish Art*, 9 (1982), 84–104, and ead., 'Origins of the Jewish Jesus', in Matthew Baigell and Milly Heyd (eds.), *Complex Identities: Jewish Consciousness and Modern Art* (New Brunswick, NJ, 2001), 51–86.

[8] The Anderson Galleries were sometimes used for less modern and cutting-edge exhibitions at that time. Apparently Stieglitz took a liking to Rubin's work and remained in touch with him later.

The painting depicts five people in the desert. A gaunt, upright figure in the centre, his head bathed in a soft aura, is surrounded by three men and a woman lying on the ground; one of the men gazes in horror as the woman tries to pull off the central figure's garment. In an interview that took place in 1921, Rubin identified this central figure as a self-image. The aura suggests a halo, possibly linking him with the saints or with Jesus himself. Other paintings and letters written during this period indicate that Jesus fascinated Rubin, arousing deep feelings of identification. Additional hints in the painting lead to a possible interpretation of it as a direct reference to the Nazarene.

The scene it depicts can be linked to two central episodes in the life of Jesus: his praying in the garden of Gethsemane (Matthew 26: 36–46; Mark 14: 32–42; Luke 22: 39–46) and his encounter with Mary Magdalene after his resurrection (John 20: 14–18). Although, as discussed below, the painting's title would seem to make the temptation in the wilderness the primary reference, the lack of sexual content in this New Testament episode (Matthew 4: 1–11; Mark 1: 12–13; Luke 4: 1–13), where Satan tempts Jesus with worldly wealth and power rather than sex, leads me to take Gethsemane as my primary interpretative key.

After the Last Supper, Jesus set out to pray at Gethsemane in the company of Peter and the two sons of Zebedee, James and John. He prayed three times, and each time, when he returned to his disciples, he found them asleep. In this deeply sorrowful scene, Jesus asks God to spare him his imminent and terrible fate. In a purely human rather than divine act, he beseeches: 'My Father, if it be possible, let this cup pass from me; nevertheless, not as I will, but as thou wilt' (Matthew 26: 39). The presence of the sleeping disciples heightens Jesus's feeling of loneliness in the face of what awaits him. Soon after, the Roman soldiers arrive, led by Judas Iscariot, to arrest him.

Both the expression of suffering on the face of the central figure in *Temptation in the Desert* and the fact that he is surrounded by three prostrate men link the painting to this scene. The self-embracing posture of the central figure can then be interpreted as an imploring gesture, an appeal to be spared. Indeed, in many depictions of the scene from the Renaissance onwards, Jesus is seen kneeling, as if begging to be saved, in front of a single angel or several angels holding a large golden cup; the three disciples are seen sleeping nearby. Although Rubin's painting does not unambiguously depict Gethsemane—it is devoid of angels or Roman soldiers—it nevertheless includes some central elements of the scriptural account. The location of the scene in the desert, in a place unconnected with the garden described in the Gospels, differs, however, from other portrayals of Jesus's prayer at Gethsemane. The choice of the desert, a kind of 'extraterritorial' location, weakens the obvious Christian context in favour of a personal and mythical interpretation. The scene seems to be occurring in a 'non-place', outside the familiar world.

Although Rubin did not refer explicitly to Jesus when writing about his identification with the central figure, this association can be deduced from the painting. Previously, Paul Gauguin had painted himself as Jesus at Gethsemane, seated in a bent posture, lost in thought. Although Rubin was generally familiar with Gauguin's work, we do not know whether he had seen this specific painting, but it is difficult to deny the clear similarities between Gauguin's depiction of impending martyrdom and Rubin's vision.

Just as he doesn't reproduce the physical detail of a garden in this painting, neither does Rubin follow the New Testament story exactly. For example, the New Testament doesn't mention a woman's presence at Gethsemane, and the female figure in the painting thus suggests a link to a different episode in the Gospels: the encounter between Mary Magdalene and Jesus after his resurrection. As described in John (20: 14–18), Mary tries to touch Jesus's garment, but he says to her 'Touch me not' (the Greek original literally reads 'Don't try to embrace or hold me'), and commands her to notify his disciples and, through them, the whole world, of his victory over death: 'go to my brethren and say unto them, I am ascending to my Father and your Father, and to my God and your God' (John 20: 17). Some scholars believe that this scene singles out Mary Magdalene not only as the herald of 'the new life' but also as the first apostle (the *Apostola apostolorum*, or the apostles' apostle).[9] Yet she must not touch Jesus as she can no longer regard him as a mortal.

Christian sources contain some hints to the effect that Mary Magdalene and Jesus were particularly close.[10] Although their encounter following the resurrection (the best-known depiction is that by Titian, 1510/11) was not usually interpreted as a temptation scene, many portrayals of Mary emphasize her sexuality, sometimes even with the suffering figure of Jesus placed by her side. Auguste Rodin, for example, created a sculpture of the crucified Jesus embraced by a naked Mary Magdalene (1894), and Rubin may have seen this work while visiting Rodin's Paris studio during his stay in Paris in 1914. Although Rubin did not mention the encounter between Mary Magdalene and Jesus when discussing the *Temptation in the Desert*, the episode does seem to be hinted at in his thoughts about it: 'That figure in the middle is I . . . It is I resisting temptation, continuing on my way of suffering in spite of the hands that reach out to grasp me . . . she is trying to hold me back, but I am going on. I shall go on!'[11] Rubin's protagonist seems to be

[9] Susan Haskins, *Mary Magdalen, Myth and Metaphor* (New York, 1944), 10; see also *New Catholic Encyclopedia* (Palatine, Ill., 2002), ix. 285–7.    [10] Haskins, *Mary Magdalen*, 38–40.
[11] Reuven Rubin, interview in the catalogue of his 1921 New York exhibition. See Louis Bernheimer, 'Tragic Fire of the East in Roumanian Paintings', in *Rubin and Kolnik: Paintings and Sculptures* (New York, 1921), unpaginated.

addressing the woman, telling her not to touch him or divert him from his chosen path: devotion to his art.

The painting's clearest reference to the New Testament seems to be in its title, but, as noted above, this is not as direct or obvious as it may at first appear. In choosing the title Rubin was, apparently, alluding to an additional Christian theme, the earthly temptations inflicted upon saints and martyrs, most famously, the story of St Anthony (251–356 CE), considered the father of monasticism. Anthony was subjected by the Devil to various ordeals, including sexual temptations.[12] In many Renaissance paintings he appears alongside grotesque, gruesome, and demonic creatures, and in the nineteenth century depictions of Anthony began to take on the connotations of sexual temptation, as part of an artistic trend that swept the fields of literature, theatre, and the plastic arts in which the female was presented as tempting and destructive, a *femme fatale*.

Although Rubin identifies himself with the key figure in the *Temptation*, the painting is not a direct self-portrait. In the 1921 interview cited above, he referred to the death of his brother Baruch: 'He [the central figure] has the face of my brother, who died in the war, I saw him on his deathbed and his head is [depicted] on many of my canvases.' From the summer of 1916, when Romania joined the war, daily life was disrupted and many people died of disease and cold. Rubin himself fell ill; Baruch contracted meningitis and died. Rubin considered his brother a victim of the war since it had caused the epidemic, and he recalled that following Baruch's death he sank into depression, since he was 'closest to me in age and sympathy'.[13] The depression and mourning might also have involved feelings of guilt for having survived. Speaking of the painting, Rubin initially said that the central figure was a portrait of his brother and only later that it was actually a self-portrait. Rubin and his brother thus merge in this painting into one figure, which, as outlined above, is linked to the figure of Jesus. Knowingly or otherwise, Rubin joins other artists such as Max Beckmann and Jacob Epstein, who during this period depicted Jesus as a symbolic victim of the horrors of the First World War.

To sum up, the *Temptation in the Desert* represents a synthesis of influences: two central scenes from the New Testament—the prayer at Gethsemane and the encounter of Jesus and Mary Magdalene after Jesus's resurrection; the theme of the *femme fatale*, which fascinated many artists at the turn of the century; the image of Jesus as symbolizing the horrors of the First World War; and Rubin's personal connection with the war: his brother's death. If, indeed, the figure of the artist refers to Jesus, then this work is one of the few early examples of a Jewish artist daring to identify with this controversial

[12] G. Duchet-Suchaux and M. Pastoureau, *The Bible and the Saints*, trans. David Rodzinowicz Howell (Paris, 1994), 37–8.

[13] Reuven Rubin, *My Life—My Art* (New York, 1969), 98.

figure in a personal context rather than in a socio-historical one in which the suffering of the Jewish people is seen as the result of Christian antisemitism. As we shall see, this was not the only instance in which Rubin associated himself with Jesus.

Artists throughout history have employed the idea of the artist as Christ: Dürer depicted himself as the proud and powerful Christ; James Ensor depicted the crucifixion with the name 'Ensor' (instead of the legendary INRI) inscribed on the plaque above the crucified Christ; Van Gogh painted his own face as Christ in a work after Delacroix's *Pietà*; and in moments of distress and anguish Gauguin depicted himself at least twice as Jesus. Rubin mentions Van Gogh and Gauguin as central influences at this time, and he seems also to have recognized their connection to the figure of Jesus. His own identification with the suffering Jesus is expressed in a letter written in 1922 to a childhood friend. He describes the hardships that he was then undergoing and concludes by saying: 'The wounds of Christ are burning me and my sufferings are understood by no one.'[14]

This kind of identification is hinted at in a self-portrait from 1921 (Plate 4), which depicts the artist with a tormented visage and with his hands spread out, facing the viewer, in a way reminiscent of the image of the 'man of sorrows'—one of the traditional depictions of Jesus, going back to the Middle Ages, in which he displays his wounds for all to see. Such works were designed to show the agonies that Jesus had to endure in order to redeem the world of its sins.

The posture of the artist's hands in this self-portrait is close to the posture of the hands in another painting: *The Encounter (Jesus and the Jew)* (Plate 5) painted about a year later in Bucharest, not long before Rubin emigrated to Palestine. This is an important work of Rubin's early period and marks a change in his attitude towards the meaning of Jesus for him: it does not portray Jesus as the artist but as a figure who, as we shall see, has a compelling symbolic meaning in the context of the Jewish diaspora. To understand this painting, we must first look at the figure of the elderly Jew seated on the bench on the left, fatigued and bowed down. His encounter with Jesus suggests that he represents the mythical figure of the Wandering Jew (sometimes known as Ahasverus), who was depicted many times in Christian artworks and, from the late nineteenth century, in various works of art by Jews.

If Rubin is indeed here referring to the Wandering Jew, then this image differs from the usual depiction of Ahasverus. He is usually portrayed in motion—the central feature of his punishment—and facing the figure of Jesus, who hovers above him as a constant reminder of his sin. The historian

---

[14] Rubin to Bernard Weinberg (a friend living in Paris), 27 May 1922 (Rubin Museum Archive (RMA), Tel Aviv). Translated from the Hebrew by David Giladi; original in Romanian. Rubin's letters were compiled and published in the newspaper *Ma'ariv* in 1981.

Richard Cohen suggests that the painting is a depiction of a 'ceasefire', a kind of end of the race in which no one is the winner. Both Jesus and the Jew look exhausted. According to Cohen, Rubin points in this painting to the creation of a new world now that the Wandering Jew has endured his punishment to the full.[15]

In 1929 Itzik Manger, the renowned Yiddish poet active in Czernowitz at the time of Rubin's stay there, published a collection of poems titled *Shtern oyfn dakh* (Stars on the Roof) that included poems composed during the 1920s. One of the poems in the collection is the 'Ballad of the Crucified and the Verminous Man'.

On the darkening road, stands the verminous man
Who rouses from sleep the crucified one.

'Tell me, O Jesus, where did you hear
That your crown is holier than my tear?

Jesus, tell me, who says that your crown
Is holier than all my pain?'

King Jesus stammers, 'I'm only a child
Whose home is the wind where I'm crucified.'

King Jesus stammers, 'Woe and thrice woe
To my scarlet spring amid fallen snow.'

Feverish, the verminous man says, 'My home
Is cobwebs and night and wind and loam.

Forever a stranger, wherever I go,
Lice flicker like stars in my shirt—they glow.

You are rocked on the wind by two women so mild.
One murmurs, "Beloved", the other says, "Child."

There are pitying lips for each of your wounds;
They hallow your flesh, O crucified man,

While I am like shadows or dogs that bark
Or howl, abandoned on roads after dark.'

King Jesus stammers, 'O wretch, I believe
Your dust is more holy, more holy your grief.'

From the crucified trickles a thin, silver cry;
Smiling, the verminous man turns away

[15] Richard Cohen, 'Entre errance et histoire: Interprétations juives du mythe de Gottlieb à Kitaj', in *Le Juif Errant: Un témoin du temps*, exhibition catalogue, Musée d'Art et d'Histoire du Judaïsme (Paris, 2001), 165.

With heavy step toward the evening town
For a loaf of bread and a pitcher of wine.[16]

It is interesting to note the overlap between Manger's poem and Rubin's work. Admittedly, in the painting Jesus is seated in a proud, upright posture, while the Jew is stooped and slumped, which does not accord with the 'victory' of the Jew over Jesus in the poem. Yet Rubin's scene does recall the situation described in the first few verses, in which the Jew imagines the figure of Jesus. Perhaps the painting portrays the beginning of the conversation between Jesus and the Jew—a conversation that ends with the descent of the Jew, encouraged by Jesus's empathy, down into the village described in both the poem and the painting.

Despite the poem's somewhat whimsical tone, it does express the Jews' sense of the injustice committed by those who used the name of Jesus against them—a sentiment shared by many Jewish thinkers and artists. Jesus's admission that the suffering of the Jew is holier than his own can be read as criticism of the Church, which has turned Jesus's message into a justification for persecution and antisemitism.

It is not certain whether Rubin read Manger's poem, as the exact date of its writing is unknown; moreover, the painting apparently dates from Rubin's Bucharest days and not from his time in Czernowitz. Yet Rubin would surely have been familiar with Manger's poems—he had contacts among the Yiddish literary circle active in Czernowitz, contacts that he retained in later years, even after leaving Romania—and he would have been aware of Manger's interest in the relationship between the Jews and the figure of Jesus, a theme explored by many Yiddish poets at the time.[17]

Yet the painting also suggests another interpretation: a central element of *The Encounter* is the tree growing alongside Jesus, which parallels his erect posture, in contrast to the wilting tree beside the elderly Jew with his downcast head. The young tree next to Jesus is even propped up by a support, meant to ensure its upright growth. Feebleness and decline, representing the exilic Jew, contrasted with renewal, growth, and uprightness, is a familiar theme from images associated with Zionism: in an iconic postcard for the Fifth Zionist Congress, drawn by Ephraim Moses Lilien in 1901 (Plate 6), a stooped elderly Jew is depicted seated among curvilinear thorns, his cane in his hand and his downcast head leaning on the cane. To the right, on the horizon, a figure of a Jew can be seen ploughing the field in the direction of the rising sun, and beneath him, the ears of grain symbolize the promise of fertility and renewed growth in Palestine.

[16] Itzik Manger, *The World According to Itzik: Selected Poetry and Prose*, trans. Leonard Wolf (New Haven, 2002), 73–4.

[17] Avraham Novershtern, *Magic Twilight: Apocalypse and Messianism in Yiddish Literature* [Kesem hadimdumim: apokalipsah umeshiḥiyut besifrut yidish] (Jerusalem, 2003), 243–4.

The similarity between the elderly figures in the two paintings is clear. Extending the analogy, Jesus in Rubin's painting can be equated with the grain and the pioneer in Lilien's postcard—expressing an upsurge of vitality as opposed to the despair of the exilic Jew. Jesus's resurrection is a Christian symbol of life after death and of victory over death. In this painting, Rubin creates a symbolic analogy between the Zionist movement, reviving the Jewish people after its long exile, and the figure of Jesus, resurrected after his agonized death (emphasized by the bleeding stigmata on his hands). The symbolism of resurrection in *The Encounter* is also expressed in the blue flowers growing on the ground. According to this interpretation, Rubin's depiction of the Jew differs significantly from the description in Manger's poem, in a way that tips the balance between Jesus and the Jew: the latter's desperate need for recognition for his suffering is overshadowed by the figure of Jesus himself as a symbol of the 'new Jew', arisen from the death of exile, to be reborn in the Land of Israel.

Very similar in composition to *The Encounter (Jesus and the Jew)* is the painting *Jesus and the Last Apostle* (1922; Plate 7), which Rubin painted prior to his arrival in Palestine. The two works appear to be linked. In both the figure of Jesus is depicted as the counterpart of another figure, seated on a bench in a rural landscape, but in *Jesus and the Last Apostle* it has undergone an interesting transformation. In *The Encounter*, he is seated with his body upright and his head held high, his wounds displayed for all to see and his expression pained but proud, while the Jew is stooped and frail. In *Jesus and the Last Apostle* the tables are turned—it is Jesus who is now seated on the left, his face downcast, resting on his right arm, and completely concealed.

The key to the painting is the second figure—the 'last apostle'. Writing about the work in a letter, Rubin mentions that the model for this figure was Gala Galaction (1879–1961), a famous Romanian priest, writer, theologian, poet, humanist, and intellectual who fulfilled various roles in Romanian politics, especially between the world wars. In 1927 he translated the Bible into Romanian, and his prose style recalls that of the Bible. He was on friendly terms with rabbis and Jewish intellectuals and published articles in the Zionist periodical *Hage'ulah*. He expressed great admiration for Theodor Herzl, considering him the heir of the biblical prophets, and even wrote a book about him. His peers considered Galaction to be a true spiritual leader. His appearance was that of a biblical prophet, and many artists painted and sculpted him as such. Galaction was a charismatic and influential figure in Romanian culture and politics and also, more relevant to our context, served as a mediator between Jews and Romanians—in opposition to the endemic antisemitism prevailing in Romania during those years.

Galaction's benevolent disposition towards the Jews and Zionism is apparently what caused Rubin to ask him to serve as a model for the painting, as a figure placed in contrast to Jesus.[18] Jesus, showing his wounds, seems to be apologizing for the great suffering endured by the Jewish people on his account. The placement of Galaction—an opponent of antisemitism and a champion of Zionism—alongside Jesus is perhaps meant to depict the possibility of reconciliation between the Jewish people and Jesus. The latter has undergone a transformation: from a martyr and model whose crucifixion is blamed on the Jews, he becomes a figure apologizing to the Jews for the suffering inflicted on them in his name. Galaction performs the role of mediator, a new kind of apostle—the 'last apostle', bringing a message of mutual understanding between the two religions.

The Romanian public, which was in general unsympathetic to the Jews, saw Galaction as a man vested with religious authority; a painting by a Jewish artist that linked a philosemitic Romanian to the suffering of Jesus could be read, then, as a call for reconciliation. This, as we may recall, was also the intention of other Jewish artists who depicted Jesus, such as Mark Antokolsky and Marc Chagall.

*Meal of the Poor* (1922; Plate 8) is another painting from Rubin's Bucharest period that was shown in his exhibition there at the end of 1922. The painting, in which the figures of seven careworn Jews are seated at a table, in a kind of hasidic *tish* or celebratory gathering, also suggests Christian motifs. At the head of the table sits a rabbi-like figure dividing the bread. All the figures are surrounded by an aura, which can most clearly be seen around the old rabbi and the figure on his right. On the oval table are slices of watermelon (the cheapest kind of food, which was also used to feed cattle), loaves of bread, a plate of fish, and a vase with a white lily. The lily serves as a symbol of the annunciation in many paintings, appearing in the hand of the angel bringing Mary the news of her miraculous conception. The fish is also an important Christian symbol (the Greek word for 'fish', *ichthus*, supplied early Christians with an acronym for 'Jesus Christ, God's Son, Saviour'); it was also associated with the miracle of the loaves and fishes and with Jesus's disciples, many of them Galilee fishermen. Although the guests at the table include two women, the seating arrangement could suggest the disciples placed around the table at the Last Supper, with one important difference—the number of those present, which at the Last Supper was, of course, twelve besides Jesus. If the figure of the old rabbi at the head of the table is analogous to Jesus at the Last Supper, then only six of the disciples are present at this meal; it is perhaps for this reason that the table is incompletely laid, its cloth prominently cut off in front of the viewer. Although there is no written evidence to suggest it, one might speculate:

---

[18] Rubin kept up his contacts with Galaction after arriving in Palestine, and Galaction even wrote an appreciative article on Rubin's Land of Israel paintings, published in the Romanian newspaper *Adevărul* in November 1924.

could Rubin have been hinting that the absent disciples of this 'Jesus' are on their way to Palestine? This meal of the poor, tasting of hardship and suffering, is one of Rubin's last paintings before his own emigration there.

In 1922 Rubin painted the work called *The Madonna of the Homeless* (Plate 9), shown at his Bucharest exhibition at the end of the same year, a painting that is also associated with scenes from the New Testament and with the figure of Jesus. In the vein of *The Encounter*, Rubin creates an analogy between the Jesus-like infant and the figure of the pioneer, spiritually reborn on the soil of Palestine. The tones of the painting are lighter, and it displays the first signs of Rubin's new Land of Israel style. In contrast to the anguish reflected in his previous paintings, this work seems to indicate Rubin's optimism in anticipation of his *aliyah*. The emphasis placed on Jesus the infant rather than on the suffering of the crucified Christ lends strength to this interpretation. In *The Madonna of the Homeless* the baby is lying on his back on the ground, as in adoration scenes from the late fourteenth century, of which Rubin probably saw many examples during his journey through Italy in 1915. The depiction of the Madonna and child in the nineteenth century had gradually departed from such traditional representations, whether in works by James Tissot, who painted Mary as an Arab woman in an attempt at historical accuracy, or in the works of Jean-François Millet, who presented her as a simple villager. The Impressionists opted for a more prosaic style, while Van Gogh, Gauguin, and Émile Bernard, each in his own way, rediscovered the religious dimension of this image. Gauguin portrayed his Madonnas in the local landscape and attire of Tahitian women. He perceived a contrast between European forms of faith, which he associated with the Eve of the Hebrew Bible, and the beliefs of Tahiti, which, he felt, were closer to the 'second Eve'—Mary. Gauguin considered the women of Tahiti wholesome and pure, unlike the decadent women of Europe.[19] Rubin, as we know, was influenced by Gauguin, and his Israeli paintings have often been compared to Gauguin's works from Tahiti in their attempt to express the primal, the innocent, and the pure. Perhaps, like his French counterpart, Rubin saw Mary's role in this painting as that of a second Eve: like the women of Tahiti, she is good and pure, in the tradition of the 'noble savage', in contrast to the decadent, seductive European woman—depicted, for example, in *Temptation in the Desert*.

Indeed, in many ways, *The Madonna of the Homeless* is diametrically opposed to the earlier *Temptation in the Desert*. The composition of the two paintings is very similar: in the *Temptation*, three figures lie behind the protagonist in the centre, with another lying in the foreground. In *The Madonna of the Homeless* the woman is the central figure; behind her lie four men, and in front of her

[19] Ziva Amishai-Maisels, *Gauguin's Religious Themes* (New York, 1985), 291.

is the naked infant. The gentle, smiling face of the Madonna replaces the
tortured countenance of the central figure in *Temptation in the Desert*. The
smiling Madonna is, furthermore, the opposite of the seductive woman. Her
bare breast symbolizes fertility and health rather than temptation.

*The Madonna of the Homeless*, painted a short time prior to Rubin's arrival
in Palestine, can be considered a turning point—from his anguished, 'exilic'
depictions and the portrayal of ascetic prophets and the suffering Jesus to a
painting devoted to Zionist renewal, realized by Rubin himself with his emigration in 1923. Rubin's Mary is not praying to Jesus, a fact that lessens
somewhat her Christian identification as the mother of God. Her bared
breast emphasizes the idea of fertility; her position, seated on the ground, is
an image of simplicity and vitality. The sleeping child seems to symbolize
the Jew reborn in the Land of Israel while also expressing the vital powers of
birth and growth. The sleeping male figures behind the Madonna are the
'homeless', the pioneers who have come to build their new home in
Palestine.

This work continues Rubin's exploration of Christian symbols but, in
contrast to the other paintings, it is imbued with a sense of hope and renewal
(the theme of suffering is merely hinted at by the red flowers in the
Madonna's hands). Above all, it presents Jesus's other image—as the child
bringing the promise of salvation, the child whose birth is a symbol of victory over death. Indeed, this image might indicate Rubin's identification
with another important aspect of the figure of Jesus—his resurrection.

In *The Encounter*, Jesus can be interpreted as a symbol of the Zionist pioneer; in *The Madonna of the Homeless*, this symbolism is even more explicit.
Jesus the child appears here as the symbol of Zionism and the Jew reborn on
his native land, resurrected from the death of exile. Perhaps the figure of
Jesus here—the infant born on the soil of Palestine—can be considered a
'self-portrait' of the artist, soon to arrive in the Land of Israel.

Rubin's first year in Palestine was notably the most important one in his
artistic development. In that year, gradually abandoning his old approach, he
developed his Land of Israel style, and made a transition to new subject matter. His treatment of the figure of Jesus at this time is important in understanding Rubin's self-image at a turning point in his career: it must be seen in
the context of other cultural spheres developing within the emergent Yishuv,
primarily the field of poetry.

The third wave of Zionist immigration, during the years 1919–23,
brought to Palestine important cultural figures, such as the poets Uri Zvi
Greenberg and Abraham Shlonsky, both of whom explored the themes of
messianism and prophecy. Messianic poetic imagery was at the time a
conventional way of representing the revolutionary pioneer spirit in general,
and an expressly messianic semantics was characteristic of the public

discourse of the times.[20] In the context of religiosity and the controversies between holiness and secularity that gripped Hebrew poetry during the Third Aliyah, a special place was reserved for the figure of Jesus, originating in the new conceptions of his historical role among Jewish thinkers and scholars in Europe. Greenberg, Shlonsky, and others saw Jesus as an ideal figure and sought to 'repatriate' him, uprooting him from his Christian, antisemitic context and replanting him in the Jewish world, especially in the world of the pioneer settlers building the country with hard labour and great endurance. The link between the pioneers and early Christianity, as embodied by Jesus and the apostles, is articulated in Shlonsky's poem from 1927, 'Yizre'el (Jezreel)':

> Who is great here? Who is small
> In the kingdom of labour and flesh?
> The earth unfurls here—a New Testament scroll
> And we are—the Twelve.[21]

Even before Uri Zvi Greenberg reached Palestine his poetry was already heavily messianic, extolling the virtues of suffering and affliction. The poems from his years in Warsaw and Berlin (1921–3), throbbing with pathos, emotional turmoil, and deep religiosity endow Jesus with crucial significance. After his arrival in Palestine, Greenberg continued to employ the figure of Jesus in his poetry. In part 8 of *The Earthly Jerusalem* (*Yerushalayim shel matah*; 1924), he calls on Jesus to emerge from the monasteries and go to the valley of Jezreel:

> And now, my brother, go forth from the monasteries—for the appointed time has come. Go up to Meah She'arim and buy there a *talith* . . .
> Or better still: Buy there shorts and a blouse, garments of a *halutz*, and ask in Hebrew: 'Where is the road to Emek Jezreel, that is, *Yerushalayim shel matah*?'—and they will tell you whither.[22]

Following a visit to the Jezreel valley, Rubin wrote: 'After [the American pilgrims in Nazareth] had played 5,675 games of polo, they realized they had to play another game in Nazareth, the place where a worthy Jew with

---

[20] Hanan Hever, *Imprisoned in Utopia: An Essay on Messianism and Politics in Hebrew Poetry in Palestine between the Two World Wars* [Beshevi ha'utopyah, masah al meshiḥiyut upolitikah bashirah ha'ivrit be'erets yisra'el bein shetei milḥamot ha'olam] (Beersheva, 1995), 64.

[21] Abraham Shlonsky, *In the Circle: Songs and Poems* [Bagalgal: shirim upo'emot] (Tel Aviv, 1927), 123; this is a literal translation by Anat Schultz. This part of Shlonsky's poem may have been inspired by the poem 'The Twelve' (1918), by Russian poet Aleksandr Blok, which describes the march of twelve unruly Bolshevik guards and equates them with the twelve apostles being led by Jesus. Shlonsky was a great admirer of Blok's work and translated this poem into Hebrew in the late 1920s.

[22] Uri Zvi Greenberg, *Jerusalem: Yerushalayim Shel Matah*, trans. Charles A. Cowen (New York, 1939), 42.

nothing to do once rose and began to preach the truth.' He goes on to describe the Jewish farmers whom he met in the valley as the antithesis of the American pilgrims, who seemed inauthentic to him: 'I want to tell you of the present-day "cross-bearers", they, these worthy Jews, excite me and it is about them that I want to cry out the furor in my soul to someone, and offer him my logic.'[23]

Rubin thus perceived a deep connection between the pioneers and the figure of Jesus on the cross, and he saw their labour as a kind of 'crucifixion' that would bring about national salvation. In describing himself as a pioneer of art, a painter, a martyr, and even as Jesus, Rubin identified with the pioneers he admired and saw himself as one of them. Having drawn an analogy between Jesus and Zionism while still in Romania, it was only natural for him to adopt the view of the pioneer as a Jesus-like figure. Yet we should keep in mind that, though Yiddish and Hebrew poetry made a link between Jesus and Zionism, in Jewish and early Land of Israel painting this link was non-existent. In the Palestine of the 1920s, Rubin's path was thus unique.

In a letter of 1923, the year of his arrival in Palestine, Rubin laments the condition of the Bezalel school and claims he will do away with old-fashioned artistic trends: 'No one has the courage to get up and sweep away all of the merchants and peddlers from within the temple. The temple must be cleaned!'[24] Referring to Jesus, who entered the temple in Jerusalem and drove out the moneylenders, Rubin sees himself as the bearer of the new artistic message, the prophet and even the messiah, sweeping away all that is old, corrupt, and decrepit and driving it out of the temple of Land of Israel art. These assertions are important both as a reflection of Rubin's view of the central artistic establishment in Palestine of those days and because of their radical tone, but perhaps above all because of the explicit way in which he identifies with Jesus.

In *Self-Portrait with a Flower* (1923?; Plate 10[25]) Rubin depicts himself in a white garment against the background of the Tel Aviv dunes, with tents, two houses, and a stretch of sea with a ship. His monumental figure fills most of the canvas; he is looking at the viewer out of the corner of his eye, with a penetrating, confident gaze. The melancholy expression still recalls the atmosphere of the Romanian paintings, but at the same time this work reveals the central characteristics of Rubin's Land of Israel style—light colours, flattened surfaces, wide, thinly painted areas of colour. The

---

[23] Rubin to Weinberg, 24 Aug. 1925, RMA.

[24] Rubin to Weinberg, 19 July 1923, RMA.

[25] Although the date on the painting is 1922, it appears nevertheless to have been painted after Rubin's arrival in Palestine in 1923. It is possible that Rubin added the (mistaken) date at a later time. This assumption was also confirmed by tests on the painting made in the Israel Museum's restoration laboratories, which showed a different use of paint in the area of the date.

construction of the face also suggests characteristics of African sculpture—characteristics that attracted many modernist artists. In his left hand Rubin is holding a white lily, the symbol of the annunciation, which we have already seen in *Meal of the Poor* (Plate 8). Here it seems to announce the birth of the messiah of labour and the renewal of the land.

Rubin depicts himself in this portrait as a pioneer. This can be seen both in his white clothing (his shirt is the typical one worn by the pioneers) and in the background—the tents of a new neighbourhood in Tel Aviv. His strong grasp of the brushes is thus analogous to the grasp of a hoe or pick-axe in the hands of a pioneer, and the artist is thus himself depicted as a kind of pioneer, holding in his hands the sign of salvation in the form of the flower, and his work tools—the paintbrushes. The severe expression on his face tells of the long and difficult road ahead before the redemption of the homeland. Similarly, saints and martyrs and the figure of Jesus in paintings of the Middle Ages and in later times appeared holding in their hands their instruments of martyrdom or other attributes (see Plate 11). In Rubin's painting there is a close connection between the brushes, recalling the tools of martyrdom, and the flower of the annunciation, representing redemption.

The series *The God-Seekers*, which Rubin created in 1923, includes twelve prints, and was bound in an album published in a numbered edition of 115 copies. The themes and style of the series represent, in a sense, a gesture of farewell, bringing to a close Rubin's Romanian period. The technique is significant: this is the only series of woodprints Rubin created; apparently he felt that this technique (rather than painting with oils) would allow him to better express his stormy feelings during his first year in Palestine. Some of the depictions reflect the artist's loneliness and sense of mission, others life in the diaspora, while yet others illustrate secular and religious aspects of the way of life in Palestine.

In one of the prints in the series that is particularly relevant to our subject, *The Prophet in the Desert* (Plate 12), Rubin alludes to Jesus directly, without mentioning or even hinting at his name in the title of the work. This avoidance might have been motivated by a desire to avert attacks from religious circles or forestall a loss in sales. The depiction of the figure with its hands pierced by wounds is based on the traditional portrayals of Jesus as the 'man of sorrows', although here, rather than a delineation of the suffering Jesus, the image seems to be of Jesus proudly displaying his wounds after the resurrection. This is how he appears, for example, in Matthias Grünewald's Isenheim altarpiece (*c*.1515). Despite the presentation of his wounds, this Jesus is not the 'man of sorrows' but rather the saviour, victorious over death. As in *The Encounter* (Plate 5), the image of the resurrected Christ can be connected here to the Zionist renewal of the land.

The figure of Jesus disappears from Rubin's works in 1924 but it returns for a last 'guest appearance' in the painting *First Seder in Jerusalem* (1950; Plate 13).[26] Jesus appears here at the *seder* table, seated next to many other figures: the artist, his wife and son, a rabbi, a soldier, and typical Israeli figures, some of which appeared in earlier paintings by Rubin. According to Christian tradition, the *seder* meal was the Last Supper, in which Jesus predicted his own death and after which began his passion, ending with the crucifixion. In this painting, Jesus joins the festive *seder* meal, presided over by a rabbi, following the establishment of the State of Israel. He is seated on the left, opposite Rubin; his hands are spread in a gesture reminiscent of the display of the stigmata, but this time he is blessing those present, perhaps expressing his approval of the establishment of a Jewish state. Here, Rubin's interest in the figure of Jesus comes full circle. After twenty-six years, Jesus's appearance in the context of the new state and of the *seder* meal celebrating the release from bondage to freedom supports the interpretation that, in Rubin's early works, Jesus signified the resurrection and rebirth of the Jewish people in its land.

Rubin employed the figure of Jesus on two planes, both exceptional for a Jewish Zionist artist at the beginning of the twentieth century: on the personal plane—as the artist identifying with Jesus's suffering, and on the national one—surprisingly enough, to express Jewish national sentiments, that is, Zionism. Rubin's identification with Jesus as a symbol of suffering and personal sacrifice is extraordinary for a Jewish artist of the period. Although, as mentioned above, there were Jewish artists—Chagall, among others—who linked the figure of Jesus with the suffering of the Jews, nowhere do we find a Jewish artist identifying with Jesus the man outside the Jewish context, to the point of creating a Jesus-like self-portrait.[27] The background to Rubin's identification with Jesus in his self-portrait (1921) and in *Temptation in the Desert* is not the general suffering of the Jews but rather Rubin's personal tribulations. Seeing himself at the time as part of the European rather than the Jewish artistic tradition that he absorbed at Bezalel, and regarding himself as a follower of Van Gogh and Gauguin, it

[26] Proof that this is indeed Jesus (and not the Prophet Elijah, the traditional *seder* guest) appears in the autobiography of the American artist of Jewish origin Raphael Soyer. Soyer describes his visit to Rubin's studio in 1968: while showing the visitor the painting *First Seder in Jerusalem*, Rubin commented: 'I even invited Jesus to this party.' See Raphael Soyer, *Self-Revealment: A Memoir* (New York, 1969), 109.

[27] Ziva Amishai-Maisels mentions the possibility that, in a preliminary study for the painting *Dedicated to Christ* or *Golgotha* by Marc Chagall (1912), the inscription above the head of the crucified Jesus was replaced by the word 'Marc'. The inscribed word is unclear, and this is a study rather than the finished painting. If it does indeed say this, however, then Chagall is here expressing his identification with Jesus in the sense of Jewish suffering and in the context of the Beilis blood libel, which gave rise to the painting. See Ziva Amishai-Maisels, 'Chagall's *Dedicated to Christ*: Sources and Meanings', *Jewish Art*, 21–2 (1995–6), 74.

was, after all, quite natural for Rubin to identify with a figure so controversial in the Jewish context.

Even more uncommon was the use Rubin made of Jesus's figure as a symbol of redemption and resurrection connected with Zionism when he contrasted Jesus in *The Encounter* with the Jew of the diaspora, or when he depicted Jesus the child in *The Madonna of the Homeless* as a Zionist symbol of renewal in the Land of Israel. Rubin set a precedent in the Zionist art of the period by portraying Jesus as a representation of the 'new Jew' destined to replace the diasporic Jew. In *Self-Portrait with a Flower*, painted in Palestine, depicting himself holding the white lily, the symbol of the annunciation and the birth of the Christian messiah, Rubin drew a connection between himself as the new Israeli artist and the figure of Jesus. In this seminal work we thus see Rubin's unique utilization of Christian symbols to express his artistic, personal, and Zionist ideals.

# FOUR

# MIHAIL SEBASTIAN
## *A Jewish Writer and his (Antisemitic) Master*

LEON VOLOVICI

A STUDY OF MIHAIL SEBASTIAN (1907–45) focusing on his Jewish dilemmas and his right-wing friends can illuminate the condition of an important category of Jewish intellectuals in Romania between the two world wars. His experience exemplifies the complex relationship between those Romanian Jews who were integrated into the culture of the country and the Romanian cultural circles that, to some degree, accepted and promoted them. In this essay I will deal specifically with the relationship between the artist Sebastian and his spiritual master, the philosopher Nae Ionescu ('our leader of conscience', as Sebastian termed him), who at important stages of his intellectual development adhered to a nationalistic trend of thought that included antisemitism as one of its integral components. To some degree, this relationship resembles that between Maurycy Gottlieb and Jan Matejko, extensively explored in Ezra Mendelsohn's book on the Polish Jewish painter.[1]

Sebastian's painful interaction with his master unfolded under far more dramatic historical circumstances than that between Gottlieb and Matejko—not in late nineteenth-century Poland, but in the mid-1930s in a Romanian intellectual environment that was captivated by extreme right-wing political ideas. The drama of Sebastian's life was also enhanced by the fact that, though he lived in a place and at a time when the Jewish intelligentsia had attained a much more advanced level of acculturation, the ultimate failure of the integration process and of the so-called 'symbiosis' between Jews and the surrounding society was becoming ever more apparent.

Sebastian was thus much more estranged than Gottlieb from the Jewish cultural world. He never sought to deny his Jewish identity, defined rather metaphysically, but he wanted to be—and was—a *Romanian* writer. The Jewish writers of the generation preceding Sebastian's were, generally speaking, connected to two cultural traditions—Jewish in their family environment and Romanian with regard to their intellectual development. In a

[1] Ezra Mendelsohn, *Painting a People: Maurycy Gottlieb and Jewish Art* (Hanover, NH, 2002).

recent synthesis, Israeli literary historian Abraham Joffe noted the existence over the first three decades of the twentieth century of no fewer than fifty Jewish writers who produced their literary output in Romanian and who were acknowledged to a greater or lesser extent by Romanian critics and literary historians.[2] Some of them are considered outstanding writers even today, among them Beniamin Fundoianu, Felix Aderca, Max Blecher, Ilarie Voronca, Isac Peltz, and Ion Călugăru.[3] Aderca and Fundoianu (later known as a French poet and philosopher under the name of Benjamin Fondane), for example, published in the Romanian-language Zionist press just as frequently as in Romanian literary magazines. Both were initially captivated by the Zionist dream and regarded A. L. Zissu as their spiritual guide. A charismatic, radical ideologist who was very influential among the young, Zissu had a cordial relationship with Nae Ionescu, whom he resembled in many ways. He, too, supported a 'pure' form of nationalism (Jewish in his case) and he argued that Jews should keep out of the culture and political life of other ethnic groups. By contrast, Sebastian was exclusively a product of Romanian and European culture, loosely connected to the Jewish tradition, which he did not reject outright but which he viewed as belonging only to the past—a past that he regarded alternately with irony and nostalgic condescension.

Surprisingly, this most 'Romanian' of the Jewish writers of his generation—a generation that won recognition after the First World War—was also the one most preoccupied by the dilemmas of Jewish identity. His treatment of the issue, however, was diffuse, sentimental, and abstract. Sebastian, who was to become popular with critics and readers alike, belonged to the young intellectual circle that gathered around Nae Ionescu, a professor of logic and metaphysics who was also a journalist and politician at the time.[4] These young people wrote for the newspaper *Cuvântul* (The Word), edited by Ionescu. Already in the autumn of 1933 Ionescu and his young followers—headed by Mircea Eliade, Emil Cioran, and, later, Constantin Noica—had begun to back the fascist Iron Guard (Garda de Fier).[5]

[2] Abraham B. Joffe, *In Foreign Pastures: Jewish Writers in Romania, 1880–1940* [Besadot zarim: soferim yehudim berumenyah, 1880–1940] (Tel Aviv, 1996).

[3] For their approach to Jewish and Romanian identity, see Leon Volovici, 'Romanian Writers—Jewish Writers: The Dilemmas of Cultural Identity', *Studia Judaica*, 13 (2005), 151–60.

[4] Irina Livezeanu, 'A Jew from the Danube: *Cuvântul*, the Rise of the Right and Mihail Sebastian', *Shvut*, 16 (1993), 297–312.

[5] See Leon Volovici, *Nationalist Ideology and Antisemitism: The Case of Romanian Intellectuals in the 1930s* (Oxford, 1991), 132–40; Norman Manea, 'Felix Culpa', in id., *On Clowns: The Dictator and the Artist* (New York, 1992); Zigu Ornea, *Anii treizeci: Extrema dreaptă românească* (Bucharest, 1995); Marta Petreu, *Un trecut deochiat sau Schimbarea la față a României* (Cluj, 1999), English version: *An Infamous Past: E. M. Cioran and the Rise of Fascism in Romania* (Chicago, 2001); Alexandra Laignel-Lavastine, *Cioran, Eliade, Ionesco: L'Oubli du fascisme* (Paris, 2002).

Without an understanding of the political context of the antisemitic psychosis that gripped Romania in the 1930s and the obsessive preoccupation with the 'Jewish question' characteristic of the period, it is difficult today to comprehend the terrible scandal and fierce debate that surrounded Sebastian's novel *De două mii de ani . . .* (For Two Thousand Years). The novel appeared in 1934, and contained an appallingly antisemitic preface by Ionescu. Written in the form of the diary of a young Jewish intellectual confronted with the traumatic and demeaning experience of Romanian antisemitism, it was a brilliant attempt to give literary expression to the situation of the Jewish intellectual in Romanian society. The hero seeks his own answer to the torments and quandaries arising from his sense of oppression, but finds himself unable to accept any of the usual ideologies then to hand: Zionism, Marxism, or self-segregation in the 'ghetto of tradition'. As he says at one point:

In my eyes, the debate over a political solution to the Jewish problem is totally unproductive. I am interested in only one solution—the psychological, the spiritual. I think that the only way to determine anything with respect to this painful question would be for me to try, for my own sake, to loosen the hostile bonds and the conflicts that connect me to Romanian life. And I do not see this seclusion as a way of escaping, an expression of a lack of solidarity with my people [i.e. the Jewish people], but, in fact, the contrary—for it is not possible that the experience of one man, who forthrightly accepts and endures his drama, should not be of help to others as well.[6]

The first-person narrative presents passionate conversations between the protagonist and his friends in the Romanian intellectual elite on the subject of Romanian antisemitism and its root causes. Unlike other novels of the period, it talks about the apathy of those in the hero's circle, including his Romanian friends, in the face of antisemitic hostility and propaganda. 'When I think of it', he declares, 'it's not so terrible that three fellows can stand on a street corner and shout "Death to the Yids!" What's terrible is that their cry doesn't arouse any reaction. No one pays any attention to it—as if it were the screeching of a passing streetcar.'[7]

As early as 1931, Sebastian had asked Ionescu to write a preface to the novel, and although, in November 1933, his mentor had joined the right-wing Legionnaire Movement (Mişcarea Legionară). Sebastian expected him to stay loyal to their past relationship and to his old ideas on Judaism. However, the preface turned out to contain an overt theological rationalization of antisemitism, and became one of the primary reasons for the scandal that surrounded the book.[8]

---

[6] Mihail Sebastian, *De două mii de ani . . .* (Bucharest, 2006), 247. All translations without a specific source in English are my own.      [7] Ibid. 225.

[8] Ovid S. Crohmălniceanu, *Literatura română între cele două războaie mondiale*, 3 vols. (Bucharest, 1975), iii. 106–9; Volovici, *Nationalist Ideology*, 99–105; Matei Călinescu, 'Romania's 1930s Revisited', *Salmagundi*, 97 (Winter 1993), 133–52.

In 1934, referred to by Sebastian as 'an antisemitic year', Jewish and Romanian intellectuals were unable to contend with the novel's sceptical personal reflections on the urgent 'Jewish question'. Sebastian was caught in the crossfire from every direction; the book, including its shocking preface, was attacked in the extremist antisemitic press, the democratic press, and the Jewish nationalist press, headed by I. Ludo. In 1935 Sebastian responded to all his attackers in a brilliant essay entitled *Cum am devenit huligan* (How I Became a Hooligan), in which he analysed the stormy response to his book, defined his position regarding the dilemma of dual identity, and summed up his relationship with Ionescu. Despite his success as the most 'integrated' Jewish author in Romanian literature, Sebastian rejected the 'comedy of assimilation', considering it a betrayal. Nevertheless, he expressed his faith in the possibility of forging a link between the Jewish tradition that was his legacy and the culture in which he functioned. In the face of brutal antisemitic attacks, and despite the denial by his opponents of his right to be a Romanian writer, Sebastian persisted in believing in the 'dual' option: 'You are a Jew and will remain a Jew, but you will nonetheless try to define your place in Romanian culture and society; your debts toward them are clearer now that you no longer have any illusions.'[9]

His relationship with Ionescu is more difficult to decipher. Certainly, the Romanian ideologue of an integral and xenophobic nationalism was the literary and intellectual godfather of his teenage years. His attachment to him was total, a youthful passion for an intellectual and cultural model, an attachment that also determined the intellectual path that he ultimately chose. Given this almost filial relationship, Ionescu's sinister preface had a cataclysmic effect on the writer: 'a total feeling of ashes and death', Sebastian wrote.[10] Using Sebastian's real name, Iosef Hechter, as a prototype of the eternal Jew who is eternally doomed, Ionescu pronounced a sentence of eternal damnation:

You are sick, Iosef Hechter. You are substantially sick because you have to suffer; and because your suffering is bottled up. Everybody is suffering, Iosef Hechter. We Christians also are suffering. But we have a way out, because we can save ourselves. I know you are hoping, hoping that he for whom you wait will come. The Messiah, on his white horse, and then you will rule the earth. You are hoping, Iosef Hechter. It is the only thing left to you.

But I cannot do anything for you. Because I know: the Messiah will not come. The Messiah has come, Iosef Hechter, and you did not recognize him. All you were asked to do in exchange for all the good things God gave you was to be vigilant. And you were not vigilant. Or you did not see, because pride closed your eyes.
. . . Iosef Hechter, don't you feel the grip of the cold and darkness?[11]

⁹ Sebastian, *De două mii de ani . . .*, 24.     ¹⁰ Ibid. 74.
¹¹ Nae Ionescu, preface to Sebastian, *De două mii de ani . . .*, 25.

'It is a preface of cold, methodical, and indifferent cruelty', commented Sebastian a year later.[12] The fact that 'our leader of conscience', as Sebastian termed him, could write such a text was much more serious and more irreparable than its being published. 'Against this preface', added Sebastian, 'I could have just one revenge that was at the same time a duty—publish it.'[13] Before he read the preface Sebastian had been naively convinced that it would not reflect Ionescu's recent radical change of political stance. 'Today I have to admit', Sebastian wrote, 'I was wrong.'[14]

Was Sebastian also wrong about the previous period? It is obvious from an examination of Ionescu's political and ideological journalism that at least some of the ideas to be found in that shocking preface were evident as much as ten years earlier. How, then, can one explain Sebastian's illusions? Replying to Ionescu's critics, who had long suspected him of antisemitic ideas, Sebastian wrote:

His sympathy for Jewish issues was known, his justification in speaking about this was unquestionable. People ignore carelessly, or just recklessly, the few years in which he developed an attitude of understanding, sympathy, and objective know-ledge with regard to the Judaic phenomenon in its political aspects, but primarily on its spiritual level. The *Cuvântul* collection from 1926 until the autumn of 1933 bears witness to that.[15]

Sebastian is referring here to a series of four articles on 'The Crisis of Judaism', published in *Cuvântul* in 1926, in which Ionescu set out to prove that, together with Judaism, a foreign and unfamiliar element had pene-trated Christian culture: 'But the European world', he stated, 'is directly or indirectly Descartes' world.' From Descartes derived the 'falsification of the concept of reason' along with, among other things, individualism, scientific nominalism and free examination, democracy, socialism, and economic or political liberalism.

But let us be honest with ourselves: who among the thinkers who followed the line of European thought, assuming it and making it their own, did not stumble in the face of the Renaissance and of Descartes; who among them was able to identify for a moment with—and participate in the monumental architecture of—Spinoza?

Didn't we all feel that a foreign and unknown element had suddenly permeated our spiritual history and changed its course? Whence does the new evolutionary pantheism acquire its explosive power—the theory that Dilthey rightly presents as the most expressive and most characteristic spiritual movement of the new age? Oh, certainly, the problem is not so simple. But I discovered something when I found out that the metaphysics of kabbalah—if its content can be called metaphysical—explains and unifies more than three-quarters of Goethe's great tragedy, *Faust*. . . .

---

[12] Mihail Sebastian, *Cum am devenit huligan* (1935; Bucharest, 2007), 74.     [13] Ibid. 89.
[14] Ibid. 67.     [15] Ibid. 59.

After all, it is only natural for us to want to know how European consciousness has been falsified in the last four hundred years.[16]

Whereas Ionescu clearly perceives here a subversive infiltration perverting the Christian spirit of Europe, Sebastian read his words as conceding some kind of praise for Judaism.

Accused of antisemitism as early as 1926, Ionescu clarified his stand:

When we were called 'antisemites', I reacted categorically and clarified: we are not antisemites, but nationalists. Not because we were afraid of a word but because it affronted our concern for the proper term. Antisemite—this is a definition by negation. This would mean that I exist only relative to my enemy. This is a humiliating and, from a tactical point of view, a dangerous situation; being simply an antisemite means adopting an inferior position by placing yourself on the defensive. Nationalism, on the other hand, is an affirmative stand: I affirm the right of my nation to perfect its own development within our state, and I declare that the other nations have to accommodate the majority nation.[17]

In 1928 Ionescu again spoke of a 'Judaization of the European spirit' in a polemic with a Hungarian politician in Transylvania who was worried about the 'Judaization' of Hungarian culture:

Count Bánffy lacks certain more precise and more scholarly information. Otherwise he could have traced the Judaization of the European spirit to as early as the Renaissance and the Reformation, so much so that not even Goethe could escape such influences. The recrudescence of the Judaic spirit in contemporary literature is made easier nowadays by the dissolute atmosphere in which we live. . . .

Thus the reaction against the Judaic spirit will also occur in Hungary, as it occurs everywhere by differentiating the national cultures and through awareness of their differences. As long as the Jews did not emphasize the permanent values of Judaism, they could formally integrate into the culture of their respective country and could deform it. Today this process is no longer possible.[18]

Today, it is obvious that Sebastian mistakenly attributed 'democratic' and 'liberal' ideas to Ionescu. Even in the essay of 1935 in which Sebastian brilliantly exposed the sophisms of Ionescu's preface, he still held the same unrealistic view of his mentor's 'democratic' antecedents. 'He has always envisaged', Sebastian wrote, 'a policy of broad public and cultural liberties for all minorities and especially for the Jews (for the issue is raised more often and more acutely with regard to them).'[19] The incompatibility of their fundamental beliefs had existed, in essence, even before 1933, but Sebastian

---

[16] 'Ce crede Julien Weill', *Cuvântul*, no. 509, 18 July 1926; repr. in Nae Ionescu, *Între ziaristică și filosofie* (Iași, 1996), 192–3.

[17] Nae Ionescu, 'Reacțiune și altceva', *Cuvântul*, no. 549, 3 Sept. 1926; repr. ibid. 15–16.

[18] Id., 'Ideile domnului Bánffy', *Cuvântul*, no. 1068, 12 Apr. 1928; repr. ibid. 242.

[19] Sebastian, *Cum am devenit huligan*, 59.

did not or could not see it. Ionescu's thinking was from the very beginning profoundly anti-democratic.[20]

Unlike Ionescu's other disciples, Sebastian was never attracted to his non-democratic ideas or to the cult of dictatorship, whether of the right or of the left (Ionescu was initially also an admirer of Stalin), but he seemed not to have noticed the early totalitarian preferences of his master. Until 1933, Sebastian failed to perceive the true nature of Ionescu's political stance—his radical, anti-liberal, and anti-democratic ideas, as well as his antisemitism.

In 1931, reprimanding those young Romanians who were organizing antisemitic attacks on Jews and their property ('a terrible waste of energy'), Ionescu conceded that antisemitism could serve an educative role during the formative years of the younger generation. But, he argued, it should be subsumed within an overarching nationalist movement:

With regard to today's youth, what is still happening now—and did not happen before!—is sad and indicative of decline. We used to know, or merely instinctively understood, that the school of antisemitism or of socialism was good on one condition . . . that one advanced beyond it. Accept it, even seek it, in a shower of enthusiasm, of generosity, or as an antidote to personal egocentrism. But no more than that! The 'violent' youth of today, less critical than we were, unfortunately take their 'doctrine' seriously. . . . This is not what we expect of the young. Not this stubborn attachment to some singular and deserted position but integration into the rhythm of the nation and of life, ready for any sacrifice.[21]

Finally, in 1933 Ionescu contested the Jews' right to involve themselves in the political life of the country, labelling those Romanians who opposed the antisemitic movements 'philosemites'[22] and 'camouflaged Jews'.[23]

Ironically, Ionescu's influence on Sebastian is noticeable in the latter's ideas on Judaism as expressed in *Cum am devenit huligan*. Both men were now opposed to the 'assimilation' of the Jews—Sebastian's 'comedy of assimilation' was a phrase first used by Ionescu. But the disciple ignored the xenophobia at the core of the professor's ideology. Ionescu stated clearly in 1933 that 'the Jews do not have the right or the qualities to influence the public life of the country',[24] but Sebastian's message was completely different: in a free society, the Jew should, as a matter of free choice, assert his own

---

[20] For an extensive analysis of Ionescu's political ideas, see George Voicu, *Mitul Nae Ionescu* (Bucharest, 2000).

[21] Nae Ionescu, 'Peste limita de vîrstă', *Cuvântul*, no. 2048, 3 Jan. 1931; repr. in id., *Între ziaristică*, 86–7.

[22] Nae Ionescu, '. . . Şi un cuvînt de pace', *Cuvântul*, no. 3076, 17 Nov. 1933; repr. ibid. 161.

[23] Nae Ionescu, ' "Zdrobitoarea majoritate" a evreilor naţionali', *Cuvântul*, no. 3099, 10 Dec. 1933; repr. ibid. 176.

[24] 'Între "agresivitate" antisemită şi "pasivitate" filosemită', *Cuvântul*, no. 3085, 26 Nov. 1933; repr. ibid. 168.

separate identity. Furthermore, in contrast to Ionescu's writing a decade earlier, which explained the sufferings of the Jews by reference to the internal contradictions within Judaism, or to the tension between religion and ethnicity or between mysticism and rationality, his preface to *De două mii de ani* . . . attributed their misfortunes to the sin of rejecting Jesus as the messiah.

How, then, can we explain Sebastian's idealized image of Ionescu and his political ideas? What appears to have been at work was the personal fascination exerted on him by Ionescu, together with an attachment to the thinker who had introduced him to the enchanted realm of ideas. Comparing the relationship between Ionescu and Sebastian to that between Richard Wagner and his Jewish disciples, Matei Călinescu does not hide his perplexity in seeking to understand the intellectual bond between an antisemitic master and the Jewish disciples who worship him:

It is amazing, from a distance, that such antisemitism did not exclude personal relationships, sometimes intense, made up of a mixture of emotional attachments, admiration or intellectual appreciation, compassion offered and accepted (it is true that Sebastian rejected the compassion offered by Nae Ionescu, so harshly expressed in the preface to *For Two Thousand Years*, but he continued to remain close to him). I try to reconstruct the context in which such things became possible, but I cannot understand it; everything remains abstract, unreal. What I am missing is the spirit of dialogue that could have existed under such circumstances.[25]

The same questions appear in the late confession of a former student of Ionescu, the writer Mariana Şora, who refers to a pervasive atmosphere that made possible the good-tempered or cynical acceptance of radical attitudes among the young intellectuals:

For example, I cannot entirely explain—but I understand, I *feel* how it was—why we were not alienated from Nae Ionescu by his famous preface to Sebastian's novel. It is a shocking text on a theoretical level in its false Christian approach that seeks abusively and sophistically to give antisemitism a permanent theological justification, and on a human level by insulting his faithful admirer and collaborator on *Cuvântul*, who had come to him so trustingly, asking for a few introductory pages. . . . And, finally, I do not understand why it took me four years, from the autumn of 1934, when discussion of the preface was at its height and I had just become a student (and a student of Nae's) in order fully to grasp that the fascination evoked by the professor and the value of what he was saying were two different things.[26]

[25] Matei Călinescu, *Un fel de jurnal* (Iaşi, 2005), 76–7.
[26] Mariana Şora, 'Intelectualul şi agora', in Iordan Chimet (ed.), *Momentul adevărului* (Cluj, 1996), 289.

In a talk delivered at the French Institute in Bucharest in 1935,[27] Sebastian spoke about the scandal set in motion by his work:

It was a novel—the story of a young Romanian Jew who is forced, somewhat unexpectedly, and in a brutal manner, to question his social and spiritual affiliation. Who is this man? Is he a Jew? Is he Romanian? Maybe he is both at the same time? He feels Romanian by virtue of many things: the language he speaks, the landscape of his birthplace, the Danube of his childhood, the books he loves, the friendships he has. But at the same time he recognizes himself as being a Jew, by virtue of certain aspects of sensitivity and intelligence, some sort of intellectual feverishness, and a particular sense of the tragic.

He does not see himself as being forced to choose between these two forces— his Judaism and his Romanianism . . . He thinks he can unite the two forces in the life of one individual; he thinks he can reach an inner agreement between the Romanian and Jewish values that comprise his being and his spirit. . . .

The scandal—because there was one—was caused by the preface of Nae Ionescu, my professor, a Romanian theoretician of the right and at the same time a theoretician of that 'national specificity' about which we will speak in a moment.

A real war flared up around this novel and its preface, a war going beyond literature, and with a purely political plane as its battlefield. Politicians of the right and those of the left, Marxists and fascists, national Jews and antisemites, everyone considered himself attacked by a book that had had the courage, the naivety, or the imprudence to state that being Romanian is not incompatible with being a Jew.[28]

His drama, Sebastian observed, was no different than that described by Jacob Wasserman in *Mein Weg als Deutsche und Jude*, or by Benjamin Crémieux in his autobiographical novel *Le Premier de la classe*. In 1935, contemplating his own life, Sebastian still considered that his 'two voices, the Jewish and the Romanian one', were 'but one', despite the opposition of those, both Romanian and Jewish, who believed in an irreducible 'biological' national essence. His rejection of a theory and a national ideology that excluded *the different* in the name of some inherent biological identity is understandable. More surprising is his championing of 'otherness' as individual experience and freedom of choice rather than some alternative 'abstract idea' as he calls it—that is, some all-encompassing political ideology. According to Sebastian, it is the right of the individual to be different and to integrate himself, in his own way, into a national identity that he can enrich by the introduction of an alternative perspective.

[27] The hitherto unpublished text of the talk appeared in Leon Volovici, 'Comment expliquer aux étrangers le "spécifique national": Une conférence de Mihail Sebastian', in *Nation and National Ideology: Past, Present and Prospects*, proceedings of the International Symposium, 6–7 Apr. 2001 (Bucharest, 2002), 128–37.

[28] Mihail Sebastian, 'On National Specificity, 1935', *Plural. Culture and Civilization*, no. 29 (Jan. 2007), 337–8.

Sebastian died in an accident in May 1945. His diary wasn't published until fifty years after his death. Started in 1935, shortly after the scandal around *De două mii de ani . . .*, it strikingly demonstrates that not even the terrible crisis caused by Ionescu's preface and not even his 'conversion to the Guard' could break up their relationship. The diary shows, however, an inevitable and clear break at the level of political ideas. It is surprising, but perhaps still comprehensible, that neither Ionescu nor any other of Sebastian's friends who had become fervent devotees of the Iron Guard broke up their relationship with him. By maintaining amicable relations they were creating the illusion, or perhaps the pretence, that their extremist political commitment was neither immoral nor a denial of old loyalties and friendships. Sebastian was unwillingly offering them a kind of guarantee that their transformation did not also entail being cast off by an intellectual who did not share their new political beliefs.

A paradoxical remark shocks today's readers of Sebastian's diary, a remark that has sometimes made him the object of sharp criticism: he once went so far as to describe his attachment to Ionescu as filial—despite the fact that, as he noted, he no longer had anything in common with him on an ideological or intellectual level, still less on the level of his destiny. His persistence in retaining contact with his 'converted' friends (above all Mircea Eliade) was due not only to a strong and enduring personal attachment but also to a stubborn, desperate conviction that, despite the abyss that had opened up between them, it might still be possible to rebuild the pluralist intellectual ambiance of earlier years.

In a private letter to Tudor Vianu in 1945, Eugène Ionesco, the Romanian-born dramatist and Sebastian's friend during the Second World War, said that he considered Nae Ionescu's influence to be the main cause of the catastrophic pro-fascist orientation adopted by the younger generation of Romanians in the 1930s. 'Only Mihail Sebastian', he wrote, 'managed to preserve a clear head and genuinely human feelings. Too bad he is no longer among us.'[29] Ionesco's political assessment was correct. However, regarding Sebastian's personal relationship with Ionescu and his followers, the situation was more complicated and ambiguous. Many blamed Sebastian then, and still do so today, for remaining in touch with people who had become members of the Iron Guard and aggressive antisemites. But it has to be understood that he was fatally dependent on this environment: it was his oxygen reserve, and he had no other option, even after 1935, when he perceived the mounting signs of total impasse. He could not overcome this dilemma even though his circle had, for the most part, cast its lot with a radical, anti-intellectual, and totalitarian political movement that excluded Sebastian the Jew, denied him the right to exist as a Romanian writer, and eventually even the very right to exist. To

[29] An English translation of Ionesco's letter can be found in Petreu, *An Infamous Past*, 58–9.

break with Ionescu's circle would have meant to remove the veil of illusion that Sebastian had created for himself during his formative years. Steven Aschheim has commented perceptively on the similar case of Victor Klemperer's dependence on Germany and Germanism,[30] and Sebastian too came to understand, as time went on, that the greater his attachment to Romania and its culture, the greater his vulnerability.

Despite maintaining relations with his friends and with their spiritual guide, after 1935 Sebastian began increasingly to shed his illusions. The notes in his diary on Ionescu, always written with much sympathy, are nonetheless lucid and critical. Sebastian's bitter irony does not miss the professor's sophisms, his political opportunism, his pathetic pro-Iron Guard and pro-Hitler sympathies, or the frequent illogical statements caused by political calculation, megalomania, or his irrepressible impulse to amaze and provoke.

'Poor Nae! How rapid is his descent', exclaimed Sebastian in one diary entry of November 1935. 'What a poseur that man can be!' he wrote in March of the same year. But soon after, on 17 June, his admiration was still intact: 'He is undoubtedly the most interesting and the most complex person I have ever known.' However, 'there is something demonic in Nae', he later concluded (14 March 1936).[31] When the professor was arrested in the midst of one of a series of political crises Sebastian was deeply concerned, dreamed about him, missed him, and was happy to see him free again.

Nae Ionescu died unexpectedly in March 1940. Here is Sebastian's laconic note: 'Nervous, uncontrollable sobbing as I entered Nae Ionescu's house yesterday morning, two hours after his death. He takes with him a whole period of my life, which is now—only now—over for good.'[32] Three years later Sebastian was still mentioning his mentor and dreaming about him. One dream he recorded, on 29 December 1943, is remarkably transparent:

I'm at the university. I meet Onicescu[33] in a corridor. He is leaving for Berlin—and tells me to leave with him. A moment later I am in a small room, at Nae Ionescu's seminar. Here he comes. He asks me the time and notes my answer on a piece of paper. Then he asks the same question of the other students in turn, noting each reply under a special heading. The times given are not the same. Then Nae asks each of us to determine the right time—and gets us to sign our names. He turns to me and tells me that I speak with a Jewish accent. But immediately after that, he puts his hand on mine and adds: 'You'll leave on Saturday evening for Berlin.'[34]

[30] Steven E. Aschheim, _Scholem, Arendt, Klemperer: Intimate Chronicles in Turbulent Times_ (Bloomington, Ind., 2001), 83.

[31] Mihail Sebastian, _Journal, 1935–1944_ (Chicago, 2000), 8, 17, 29, 37.  [32] Ibid. 278.

[33] Octav Onicescu (1892–1983), a well-known Romanian mathematician, was a disciple of Ionescu, and a member of the Iron Guard.

[34] The last sentence is incorrectly translated in the English edition as 'But immediately after that, he puts his hand on mine and adds that he[!] is leaving on Saturday evening for Berlin' (p. 584). In the original: 'Dar imediat după asta pune mîna pe mîna mea şi adaugă: Pleci sîmbătă seara la Berlin' (Mihail Sebastian, _Jurnal, 1935–1944_ (Bucharest, 1996), 537).

We can find the source for the dream 'departure to Berlin' in a note of the same year (2 June 1943). After an encounter on the street with the philosopher Constantin Noica, who was about to leave for Berlin to participate in a conference on 'the internal tension within Romanian culture', Sebastian commented: 'It seemed so grotesque, that I could not help laughing.'

In the dream involving Ionescu what overtly disturbs the normal relationship is the 'Jewish accent', as the professor calls it. At that time, such an accent rendered impossible any type of active relationship between Sebastian and his friends—between Sebastian and the new order prepared by Ionescu. And in 1943 the dream can be read as having an ominous significance: sending Sebastian to Berlin in December of that year—with 'his hand on mine'—was a tender way of sending him to his death.

The political circumstances of the 1930s and of the Second World War forced Sebastian, like many other Jewish intellectuals in Europe (for example Victor Klemperer, to whom Sebastian has frequently been compared[35]) into a painful meditation on his options. During the war years, terrorized by the danger of a pogrom or by the spectre of deportation, he returned, against his will, to an exclusively Jewish environment as a literature teacher in a Jewish school. He accepted in his own way the condition of being Jewish and of being doomed. He was dismayed by the 'rhinocerization' of his maestro and of other old friends who had gone over to the side that preached or justified ideologically his social and perhaps his physical exclusion. In the most critical phase, he meditated in solitude in his diary on the tragic impasse that called into question not only his own destiny but also that of the people to whom he belonged.

Ironically, those writers—like Sebastian—who vacillated and were torn between two identities that had then entered a fatal collision succeeded best at the level of creativity. It was their only revenge.

[35] See e.g. Peter Gay, 'Witness to Fascism', *New York Review of Books*, 4 Oct. 2001, pp. 44–7.

# FIVE

# INSIDERS/OUTSIDERS

## *Poles and Jews in Recent Polish Jewish Fiction and Autobiography*

### KAREN AUERBACH AND ANTONY POLONSKY

IT IS A PARADOXICAL FACT that, with Poland no longer one of the great centres of the Jewish world following the Second World War, there has emerged what has been described as a 'Jewish school of Polish literature',[1] a group of writers who have explored the main dilemmas faced by Polish Jewry, and in particular the problem of the dual identity or 'insider/outsider' status of a Jew writing in the Polish language. The word 'school' perhaps overstates the unity of this group, which consists of two subsections—the older generation, whose most important members, Julian Stryjkowski, Adolf Rudnicki, and Stanisław Wygodzki, came to maturity before the war; and the younger group, the most notable of whom are Ida Fink, Henryk Grynberg, Bogdan Wojdowski, and Hanna Krall, who grew up during the war. In the 1990s some additional members of this second generation have found their voices, and writers of a third generation, born after 1945, have made their debut.

The end of communism imparted a new creative lease on life to Grynberg and witnessed the emergence of a number of other writers who had either never referred to being Jewish in their works or who now for the first time discussed their Jewish origins. In this category we will examine the works of Wilhelm Dichter, who, like Grynberg, emphasizes the post-Second World War period in his narrative; Joanna Olczak-Ronikier and Krzysztof Teodor Toeplitz, who describe the processes of their families' integration into Polish culture and society; and Antoni Marianowicz, Michał Głowiński and Arnold Mostowicz, whose memoirs focus on surviving the Holocaust. The Second World War is a dominant concern for all of these writers except Toeplitz, whose wartime experience differed as he was not considered Jewish according to Nazi racial definitions. For the others, writing about wartime survival as Jews became part of a delayed process of integrating these experiences into their often fractured identities.

[1] Jan Błoński, 'Is There a Jewish School of Polish Literature?', *Polin*, 1 (1986), 196–211.

Grynberg's *Memorbuch* (Memorial Book)[2] is the only work among those analysed here that seeks to understand fully the spectrum of pre-war, wartime, and post-war history. Born in Warsaw in 1936, Grynberg survived the war together with his mother, partly in hiding and partly because he had 'Aryan' papers. He made his reputation with a lightly fictionalized version of his own life, which he described as follows, 'All these works exist independently, completely separate from each other, but they are linked together by their common narrator and by his fate, as well as by the fate of those closest to him, of the circles in which he moved and of the country from 1942 to 1968.'[3] Unlike this earlier cycle, *Memorbuch* is not directly autobiographical. Grynberg left Poland in 1967 and did not deal in his earlier fiction with the 'anti-Zionist' campaign of 1968 because, in his words, he 'lacked the experience to describe what took place there'.[4] *Memorbuch*, then, addresses what was previously an 'omission . . . in his autobiographical cycle'.[5]

*Memorbuch* deals with the vexed question of the Jewish relationship to communism in the form of a lightly fictionalized biography of a Jewish communist, Adam Bromberg, from his childhood in a wealthy Jewish family in Lublin to his expulsion from the Communist Party and subsequent emigration from Poland during the 'anti-Zionist' persecutions of 1968. In an author's note Grynberg explains that the narrative is culled from Bromberg's extensive writings and recordings, which he acquired after the latter's death and which he supplemented through interviews with Bromberg's family and friends. He asserts that he did not invent any characters or events, and changed names only when privacy was an issue.

The choice of Bromberg to tell the story of post-war Polish Jewish life in the context of 1968 determines *Memorbuch*'s historical and literary themes and is revealing of how Grynberg interprets the events he describes. Bromberg was a pre-war communist who nevertheless retained his Jewishness, an assimilated Polish Jew who remained in Poland after the Second World War but, unlike many, never changed either his first or last names. He became involved in book publishing in Warsaw in the years before the war, and as a publisher and editor under the communist government he struggled, according to Grynberg's account, to preserve historical

---

[2] Henryk Grynberg, *Memorbuch* (Warsaw, 2000).

[3] 'Od autora', *Życie ideologiczne, życie osobiste* (Warsaw, 1992), 5. Grynberg's *Żydowska wojna* [Jewish War] (Warsaw, 1965) and *Zwycięstwo* [Victory] (Paris, 1969) describe his and his mother's survival of the Second World War and the early post-war years; *Życie ideologiczne* [Ideological Life] (London, 1975) describes his years of study under Stalinism; *Życie osobiste* [Personal Life] (London, 1979) relates his experiences in the Yiddish theatre in post-war Poland; *Ojczyzna* [Fatherland] (Warsaw, 1999) describes his break with Poland; and *Kadisz* (Kaddish) (Kraków, 1987) recounts his emigration to the United States. Unless otherwise noted, translations from Polish sources are the authors'.

[4] Antony Polonsky and Monika Adamczyk-Garbowska (eds.), *Contemporary Jewish Writing in Poland: An Anthology* (Lincoln, Nebr., 2001), p. xxxv.                    [5] Ibid.

truth and Polish cultural integrity despite the politicization and falsification of history under communist rule. This focus on books and publishing contributes to the centrality of the meaning and misuse of history in Grynberg's message.

Grynberg's narrative, written in the first person through Bromberg's voice, begins with the arranged marriage of Bromberg's parents by a traditional matchmaker at the beginning of the twentieth century and ends with Bromberg's post-1968 life in Stockholm. It seeks to explain the roots and the nature of Bromberg's identity as an assimilated Polish Jewish communist as well as the historical factors that led to his forced exile in 1968. Assimilated Polish Jewry, whom Diana Pinto has described as 'the great forgotten current of postwar Jewish history . . . [those] who lived in Poland in the fullest sense of the term',[6] comprised a growing minority of Jews in Poland before the Second World War but eventually became the majority in post-war Poland. The struggle to integrate Polish and Jewish identities and to reconcile feelings of Polishness with experiences of antisemitism before the war, during the Holocaust, and in post-war Poland was even more complicated for Jewish communists. Many Poles regarded communism as a betrayal of Polishness, while communism's internationalist, anti-religious ideology entailed at some level a renunciation of Jewishness. Bromberg, however, asserts his continued loyalty to both parts of his identity in Grynberg's narrative. In this sense, *Memorbuch* is an attempt to address the involvement of a minority of Jews in the Polish communist regime, a phenomenon that is rooted in historical circumstances but one that antisemitic circles have greatly exaggerated by labelling communism a Jewish phenomenon.

Grynberg indicates his approach to this history through the book's title, which recalls the Jewish tradition, begun in the Middle Ages, of recording the victims and locations of persecution as well as the names of a Jewish community's distinguished individuals. The title thus seeks to include the events of 1968 within the broader memory of Jewish persecution and to place this period in a historical context, evoking the underlying sense of exile that, for Grynberg, is at the heart of European Jewish history. The book's structure reinforces this theme. For each city that figures significantly in the narrative Grynberg provides the historical background of Jewish life there, building a picture of the broad sweep of European Jewish history as made up of cycles of acceptance and expulsion. We can see this approach particularly clearly in the chapter entitled 'Honeymoon' in which, just before the events of 1968, Bromberg and his wife Hanka take a belated honeymoon through Europe. The chapter sketches the history of various European Jewish communities (from those in France to those in Bratislava, for example), demonstrating

---

[6] Diana Pinto, 'Fifty Years after the Holocaust: Building a New Jewish and Polish Memory', *East European Jewish Affairs*, 26/2 (1996), 92.

how, in Grynberg's view, flourishing Jewish life over centuries was interrupted, with repetitive monotony, by periodic persecution until finally the Holocaust left only a remnant surviving. Through the juxtaposition of this chapter and the events of 1968, Grynberg places the 'anti-Zionist' campaign in the context of this European cycle. Furthermore, he links his account of post-war Polish Jewish history to the larger history of Jewish exile: in describing the destruction of a community during the Khmelnytsky massacres of the seventeenth century, he writes: 'The *memorbuch* was taken along in exile and continued.'[7]

The two families at the core of *Memorbuch* are those of Bromberg and Hanka, both the children of wealthy, acculturated parents. Bromberg's relationship with his father appears as the primary influence in his early life, and through it Grynberg explains both his protagonist's understanding of Jewishness and the development of his political beliefs. In the father's world of wealth lie the seeds of Bromberg's gravitation towards socialism and a communism that sought to overturn the very social order that allowed his father to prosper. Bromberg's father was a self-educated brush trader from Międzyrzec who inherited his father-in-law's business in hops in Lublin. Although in *Memorbuch*'s opening paragraph his father is said to have 'discarded' his gabardine and beard along with his traditional Jewish life when he married Bromberg's mother, he remained very much a part of Lublin's Jewish circles. He was a leader of the city's Jewish community and was involved in what *Memorbuch* describes as 'conservative' Jewish politics. Hanka's family, too, was acculturated yet not entirely assimilated, looking askance at Jews who sought to deny their Jewishness.

Bromberg's relationship with his father is his frame of reference for explaining his own identity and choices. In a larger sense, *Memorbuch* depicts the development of twentieth-century Jewish history through the lens of generational rebellion. The loosening of tradition in order to prosper in modernity and the development of the new, secular Jewish politics of Zionism and socialism are evident within both Bromberg's and Hanka's families. The children's political choices reflect the spectrum of secular Jewish politics in inter-war Poland and represent a challenge to their fathers' world-view.

Grynberg also emphasizes this generational dynamic when describing the events of 1968: in addition to relating the experiences of Bromberg's daughters and his niece at this time, Grynberg digresses from the focus on Bromberg and Hanka's families in order to provide the family histories of the other young people caught up in the political turmoil of that year. In these narratives the generational cycle highlights continuities in the experience of persecution during the Holocaust and in 1968. For example,

---

[7] *Memorbuch*, 253.

one woman, a Holocaust survivor, cries at the time of her twin daughters' twentieth birthday, which falls in March 1968. This was the period during which her daughters and other assimilated Polish Jewish students were being singled out for their Jewish roots as the government transformed university protests against censorship into an 'anti-Zionist' campaign of propaganda and harassment. In *Memorbuch* the mother, who has never before talked to her children about her life during the war, explains to her daughters the reason for her despair: 'Because when I reached the age of twenty, this is when the ghetto began.'[8]

According to Grynberg's narrative in *Memorbuch*, the experiences of 1968 revealed the limits of Jewish integration into Polish society, as indeed did Bromberg's experiences in pre-war Poland. When he was a boy, his family 'lived in a Polish part of town and spoke only Polish, but we did not have Polish friends'.[9] When he was forced to leave Poland for Vienna as a young man after being arrested for printing and distributing communist leaflets, he again belonged to secular Polish Jewish circles despite the internationalist ethos of communist ideology. Only when he served time in prison for his communist activities in the 1930s did he enter a social circle that included both Jews and non-Jews. The limited nature of social integration even among those who supported the ideology of assimilation persisted until the generation of survivors' children became organically part of Polish society in the post-war period.

Wartime experiences exerted a contradictory influence on post-war Jewish life. On the one hand, the experience of being persecuted specifically as Jews solidified their sense of being different from other Poles. Yet the assimilated character of post-war Jewish life became more pronounced after most of those who identified primarily as Jews emigrated immediately after the war or between 1956 and 1960. In addition, some Jews who had survived the war and remained in Poland had assumed Catholic identities in wartime or afterwards, or had married Catholics.

The difficulties of identity for assimilated families of Jewish background in post-war Poland were complicated by the nature of post-war politics and the communist allegiance of a minority of Polish Jews who remained. Bromberg's narrative seeks to elucidate his belief in communism and his involvement in the communist regime. His older (and disabled) sister, a voracious reader, introduced him to political thought and radical thinkers as a child, and he first took part in Communist Party activities as a youth in Lublin. His initial disillusionment came even before the Second World War, during his first imprisonment, when anyone who expressed doubt about the party line was seen as potentially disloyal. 'We stayed in the party', he explains, 'because we believed that it was the only uncompromising enemy

[8] *Memorbuch*, 337.        [9] Ibid. 34.

of Hitler, we feared that soft Western democracy would come to a compromise with Hitler. Moscow was for us the only certainty.'[10] (The Soviet Union's non-aggression pact with the Nazis was incomprehensible to him, he recalls.)

The seeming contradiction in Bromberg's allegiance to communism in light of his loyalty to both Polish and Jewish identities reflects the predicament of Polish Jews both in inter-war Poland and in wartime. Grynberg includes in *Memorbuch* nearly fifty pages of excerpts from debates in the Polish parliament from 1935 to 1938 on the role of the Jews in the economy, as well as government officials' expressions of support for boycotts of Jewish businesses and large-scale emigration. This chapter reflects the increasingly hostile atmosphere in the second half of the 1930s for Polish Jews, as ethnic Polish nationalism, economic depression, and the influence of Nazi Germany led to anti-Jewish violence and boycotts as well as other forms of discrimination such as 'ghetto benches' at the university.

For Bromberg, who survived the war in a Soviet labour camp while his parents and siblings, who stayed behind in eastern Poland, were killed, involvement in the communist government during and after the war was both an outgrowth of his earlier beliefs and a choice between the 'lesser of two evils', one that, in his view, did not preclude his continued loyalty to Poland. During the Soviet occupation of eastern Poland he helped to translate Russian schoolbooks into Polish, and he fought in the Polish army organized on Soviet soil under General Zygmunt Berling. As the soldiers deployed across the river from Warsaw while the Germans put down the 1944 Warsaw uprising, Grynberg writes that Bromberg 'did not understand . . . why we did not go to help'.[11] He thought that 'the Poland for which we are going to fight will be sovereign, without collective farms or any other foreign models'.[12] The narrative here becomes quite apologetic: 'Why did everyone take part in this farce, of which we were unaware? Because we had no other way to approach the enemy with weapons.'[13]

Despite Bromberg's early disillusionment with a regime that did not conform to its purported ideology, he became involved in the post-war communist government while still fighting to remain faithful to Polish history and literature through his work in publishing. In Grynberg's narrative he expresses bitterness at accusations of disloyalty when he found himself a target of the 'anti-Zionist' propaganda in 1968. As director of the state Scientific Publishing House he had helped to organize the publication of the *Wielka Encyklopedia Powszechna* (Great Universal Encyclopedia), generally regarded as the single most important post-war achievement of Polish book publishing.[14] Government officials and the state-run press seized on an

[10] Ibid. 75.    [11] Ibid. 162.    [12] Ibid. 149.    [13] Ibid. 151.
[14] Paul Lendvai, *Antisemitism without Jews: Communist Eastern Europe* (New York, 1971), 189.

entry in the encyclopedia that distinguished between concentration camps and death camps, between the fate of Poles and that of Jews killed in the Holocaust. 'The contents of some entries in the *Wielka Encyklopedia Powszechna* not only stand in glaring contradiction to objective historical truth, but also, as in the case of the entry "Hitlerite concentration camps", constitute an outright affront to the Polish nation', asserts one accusation cited in *Memorbuch*.[15] Bromberg was fired and expelled from the party; he was also accused of misusing government funds as part of a Jewish conspiracy. He was arrested and imprisoned, and thirty-four Jewish employees of the publishing house were fired.[16]

The political events of 1968 posed a challenge to the integration of Polish and Jewish identities that Bromberg sought. This is encapsulated in a bitter exchange between one of his friends and a security police interrogator:

'Are you a Pole or a Jew?' asked the specialist, putting his pistol on the table.
'Both a Pole, and a Jew', responded Leon.
'Either one is a Pole, or a Jew!'
'I am an example that it is possible to be both one and the other.'
'And you are connected with Polish culture?'
'Yes.'
'Then recite something from *Pan Tadeusz*.'
'Jankiel through the whole winter stayed one knew not where, now suddenly with the main staff of the military he made his appearance . . .'[17]

In retelling the events of 1968 in the context of twentieth-century Polish Jewish history, Grynberg also searches for the deeper roots of antisemitism. He sums up his analysis through a conversation with Isaac Bashevis Singer in *Memorbuch*'s last scene. Bromberg and his daughter have set up a small press in their home in Stockholm, where they emigrated after 1968, and among their publications are Polish translations of Singer's works. During visits to Stockholm, Singer 'asked me about Lublin. My assimilated, *nouveau riche* environment was little known to him and he listened very attentively.' Bromberg continues:

[Singer] was starved for information, he was enraptured when he discovered something, and he wrote down everything because he was already losing his memory.
I told him as well about our survival over the recent years.
'This is neither communism nor fascism, this is much older', he [Singer] said.

---

[15] *Memorbuch*, 285.                               [16] Lendvai, *Antisemitism without Jews*, 189.
[17] *Memorbuch*, 311. In a 1962 English translation of *Pan Tadeusz*, this line reads in full, within parentheses in the original: '(Since that night of storm, Jankiel had spent the winter none knew where; But now he suddenly had joined them there, In company with Poland's General Staff.)'. Adam Mickiewicz, *Pan Tadeusz, or The Last Foray in Lithuania*, trans. W. Kirkconnell (Toronto, 1962), 362–3.

Hanka always read him with great interest, but already at the first dinner she said openly:

'How can you, after everything, write that there is a God?'

'But I never wrote that there is no Satan.'

'And what, you believe in all these demons which you describe? Such a writer as you? Where did you see them?'

'What do you mean, where? In man . . .'[18]

Whereas Grynberg attempts to create a unified narrative of Polish Jewish history from the early twentieth century to 1968, the other authors whose works are described here confine their writing to more limited periods, avoiding Grynberg's more explicit attempt to offer an integrated explanation and definition of the underlying phenomena of twentieth-century Polish Jewish experience. Aside from Grynberg, only Wilhelm Dichter focuses extensively on the post-war period. Dichter came to writing late. Born in 1935 in Drohobych, he survived the war on 'Aryan' papers with his mother. After the war, in which his father died, he moved with his mother and stepfather to Warsaw, where Dichter became an engineer. Forced to leave Poland in the 'anti-Zionist' campaign of 1968, he settled near Boston. His first novel, *Koń Pana Boga* (God's Donkey) describes his wartime experiences, while the second, *Szkoła bezbożników* (A School for Atheists) describes his adolescence in the Warsaw of the late 1940s and early 1950s.[19] The insecurity he had felt during the war did not come to an end with liberation. He was very conscious of the pervasive antisemitism of society and of the widespread Polish belief that the new regime was entirely dominated by Jews. As the popular saying went, 'Żydzi rządzą nami i już' ('The Jews rule us—what more is there to be said?'). Even attending Catholic classes in his school did not offer sanctuary because there he was held responsible for the death of Jesus. To spare him these constant humiliations and threats of violence, his mother and stepfather registered him in a special school supported by the regime for its adherents in the Warsaw suburb of Żoliborz.

*Szkoła bezbożników* describes his initial infatuation and subsequent disillusionment with communism. His break with Marxism is the result partly of his innate common sense and partly of an adolescent love-affair. The great strength of the book is its penetrating account of the vicious circle of Polish–Jewish relations after the war. Polish society, seeking a scapegoat for post-war oppression, found one in the Jews. The Jews, for their part, felt used by the regime on which they depended for their security. For the majority on both sides, the solution was to remove the Jews from Polish society. This was particularly painful for families such as the Dichters, who felt Polish and wished to remain in Poland. Certainly, Dichter's work is

[18] *Memorbuch*, 357.

[19] Wilhelm Dichter, *Koń Pana Boga* (Kraków, 1996); *Szkoła bezbożników* (Kraków, 1999).

one of the most sophisticated contributions to the whole debate about *Żydokomuna*.

The post-war identity struggles within the context of Polish politics described by both Dichter and Grynberg exist in the other works analysed here as well, but only in the background. Our other writers focus on pre-war or wartime experiences; yet they nevertheless frequently echo one another in describing their reasons for writing as an attempt to repair their fragmented post-war identities that resulted from a break with their own and their families' pre-war and wartime lives.

Joanna Olczak-Ronikier and Krzysztof Teodor Toeplitz, in particular, describe similar underlying motivations for their family memoirs. Both authors lament the loss of an idyllic childhood in Warsaw that ended prematurely with the outbreak of the Second World War, and for both the reconstruction of the past is shadowed by the wartime imposition of a Jewish identity. On the one hand, their search for the past is an attempt to understand that identity. Olczak-Ronikier, in *W ogrodzie pamięci* (In the Garden of Memory) and Toeplitz, in *Rodzina Toeplitzów: Książka mojego ojca* (The Toeplitz Family: Book of my Father),[20] are seeking to repair broken family ties that were ruptured during and after the war; the Jewish past, for Olczak-Ronikier especially, is the key to mending those ties. At the same time, the overall storyline of both memoirs is the way in which each family became such an integral part of Polish society by the outbreak of war that their social networks enabled them to avoid the fate of those enclosed in ghettos and sent to death camps.[21] In this context, Olczak-Ronikier and Toeplitz seek to explain how their families became part of the 'universe of obligation'[22] of Polish society.

*W ogrodzie pamięci* and *Rodzina Toeplitzów*, published three years apart, intersect with each other in both their narrative development and their overarching themes. Both are histories of a Jewish family's path to assimilation into Polish society: the Toeplitz family beginning at the end of the eighteenth century, Olczak-Ronikier's in the last third of the nineteenth century. The two works are also strikingly parallel in their overall structure. Both begin by rooting the author's ancestors in the town from which the family's last name is taken, and both take as a starting point an ancestor who was a rabbi. They then describe the gradual process of assimilation over three or four generations—first by making tentative steps towards integration with Polish society but at the same time maintaining traditional Jewish observance; then by

[20] *W ogrodzie pamięci* (Kraków, 2003); *Rodzina Toeplitzów* (Kraków, 2004).
[21] For further study of the role of social networks in hiding Jews in the Polish capital during the Second World War, see Gunnar S. Paulsson, *Secret City: The Hidden Jews of Warsaw, 1940–1945* (New Haven, 2002).
[22] Helen Fein, *Accounting for Genocide: National Responses and Jewish Victimization during the Holocaust* (New York, 1979), 4.

abandoning Jewish religious tradition but maintaining a Jewish identity; and, finally, by leaving behind Jewishness altogether through intermarriage and conversion. More generally, the memoirs are explorations by members of the Polish intelligentsia, only partly Jewish, of the Jewish branch of their family (although *Rodzina Toeplitzów* includes a chapter on the author's non-Jewish grandmother and her family).

Family memoirs are revealing not only because of the histories that they describe but also because they reflect the author's own individual preoccupations. *W ogrodzie pamięci* and *Rodzina Toeplitzów* diverge significantly in this respect, despite the similarities in their authors' broader motivations for writing. Olczak-Ronikier, whose Jewish mother was baptized into the Protestant faith upon marriage, writes as a child survivor revisiting suppressed wartime traumas and seeking to understand the family's pre-war path to assimilation that made her survival possible. The Second World War therefore comprises a significant portion of *W ogrodzie pamięci*. Toeplitz, on the other hand, ends his main narrative in 1939, dedicating only a four-page epilogue to the German occupation. This cursory discussion of the war can be attributed to the fact that, while Olczak-Ronikier was considered Jewish by Nazi racial laws and was forced with her mother and grandmother to go into hiding, Toeplitz was only one-quarter Jewish, and his wartime experience was therefore basically that of non-Jews. Whereas *W ogrodzie pamięci* centres on the irony of the family's having to struggle for survival as Jews in the war despite their distance from Jewishness, *Rodzina Toeplitzów* is in part a defence of the family's contributions to the Polish economy and culture despite the communist activism of later generations.

*W ogrodzie pamięci* follows two narratives: first, the family's path to Polishness along with its survival of the war, and second, Olczak-Ronikier's search for her family's past. The first story is told at length, weaving together the family's experiences with the larger context of Polish and Jewish history. The latter thread, though arguably as important, is nevertheless circumscribed and limited to the author's description of meetings with distant family members and reflections on her identity as a hidden child during the war; she rarely explores directly how Jewishness affected her adult life in post-war Poland.

Olczak-Ronikier explores her family's path from Jewishness to Polishness mainly through the loosening of their religious observance, their life-cycle events, their education and social circles, and their language. She also seeks to understand the polonization of her family and the limits of their inclusion in Polish society by analysing the role of assimilation and antisemitism in the development of identity, the entrance of her grandmother and mother into the Polish intelligentsia through publishing, and the political involvement and political fate of her grandmother's generation. She focuses on her grandmother and her grandmother's siblings as members of a transitional generation that became part of the Polish intelligentsia in the late nineteenth and early twentieth centuries, and on the degree to which becoming Polish entailed shedding their Jewishness. Yet the fate of the family during the Second World War remains the main thread in recounting her family's past.

The process of becoming Polish occurred in one branch of Olczak-Ronikier's family—the Horwitzes—largely in the space of one generation at the end of the nineteenth century. The author's great-grandfather, Gustaw Horwitz, a descendant of rabbis, was the son of a progressive-minded chief rabbi of Vienna in the early nineteenth century. Gustaw's doctoral degrees in theology and philosophy and his doctoral work on Spinoza indicate his attempt to harmonize Jewishness with a modern European identity. He went to Warsaw to work in a salt-importing business, marrying Julia, the daughter of the business's owner Izaak Kleinmann, 'an emancipated, modern Jew, a cosmopolitan, who used German more fluently than Polish and felt better in Berlin or Vienna than in Warsaw. He [Kleinmann] did not like Polish Jews because of the fanaticism of the Orthodox circles and because the adherents of assimilation had, in his opinion, a too servile attitude to the Poles.'[23]

While Gustaw was alive the family maintained a firm connection to Jewishness, and its members retained their status as outsiders within Polish society despite their modern ways. However, with his premature death in 1882 the family's polonization began in earnest. Olczak-Ronikier writes that her grandmother, Janina, one of Gustaw and Julia's children, saw Gustaw's death as the point at which the family began to abandon its Jewish roots and enter Polish society. She argues that the turn to secularization after Gustaw's death resulted in a vacuum of identity for Janina and her siblings that they sought to fill by adopting the values of the Polish intelligentsia. Yet Jewishness remained significant for that generation because of the continued role of Jewish ritual during life-cycle events and because of the limits of their social integration into Polish society, in part because of the spread of antisemitism. The result was an identity crisis that led several members of that generation down the path to socialism and radical politics. Olczak-Ronikier links their radicalism not only to their rejection by segments of Polish society but also to the process of secularization.

Olczak-Ronikier notes that the Horwitz family, with the exception of her own mother, did not formally leave Judaism even in the second generation after their polonization. Her father, Tadeusz Olczak,

was the first and only non-Jew who entered the family. Did this have some kind of significance? He himself was devoid of antisemitic prejudices; however, in pre-war

[23] *W ogrodzie pamięci*, 10.

times such mixed marriages inspired distaste in the surrounding society. The wedding took place in 1933, in the Evangelical Augsburg parish in Warsaw. Mother was the first in the family who changed her religion, which did not evoke any special reaction among her closest [relatives]. Aside from the pious Samuel Beylin [who married Janina's eldest sister, Flora], none of the family members was religious. They remained 'in the Mosaic confession' with a feeling of independence. They did not want to renounce it in order to make their lives easier.[24]

Education was, perhaps, the most significant path to polonization. It was through Polish private schools and higher education that the Horwitz family entered the Polish intelligentsia, providing both knowledge of the Polish language and literature and entry into new social circles. Olczak-Ronikier notes that 'In 1882, when my grandmother [Janina] began her education, the tsar's politics of russification in the [Polish] Kingdom reached its apogee.'[25] As a result, her grandmother's education was imbued with the spirit of Polish national resistance. In the private Polish girls' school of Leokadia and Bronisława Kosmowska, the author writes, 'there dominated the spirit of resistance in the face of the [anti-Polish] partitions, the cult of independence, and Romantic poetry—all of this acted upon the imagination of the girls and built a love for Poland, among Jewish students as well. But this love, as we know, was not always reciprocated.'[26] She cites the taunts of young boys who pretended to 'baptize' the young Jewish pupils in the waterworks as they returned home from school, as well as the 'antisemitic provocations [that] evoked fury' in 11-year-old Maks, one of her grandmother's brothers, at school.[27]

When Olczak-Ronikier's grandmother Janina and Janina's husband Jakub Mortkowicz purchased Gabriel Centnerszwer's bookshop in 1903, they drew on a long tradition of Jewish involvement in the Polish intelligentsia through bookselling. Aleksander Hertz comments that 'Great Polish booksellers of Jewish origin are a tradition that reaches from Glucksberg to Jacob [Jakub] Mortkowicz.'[28] It is noteworthy that in the third volume of Jakub Shatzky's *History of the Jews in Warsaw*, which covers the period from 1863 to 1896, nearly half of the chapter on Jews in Polish cultural life is taken up with the history of Jewish booksellers, who were a significant factor in Polish cultural life as early as the middle of the nineteenth century.[29]

Janina and Jakub Mortkowicz's publishing activities combined a European outlook with Polish patriotism and participation in Polish intellectual life. While active in Polish publishing organizations, Jakub sympathized with the Polish Socialist Party, which promoted both socialist revolution and national

[24] *W ogrodzie pamięci*, 209.     [25] Ibid. 29.     [26] Ibid. 30.     [27] Ibid. 30–1, 39.

[28] Aleksander Hertz, *The Jews in Polish Culture* (Evanston, Ill., 1988), 229.

[29] 'Varshever yidn in poylishn kultur-lebn', in Jacob Shatzky, *History of the Jews in Warsaw* [Geshikhte fun yidn in varshe], vol. iii (New York, 1953), 406–23.

independence. The prominent writers whose works they published became personal friends of the Mortkowiczes, and their bookshop became a gathering-place for the Polish intelligentsia. Yet Olczak-Ronikier wonders about the continued impact of her grandfather's Jewish background in light of his desire to be fully part of Polish society at a time when ethnic Polish nationalism challenged that possibility. Jakub Mortkowicz had grown up in a family that was more traditional than the Horwitzes. His father had owned a secondhand bookshop in Radom before he came to work in his son's bookshop, and Olczak-Ronikier notes that Jakub employed his father in the back rather than to serve customers, perhaps, she writes, indicating his embarrassment at his father's overt Jewishness.

Olczak-Ronikier notes the unease that secularization and acculturation created for her mother and grandmother. Her mother continued to be 'bothered by a feeling of inferiority' and to struggle for inclusion in Polish society. At the same time, the manner in which they survived the Second World War underlines the extent to which they had become part of Polish society and separated from the Jewish masses. The establishment of the ghetto in Warsaw in October 1940 threatened twelve members of Olczak-Ronikier's family still living in the Polish capital, and forced them to decide with which community, Jewish or non-Jewish, to cast their fate. All but two, Janina's eldest brother Ludwik and his wife Genia, made the decision to hide on the 'Aryan' side; all but Ludwik and Genia survived.[30] Although most family members opted to cast their lot with the non-Jews, Olczak-Ronikier nevertheless links her narration of the family's survival to the fate of the Jewish masses in the Warsaw ghetto. She introduces the various phases of her family's wartime survival by noting the major events within the ghetto: its establishment, its liquidation, and the uprising. This device emphasizes the difference between the fate of the Jewish masses and that of her own family, whose integration into the Polish intelligentsia was largely responsible for their survival.

In *W ogrodzie pamięci* Olczak-Ronikier does not shy away from addressing the difficulties of Polish–Jewish relations and antisemitism during the war. This is particularly evident in a chapter on the fate of her cousin Ryszard Bychowski,[31] who escaped from Warsaw after the outbreak of war in 1939, eventually settling in the United States in 1941 before returning to Europe as part of Sikorski's forces in London and being killed in a bombing raid over

[30] Janina's eldest sister, Flora, died of natural causes in 1945. About the fate of Ludwik and Genia, Olczak-Ronikier writes: 'In January 1943, grandmother's brother, Ludwik Horwitz, and his wife Genia were arrested. In February they were both shot. . . . Lutek had been working in the State Geological Institute in Warsaw. He spoke excellent German and was not afraid of the Germans. He did not pay attention to news of anti-Jewish decrees, he did not put on armbands, he did not try to hide under changed names. . . . He was sixty-eight years old when he died.' *W ogrodzie pamięci*, 285.          [31] 'Chłopiec z nieba' (ibid. 314–32).

Germany. Olczak-Ronikier cites his last letter to his father, written in December 1943, in which he expressed his disillusionment at the prospect of Jewish integration in Poland in the face of the indifference to, and contempt for, the fate of the Jews that he encountered among his fellow officers in the Polish air force.

Intertwined with the narrative of her family's past, Olczak-Ronikier's second theme—her search for that past—begins with the memoir's opening lines: 'On 28 October 1998, a Tuesday, in the Centre for Jewish Culture in Kraków, I had a metaphysical experience. My great-great-grandfather, or rather the shadow of his shadow, appeared there unexpectedly.'[32] She explains that she had attended a performance of Yiddish songs by the chief rabbi of Austria with the hope that he might help her learn about her great-great-grandfather, Lazar Horwitz, who had been chief rabbi of Vienna in the first quarter of the nineteenth century:

'Is there some kind of possibility of finding his traces?' I asked. 'Horowitz', he corrected me [regarding the spelling of Lazar's last name]. 'What does this mean, to search for traces? It is not necessary to find his traces. His portrait hangs in my office over the desk. He is a very well-known figure, an enlightened individual, one of our greatest rabbis.' That conversation brought from the dead a figure barely existing in memory, who, the more I found out about him, the more he became distinct.[33]

Olczak-Ronikier's reflections on the reasons for undertaking her search are usually linked to family events such as births and deaths. The passage in which she comes closest to an explanation of her motivation for writing follows the recounting of her mother Hanna's birth. She expresses ambivalence about citing her mother's birth certificate:

Perhaps I have remorse that I bring into the light of day the carefully hidden feelings of my closest ones. As if I broke into someone else's closed drawer. But I am attempting only to get closer to the truth about them. . . . I am trying also to approach the truth about myself. It seems to me that in overcoming the reluctance to cite these documents, I overcome fear. One's own and inherited. During the war, after all, these passages from an act of civil records represented a death sentence. . . . I will say sincerely that even a few years ago I would not have summoned up the courage to publish them. I would have thought that this is the long-forgotten past. It was. It passed. There is nothing to return to. Anyhow, what for? Who knows what could come about once more? But perhaps the time has finally come to shake off this feeling of fear and shame coded in one's genes, hidden deep in the soul. It is high time to find the effaced traces of the path.[34]

---

[32] *W ogrodzie pamięci*, 7.

[33] Ibid. It is unclear when the family name was changed from Horowitz to Horwitz and which family members made this change. In order to avoid confusion, the name is spelled throughout this essay as 'Horwitz', with the exception of the quotation in this passage.

[34] Ibid. 98–9.

In describing her attitude towards her wartime survival, Olczak-Ronikier refers repeatedly to the absence of emotions and avoidance of conversations connected with the war. The trauma of her wartime experiences also shadowed her pre-war memories, so that 'there did not remain in my memory any trace of the colours, tastes, or smells of childhood'.[35] Even happy memories of her pre-war childhood become intertwined with the fateful wartime history superimposed on the pre-war landscape.

The reconstruction of her family's history is an attempt not only to reconstruct her own identity but also to renew the family links broken by the wartime dispersal. During a meeting of the family's far-flung branches in April 2001, one of Olczak-Ronikier's cousins told the gathered descendants that

he consider[ed] our meeting to be a great victory over fate. Two diabolical powers conspired to annihilate us. German totalitarianism murdered people, Soviet totalitarianism killed and destroyed people and also broke the ties between us. It deprived us not only of dignity and the feeling of safety but also of communal belonging, family tradition, and one's own identity. People who are uprooted, stripped of memory, of attachments, of values transmitted through previous generations, do not know what they are living for, and they do not have anything to transmit to their own children. Luckily, we survived all of these threats; we found one another and our common past, which allowed us to understand better who we are and where we are heading.[36]

Olczak-Ronikier's lament at a family's dispersion and the attempt to reconnect broken family ties through a reconstruction of the past are echoed in Krzysztof Teodor Toeplitz's family memoir. *Rodzina Toeplitzów* resembles *W ogrodzie pamięci* in the author's attempt to understand the nature of his family's Jewishness by tracking down sociological markers of identity, in its constant reference to the wartime fate of family members in the course of recounting earlier history, and in its particular attention to the wartime fate of the family archives. Like Olczak-Ronikier, Toeplitz also seeks to explain the socialist and communist leanings among some family members while avoiding an emphasis on the post-war period, despite making indirect references to antisemitism in communist Poland.

The Toeplitz family's path to integration into Polish society as pioneers of the capitalist economy precedes the events described in Olczak-Ronikier's memoir by nearly a century. Jehuda Lejb, a rabbi who settled in Leszno and died there in 1806, was the first family member to take the last name Toeplitz, which probably derives from the Czech town of Teplice. Jehuda Lejb's two sons were the last family members to uphold traditional Jewish observance. One of the sons, Samuel, who became a banker, moved to

---

[35] *W ogrodzie pamięci*, 212.     [36] Ibid. 343.

Warsaw at the start of the nineteenth century, when the city was beginning to feel the effects of the Berlin Haskalah. The Toeplitzes were among the first Jews to be accepted into Polish economic institutions in the nineteenth century, and they also participated in government committees and delegations concerned with Jewish issues.[37]

Toeplitz seeks to elucidate the path leading from a rabbi's move to Leszno at the turn of the eighteenth century to complete assimilation into Polish society in the author's own lifetime. He emphasizes the very gradual nature of this process, while stressing the Polish patriotism of his family (which he shares) as well as the family's contribution to the Polish economy and to Polish culture through its financial support for musicians, writers, and artists. Like Olczak-Ronikier, Toeplitz pays particular attention to life-cycle events in trying to understand his ancestors' identity as Jews. In particular, he notes the numerous marriages within a circle of several dozen Jewish plutocratic families in Poland throughout the nineteenth century.[38] By the outbreak of the Second World War, however, the Toeplitz family had become assimilated into Polish society through intermarriage with non-Jews to a greater degree than Olczak-Ronikier's family. Toeplitz's grandfather, Teodor, had married a noblewoman and his father also married a non-Jewish woman; he was therefore only one-quarter Jewish and hence not defined as 'Jewish' by the Nazi racial laws, although his Jewish roots remained a danger during wartime. Perhaps as a result of this relative immunity, wartime survival does not loom as large in Toeplitz's memoir as it does in Olczak-Ronikier's. Yet its frequent references to the Second World War indicate that wartime experiences were not as separate from the family's earlier history as Toeplitz asserts in his introduction.

Toeplitz comments ironically in this context on his grandfather Teodor's descriptions of Jews whom he encountered in Berlin during his studies there in the early 1890s. In a letter home, he notes the stereotypically 'semitic gestures and manner of speaking' of one of his professors, while remarking that a second Jewish professor possesses none of these traits. Toeplitz comments that, while his grandfather refers in the same letter to Russian Jews as his closest neighbours, the term 'Russian Jew' echoes with a 'feeling, carried from home, of a distance between the circle of maskilim and the orthodox Jewish masses'. He continues:

[37] Artur Eisenbach notes that, when the Merchant Confraternity of Warsaw admitted Jews for the first time in 1828, Teodor Toeplitz was one of two Jews elected as deputy elders, and later Henryk Toeplitz was among a group of Jews elected to a committee of the Confraternity assigned to reorganize the Warsaw stock exchange. Eisenbach, *The Emancipation of the Jews in Poland, 1780–1870*, ed. Antony Polonsky (Oxford, 1991), 236, 238.

[38] *Rodzina Toeplitzów*, 117–19.

Let us recall this tangle of emotions that determined, and perhaps determines to this day, the attitude of many 'assimilated' and 'enlightened' people, coming from Jewish circles, being aware, in addition, that not a full half-century later, history clarified in a brutal enough way all of these hesitations and my grandfather, if he had not died in 1937, two years later would for certain have shared the fate of those 'Russian Jews', as occurred with other members of the family.[39]

Perhaps the most interesting comparison between *W ogrodzie pamięci* and *Rodzina Toeplitzów* concerns their respective authors' approaches to the socialist and communist politics of some family members. In Olczak-Ronikier's family, two of her grandmother's siblings became communists during the party's clandestine period, including Maks Horwitz, who was a founder of the Communist Party of Poland before being executed in the Soviet Union during the Great Purge. Another sibling, Kamilla, avoided that fate but spent ten years in a Siberian labour camp before being freed in 1944. (Kamilla's son, the historian Jan Kancewicz, likewise consigned to the Gulag as a child, was released a year before his mother.)

In Toeplitz's capitalist family, his great-uncle Ludwik, Teodor's brother, was the first to become involved in socialist circles, while living in Geneva. Ludwik was arrested in Poland in 1888 for smuggling socialist periodicals into Poland. Teodor was active in the Polish Socialist Party and a founder of the Warsaw Apartment Co-operative. Toeplitz's father, meanwhile, turned to communism and was sentenced in inter-war Poland to four years in prison following allegations that, among other things, he had spread communist propaganda among Polish soldiers while fighting for Poland during the Polish–Soviet war. The author himself was active in the Communist Party in Poland after the Second World War and even after the events of 1968, but he does not address his own political activism. The closest he comes to doing so is his description of a conversation in 1947 with his great-uncle Ludwik in which Toeplitz praised the socialist system being built in Poland, but by that time Ludwik was critical of communism.[40]

Although Olczak-Ronikier cites the effects of secularization on the leftist politics of several of her grandmother's siblings, both she and Toeplitz explain these family members' attraction to communism as in large part a reaction to the resistance that assimilated Jews encountered in their attempt to be fully part of Polish society. Maks Horwitz, Olczak-Ronikier's great-uncle, expressed this view in a pamphlet entitled *W kwestii żydowskiej* (On the Jewish Question), which he wrote in 1905 at the age of 28 after serving a prison sentence for his political activities. In it, Olczak-Ronikier notes, Maks referred to assimilation as 'the bankrupt ideology of the Jewish bourgeoisie and intelligentsia', and she comments: 'He had long ago ceased being the

---

[39] *Rodzina Toeplitzów*, 197.     [40] Ibid. 160.

romantic boy who fell in love with Polishness and believed that it is enough to dedicate one's life to struggle for freedom and justice in order for Poland to love him as a native son. . . . He already knew that he would always remain an undesired parasite.'[41] Paraphrasing Maks's criticism of assimilated Jews, she writes:

The prescription for avoiding contempt seemed simple to him: 'A Jew, in order to become a person, had to stop being a Jew, had to become a Pole . . .'. It was necessary to commit a dual betrayal. To renounce one's non-assimilated fellow-citizens. That is, one's roots, one's history, religion, tradition. And also to renounce one's very self, one's identity shaped over centuries. To hide carefully one's 'I', one's psychic, intellectual, and cultural difference, to imitate someone else, 'to become entirely a Pole, to the point of illusion'.

It was not possible to keep pace with such mimicry. So there remained shame. About whom was Maks speaking? About himself? About his family? 'They were ashamed of their roots. It is understood that they did not deny them where they were well known. But also here they tried in deed, word, and gesture to prove and convince that they felt completely, that is, completely, like Poles, that they had overcome their Jewishness as completely as possible.'[42]

Toeplitz, for his part, bitterly describes his father's experiences fighting on behalf of Poland in the Polish–Soviet war of 1919–20, referring to the stereotype encountered by his father and other soldiers that 'this entire revolution is Jewish work',[43] as well as to the Polish internment of Jewish soldiers in the Jabłonna camp during the war. After the arrest of Toeplitz's father in 1922, his grandfather Teodor pointedly told a newspaper that his son would not leave Poland to avoid his prison sentence. *Rodzina Toeplitzów* does not explore in greater depth the roots of the stereotype of *Żydokomuna* or its effect on the author's own life, beyond his ironic observation: 'Perhaps some kind of logic explains why the road that began with the Haskalah had to lead to socialism?'[44]

Both Olczak-Ronikier and Toeplitz describe only briefly their own experiences as assimilated individuals of Jewish background in Poland after the Second World War. *W ogrodzie pamięci* occasionally refers indirectly to postwar events. In an interview Olczak-Ronikier recounted that her mother and grandmother did not return to Warsaw after the war, resettling instead in Kraków, where they initially sought to rebuild their publishing house. When the firm was closed down during the consolidation of the communist regime they took up literary activities—her grandmother as a translator and her mother as a writer. Her grandmother died in 1960 and her mother in 1968.[45]

This is the extent of Olczak-Ronikier's treatment of the post-war period in *W ogrodzie pamięci*. The only reference to the anti-Zionist campaign in

---

[41] *W ogrodzie pamięci*, 121.    [42] Ibid. 122.    [43] *Rodzina Toeplitzów*, 296.
[44] Ibid. 161.    [45] Interview with Karen Auerbach, Kraków, 4 Sept. 2004 (unpublished).

1968 is a cryptic description of her cousin Paweł Beylin, who became a philosopher and a professor of art:

In *Gazeta Świąteczna* on 21 October 1999, Andrzej Seweryn, describing March '68, recalled how at that time the 'red' rector of the Theatre School urged the students to be quiet. And he instructed: 'Do not lose your heads.' . . . Then our beloved lecturer in philosophy, Professor Paweł Beylin, stood up: 'Yes, yes, it is not permissible to lose one's head, but it is also not permissible to save face [literally to lose face].'[46]

In the same interview Olczak-Ronikier explained that, although she was living in Warsaw in the first half of 1968 and was a member of the circles in the capital that were deeply affected by the anti-Zionist campaign, for her, personal upheavals overshadowed political events that year. In addition to suffering her mother's death shortly before the March events, she was also in the process of separating from her husband, a German foreign correspondent whom she had met in 1956. In June 1968 she moved to Kraków with her daughter Kasia, then 6 years old. In recent years Kasia's involvement in the present-day Jewish community in Kraków has prompted Olczak-Ronikier to attend occasional communal events.

Despite her reticence in *W ogrodzie pamięci* about her own Jewishness, indirect references indicate how Olczak-Ronikier might have interpreted her grandmother's struggles with Jewishness through the prism of her own experiences. In referring to her grandmother's 'wise choosing of life paths and friends so that the inevitable unpleasantness would be minimal',[47] she might also have been describing her own life choices: in the same interview she said that, aside from her childhood during the Second World War, Jewishness affected her adult life perhaps only in her avoidance of a career that would have bound her to any institution where discrimination during periods of political upheaval might have affected her opportunities.

Toeplitz likewise avoids addressing his own experiences as an individual with Jewish roots in post-war Poland. However, like Olczak-Ronikier he makes occasional connections between the experiences of previous generations and his own. For example, in describing the 'Endek' criticism of his grandfather Teodor, who was actively involved in agricultural affairs in the early inter-war period, Toeplitz notes, 'This Endek "way of thinking" with regard to Poles with Jewish roots has not been rectified even today.'[48]

The indirect references to the present indicate that *W ogrodzie pamięci* and *Rodzina Toeplitzów* are as much about their authors' attempts 'to approach the

---

[46] *W ogrodzie pamięci*, 215.                                          [47] Ibid. 31.
[48] *Rodzina Toeplitzów*, 279. 'Endek' refers to the term *endecja*, short for National Democracy, the camp of Roman Dmowski in independent Poland. Dmowski's rightist ideology, in contrast with that of Józef Piłsudski, privileged ethnic Poles over national minorities in the Polish state. Dmowski viewed the involvement of Jews in Polish trade as the main cause of Poland's political weakness.

truth about myself', as Olczak-Ronikier writes, as they are histories of their families. Yet their hesitation in addressing the post-war period directly points to their ambivalence about the meaning of the connections that they make between the past and the present. This ambivalence reflects the nature of attitudes in Poland towards the place of the Jews in Polish society since 1945. The reluctance to deal with the post-war period can be attributed in part to the continued strength of the stereotype of *Żydokomuna*, which blames communists of Jewish origin for the post-war imposition of communism. In avoiding this post-war history, Olczak-Ronikier and Toeplitz create incomplete portraits of their families' paths to assimilation into Polish society. After all, their own apparently complete integration into the Polish intelligentsia is as significant with regard to the history of the assimilated minority as was the 'anti-Zionist' campaign for the larger history of Polish–Jewish co-existence.

Our next three authors, Michał Głowiński, Arnold Mostowicz, and Antoni Marianowicz, also refrain from emphasizing the post-war period in their memoirs, although, like Olczak-Ronikier and Toeplitz, they reflect on questions of Polish Jewish identity that are relevant to their post-war lives. The memoirs by Głowiński, Mostowicz, and Marianowicz are narratives of wartime survival as Jews by individuals who were active in Polish literary and journalistic circles after the Second World War.

In the works of these three authors, the pre-war period figures prominently only in Antoni Marianowicz's beautifully written and carefully crafted memoir, *Życie surowo wzbronione*, which provides an unusual and striking picture of Jewish life in Warsaw before and during the Second World War.[49] The first part, in the form of a series of interviews with the Polish theatre critic Hanna Baltyn, outlines the experiences of the author and his parents under the German occupation. The second is a finely chiselled account of their life and that of their circle before the war. This circle was that of the minority of acculturated and polonized Jews who were well integrated into Warsaw society. It is a milieu that Marianowicz was well placed to describe. His paternal grandfather was a successful textile manufacturer who converted to Protestantism, and his father was a prosperous businessman who lived a comfortable life before the war, with an apartment on Świętokrzyska Street in the centre of Warsaw and a villa in the summer resort of Konstancin, outside the Polish capital. His mother (who was never fully accepted by his father's family) came from Dynaburg in Latvia. They associated largely with acculturated Jews like themselves and were either related to or connected with many of Warsaw's Jewish elite.

---

[49] *Życie surowo wzbronione* (Warsaw, 1995); trans. into English by Alicia Nitecki as *Life Strictly Forbidden* (London, 2004). Antoni Marianowicz is the name he assumed when he fled from the ghetto with his mother in the summer of 1942. His original name was Kazimierz Jerzy Berman, and throughout his life he was known by the nickname Kazio.

Marianowicz is well aware of the complexities of his background, which is perhaps the main reason why he began describing his pre-war and wartime experiences so late in his life. Hanna Baltyn's questioning also brings this out: 'Many people are unaware that you are a Jew. Neither your surname nor your appearance indicates that. You weren't maligned in the press, you didn't leave after 1968. Tell me why you want to talk about all that. What drives you to do so?' Marianowicz responded:

If I couldn't tell everything about myself today, I wouldn't know why I had survived that war. Someone might think that I was ashamed of my roots, and that would be to misjudge me. I come from a Jewish family and I think that not a single drop of Aryan blood flows through my veins. . . . At the same time, I've never been a Jew in the religious sense. . . . And I consider myself a Christian because Christian ethics speak to me more strongly than any other ideology. . . .

The fact that I'm a Pole, on the other hand, isn't out of choice, and I don't necessarily like it. I'm a Pole because I am. This land is my land, this language my language. My relationship with Poland is like the relationship one has with one's family. Sometimes I love it, sometimes I can hardly stand it, but I don't think that anyone, regardless of position or title, has the right to teach me patriotism.[50]

As these comments suggest, like many people who were both Poles and Jews he is acutely conscious of the strength of antisemitism in Poland and the way it poisoned the atmosphere in the inter-war period. In a striking vignette he describes Antoni S., the gardener at his father's Konstancin villa, who was a trusted employee and who, with his wife, lunched every Sunday with the family. At the same time, he was a devoted reader of *Mały Dziennik*, an antisemitic broadsheet whose managing editor was Fr. Maximilian Kolbe. When the Nazi invasion began, Antoni S. turned out to be a vicious antisemite and Nazi collaborator, and after the war, when the Nazi, Schulz, who had lived in the villa during the occupation fled, Antoni S. appropriated all the family's property. The main reason why Marianowicz's family decided to move to the ghetto in 1940 was, as Marianowicz later put it, 'because conditions there were better for us'. He explains why so many Jews in hiding on the 'Aryan' side were taken in by the Hotel Polski scheme, in which the Germans offered safe passage out of Poland for those willing to pay a large sum only to dispatch them to their deaths in Auschwitz. In response to Hanna Baltyn's question, 'What do you think finally persuaded some very experienced people to take such a huge risk?', he responded: 'The hopelessness of that half-life in hiding; a loss of faith in survival; fear each time a door squeaked or something rustled. Have you ever been really afraid?'[51]

At the same time, he gives a nuanced picture of the attitude of Polish society to the Holocaust and shows how, particularly in the small town of

[50] *Life Strictly Forbidden*, 4–5.          [51] Ibid. 36.

Wołomin near Warsaw, there were many people either willing to aid Jews or to close their eyes to the fact that others were doing so. This was also true, as he indicates, of the German occupiers. He sums up the average Polish response to the mass murder of the Jews when Baltyn asks him about the Germans' distribution to Polish workers in Wołomin of bloodstained clothing clearly obtained from murdered Jews:

[HB] Did the workers who had been given these things by their German employers realize to whom the clothes had belonged? Did the red stains draw comments?

[AM] Of course. It was talked about, but with no emotion or interest. The fact that the clothes had belonged to Jews evoked neither commiseration for the former owners nor joy that they had fallen victim to the Reich. The attitude to the clothes was purely utilitarian; the comments were exclusively about their usefulness.

[HB] Didn't that enrage you?'

[AM] I bore no ill will to those who made use of the Jewish clothes. One might say, like the poet, that the people of Warsaw, like those of Rome, and also of Wołomin, 'trade, play, make love, as they pass by the heaps of martyrs' (Czesław Miłosz)—often in the clothes of those who fell victim to genocide.[52]

Marianowicz was very much influenced by Antoni Słonimski, a writer with a distinguished Jewish lineage who had been baptized as an infant by his socialist father, but who always regarded himself as a 'Jew of antisemitic origins'. Like Słonimski, who was married to Marianowicz's aunt, Marianowicz believed that philosemitism was not significantly preferable to antisemitism. What was needed was 'anti-antisemitism', and the best way to deal with anti-Jewish prejudice was by mocking its stupidity, a view shared by another Polish Jewish writer, Julian Tuwim. In his *Wyciąg na szklaną górę: Dziennik roku przestępnego 2000* (Climbing a Glass Mountain: Diary of the Leap [or Criminal] Year 2000), Marianowicz describes a reception for Mayor Ed Koch of New York. Asked by the mayor, 'How is it that after the massive emigration of Jews from Poland in 1968, there is still antisemitism in that country?' he responded, 'Simple! The antisemites didn't emigrate!'[53]

As part of the Jewish elite that lived in the ghetto on Chłodna Street, Marianowicz is well placed to describe the milieu of the chairman of the Jewish Council, Adam Czerniaków. This he does with great subtlety and empathy, providing the best account of those who thought that they were compelled by impossible circumstances to try to mitigate the worst effects of German rule. Very few of these people or of the author's own family were to survive the war, and some of them, as Marianowicz points out bitterly, such

---

[52] *Life Strictly Forbidden*, 121. The reference is to Czesław Miłosz, 'Campo di Fiori', written in Warsaw in 1943; see the English translation by Adam Gillon in Jan Błoński, 'The Poor Poles Look at the Ghetto', *Polin*, 1 (1986) 332–4.

[53] *Wyciąg na szklaną górę: Dziennik roku przestępnego 2000* (Warsaw, 2002), 91.

as the eminent neurologist, Władysław Sterling and his wife, or the historian Marceli Handelsman, were murdered by 'native fascists' in the last stage of the war. Living on the 'Aryan' side in the town of Wołomin after fleeing from the ghetto, he provides a valuable picture of another side of the German occupation—the casual brutalization and widespread corruption that it created. Only someone from his background could have described so effectively two such different settings. One striking feature of his description of Polish society under the occupation, a feature it shared with Jewish society in the ghettos, was its obsession with mystical predictions of a German catastrophe.

The most tragic episode in the book is one that Marianowicz apparently felt unable to share with Hanna Baltyn and which he recounts only towards the end of the second half of the memoir. His father found the humiliation and forced inactivity of the ghetto extremely difficult to bear. The last straw for him was when his son, who inadvertently had not raised his hat to a young German officer (as all Jews were required to), was beaten up and came home with blood streaming from his head. He encountered his father on the stairs of their apartment building, where many social encounters occurred. As Marianowicz continues:

At the moment I appeared on the stairs, Father was standing with a few neighbors discussing the Sienna Street Affair [when a number of Jews had been shot]. Silence descended. In a voice choked with tears, I blurted out what had happened. Then my father looked strangely at me, and in a very quiet voice, as though talking to himself, said, 'I'm not going to survive this.'[54]

Although he was only 54 his heart was already weakened, and he died of a heart attack that same night.

Among the most memorable passages in this book is the description of pre-war Konstancin. Marianowicz is clearly in love with his memories of this resort (he mentions that today it is a shadow of its former self ): 'If I never thought seriously about leaving Poland, surely a large part of the reason was Konstancin, that odd place unlike any other, where across abandonment and neglect, a beauty looks down on us that can be recaptured only in memory.'[55] He quotes Antoni Słonimski's monologue 'How It Really Happened', a comic piece whose light touch hides its deeper and more tragic message. Słonimski recounts how Jesus returns to Warsaw to comfort the last Jewish tailor on his deathbed. He vouchsafes him a vision of the afterlife, which turns out to be very like pre-war Konstancin:

When Rayzeman woke up and I gave him Dr. Walicki's drops, he felt a little better, and he told me that he wasn't afraid of dying, and he wasn't even worried about this eviction order with no right of appeal that he had received because he had had

<hr>

[54] *Life Strictly Forbidden*, 230.         [55] Ibid. 257.

a very long conversation with the Departing Person, and there was no doubt that the Person would take care of him, and most importantly, he already knew what it was like on the other side of life, in the embrace of darkness.

'You see, how can I describe it to you, there is something very comforting there, something like Konstancin anno 1912.' And he started telling me about some *boutonnieres* and butterfly nets and what the smell of the ether was like, and how cold it was, and how the food was just like the kielbasa before the First World War, and the bagels you can't get anymore, and cold milk, and figs and challah in the evening, and after supper how everyone goes to the train station to wait for the Warsaw train. You hear the engineer, old Charonovich, giving the whistle a long, steady blow, and the train pulls in, and you look to see who's coming on it, because all the passengers are our beloved dead. And how when he, Rayzeman, gets there, there on the wooden platform lit with gas lamps, his father will be waiting for him, and N., and all his old friends, they'll ask him about everything, and talk long into the night, around the oil lamp in his old house, about the movies, the books and jokes that came after they had already passed on.

'And later', he said, 'I'll go with them to the station every evening to wait for the travelers from the other side of life. And if someone had many friends and well-wishers in life, then he will have many people there to wait for him and to talk with, but if someone was disliked, he'll have to stand on the side and envy the others. We'll all be young again, kissing girls from the *Leliwa* pension, and holding a girl's small warm hand in our hand, we'll walk in the garden after the rain when everything smells, and you can breathe deep and strong, and all the way, like I haven't been able to for a long time.'[56]

Marianowicz had a successful literary career in post-war Poland as a journalist, writer for cabarets, feuilletonist, and translator. He had begun writing in the ghetto, producing cabaret sketches and poems. One of them, *Ptak* (The Bird), was reprinted in Michał Borwicz's post-war collection of ghetto literature, *Pieśń ujdzie cało* (The Song Will Survive).[57] From 1946 to 1948 Marianowicz served as the correspondent of the Polish Press Agency and Polish press attaché in Brussels; between 1949 and 1955 he was the deputy editor of the satirical magazine *Szpilki*, for which he continued to work throughout his life. He died in June 2003 at the age of 79.[58] (Let us hope that

[56] Antoni Słonimski, 'How It Really Happened', in Polonsky and Adamczyk-Garbowska (eds.), *Contemporary Jewish Writing in Poland*, 340–1.

[57] Michał Borwicz, *Pieśń ujdzie cało: Antologia wierszy o Żydach pod okupacją niemiecką* (Warsaw, 1947).

[58] In post-war Poland Marianowicz wrote texts for cabarets, including the Syrena theatre and the radio cabaret 'Eterek' (Little Ether). In the 1960s he wrote feuilletons for *Kurier Polski* and translated into Polish many children's books, including *Winnie-the-Pooh* and *Alice in Wonderland*. He initially translated *Alice*, which he adored, during the occupation, but that version was lost, and he was forced to reconstruct it after the war, so that it appeared for the first time in 1949. He was a writer and collector of limericks, and translated the librettos of a number of musicals, including *Hello Dolly!* and *Fiddler on the Roof*, which enjoyed great success

he is now in the heavenly Konstancin and that many people came to greet him at the station.)

Michał Głowiński, after surviving the war on the 'Aryan' side, subsequently became one of Poland's leading literary scholars and has written extensively both in *Tygodnik Powszechny* and various literary periodicals, including those of the 'alternative' press (*drugi obieg*). Only in his memoirs, *Czarne sezony* (Black Seasons), did he finally reveal his Jewish background, providing a horrifying picture of what it meant to 'pass' as Polish during the war.[59] The historical realities of the period are filtered through the experiences of the author's child persona, who, because of his Jewish appearance, is constantly threatened with death. Survival becomes a matter of pure chance.

The narrator comments at several points on the importance of having a good (i.e. 'Aryan') appearance. He describes how he is brought to Warsaw by his Aunt Maria, who had what were at that time called 'good features' that were not only a privilege but also a veritable gift from the heavens: 'Maria had wonderful features, [she was] an attractive blonde who came across as having descended upon the world not into a Jewish merchant family but into a household of Polish nobility [*szlachecki dworek*]. Unless you knew her well, you would never guess what origin lay behind that impeccable Slavic beauty.'[60]

His aunt is compelled to leave him in a bakery and he soon becomes aware that he has attracted the attention of those working there. '"A Jewboy" [*Żydek*], said one, "definitely a Jew." "Not her, for sure, but he's a Jew", replied another. "She dumped him on us", said a third.' The discussion intensifies and involves more people. 'We have to tell the police',[61] the boy began to hear more and more frequently. Głowiński understands the difficulty of these women and the penalties they might face if caught with a Jewish child, but the ordeal remains nightmarish. Although it is brought to an end by the return of his aunt, it casts a revealing light on Polish attitudes to Jews during the war. Certainly the memoir is one of the most powerful evocations of the inhuman world of the Nazis and the way Poles accommodated to it.[62]

Like Marianowicz and Głowiński, Arnold Mostowicz was a well-known Polish intellectual who late in life wrote about how he survived the Second

in the 1990s after the collapse of communism. He was an active member of the Polish Writers' Union (Związek Literatów Polskich) and, after its dissolution in 1981 by the government, of the Polish Writers' Association (Stowarzyszenie Pisarzy Polskich). From 1996, he was chair of the Authors' Association—ZAiKS.

[59] Michał Głowiński, *Czarne sezony* (Warsaw, 1998); the book has now appeared in English: *The Black Seasons*, trans. Marci Shore (Evanston, Ill., 2005).

[60] *Czarne sezony*, 91–2.  [61] Ibid. 93–4.

[62] See also Gilbert Rappoport, 'Review of Michał Głowiński, *Czarny sezony*', *Polin*, 14 (2001), 408–13.

World War as a Jew. Whereas Mostowicz later pursued a literary career as a journalist and editor of various publications, his initial training was as a medical doctor. In *Żółta gwiazda i czerwony krzyż* (Yellow Star and Red Cross) he writes of his ghetto experiences in Łódź from the unique perspective of an individual charged with the health of the ghetto and with the relative freedom of movement that it provided.[63]

Mostowicz was born in 1914 into a large and diverse Jewish family in Łódź. His father, who was born in Krośniewice, near Kutno, earned his living in the textile industry but also pursued his literary and theatrical interests and wrote for the local Yiddish press. Mostowicz senior fled to Warsaw at the beginning of the war and was a successful actor in the Yiddish theatre in the ghetto. He was deported to his death in Treblinka in 1942.

Before the war Mostowicz was unable to obtain entry to medical school in Poland because of the anti-Jewish restrictions, so he enrolled as a medical student in Rouen (his family could not afford to send him to the more expensive Paris). He returned to Poland, having just qualified as a doctor, shortly before the outbreak of war, fleeing in September 1939 from his native Łódź to Warsaw, where he worked in a hospital during the German siege of the Polish capital. Returning to Łódź after the Polish defeat, he became a doctor in the 'Sanitary Service' of the ghetto. After the ghetto's liquidation he was deported, first to Auschwitz, then to a labour camp at Jelenia Góra, where he worked in an artificial fibre factory and nearly died from typhoid, and later to other labour camps, where he lived out the war. Following his liberation, Mostowicz opted to remain in Poland. He had already become active in the communist movement while a student in France, and he now joined the Polish Workers' Party, working as a journalist, first in Silesia, where he was editor of *Trybuna Dolnośląska*, and later in Kraków, where he was on the editorial board of *Gazeta Krakowska*. He observed subsequently: 'I do not regret my support for communism. Stalinism caused suffering, but I accepted it because I was certain that it would be replaced by something better. And in 1956 things did change.'[64]

In 1955, as the Thaw got under way in the Soviet Union, Mostowicz was appointed editor in chief of the humorous magazine *Szpilki*, where he assembled a very lively and creative team of writers. He lost this position in 1969 as a result of the 'anti-Zionist' purge begun in 1968. He worked first in the monthly *Ty i Ja*, where many of those who lost their jobs as a result of the purge found employment. When this publication was closed down, he

---

[63] Arnold Mostowicz, *Żółta gwiazda i czerwony krzyż* (Warsaw, 1988); trans. into German by Karin Wolff and Andrzej Bodek as *Der blinde Maks: oder, Passierschein durch den Styx* (Berlin, 1992), and into English by Henia and Nochem Reinhartz as *With a Yellow Star and a Red Cross: A Doctor in the Łódź Ghetto*, with a foreword by Antony Polonsky (London, 2005).

[64] Interview with Joanna Podgórska, *Polityka*, 5 Apr. 2001.

earned his living by writing scientific and medical articles. He refused to leave Poland, partly because he did not want to abandon the grave of his 15-year-old son, who had died in 1964, and partly because, as he explained in an interview in April 2001, 'If I had emigrated, I would have done what they wanted me to do.'[65] He became increasingly active in Jewish life in Poland as it was becoming revitalized, and was one of the founders in 1991 of the Stowarzyszenie Żydów Kombatantów i Poszkodowanych w II Wojnie Światowej (Association of Jewish Combatants and Victims in the Second World War).

In addition to *Żółta gwiazda i czerwony krzyż*, Mostowicz published a number of other books, including *Biologia uczy myśleć* (Biology Teaches You to Think), *Łódź, moja zakazana miłość* (Łódź, My Forbidden Love); *Karambole na czerwonym suknie* (Ricochets on a Red Skirt), and *Lekarska ballada* (Medical Ballad).[66] He was also the narrator and scriptwriter for the 2001 film *Fotoamator* (Camera Buff), directed by Dariusz Jabłoński, which contrasted the beautiful colour slides taken during the war by the Austrian chief accountant administering the Łódź ghetto with the death and degradation that characterized ghetto life. Mostowicz died in 2002.

In April 2001 he concluded the interview with Joanna Podgórska with the following words: 'What am I today? More a Jew or more a Pole? I don't know. I feel myself a patriot and, as George Bernard Shaw used to say, a true patriot is one who is dissatisfied with his homeland.' This double perspective of a Jew and a Pole, while echoing the other works described here, is especially striking in *Żółta gwiazda i czerwony krzyż*. It took Mostowicz over forty years before he was able to return to his traumatic past. He generally describes his experiences in the third person, as if his connection with the person who lived through these nightmarish occurrences is too painful to acknowledge directly. Instead of giving a chronological account, Mostowicz provides a series of vignettes that capture the essence of the tragic years of Jewish martyrdom and also frequently refer to Jewish life in inter-war Poland and to the history of his own family. These finely wrought and often deceptively artless accounts give a remarkable picture of what it was like to live through what he calls the 'time of indifference',[67] when the world dispassionately witnessed the mass murder of the Jews. Each chapter, which portrays a different aspect of the nightmarish world of the Nazis, is infused with Mostowicz's subtle commentaries on human nature.

In the first, he depicts the brutality that accompanied the establishment of the ghetto. Diarists, photographers, and, later, memoir writers and filmmakers

---

[65] Interview with Joanna Podgórska, *Polityka*, 5 Apr. 2001.
[66] *Biologia uczy myśleć* (Warsaw, 1988); *Łódź, moja zakazana miłość* (Łódź, 1999); *Karambole na czerwonym suknie* (Warsaw, 2001); *Lekarska ballada* (Łódź, 2003).
[67] *Żółta gwiazda i czerwony krzyż*, 112.

have tried to describe the horror and confusion of Jews who were given a few minutes' notice to gather their belongings and leave their homes for ever. As a physician, however, Mostowicz is able to relate this tragic experience from the viewpoint of one responsible for treating those unable to keep up and recording the fate of those who were killed by this brutal evacuation. He describes his neighbours' behaviour during the 'resettlement', noting the actions of one Polish woman who assisted Jews in the only way she knew how, through kneeling down in the courtyard and praying over the body of a fallen Jew.[68]

In the second chapter, a visit to the Gypsy (Roma) camp, Mostowicz writes from the unique experience of one of the few Jews allowed inside this section of the ghetto. Very little primary source documentation of that area survived the war. The Nazis killed all of the Roma interned in the Łódź ghetto, leaving no witnesses. A few Jewish sources offer fragmentary evidence of the Roma experience and only a few remaining pages in the German records testify to the tragedy of the Roma in the ghetto. Illegal photographs were taken of this portion of the camp, but they were destroyed during the 1948 War of Independence in Israel when the kibbutz in which the photographs were housed was bombed. Mostowicz thus stands alone as a first-person witness of the last days of a people who were being systematically killed by the Nazis.

He also had entry to the homes of people from all walks of pre-war and ghetto life. Even before the war, the majority of Łódź's Jewish community had been poor, consisting mostly of artisans and textile workers. In addition, there existed a significant minority of industrialists, intellectuals, and professionals. The pre-war Jewish community was diverse not only in its economic stratifications but also in its religious observance. Although the great majority of Jews were religious, there were a variety of traditions, including various hasidic sects. Mostowicz's descriptions reflect this diverse pre-war community.

The text of *Żółta gwiazda i czerwony krzyż* becomes personal in Mostowicz's description of his extended family—a group that likewise encompassed a range of economic and religious backgrounds. In one place, for example, he records how religious feeling played a role in aggravating the anguish of one of his cousins, a deeply religious Jew who, because of malnutrition and illness, could not fulfil his religious obligation to have intercourse with his wife.[69] One of the most memorable pieces is in the style of the *szmonces*, the humorous Jewish monologue with a hidden deeper meaning, in which he describes how the Jewish underworld's crude but effective way of enforcing justice in Łódź in the inter-war period came to an end. In this piece, Mostowicz condemns Jews who willingly collaborated with the Gestapo. He is more reflective in his evaluation of others who found

[68] Ibid. 9.    [69] Ibid. 66.

themselves forced into doing the Nazis' dirty work. For example, he gives his own assessment of Mordechai Chaim Rumkowski in a chapter tellingly entitled, 'There Once Was a King . . .'. In it he questions the usual attempt to contrast the moral heroism of Adam Czerniaków, who committed suicide rather than comply with the German demand that he assist in the deportation of the Jews of Warsaw, with the constant attempt of Rumkowski to placate the Germans. Given the total abandonment and isolation of the Jews, their leaders could only count on a miracle to save them. Had the Soviets broken through the German lines in 1944 or had the plot against Hitler's life succeeded, that miracle would have occurred. Rumkowski would still have been condemned for his many acts of cravenness. But he would have saved perhaps 60,000 Jews. Even without this miracle, Mostowicz remarks, 'from the Łódź ghetto ultimately there remained alive more than 10,000 Jews whom death in the camps had not had time to swallow. Almost no one survived from the Warsaw ghetto, except those few who found shelter on the "Aryan" side.'[70]

The last chapters describe Mostowicz's experiences first in Auschwitz, and then in the labour camps of Jelenia Góra, Warmbrunn, Dörnhau, and Erlenbusch. As the war approached its end, the Nazi world began to exhibit some strange contradictions. A number of SS men ask individual prisoners whether it is true that Jews are being murdered *en masse* in Auschwitz. Acts of humanity, such as the organization of a football match between the SS and their prisoners, alternate with mindless brutality and killing. A previously 'humane' guard loses his temper and viciously beats up Mostowicz, a sign that the Soviet offensive is succeeding. The prisoners also sometimes behave bizarrely. As a group of prisoners is being marched to the camp in Hirschberg, a German Jewish doctor asks to change places with Mostowicz in the column. He is frightened that someone who knew him from the days when he came skiing in this area will recognize him in his shameful concentration camp garb.

In one of these later chapters, Mostowicz describes how, in the 'memorable year 1981', which saw the flourishing of the Solidarity movement in Poland, he was invited to a scientific conference in Cieplice, where, as a camp prisoner, he had nearly died of typhoid as the war came to an end. He comments:

The evacuation of the Cieplice camp was an entirely different story. When he started out at that time on an unknown road, he left behind a stage of suffering that, while occupying little space in his biography, had engraved deep traces in him. He was not always aware of the existence of those traces, or rather scars. He thought that the current of life would erase those traces as the sea erases footprints in the sand on the beach. But this was an illusion. He was returning to the Cieplice

[70] *Żółta gwiazda i czerwony krzyż*, 125.

of his memories and, what was worse, he was returning to it in his nightmares. He had never returned to a place to confront his memories and his dreams with reality. At least, with what remained of the reality of that other time. Perhaps it was laziness. Perhaps it was a superstition that he could not understand. In a certain period, it was fear. The fear of delving too much into his own past, because that meant that he was getting old. For the same reason, he did not like to look at photographs that recalled the old days . . .

Standing then in front of the five buildings that at one time had comprised the Cieplice camp, he felt a kind of regret that he had treated his past that way. And not only his past at the camps. He had treated it as if it belonged to someone else. And this was, after all, a deception. One cannot create an artificial separation between the different periods of one's own life as he had done—between the period of his life that ended with the liberation and that which began with the liberation. You are what you are: the tears of your mother, the laughter of your friend, the stone that was thrown at you because of your ethnic origin, the song with which you bid farewell to the train with volunteers that went to the Spanish front—the yellow star that you wore attached to your chest, the dead person's bread that saved you from death. Is it too late to repair this deception?[71]

These ruminations reveal a motivation for writing that echoes Olczak-Ronikier as well as the less explicit references of the other authors we have looked at here. In writing about their Jewish past and wartime traumas, these authors seek to bring together the various parts of their past and present: the acculturated Jew of the pre-war period for which Polish society in the first half of the twentieth century could not find an appropriate place; the hidden child or ghetto dweller of the Second World War; and the Pole of Jewish background who belonged to the intellectual circles of post-war Poland. In explaining his need to overcome this fracturing of identity, Mostowicz, like Olczak-Ronikier and Marianowicz as well as Bromberg in Grynberg's *Memorbuch*, refers to the wartime fear long associated with his Jewish past. These authors' process of writing about their Jewish background and wartime experiences can be seen as an attempt to disconnect their Jewish past from this feeling of fear and reconnect it with the families and communities that they now describe.

The openness with which the memoirs address their authors' Jewish background indicates an attempt to normalize attitudes, at least among some segments of the Polish intelligentsia, towards Jewish integration into Polish society and the Jewish contribution to Polish culture. The memoirs are part of the continued effort in Poland to overcome the taboo connected with discussing the Jewish past, a taboo that has been turned inside out by the current fashion among certain circles for all things Jewish.

[71] Ibid. 210–11.

It is worth noting, however, the difference in emphasis between those writers who emigrated in 1967–8 (Grynberg and Dichter) and those who remained in Poland. The post-war period, and particularly the 1968 events, are still largely unaddressed in the memoirs of those writing from Poland, whether because these events had a lesser impact on those who chose to remain or because the experiences of those years still are too close to the present.

These works are significant beyond the writers' own relationship to their Jewish background, however. Looking at the past through the perspective of being both a Pole and a Jew, both insider and outsider, they are seeking to integrate the Jewish past not only into their own identities, but also into a broader understanding of recent Polish, and Polish Jewish, history. It took the end of communism to bring these voices to the surface.

# PART II

## ACCULTURATION, ASSIMILATION, AND IDENTITY

# NEGOTIATING CZECHOSLOVAKIA
## The Challenges of Jewish Citizenship in a Multiethnic Nation-State

### HILLEL J. KIEVAL

S TUDENTS OF JEWISH LIFE in inter-war Czechoslovakia often confront the aphorism—and may even be guilty of spreading it—that claims the only 'true Czechoslovaks' between the two world wars were the Jews. A similar simplifying proverb makes the rounds concerning Jews of the Habsburg monarchy: the only true 'Austrians' before 1914, we are told, were the Jews. Behind both claims are the assumptions that Jews, alone among east-central Europe's ethnic groups and nations in the making, did not challenge the legitimacy of the imperial or the multiethnic state in the name of a presumptive nation, remained aloof from nationalizing pressures and processes, and chose instead to identify politically with the state as a supranational construct.[1]

Like most proverbial assertions, Jews as the only 'true Czechoslovaks'— or as the only 'true Austrians', for that matter—does not stand up long to scrutiny. First, it assumes that members of ethnic nationalities in imperial states do not, or will not, identify politically with the state; this is, at best, an untested hypothesis based largely on the political rhetoric employed by the more extreme nationalists themselves; it represents a position which, for most of the nineteenth century at least, was not shared by the majority of the population. The statement also bears traces of the position—itself born of the ideological struggles of the nineteenth century—that the Jews, unlike all of their neighbours, did not constitute an ethnic group or, alternatively, that *their* ethnicity, exceptionally, was not tied to territory and thus could not constitute a threat to the imperial state. Finally, it suggests a mutuality between the new state of Czechoslovakia and its Jewish population that

---

[1] Marsha Rozenblit offers a more subtle formulation regarding the Jews of Austria-Hungary before the First World War. Jews felt deeply loyal to the Habsburg monarchy, she argues, because 'the supranational state allowed them the luxury of separating the political, cultural, and ethnic strands in their identity'. With regard to Habsburg Austria, she writes, Jews developed a 'tripartite identity', according to which they identified *politically* as Austrians, *culturally* as German, Czech, Polish, etc., and *ethnically* as Jews. Marsha L. Rozenblit, *Reconstructing a National Identity: The Jews of Habsburg Austria during World War I* (New York, 2001), 3–4.

never, in fact, existed: on the one hand, that the state never had reason to
regard the Jews within its borders as threatening or problematic, and on the
other, that the Jews recognized in Czechoslovakia not a nation-state in
the Wilsonian model but a supranational construct—the 'nationalities state'
that the Habsburg monarchy had claimed to be.

In fact, as this essay will show, Jewish integration in inter-war Czechoslovakia was a complex and often difficult process, which involved delicate
negotiations with a triumphant national movement, uncertainty over the
eventual extent of Jewish national expression and/or autonomy, and—for
many Jews in the new state—a sudden disruption of long-standing patterns
of acculturation and national identification. Jews were indeed viewed with
suspicion by the government of Masaryk, Kramář, and Beneš—particularly
the former Hungarian citizens in Slovakia and German-speaking Jews in
Bohemia and Moravia, but, to a certain extent, Jewish nationalists as well;
and the strategic identification of Jewish spokespersons—including the
Zionists—with the state involved not so much an appeal to a supranational
political model as an acknowledgement of the reality of 'Czechoslovak'
domination in the new political order. My goal here will be to assess both the
foundations and the limits of Jewish citizenship in the new state by focusing
on the intersection of language, culture, and politics. What is at stake in this
investigation is the question as to whether, or to what degree, Jews developed a 'Czechoslovak' political identity during these years and, if so, with
what consequences for their political, social, and cultural integration into
the new state?

My point of departure will be the dissolution of the Habsburg monarchy
and, with it, the ending of the distinctive political structures that had established the framework for the cultural and political choices of Jews in three
different environments: the lands of the Czech Crown (Bohemia, Moravia,
and Silesia), Upper Hungary (Slovakia), and Carpatho-Rus (in today's
Ukraine). The questions that I would like to raise are the following. To what
extent did attitudes and behaviours whose origin lay in accommodating
Austrian and Hungarian conditions carry over to the new nation-state?
What was the relationship between culture and citizenship in Czechoslovakia? (Did 'insider' status, or a sense of belonging to the new state,
depend on meeting specific cultural/linguistic requirements?) How many
Jewish cultural orientations can be said to have been in play in this part
of east-central Europe? Did Jews achieve a successful integration as
'Czechoslovaks'? Finally, how did Jewish nationality function as a set of
norms around which to organize group politics and social identity?

Under the late Habsburg monarchy, Jews from the various regions that
would come to form the Czechoslovak state developed distinct responses to
the challenges of acculturation and political integration. In Bohemia, the

rise of a politically articulate (and demanding) Czech middle class—which achieved complete dominance of the Prague government, if not of its cultural life, by the 1880s—combined with the migration of bilingual Jews from the Czech countryside to the cities, produced shock waves in what for nearly a century had been a steady, calm voyage of acculturation to the linguistic culture of the court and loyalty to the dynastic state, achieved largely through the medium of the German Jewish *Normalschulen*—state-supervised schools with a modern curriculum. The late imperial period produced the first modern Czech Jews, committed to employing the language of the majority and to displaying overt sympathy for its larger political goals. It also had the dual effect of, first, tempering the enthusiasm and confidence with which German-speaking Jews continued to pursue the previous acculturation (attenuating, as it were, the 'German–Jewish embrace'), and removing from it any sense of national identification, and, second, initiating a fascinating experiment with Jewish cultural nationalism (the so-called 'Prague Zionism') on the part of young, urban Jews—mainly artists and intellectuals, but also members of the commercial middle class.[2]

This sea change in political culture was not as fully achieved in Moravia, where proximity to Vienna, German dominance of the Landtag, and the survival of autonomous Jewish municipalities (*politische Judengemeinde*) decades beyond the revolution of 1848 prolonged the germanocentric orientation of a large portion of the Jewish community. The existence of Jewish political communities alongside Christian towns, in a structure that seemed to blend aspects of the pre-modern, corporate status of the Jews with their new role as citizens, also encouraged the articulation of an autonomous Jewish politics not found in Bohemia.[3]

The overall consequence of the new demographic, cultural, and political realities in Bohemia and Moravia—in the context of late Habsburg institutional arrangements—was the production of a modern Jewish community that managed to remain *staatstreu* (or, at least, *regierungstreu*). At the same time, it positioned itself to meet the rules and expectations of a very different kind of state, a multiethnic nation-state, which, while recognizing the rights of its national minorities, would nevertheless be unabashedly committed to furthering the interests—and expressing the sovereignty—of its dominant group.

[2] These processes are described more fully in Hillel J. Kieval, *The Making of Czech Jewry: National Conflict and Jewish Society in Bohemia, 1870–1918* (New York, 1988), and, more recently and from a more long-term perspective, in id., *Languages of Community: The Jewish Experience in the Czech Lands* (Berkeley, 2000).

[3] On the political culture of Moravian Jews—and the unique structural characteristics of Moravia—see Michael L. Miller, 'Rabbis and Revolution: A Study in Nineteenth-Century Moravian Jewry', Ph.D. diss., Columbia University, 2004; id., 'Reluctant Kingmakers: Moravian Jewish Politics in Late Imperial Austria', *Jewish Studies at the Central European University*, 3 (2002/3), 111–23; and Jacob Toury, 'Townships in the German-Speaking Parts of the Austrian Empire before and after the Revolution of 1848/49', *Leo Baeck Institute Yearbook*, 26 (1981), 55–72.

There is a certain irony in the manoeuvring and self-refashioning that characterized much of public Jewish life in Bohemia and Moravia in the last decades of the monarchy. One could argue that the net result of the long and arduous process of what I have called 'secondary acculturation', far from transforming the basis on which Jewish politics in east-central Europe operated, merely preserved for the Jews their cherished position as a *Staatsvolk*.[4] Only the object of their devotion was new. Jews in the Bohemian lands had distanced themselves, to be sure, from Austro-German liberalism and had learned (sometimes from painful experience) to pay close attention to the shifting balance of power among the region's dominant ethnic groups, but on one important level nothing had changed. Jews continued to play their long-standing political card of choice: full identification with the state. Loyalty to the Czechoslovak state would transcend linguistic and political divisions; it would encompass veterans of the Czech Jewish movement as well as recent converts to the cause, diehard promoters of German language and culture, and committed Zionists; and it would be predicated on the self-generated assurance that the imagined community of 'Czechoslovaks' (a fiction born of the dissolution of the monarchy, in which Slavic speakers who had lived under dissimilar political conditions for the previous four centuries were proclaimed members of a single nation) was both expansive enough and generous enough to accommodate multiple languages, religions, political ideologies, and even ethno-cultural programmes.

With the proclamation of the Czechoslovak Republic on 28 October 1918, the political programme of the Czech Jewish movement—reorganized in 1919 as the Svaz Čechů-židů—was realized beyond what only a few years earlier would have been considered any reasonable expectation. Its activists were left with little more to do than mobilize Jewish public opinion in support of the new state and urge continued acculturation to the linguistic patterns of the new majority. In December 1919 the venerable Association of Czech Academic Jews (Spolek českých akademiků-židů), founded in 1876 by Jewish university and technical school students who inclined towards Czech national culture, and dedicated to effecting a cultural, linguistic, and political reorientation among Bohemian Jews, announced that, to all intents and purposes, its original mission had been fulfilled. Renaming itself the (Siegfried) Kapper Academic Society (Akademický spolek 'Kapper'— after the mid-nineteenth-century Czech Jewish poet) and amending its bylaws, the association announced its new goals to be the promotion of the well-being of the Czechoslovak state and the integration of Jews into Czech society; at the same time it opened the group's doors to non-Jewish member-

---

[4] On the concept of 'secondary acculturation', see Kieval, *Making of Czech Jewry*, 4, 8, and 198–203.

ship.[5] Along similar lines, the Association of Czech Progressive Jews (Svaz českých pokrokových židů) issued a call in autumn 1918 for the establishment of a daily Czech Jewish newspaper, focusing on business and economics while expressing progressive and democratic opinion. 'The Jews need a Czech paper', their public appeal read, 'and the Czech nation needs a business paper.'

While the newspaper was to be 'Jewish' in inspiration, in its financial backing, and, to a large extent, in its editorial staff, it would not carry the label 'Jewish' on its masthead. In this sense, the imagined publication could stand as a Czech counterpart to the German liberal daily, the *Prager Tagblatt*. The determination not to be regarded as having a distinct, Jewish agenda, moreover—expressed in the following lines from the appeal for support issued by the project's initiators—reflected the dilemma of any movement that faces the new situation of having achieved its main goals. What is the stage that follows completion?

The establishment and publication of a truly progressive and democratic paper will demonstrate to Czech Jews in practice that there is no difference between us and the rest of society . . . in our personal relationship to—and genuine love of—the fatherland. That we have the same aspirations, the same hopes as the other, the non-Jewish, sons of the Czech lands. That we feel the same burning love for it, and that it is only prejudice and mutual misunderstanding that, unfortunately quite often in recent days, erects barriers between us.[6]

It is tempting, of course, to view the assertion that 'there is no difference between us and the rest of society' as an example of 'protesting too much' in the hope of overcoming one's own doubts to the contrary. Doubtless there was some of this in the degree to which the point was belaboured. The fact remains, however, that Czech Jewish political activists did not possess a clear vision of what Jewish cultural expression should be in a context in which Czechs enjoyed national self-determination. What would the movement stand for the day after the celebration of independence? At this point, the movement had little to suggest beyond steadfast support for the state and continued Jewish integration into Czech society.

As it turned out, Czech Jews did establish a liberal daily newspaper in February 1919, which went by the name of *Tribuna*. It was edited by Bedřich Hlaváč, a close friend of Tomáš Masaryk, who had converted in his twenties

---

[5] Ibid. 183–5; 'Z organisací českožidovských', *Kalendář česko-židovský*, 38 (1918/19), 115–17; Akademický spolek 'Kapper', *Výroční zpráva akademického spolku 'Kapper' za období od roku 1914 do roku 1921* (Prague, 1921), 5–6; 'Zprávy spolkové', *Kalendář česko-židovský*, 40 (1920/1), 107.

[6] 'Přátelé', *Kalendář česko-židovský*, 38 (1918/19), 3–4. The appeal was signed by Eduard Lederer, Vojtěch Rakous, Stanislav Schulhof, Lev Vohryzek, Viktor Vohryzek, Mořic Hirsch, and Rudolf Neuwirth. See also Viktor Vohryzek, 'Česká žurnalistika', *Rozvoj*, no. 3 (1919), 1–2, and 'K projektu nového denníku', *Rozhled* (1918), no. 21, 4–5. All translations, unless otherwise indicated, are my own.

to Catholicism. Another editor, Arne Laurin (born Arne Lustig; 1889–1945), who like Hlavač was fully bilingual, would later become the editor of the state-funded German-language paper *Prager Presse*, but he never ceased writing for *Tribuna*. The paper's other collaborators included the literary and theatre critic Josef Kodíček, the journalist (and, later, Catholic martyr) Alfred Fuchs, the sociologist Jindřich Kohn, and the writers Karel Poláček and Milena Jesenská. *Tribuna's* ownership changed hands in 1922, and in 1928 it ceased publication. During its brief period of operation as a Czech-language daily devoted to economic reporting, progressive politics, and support of the Czechoslovak state, with no overt reference to the Czech Jewish community, its appearance seemed to confirm the contention of its founders that there was no longer any difference between Jews and non-Jewish Czechs in their public lives. To most readers, however—both supporters and detractors— *Tribuna* was a 'Jewish' newspaper.[7]

A large percentage of Jews in Bohemia and Moravia, though no longer the majority, continued to speak the German language, send their children to German schools, attend German cultural events, and read German newspapers.[8] Jews held prominent editorial positions and were active as reporters for a number of German newspapers in the country's capital, including the *Prager Tagblatt*, *Bohemia*, and *Die Wahrheit*, which began publication in 1927. Max Brod, Rudolf Fuchs, Willy Haas, Egon Ervin Kisch, Theodor Lessing, Friedrich Torberg, Joseph Wechsberg, Otto Pick, Pavel Eisner, and others all wrote for the German-language press; a number wrote for several papers at the same time; some for both German liberal and Zionist publications; and Eisner, Pick, and Arne Laurin for both German and Czech newspapers.[9] While virtually all of the German publications for which Prague Jews wrote in the inter-war years expressed strong support for Czechoslovak parliamentary democracy, none could rival the *Prager Presse* for loyalty to the government or reliability in presenting the state's position. This semi-official paper, which appeared from 1921 to 1938 and was intended in part for a foreign readership, was headed by the bilingual Arne Laurin—a member of the so-called Friday circle organized by the Čapek brothers. As mentioned earlier, he had been active in the Czech Jewish movement and also served as an editor for the Czech-language paper *Tribuna*.[10]

---

[7] On *Tribuna*, see especially Kateřina Čapková, *Češi, Němci, Židé? Národní identita Židů v Čechách 1918–1938* (Prague, 2005), 125–9; also Tomáš Pěkný, *Historie Židů v Čechách a na Moravě* (Prague, 2001), 540; Egon Hostovský, 'The Czech-Jewish Movement', in *The Jews of Czechoslovakia: Historical Studies and Surveys*, 3 vols. (Philadelphia, 1968, 1971, 1984), ii. 151–2 and Josef Vyskočil, 'Die tschechisch-jüdische Bewegung', *Judaica Bohemiae*, 3 (1967), 47.

[8] Čapková observes that it was primarily among the higher social strata of Jews that families sent their children to German language schools in inter-war Czechoslovakia. Middle-class and working-class Jews sent their children primarily to Czech schools, including middle school and universities (*Češi, Němci, Židé?*, 64). [9] Ibid. 67–71; Pěkný, *Historie Židů*, 538–42

[10] Pěkný, *Historie Židů*, 539; Čapková, *Češi, Němci, Židé?*, 69–70.

The active involvement of members of the Jewish Party (Židovská strana) in a number of German-language newspapers raises the question of the connections that existed among language use, cultural politics, national minority rights, and loyalty to the state in inter-war Czechoslovakia. Were German speakers more likely than Czech speakers to promote a Jewish national position in Bohemia and Moravia? Were speakers of Hungarian more likely than speakers of Slovak or Yiddish to promote Zionism in Slovakia? Were German- and Hungarian-speaking Jews induced to declare their nationality as Jewish in the 1921 and 1930 censuses in order not to be too closely identified with the formerly dominant cultures now in decline and disfavour? Did Beneš and Masaryk agree to recognize the right of Jews to be treated as a distinct national group in 1920 in order to reduce the numbers of Germans and Hungarians in the state and weaken their respective influence? Last, to what conception of the state did Jewish nationalists pledge their loyalty?

Max Brod's nationalist credo, published in the Bratislava newspaper *Jüdische Volkszeitung*, offers, as it were, an unintentionally absurd response to the first question. 'Ich bin nichts als Jude', he proclaims in his best *Hochdeutsch*—I am nothing other than a Jew. 'I belong (fully cognizant of my duties as a citizen) to no other people than the Jewish one.'[11] Brod's formulation more than a year earlier of his negotiation of the competing claims of language, culture, and national identity is a good deal more subtle:

I do not feel myself to belong to the German people, but I am a friend of Germanness [*Deutschtum*], culturally related to the German world above all through language and education, through much of what sociology calls . . . 'traditional values'—as opposed to 'generational' or 'inherited values'.

. . . Language, education, reading, and culture have made me a thankful friend of the German people, but not a German.[12]

Czech national leaders could, perhaps, be excused if they did not fully grasp the distinction between cultural affinity and core national identity and if they regarded the claims of the newfangled Jewish National Council (Národní rada židovská), established in October 1918, for Jewish minority rights with suspicion.

The fact that the Czechoslovak government was eventually won over to the idea can be attributed in no small measure to the Prague Zionists' ability to deploy the language of the nineteenth-century national revivals of east-central Europe and intuitively to grasp the real balance of power in the new

---

[11] Max Brod, 'Orthodoxie, Zionismus, Nationaljudentum', *Jüdische Volkszeitung*, 28 Nov. 919, quoted in Rebekah Klein-Pejšová, 'Building Slovak Jewry: Material Evidence of Reorientation as Citizens of Czechoslovakia', paper delivered at the Association for Jewish Studies Annual Conference, December 2007.

[12] Max Brod, 'Juden, Deutsche, Tschechen: Eine menschlich-politische Betrachtung (Juli 918)', in id., *Im Kampf um das Judentum* (Vienna, 1920), 15, 17.

state. Only a few hours before the proclamation of the Czechoslovak Republic, representatives of the Jewish National Council—including its chairman, the Czech-speaking Ludvík Singer, and vice-chairmen Max Brod and Karel Fischel—appeared before the Czech National Council (Národní Výbor) and presented it with a memorandum that argued for recognition of the Jewish nationality and the national minority rights of Jews. A close reading of the document reveals that the Jewish nationalists knew exactly how to counter the suspicions of the new government regarding their intentions: by casting their own experience with German and Hungarian acculturation in terms borrowed from Czech and Slovak national narratives, they were able to make broad promises of real benefits that would accrue to Czechoslovak legitimacy (and hegemony) through Jewish national support.

'We national Jews', the memorandum intoned, 'grant that there are some Jews who have so completely identified with the Czech or German peoples that they are capable of participating fully in the inner life of the nationality in whose midst they live.' The Zionists had no intention, it assured the Czech National Council, of placing any political obstacles in the way of individuals who had undergone such complete 'assimilation'. It then proceeded to touch on a very sensitive argument in both Czech and Slovak national rhetoric regarding 'insincere' assimilation and the role that the Austrian and Hungarian political systems had played in manipulating Jewish cultural declarations to inflate the relative weight of German and Hungarian influence, respectively, in their domains.

What we have fought against, and are still fighting against, is that vacillating, insincere sort of assimilation that is to be blamed not on the unfortunate Jewish people but on the conditions of their dispersal, and on the fact that the Austrian government (particularly under Magyar influence) consistently opposed the recognition of the Jews as a nationality group. The governments of Austria and Hungary continually sought to use the Jews as tools for oppressing the small nationalities, an exploitation that we Zionists have always emphatically deplored. The Jewish National Council regards as its primary aim the promotion of honest and frank relations between the Jewish and Czech peoples. The Czech people has equally great benefits to derive from the attainment of this goal, for the new Czech State must have domestic peace if it is to enjoy the unhampered development that we all would wish for it. Furthermore, the respect that the Czech democracy will gain among all the peoples of the world if it finds a fair solution to the Jewish problem will serve to raise the international status of the Czech State.[13]

The statement that 'the new Czech State must have domestic peace if it is to enjoy the unhampered development that we all would wish for it' signals two

---

[13] Memorandum from the Jewish National Council to the Government of the Czechoslovak State (Národní Výbor), trans. and reprod. in Aharon Moshe Rabinowicz, 'The Jewish Minority', in *The Jews of Czechoslovakia*, i. 218–19 (appendix A).

important points regarding the Zionist initiative in October 1918. First, it was the Jewish nationalists themselves who planted the suggestion that official recognition of Jews as a nationality would carry the added benefit of diminishing the size of the German and Hungarian minorities in the new state and, hence, of enhancing the ability of the 'Czechoslovak' majority to govern. Second, the Jewish National Council implied that it was prepared to support the idea of a Czechoslovak nation-state, dominated by its leading nationality. Jewish leaders had no illusions about the nature of the state that was about to be proclaimed: they did not imagine that they were about to take part in a supranational 'nationalities state' of some kind; quite the contrary, they knew the name of the game and were prepared to co-operate. They hoped in return to attain a moral victory in the war against the 'assimilationists', a position of influence in Jewish public life, and some degree of cultural autonomy, as yet undetermined.[14]

As Tatjana Lichtenstein has recently argued, Jewish activists in Czechoslovakia accommodated themselves to 'the dominant nationalizing paradigm' of the state, identifying not so much with the supranational implications of a multinational polity as with Czechoslovakia as an ethnic-national structure. Jews, then, were 'real Czechoslovaks' because they accepted the underlying terms on which the new state was established and identified with the state-nation now endowed with power. The fact that Jewish nationalists in Czechoslovakia pretty much followed suit might strike the reader as counter-intuitive or improbable. But it goes to the crux of the political strategy of accommodation and speaks to the ingenuity of the Jewish national position in the inter-war years. Lichtenstein focuses on the Czech Zionist and statistician František Friedmann (1897–1945)— whose publications painstakingly described the Jewish population of Prague and the Czech lands in terms of geographical, age, and gender distribution, language use, school attendance, and nationality declaration—and she argues that Zionists such as Friedmann, in claiming Jews 'for the Jewish nation', and in lobbying successfully for Jews to be counted as a separate national category in official censuses, actually helped to create this nation within the boundaries of Czechoslovakia, to establish it as a 'social fact'—a reality whose political implications, rather than posing a challenge to the legitimacy of the state, underscored that legitimacy.[15]

[14] Rebekah Klein-Pejšová makes a similar observation regarding the Jewish national leadership in Slovakia, which promoted Jewish politics as not only an authentic form of Jewish self-expression but also an effective way of distancing themselves from the pre-war pattern of Hungarian linguistic and political allegiance. See Klein-Pejšová, 'Building Slovak Jewry'.

[15] Tatjana Lichtenstein, 'Space and Jewish Identity: František Friedmann and the Construction of Czechoslovak Jewry', paper delivered at the Association for Jewish Studies Annual Conference, December 2007. Among Friedmann's more important statistical works are *Pražští Židé: Studie statistická*, special offprint from *Židovský kalendář na rok 5690*

Jewish nationalists in inter-war Czechoslovakia understood their principal task as uniting Jews from disparate regions and communities, separated from one another by language, acculturation patterns, religious practice, and political allegiances forged during the Habsburg past, into a single 'territorial nation', bounded by the contours of the new state—thus, a 'state-nation' par excellence, but a Jewish one. Through the use of statistics and descriptive social science, Friedmann made the Jews in Czechoslovakia 'legible as a distinct nation'. They became, as it were, a single ethnic community of some 350,000 individuals—wildly heterogeneous, perhaps, in outward appearance, standard of living, daily language, and cultural orientation, but claimed by Jewish nationalists as an essentially coherent, ethnic entity. The very existence of *this* Jewish nationality depended on the contingent fact of Czechoslovakia's existence and on the swath of territory that it cut in east-central Europe. Czechoslovak Jewry, in other words, 'was the human material that bore [witness] to the naturalness' of the state.[16]

If we turn our attention to those parts of Czechoslovakia that had been included in the Kingdom of Hungary before 1918, we see that here not only did Jews face a different set of political complications but also that conditions in Slovakia and Carpatho-Rus produced distinctive Jewish cultural responses. Bratislava (Pressburg/Pozsony)'s geographical proximity to Vienna, the presence of a strong German social element in the cities and towns of central and western Slovakia, and the relative weakness of Slovak national culture in the nineteenth century had helped to ensure a gradual, moderate (primarily linguistic) acculturation to German among a broad sector of the region's Jews—including the Orthodox population in urban centres.

In contrast to the situation in the Czech lands, however, the secondary acculturation that inevitably occurred during the last third of the nineteenth century—to Hungarian language, culture, and politics—did not evolve in opposition to the hegemony of the imperial state but, rather, as a programme *of* the state, in this case post-*Ausgleich* Hungary. As German-speaking fathers and mothers sent their sons to Magyar primary and secondary schools, they were moving from one imperial embrace to another—casting off Vienna in favour of Budapest—but they were not altering their political-cultural behaviour in any fundamental way. Their cultural and linguistic choices were still predicated on the need they felt to accommodate the requirements of the imperial state.[17]

---

*(1929–30)* (Prague, 1929), and 'Židé v Čechách', in Hugo Gold (ed.), *Židé a židovské obce v Čechách v minulosti a přítomnosti* (Brno, 1934).

[16] Lichtenstein, 'Space and Jewish Identity', 9.

[17] On Jewish linguistic and political identifications in Slovakia, see Livia Rothkirchen 'Slovakia: I, 1848–1918', in *The Jews of Czechoslovakia*, i. 72–84, and 'Slovakia: II, 1918–1938' ibid. i. 85–124; Yeshayahu Jelinek, 'In Search of Identity: Slovakian Jewry and Nationalism (1918–1938)', in Yehuda Don and Victor Karady (eds.), *A Social and Economic History of Central*

From this perspective, Jews in Slovakia were a good deal less prepared than their Czech counterparts to assume the function of *Staatsvolk* in the new Czechoslovak state after 1918. Yet we learn from Rebekah Klein-Pejšová that Slovak Jews soon went about the process of symbolically redrawing maps and boundaries, effacing traces of their Hungarian citizenship and political allegiance, and reorienting themselves and their communities to the contours of their new home state. This was to be a difficult and at times painful exercise, which involved a profound rupture of historical patterns of identification as well as a spatial/territorial about-face.[18] Perhaps nothing epitomizes the depth of the challenge better than the fact that Slovak Jews continued to be represented by religious-communal institutions that bore the Neolog, Status Quo, and Orthodox designations of their Hungarian origins. Slovak language and culture had never held the appeal for Jews in the Kingdom of Hungary that Czech language and culture had exerted over Bohemian and Moravian Jews, and, for the most part, when Jews of the former Upper Hungarian counties refashioned themselves as 'Slovak' Jews, their point of reference tended to be geographical and territorial, not national. Although the small Union of Slovak Jews (Sväz slovenských židov) urged active acculturation to Slovak language and culture and identification with the newly forged 'Czechoslovak' nation, the majority of Jews in this part of the new state understood themselves to be 'Slovak' in a more restricted sense: in Klein-Pejšová's words, as 'belonging as a group to the bound[ed] territorial unit of Slovakia and the specific set of challenges and opportunities [that] that reality presented'.[19]

For many Slovak Jews, reorienting oneself away from Budapest and in the direction of Prague and focusing imaginatively on Slovakia as *place* entailed a rediscovery of the 'local'—transforming the towns and villages in which they lived into 'Jewish home towns'. In a very real sense, this meant planting one's feet in Košice and Prešov, Bardejov and Michalovce, tracing their boundaries, walking their streets, and, ultimately, staking one's claim to them in the form of new institutional building. Noteworthy in this regard was the Jewish community of Košice, which not only established four new cultural and welfare organizations during these years but also embarked on impressive building projects that included the construction of new—occasionally imposing—synagogues to serve the town's hasidic, Orthodox, and Neolog communities. I cannot help but imagine that the monumental Neolog synagogue—completed in 1925, and with a capacity of 1,100—was intended both to evoke and to replace the great Dohány Street synagogue in Budapest, until then the architectural jewel in the Neolog crown. Oversized,

*European Jewry* (New Brunswick, 1990), 207–27; Yeshayahu Jelinek, 'Židia na Slovensku v 19. storočí: poznámky k dejinám', *Slovenský národopis*, 41/3 (1993), 271–96; and Yeshayahu Jelinek, *Židovské náboženské obce na Slovensku v 19. a 20. storočí a ich spoločenské postavenie* (Bratislava, 2002).

[18] Klein-Pejšová, 'Building Slovak Jewry', *passim*.          [19] Ibid. 3.

perhaps, for its location in a city of only 72,000 and allegedly constructed in a Magyar idiom, this edifice constituted the new 'address' of liberal Judaism in Slovakia and signalled the desire of the Neolog community to attain rootedness in the Czechoslovak environment.[20]

In the early years of the republic, Slovak Jews were not alone in puzzling over how to respond to the new balance of forces in the state. Czechoslovak officials themselves seemed unsure of the precise make-up of the Slovak Jewish community and viewed its leadership warily. During the 1920s, in fact, a complaint from the Union of Slovak Jews to the Bratislava police prompted a six-year investigation of the Neolog community and its rabbi Samuel Funk on the grounds that it might be maintaining irredentist sympathies for Hungary. Neolog Jews in Slovakia had begun to proclaim Jewish nationality in government censuses, which also worried the Ministry of the Interior, concerned that the Zionist movement in Slovakia might be providing cover for Magyar nationalists. Eventually, the state reversed its initial suspicions of Rabbi Funk and concluded that he was a loyal Czechoslovak. Opinion seems to have been divided regarding the ultimate motives and intentions of the Zionists; but the state remained highly suspicious of the Neolog establishment's continued ties to Budapest.[21]

In 1910 less than 5 per cent of the Jews in this region had declared Slovak to be their everyday language. In the inter-war period, cut off from the political and cultural orbit of Hungary, Jews in Slovakia could conceivably have tried to make up for lost time. But which language were they to adopt? Despite the nationalist fiction that had been created by the political leadership with Masaryk at its head, Czech and Slovak were, in fact, distinct languages, and behind the facade of a single Czechoslovak culture lurked the spectre of a new hegemony: a Czech cultural imperialism generated from Prague. Indeed, while the number of Slovak-speaking Jews increased considerably over the 1920s and 1930s, the temptation to pursue a direct accommodation with Czech culture and with the Czech political establishment in Prague was great. Thus, while Jews flocked to the new university in Bratislava in its early years, Jewish students from Slovakia also attended Czech institutions of higher education in large numbers, especially in Prague. In the political arena, the Orthodox Agudah chose more often than not to ally with Czech parties rather than with Slovaks.[22]

[20]  Klein-Pejšová, 'Building Slovak Jewry', 8–13.

[21]  See Rebekah Klein-Pejšová, '"Abandon Your Role as Exponents of the Magyars": Contested Jewish Loyalty in Interwar (Czecho)Slovakia', *AJS Review* (2009).

[22]  On the linguistic declarations of Slovak Jews, see Jelinek, 'In Search of Identity', 208 210–12, and Rothkirchen, 'Slovakia: II, 1918–1938', 89–95. On Jewish political orthodoxy, see Jelinek, 'In Search of Identity', 213–15; Hugo Stransky, 'The Religious Life in Slovakia and Subcarpathian Ruthenia', in *The Jews of Czechoslovakia*, ii. 347–92; and Rothkirchen, 'Slovakia II, 1918–1938', *passim*.

It also appears to have been the case that Slovak Jewry was culturally and politically the most fragmented of the inter-war Jewish communities in Czechoslovakia: Hungarian, German, and Yiddish vied with Slovak and Czech as linguistic orientations; the Hungarian tradition of dividing the Jewish community according to religious camps—Orthodox and Neolog—even for purposes of political action, made it difficult for nationalist organizations such as the Jewish Party to step in and claim to represent the population as a whole. And, while it is true that Slovak nationalist parties tended to be more antisemitic and more closely tied to the Catholic Church than their counterparts in Bohemia and Moravia, the fact is that in Slovakia they were dealing with a Jewish population that was considerably distanced from the Slovak national cause, marginalized in multiple ways, and profoundly unsure of what position it occupied in the new state.

Carpatho-Rus, by contrast, which in 1930 had a Jewish population of 102,500, presented a very different type of community. Largely rural and agricultural (with the exception of Munkács/Mukačevo and Ungvár/Užhorod), religiously Orthodox (though not in the modern, ideological sense), and Yiddish-speaking, the Jewish population in the easternmost part of the state had not been as thoroughly 'magyarized' under the monarchy as had Slovakian Jewry. The hold of Ruthenian national culture on the Jews, meanwhile, was slight. This was a region, if you will, that was ripe for colonial picking. Zionist and Czech Jewish teachers and party officials from Prague quickly set up shop in the region (as did the Prague government itself), with the aim of producing modern Jewish political subjects. Representatives of Slovakia's political Orthodoxy, meanwhile—with the support of the minister for Slovak affairs (Vávro Šrobár)—agitated successfully for the creation of an Orthodox-controlled, central office for Jewish religious affairs.[23]

Twenty-three Jewish public schools in Carpatho-Rus and Slovakia educated some 2,500 Jewish pupils in 1920–1 (many more—about 13,000 in 1923–4—attended non-Jewish schools). In sixteen of the Jewish schools the language of instruction was Slovak; in four, Magyar; in two, German; and only in one, in Mukačevo, was the language of instruction Hebrew. The number of Hebrew-language institutions would grow to nine over the next decade (950 students were attending such schools in 1923–4), but—unlike Czech, Slovak, German, Hungarian, and Ruthenian schools—they received only a small annual subsidy from the government, notwithstanding President Tomáš Masaryk's personal contribution of 10,000 Czech crowns.

[23] On Jewish life in Carpatho-Rus, see Aryeh Sole, 'Subcarpathian Ruthenia, 1918–1938', in *The Jews of Czechoslovakia*, i. 125–54; Yeshayahu Jelinek, *Carpathian Diaspora: The Jews of Subcarpathian Rus' and Mukachevo, 1848–1948* (Boulder, Colo., 2007); and Mendelsohn, *The Jews of East Central Europe between the World Wars* (Bloomington, Ind., 1983), 141–6, 152–62.

The Prague government, for its part, built a number of schools for Jewish children in remote rural areas in which the language of instruction was Czech.[24]

The question remains as to how, in the historically, culturally, and linguistically disconnected communities of Czechoslovakia, *Jewish* nationality might function as a set of norms around which to organize group politics and collective identity. The answer that I would offer is that the Jewish national camp in Czechoslovakia achieved greater success than it probably had any right to expect given that the historical profiles of the three regions of the country worked at cross-purposes to one another. In Slovakia, the major political force in the Jewish community was Orthodoxy, followed by the largely magyarized elements of the urban middle class. In the Bohemian lands, the number of Jews who identified with cultural or political Zionism was, at the outset, far smaller than those who formally proclaimed either Czech or German as their nationality (based, admittedly, on the criterion of language of colloquial use). But Bohemian and Moravian Zionism benefited greatly from several factors unique to it. First, the circle of nationally inclined intellectuals and writers that had been active in Prague on the eve of the war enjoyed considerable prestige both at home and abroad, possessing a moral and intellectual capital that far outweighed its numerical importance. Second, Masaryk and his close associates held Zionism (particularly Ahad Ha'amian cultural Zionism) in high esteem, sensing that its emphasis on self-conscious choosing and internal regeneration had much to offer the Czechs themselves. Finally, as I argued earlier, Beneš essentially accepted the claim of the Zionists themselves that allowing Jews officially to declare themselves a separate national group would have the beneficial effect of reducing the size and strength of the German minority in Bohemia and Moravia and of the Hungarians in Slovakia and Carpatho-Rus.[25] The main challenge facing Czech Zionists, then, was to create enough competition for political Orthodoxy in Slovakia to offset its dominant position in Jewish communal affairs and to capture the largely hasidic masses in Carpatho-Rus.[26]

Yet the closing months of the war seem to have caught the Zionists off-guard and unprepared for the rapid collapse of the multiethnic Habsburg monarchy.[27] While they floated the idea of convening an Austrian Jewish Congress in 1917–18, they undertook little advanced preparation for a

[24] Sole, 'Subcarpathian Ruthenia', 134–53.

[25] Kieval, *Making of Czech Jewry*, 186–97; id., *Languages of Community*, 198–216.

[26] To date the best survey of Zionist activity in inter-war Czechoslovakia can be found in Čapková, *Češi, Němci, Židé*, 197–266.

[27] Marsha Rozenblit (*Reconstructing a National Identity*, 106–27) argues that Jews of all political stripes, and throughout the western half of the Habsburg monarchy, remained committed to the idea of an Austrian *Gesamtstaat*, as the best guarantor of their civic rights and security down to the very end of the war.

Jewish national politics in the type of nation-state that seemed all but certain to emerge in the wake of Woodrow Wilson's 'Fourteen Points', which he delivered to Congress in January 1918. It was not until 14 October 1918, two days before Emperor Charles was to make his belated (and doomed) appeal to preserve the monarchy as a federation of nation-states—in which the Jews were not to be represented as they had neither territory nor parliamentary delegations—that the Zionists decided to hold a conference in Vienna in order to articulate the claims of the Jewish people in the crumbling empire. The Jewish National Council was finally established in Prague on 22 October, and, as we have seen, it was only on 28 October, the date of the Czechoslovak 'revolution', that the Zionist delegation finally met with the Czech National Council in Prague and presented it with the memorandum outlining the national requirements of the Jews. These included recognition of the Jewish nationality and freedom of individuals to profess it; full civic equality as well as national minority rights for Jews; and the democratization and unification of the Jewish religious communities.[28]

Two guides that enable us to measure the appeal of Jewish national identity in Czechoslovakia are the official declarations of nationality in the census returns and the development of a nationally oriented Jewish school system. With regard to the former, Jewish national consciousness increased as one moved across the country from west to east. By 1930, about 20 per cent of Bohemian Jews affirmed a Jewish nationality; in Moravia-Silesia, the figure was more than 51 per cent; for Slovakia, 53 per cent; and for Carpatho-Rus, apparently 93 per cent. The strongest *competing* national identity in Bohemia was Czech (or 'Czechoslovak', as the government listed it, at 46 per cent); in Moravia, German (29 per cent); and in Slovakia, Slovak (again, 'Czechoslovak', 32 per cent). It seems that the Prague government's bet regarding the effect of Jewish national minority rights on state-wide nationality ratios proved to be only partially correct, for in both Bohemia and Moravia a number of Jews appear actually to have defected from the 'Czech' to the 'Jewish' camp. (Indeed, in Bohemia the percentage of Jews who declared themselves 'Czechoslovak' actually dropped slightly between 1921 and 1930 in favour of those declaring themselves 'of the Jewish nationality'). The big losers in this competition appear to have been Germans in Moravia and Hungarians in Slovakia.[29]

In the field of education, the Zionists scored some modest victories. As I have noted, they established nine elementary schools in Carpatho-Rus, attended by 384 students in 1931–2, in which Hebrew was the language of

[28] Aharon Moshe Rabinowicz, 'The Jewish Minority', in *The Jews of Czechoslovakia*, i. 155–69.

[29] Figures on nationality declaration are gleaned from Mendelsohn, *The Jews of East Central Europe*, 131–69; see also Čapková, *Češi, Němci, Židé?*, 46–53, 197–206.

instruction; and, more impressively, two Hebrew gymnasia, in Mukačevo and in Užhorod, attended by 367 students. A national Jewish elementary school in Prague educated its students in Czech; both its sister institution and a *Reformrealgymnasium* in Brno started out teaching in German before switching over eventually to the 'proper' language of the state. These figures need to be compared, of course, to the total number of Jewish students attending school throughout the country in that year, close to 64,000. Of these, just under 36,000 were going to Czech- or Slovak-language schools; a little under 11,000 to German schools; 6,000 to Ruthenian schools; a little over 5,000 to Magyar schools; over 4,900 to schools that had more than one language of instruction; 86 to French- and English-language schools; and some 750 to rabbinical seminaries. To add a complicating note to the public/private, Jewish/state division: a number of the German-, Slovak-, and Magyar-language schools were in fact run by local Jewish communities. Additionally, it should be kept in mind that, in the case of Czechoslovakia, Jewish minority rights—and indeed Jewish national identity—were *not* tied to language. Jews, in fact, were singled out as the one exception to what was otherwise the rule. They could speak whatever language they wanted and still proclaim the Jewish nationality if they wished. Thus, even among the 64,000 students who were educated outside of the Hebrew-oriented Zionist system, some 38,400 (about 60 per cent) declared their nationality as Jewish.[30]

Jewish emancipation in inter-war Czechoslovakia came with its own 'bargain', its own particular costs and tradeoffs. Chief among these was an implicit acknowledgement and acceptance of 'Czechoslovak' (one might argue, Czech) political and cultural hegemony—a position of power that required of many Jews a new set of linguistic accommodations, and of Jewish nationalists a willingness to subordinate federalist visions of full cultural autonomy to the much more limited possibilities afforded by the nation-state model. In fact, Czechoslovak Jews never seem to have had any illusions that theirs was to be a supranational, nationalities state. For the Czech Jewish movement, the consolidation of political power by Czech nationalists corresponded to their own ideal for the future.

But liberal, German-speaking Jews also bought in to the agreement and worked towards the legitimization of the state because of the benefits to individual liberty and personal advancement that the new parliamentary democracy offered. Bilingualism had always been a pattern in their lives, and if now they had to allow greater weight to Czech language and culture, so be it. Just as interesting, Jewish nationalists promoted full 'Czechoslovak' sovereignty as well, to the point of promoting Czech 'internal colonialism' in eastern Slovakia and Carpatho-Rus while constructing a Czechoslovak Jewish nation whose contours coincided with the borders of the new state.

[30] Rabinowicz, 'The Jewish Minority', 213–17.

The semi-fiction of a Jewish national position in Czechoslovakia afforded Jews—particularly in the eastern regions of the state—a political and cultural structure within which to organize education and public life, an opportunity to distance themselves from historical patterns of acculturation, and a vehicle through which to articulate the contours of their citizenship in the new state. Through all of the diversity of the Czechoslovak Jewish experience between the wars—and despite the political, religious, social, and linguistic divisions in the Jewish community—one *can* find signs, I think, of an emerging, cohesive, *Czechoslovak* political culture among Jews. It was a culture of allegiance to a (for the most part) protective state and of increasing identification with its two main languages and literatures (Czech and Slovak). And it appears to have coexisted perfectly well with both political Orthodoxy and Jewish ethnic affirmation—a kind of Europe-centred cultural Zionism that was more conducive to the reproduction of Jewish life in multinational east-central Europe than to the encouragement of Jewish migration to Palestine.

It is not entirely clear, however, to what extent the political identity of Czechoslovak Jews *as* Czechoslovaks secured their status as citizens of the young state. Indeed, Jews were to see their rights reduced and their security threatened in the aftermath of the Munich accords. Moreover, there was something antiquated about Czechoslovak Jewish loyalism. For all of the convulsions that Jews had lived through since 1914, for all that was 'new' in Jewish political culture, it contained unmistakable echoes of Habsburg experiences and models. In a new context of ethno-national struggle, class conflict, and radical challenges to parliamentary democracy, Czechoslovak Jews once again had transformed themselves into a *Staatsvolk*. And once more the risks and benefits of this move—its wisdom, if you will—depended on the long-term viability of the Czechoslovak state. Jews made individual and collective choices as though they were in control of their own fate. But they were not.

# SEVEN

# THE DEBATE OVER ASSIMILATION IN LATE NINETEENTH-CENTURY LWÓW

### RACHEL MANEKIN

IN HIS ARTICLES on Alfred Nossig[1] and Wilhelm Feldman,[2] as well as in his book on Maurycy Gottlieb,[3] Ezra Mendelsohn analysed the complexities of Jewish identity in Galicia in the last third of the nineteenth century with respect to the paths chosen by both organizations and individuals. Mendelsohn has distinguished broadly between four political/ideological groups: the liberal and pro-German integrationist; the Orthodox; the pro-Polish integrationist; and the Zionist.

In this essay I will focus on the pro-Polish integrationist group, and particularly on the debate about 'assimilation' that erupted among its members in 1883. It is interesting that the year 1883 also marked the bicentennial anniversary of what Poles saw as their crucial contribution to the victory of Austria when the Turks stood at the gates of Vienna.[4] In 1883 Polish patriotism could thus be celebrated within the context of a Polish and an Austrian day of commemoration.[5] However, for a variety of reasons, the 1880s were hardly the best of times for a group seeking to open up a new chapter in the history of the Jews of Galicia—an exclusively Polish one.

Who were the pro-Polish integrationists? In general, they came mostly from the younger generation of graduates from the gymnasia and from the

---

[1] Ezra Mendelsohn, 'From Assimilation to Zionism in Lvov: The Case of Alfred Nossig', *Slavonic and East European Review*, 49 (1971), 521–34.

[2] Ezra Mendelsohn, 'Jewish Assimilation in Lvov: The Case of Wilhelm Feldman', in Andrei S. Markovits and Frank E. Sysyn (eds.), *Nationbuilding and the Politics of Nationalism* (Cambridge, Mass., 1982), 94–110 (first published in *Slavic Review*, 28 (1969), 577–90).

[3] Ezra Mendelsohn, *Painting a People: Maurycy Gottlieb and Jewish Art* (Hanover, NH, 2002), 6–27.

[4] On King Jan III Sobieski and his role in the battle see Norman Davies, *God's Playground: A History of Poland*, 2 vols. (New York, 1982), i. 480–6.

[5] See e.g. the poem 'The Fourth Jubilee' (Heb.), *Der Israelit*, 11 Sept. 1883, p. 1.

university students in Lwów. Joined by a small number of polonized Jews from the older generation, they saw themselves as the new Jewish intelligentsia in town. Unlike the vast majority of Jews in eastern Galicia, the graduates of the Polish educational system were already equipped with the linguistic and cultural skills necessary to facilitate their integration within their Polish surroundings. They first organized in 1881 when they founded the Polish-language newspaper *Ojczyzna* (Fatherland) to promote their views.

This newly formed intelligentsia was mentally and socially detached from broad strata of Galician Jewish society. Most of them had minimal knowledge at best of Hebrew and the Jewish religion. Some of them, aware of their limitations and inability to reach the audience they wished to influence, proposed to traditional maskilim, the supporters of the Jewish Enlightenment, or Haskalah, that they publish a newspaper in Hebrew that would appear together with *Ojczyzna*, a plan that would further the aim of fostering a sense of Polish identity and loyalty among Galician Jews. The maskilim accepted the proposal, and called their newspaper *Hamazkir ahavah le'erets moladeto* (The Recorder of Love for the Motherland).[6] The paper's logo was the Polish eagle on whose breast was emblazoned a Star of David; its motto, which appeared in Hebrew and in Polish, was the verse from Jeremiah, 'Seek the peace of the city whither I have caused you to be carried away captive, and pray unto the Lord for it; for in the peace thereof shall ye have peace' (Jer. 29: 7).

The editor of *Hamazkir* in its first year was Moses Issachar Landau, a maskil and a rabbi who wore the traditional shtreimel (fur hat) and long black coat;[7] he was succeeded by Isaac Bernfeld, the brother of the noted scholar Simon Bernfeld, who also published articles in the newspaper. A year later, in 1882, a society was established in Lwów called Agudat Ahim (The Fraternal Association), which took *Ojczyzna* and *Hamazkir* under its wing. Its membership included some veterans of the 1863 Polish revolt who had fled to Galicia and some Christian Polish public figures such as the author Jan Lam.[8] The society aimed at putting an end to the ideological and political support that Galician Jewish liberals had provided to the German centralists in Austria. In its stead they sought to strengthen the connection to Polish history and culture, while winning support for Polish liberal trends.[9]

---

[6] Jewish National and University Library Archives, Jerusalem, Yehudah Leib Landau Archive, 4° 798, file 7, p. 7.

[7] Gershom Bader, *A Country and its Sages* [Medinah veḥakhameiha] (New York, 1934), 134–6.

[8] The names of the members were listed in *Ojczyzna* starting from 15 Nov. 1882. For the list that included Jan Lam, see *Ojczyzna*, 1 Dec. 1882, p. 91.

[9] On the society see Katarzyna Kopff-Muszyńska, '"Ob Deutsch oder Polnisch"—przyczynek do badań nad asymilacją Żydów we Lwowie w latach 1840–1890', in Andrzej K. Paluch (ed.), *The Jews in Poland* (Kraków, 1992), 187–203.

But barely one year after the society was founded, the hope for an understanding between *Hamazkir*'s maskilim and *Ojczyzna*'s intelligentsia proved unrealistic. The disagreement between the groups found expression in the newspapers of Agudat Ahim and also in pamphlets published in German, Hebrew, and Polish. The groups disagreed in particular about the desirable degree of integration into Polish society or, in their words, the extent of assimilation.

Until recently, Jewish historiography tended to term Agudat Ahim an 'assimilationist' organization (*agudat hamitbolelim*), with an emphatically pejorative connotation.[10] Mendelsohn was the first to use neutral terminology in relation to Agudat Ahim, describing the ideology behind *Ojczyzna* and similar newspapers as intended to promote 'a liberal, integrationist vision of the Jewish future'.[11] Here I discuss the meanings of the term 'assimilation' as it was used by the parties to the original debate, to enable us to comprehend it in the context of its contemporary interpretations and connotations. To erase it from our vocabulary in this case would distort the experience of the people under discussion, who left us the published sources utilized here.

The first pamphlet devoted to the debate appeared in 1883 in German and bore the title *Die Assimilation der Juden*.[12] Its author was Baerish Goldenberg, a Galician maskil of the type familiar from the first half of the nineteenth century. In his youth Goldenberg had attended Joseph Perl's school in Tarnopol, and he became known later for his philological essays and for the maskilic journal, *Nogah hayare'ah* (The Glow of the Moon), which he edited and published in the 1870s and 1880s. Goldenberg was also one of the first contributors to *Hamazkir*.[13]

In his pamphlet Goldenberg grappled with what he saw as the need to define the boundaries of 'assimilation' in light of the growing shadow of antisemitism. The enlighteners, he wrote, were hammering this word daily into people's heads, until their eardrums were worn out. But they were not the only ones—many conservatives as well did not tire of claiming that assimilation was a necessity of the times. What was missing in this growing trend was an understanding of the term as applied to Judaism. Goldenberg

---

[10] See Nathan M. Gelber, *The History of the Zionist Movement in Galicia* [Toledot hatenuah hatsiyonit begalitsyah 1875–1918], 2 vols. (Jerusalem, 1958), i. 83–8.

[11] See Mendelsohn, *Painting a People*, 16. See also Jonathan Frankel, 'Assimilation and the Jews in Nineteenth-Century Europe: Toward a New Historiography?', in Jonathan Frankel and Steven J. Zipperstein (eds.), *Assimilation and Community: The Jews in Nineteenth-Century Europe* (Cambridge, 1992), 1–37.

[12] Baerish Goldenberg, *Die Assimilation der Juden* (Tarnopol, 1883). On Goldenberg see Bader, *A Country and its Sages* (Heb.), 59–60.

[13] See his Polish patriotic poem, 'Aḥ letsarah' [A Friend in Dire Times], *Hamazkir*, 15 Aug. 1881, p. 3.

considered that, with regard to Jews, assimilation should be limited to the spheres of language and dress. The sort of assimilation urged by those groups calling for the reform of Judaism (the 'Neologs' of different varieties) was not eradicating antisemitism, as they had promised; on the contrary, it was only adding fuel to the fire. After all, Jewish traditional sources called upon Jews to be sensitive to the sentiments of their non-Jewish neighbours. The Jew had always been a patriot and there was no need to turn him into one.

Goldenberg next dealt with who should define assimilation and what aim it should accomplish.[14] Was the surrender of the Jews' inherited customs the only way for them to show their Christian brothers their love and respect? What they needed now, he claimed, was not assimilation in the sense used by the Neologs but rather a return to the morality of their own religion. Goldenberg recommended a reverse assimilation—that is, assimilating into Jewish society such concepts, taken for granted in the non-Jewish world, as pride in one's national language; respect for religion side by side with *Bildung*; national institution-building; and ethnic solidarity.

Goldenberg was disappointed by the leadership of the pro-Polish Jewish intelligentsia, especially because of what he saw as its neglect of the Jewish religion. On the face of it, the intelligentsia's god was assimilation, but what they were really looking for was influence, status, and opportunities. The simple Jew was satisfied if the legal restrictions against him were lifted; he left his political representation to the country's nobility. Under Goldenberg's pen, the issue of assimilation thus became, in large part, a matter of internal Jewish politics. He rejected the intelligentsia's claim to leadership and asserted that it was the rabbis who should lead the Jewish community.[15] He belittled especially the university-educated intelligentsia, describing its members as a band of ignoramuses, idlers, and café-sitters.[16] In his view, not they but rather autodidacts such as Joseph Perl, Nachman Krochmal, Solomon Judah Leib Rapoport, Isaac Erter, and Judah Leib Mieses were the ones responsible for the Galician Haskalah.[17]

In an effort to counter the most popular antisemitic accusations of his day, Goldenberg proposed that the government convene a rabbinical synod that would offer a 'canonical interpretation' of those passages in the Talmud and other rabbinic works that pertained to non-Jews. The synod would see to it that the proper norms of behaviour, as well as correct attitudes toward the state and the non-Jewish population, would be written down in a book available in Yiddish and the language of the country, which would become required reading in all the *ḥeder*s and *talmud torah*s (lower-level religious schools) and other Jewish schools.[18]

---

[14] *Die Assimilation*, 17.    [15] Ibid. 10.    [16] Ibid. 25.
[17] Ibid. 31.    [18] Ibid. 34–5.

Goldenberg's proposal harked back to the familiar values of the early nineteenth-century Haskalah, when calls for assimilation in dress and language were viewed as radical and dangerous, and aroused great opposition. But now, in 1883, such a proposal, framed in the Haskalah rhetoric, was viewed as conservative. In the 1880s, the question of assimilation focused not on Jewish regeneration, as it had in the first half of the century, but rather on the extent of social and cultural integration into the non-Jewish surroundings.

Another pamphlet of 1883 that dealt with the same issue was *The New Haskalah or Assimilation*, which was published in Hebrew.[19] Its author was the young Judah Leib Landau, the son of the first editor of *Hamazkir* and later a Hebrew poet, playwright, and rabbi.[20] For Landau the very term assimilation (*hitbolelut bein ha'amim*) as then used was a negative one, implying radical self-negation. In his eyes, this was a new Haskalah (*hahaskalah hahadashah*), to be clearly distinguished from the original, more positive Haskalah of the first half of the nineteenth century. The new Haskalah, Landau claimed, was responsible for antisemitism in Germany, Russia, and Hungary.[21]

The heroes of the old Haskalah, men like Solomon Judah Rapoport, argued Landau, sought to revive the spirit of the people and to awaken within it the national soul; they published newspapers, books, and translations in Hebrew for this purpose.[22] The advocates of the new Haskalah, by contrast, were not only ignorant of the Hebrew alphabet, but many of them scoffed at Jewish customs and were devoid of any Jewish national sentiment.[23] To prove his point, Landau relates that one of the young adherents of assimilation proposed, at a meeting of Agudat Ahim, to close down *Hamazkir* because Hebrew was incomprehensible to him and his friends. The proposal was rejected thanks to the intervention of Adolph Lilien and Dr Filip Zucker.[24]

The 58-year-old Goldenberg and the 17-year-old Landau, though polonists, tried to assert their independence by upholding the values of the 'old Haskalah', which they preferred to the new one. Landau clothed the old Haskalah values in the modern national rhetoric, while Goldenberg admitted to adopting the nationalist rhetoric from the non-Jewish world.

The tracts by Goldenberg and Landau were attacked by *Der Israelit*, the German-language newspaper published in Lwów by the Shomer Israel society. Shomer Israel had been founded fifteen years earlier in Lwów by the

---

[19] Yehudah Leib Landau, *The New Haskalah or Assimilation* [Hahaskalah hahadashah o ha'asimilatsiyon] (Lemberg, 1883).
[20] On Landau see Yehuda Friedlander and Rafael Weiser (eds.) *Rav, meshorer umahazay: Yehudah Leib Landau / Rabbi, Playwright, Poet: Judah Leo Landau* (mainly Hebrew; foreword and one article in English) (Jerusalem, 1989).     [21] Landau, *The New Haskalah* (Heb.), 7–8.
[22] Ibid. 13–14.          [23] Ibid. 16–17.          [24] Ibid. 18.

intelligentsia of the previous generation as a liberal, pro-German society, but in the 1880s it adapted slowly to the new winds of polonization. When Agudat Ahim was founded, some of the prominent members of Shomer Israel joined it, without their seeing any contradiction between the two organizations. *Der Israelit* accused Goldenberg of abandoning his former enlightened position and crossing over to the Orthodox camp, which had recently established the Mahazikei Hadat society, likewise in Lwów. Assimilation, continued the paper, required a lot more than just language and dress, and religion was irrelevant. *Der Israelit* rejected Goldenberg's claim that contemporary German antisemitism was the result of assimilation, arguing that it was based on racial hatred.[25] The paper questioned what sort of alternative leadership Goldenberg was suggesting—the rabbis? Was he certain that his rabbinical synod would indeed stipulate tolerant and open-minded norms with respect to controversial statements in the Talmud?[26]

Goldenberg's pamphlet was likewise attacked by Isaac Bernfeld, the editor of *Hamazkir*. According to Bernfeld, assimilation was an inevitable process, as was to be seen everywhere in Europe. There was only one sort of assimilation: it applied to the political and social spheres and had nothing to do with religion or faith. Expressing views similar to those of *Der Israelit*, Bernfeld wrote that Goldenberg had become a slavish follower of the Mahazikei Hadat leaders, who considered themselves in exile and under an obligation to humble themselves before the non-Jewish world. Unlike Goldenberg, who had turned his back on assimilation, wrote Bernfeld, the members of his camp did not see themselves as strangers in their country, but as citizens with rights and obligations that they shared with all its sons.[27] For Bernfeld, as for *Der Israelit*, assimilation was thus a neutral term, depicting the inexorable consequences of emancipation.

Responding to the arguments made by Judah Leib Landau in his pamphlet, Bernfeld contended that what Landau sought hardly differed from the programme of the antisemites: the Jews' return to the ghetto and to 'Jewish isolationism'.[28] And yet, despite such attacks, Landau continued to write pro-Polish articles for *Hamazkir* until it ceased publication. Moreover, Landau and Bernfeld himself were among the first and most active members of Mikra Kodesh, the proto-nationalist society founded in Lwów in 1883, whose goal was to foster knowledge of Jewish culture and history.[29] Bernfeld served as the Hebrew secretary of Mikra Kodesh, occasionally reporting its

---

[25] 'Die Assimilation der Juden', *Der Israelit*, 13 Apr. 1883, pp. 1–2.

[26] 'Die Assimilation der Juden', *Der Israelit*, 18 May 1883, pp. 1–2.

[27] See 'What Are We?' (Heb.), *Hamazkir*, 1 and 15 July 1883, front-page articles.

[28] See 'The Antisemites and the Zealots' (Heb.), *Hamazkir*, 16 Aug. 1883, front-page article.

[29] On Mikra Kodesh see Gelber, *The History of the Zionist Movement in Galicia* (Heb.), i. 82–123; the society's name was taken from a phrase in the liturgy, and means literally 'holy convocation'.

activities in none other than *Hamazkir*.[30] In Bernfeld's eyes there was no contradiction between editing a newspaper that fostered Jewish–Polish co-operation and promoting the Jewish heritage and language. Polish national-ism was defined by people such as Bernfeld in terms of a common history, a civic society, and shared political aspirations. By contrast, for Landau and Goldenberg it was also defined in ethnic and religious terms; therefore clear limitations had to be set to assimilation in order to avoid conflict with the very essence of Judaism.

The two pamphlets I have mentioned were written by Galician maskilim associated with *Hamazkir*. They indicate not only the ideological tensions between the two groups in Agudat Ahim but also the resentment felt by the maskilim at being looked down upon by the self-proclaimed Jewish polo-nized intelligentsia.

A third pamphlet that appeared in the same year, *Klątwa galicyjskich rabinów i cudotwórców* (The *Ḥerem* of the Galician Rabbis and the Miracle-Workers),[31] was written and published by Zygmunt Fryling, the member of Agudat Ahim who had proposed closing down *Hamazkir*.[32] The pamphlet came as a response to the rabbinical ban (*ḥerem*) that had been proclaimed against any-one who voted in the provincial elections for Filip Zucker, a prominent mem-ber of Agudat Ahim. Zucker was the head of the Jewish community in Lwów and a member of the Galician Sejm. The Orthodox Mahazikei Hadat society printed the text of the ban and distributed it with its newspaper.[33]

In his pamphlet, Fryling wrote that the 'Jewish fanatics' were terrified of the success of assimilation and were intent on stopping it at any price, includ-ing threats of excommunication and curses, in order to preserve their political power and influence. Fryling responded to the Orthodox accusation that the members of Agudat Ahim were devoid of any Jewish identity and wished to assimilate entirely within Polish society and religion, an accusation that, as we have seen, was also levelled by people associated with *Hamazkir*. On the con-trary, Fryling wrote, there was a difference between Jewish assimilation in Galicia and that in Warsaw: In the Polish capital, the Jewish intelligentsia had completely lost its sense of identification with the Jewish people, and many of its members had converted to Christianity. In Galicia, by contrast, not only were there relatively few conversions but also the intelligentsia strove to enlighten the Jewish masses and to preserve their civil rights. The purpose of Agudat Ahim, and the pro-Polish Jewish intelligentsia in general, was to

[30] *Hamazkir*, 15 June 1883, pp. 44–6; 15 Jan. 1885, p. 7; 3 Apr. 1885, p. 27; 15 Apr. 1885, p. 31.
[31] Zygmunt Fryling, *Klątwa galicyjskich rabinów i cudotwórców* (Lwów, 1883).
[32] *Ojczyzna*, 1 May 1882, p. 38.
[33] See *Maḥazikei hadat*, 1 Feb. 1883. Most of the copies of this issue were confiscated by the authorities. For a copy see the Central State Historical Archive in Lviv, *fond* 156, *opys* 1, a., *sprava* 667, and in a microfilm copy, the Central Archives for the History of the Jewish People in Jerusalem, HM2/8852.6.

achieve full civil rights, to have the Jews conform to the rest of society, and to work together with the Poles on behalf of the country.

Unlike the pamphlets of Goldenberg and Landau, Fryling's booklet was not directed solely, or even mainly, at a Jewish audience. On the contrary, his aim was to draw the Poles into the debate between Mahazikei Hadat and Agudat Ahim and to persuade them to side with the latter. For this purpose he translated into Polish the entire text of the rabbinic ban, which singled out by name not only Filip Zucker but also 'his disciple Merunowicz'. This was a reference to Theophil Merunowicz, a Christian journalist and member of the Galician Sejm, who was one of the first Poles in Galicia to introduce contemporary antisemitic discourse into the public sphere.[34]

In September 1882 Merunowicz had delivered a speech in the Sejm in which he warned against the growing influence of Jews in Galicia. He called for the compulsory education of rabbis, the abolition of the *heder*s (religious elementary schools), the state supervision of Jewish communal funds, and the translation of the Talmud into Polish. Jewish courts, he noted, were authorized to judge cases according to the Talmud, without anybody knowing what the Talmud said or whether talmudic law conflicted with that of the state. Merunowicz's speech was well received in the Sejm, and his positions were widely publicized by the Lwów-based nationalist newspaper *Gazeta Narodowa*.[35]

Responding to Merunowicz in the Sejm, Zucker rejected his attack on the Talmud and his calls for supervision of the Jewish community, while at the same time supporting his proposals for the compulsory education of rabbis, the abolition of the *heder*s, and the establishment of a seminary that would train teachers of the Jewish religion. He concluded his speech with the claim that 'the improvement of Galician Jewry depends upon cooperation between the intelligentsia of all the religious confessions'.[36]

Zucker's speech managed to alienate both the Orthodox and many of the pro-Polish maskilim such as Goldenberg and Landau. The Orthodox naturally opposed his proposals regarding rabbinic education and the *heder*s, while also, of course, resenting his partial agreement with Merunowicz. Until this speech, Mahazikei Hadat had not actively opposed Agudat Ahim; they themselves had emphasized their sympathy and ideological congruence with the conservative forces within the Galician body politic.[37] The maskilim, for

---

[34] Andrzej Żbikowski, 'Rozwój ideologii antysemickiej w Galicji w II połowie XIX w.: Teofila Merunowicza atak na żydowskie kahały', *Biuletyn Żydowskiego Instytutu Historycznego w Polsce*, 167/8, no. 3/4 (1993), 53–62; 169/71, no. 1/3 (1994), 22–39.

[35] 'Mowa posła Merunowicza', *Gazeta Narodowa*, 16 Sept. 1882, p. 2; 17 Sept. 1882, p. 2.

[36] *Der Israelit*, 8 Dec. 1882, pp. 2–3; 22 Dec. 1882, pp. 2–4; 5 Jan. 1883, pp. 4–6; 19 Jan. 1883, pp. 3–4; 2 Feb. 1883, pp. 4–5.

[37] See Rachel Manekin, 'The New Covenant: Orthodox Jews and Polish Catholics in Galicia, 1879–1883' (Heb.), *Tsiyon*, 64 (1999), 157–86.

their part, felt snubbed by the intelligentsia associated with Agudat Ahim and resented their leadership claims. The pamphlets by Goldenberg and Landau have, in fact, to be understood at least partly as a negative response to Agudat Ahim's public stance when represented by such men as Filip Zucker.

Both Zucker in his speech in the Sejm and Fryling in his pamphlet implicitly called upon the Poles to intervene on the side of the intelligentsia in their dispute with the Orthodox. While it seemed natural to them that they were entitled to such support, the issue was not at all obvious to the Poles. In a report from Lwów, the highly respected conservative newspaper *Czas* considered the steps the Poles should take.[38] It concluded that, from the narrow perspective of Polish political interests, there was no good reason to support the 'Jewish progressives'. The paper reminded its readers of the political alliance between Jewish progressives and Ruthenians a decade earlier in the parliamentary elections of 1873 and the damage this alliance had caused the Poles. The Jewish liberals were untrustworthy, it suggested, having proven themselves so ready to change their political allegiances.[39] The newspaper's advice was to adopt a wait-and-see attitude.[40]

*Czas* knew full well that the Jewish intelligentsia had shifted its political orientation. In 1879, when the conservative and clerical parties came to power in the Austrian parliament and the Galician Polish club became a senior partner in the new coalition, the liberal and German-oriented chapter in Galician Jewish history had slowly begun to draw to its close. With the strengthening of Polish autonomy, the city of Lwów, once a symbol of the empire's multinationalism and multiculturalism, increasingly changed its character, and especially its language.[41] The Jewish Communal Council (Israelitische Kultusgemeinde) decided at the end of 1882 to conduct its deliberations in Polish instead of German; the proposal was made by Bernard Goldman, one of the founders of Agudat Ahim. (The council expressed the hope that other Jewish communities throughout Galicia would follow suit.)[42] In that same month Emil Byk, the past president of the Lwów Jewish Communal Council and the man who for years had symbolized the German-liberal direction of the Lwów Jewish intelligentsia, became a member of Agudat Ahim.[43] Even Bernard Löwenstein, the preacher of the Lwów Temple, the last bastion of Jewish germanization in the city, did the same.[44] When assimilation was discussed, the liberal German orientation

---

[38]  *Czas*, 20 Mar. 1883, p. 1.

[39]  Rachel Manekin, 'Politics, Religion, and National Identity: The Galician Jewish Vote in the 1873 Parliamentary Elections', *Polin*, 12 (1999), 100–19.          [40] *Czas*, 20 Mar. 1883, p. 3.

[41]  See Harald Binder, 'Making and Defending a Polish Town: Lwów (Lemberg), 1848–1914', *Austrian History Yearbook*, 34 (2003), 57–81.

[42]  *Der Israelit*, 22 Dec. 1882, pp. 3–4.          [43] *Ojczyzna*, 1 Dec. 1882, p. 91 (member no. 76).

[44]  *Ojczyzna*, 15 Nov. 1882, p. 88 (member no. 56).

was no longer considered even an option.[45] Despite Polish suspicions, what remained of the political-ideological orientation of the past was limited primarily to loyalty to the Habsburg dynasty.

Although all this was doubtless known to *Czas*, the paper was motivated by another consideration in its decision not to intervene on the side of Agudat Ahim, namely, its sympathy with the Orthodox. According to the paper, 'the obscurantism of the Orthodox is not a fact that inhibits polonization, nor is progress a necessary condition for its existence'.[46] The Polish side, so it turned out, was, for the most part, indifferent towards the new pro-Polish intelligentsia and its efforts on behalf of assimilation. Polish nationalism in the 1880s was defined not merely in historical and civil terms but also based itself more and more on ethnic and religious foundations.[47] These sentiments were diametrically opposed to the outlook of the Agudat Ahim members. With ideological dissension from within and little support from without, the prospects for Agudat Ahim thus seemed bleak.

The elections to the Galician Sejm were held in the summer of 1883. Zucker ran for re-election as the only Jewish candidate in a district where 80 per cent of the electorate was Jewish—and he was defeated by a Pole, doubtless because of the rabbinical ban against him. The initial co-operation between the intelligentsia and the maskilim, with Mahazikei Hadat a silent bystander, did not bear fruit; the assimilation movement championed by Agudat Ahim, which had nurtured hopes of widespread Polish support, now began to unravel.

At the same time, the Jewish nationalist idea started to gain ground in Galicia. The Viennese Jewish nationalist newspaper *Selbst-Emancipation* commenced publication in 1885, and immediately aimed its barbs against Agudat Ahim ('the baptism society, Agudat Ahim'; 'Agudas Akum [the society of idolaters]') and *Ojczyzna* ('the de-Judaizing newspaper').[48] When Alfred Nossig criticized *Selbst-Emancipation* for walking a fine line between (Austrian) patriotism and (Jewish) chauvinism, its editor Nathan Birnbaum responded that if the nationalists did not succeed in rousing the people ('das Volk') against assimilation, then there would not be a people left at the end of the day. Jewish nationalism, Birnbaum argued, was the most effective means of uniting the Orthodox and the progressives, as the Russian Jewish

---

[45] *Der Israelit* rejected the criticisms of *Ojczyzna*, emphasizing that it had never advocated the Germanization of Galician Jewry, but the paper continued to appear in German because under the conditions then current the German language was a cultural instrument of the highest order (*Der Israelit*, 16 Feb. 1883, p. 3).     [46] *Czas*, 20 Mar. 1883, p. 1.

[47] For an early example see *Czas*, 28 Nov. 1879, p. 1. In response to Dr Jonathan Warschauer's optimistic views on the prospects of assimilation, the paper declared that the Polish idea was a Polish nationalist one and was specifically Christian and Catholic, although it did not reject anyone who was attracted to it.

[48] See *Selbst-Emancipation*, 1 May 1885, p. 6; 3 Aug. 1885, p. 3; 2 Nov. 1885, p. 2.

example was proving. The ongoing correspondence between the two was conducted in a friendly, if frank, manner and may have been partly responsible for Nossig's subsequent conversion to Zionism. Birnbaum actually invited Nossig to contribute articles to his newspaper.[49]

In short, the intensification of Merunowicz's antisemitic activities in the Sejm, the indifference and suspicion of the conservative Poles, the active opposition of the Orthodox, and the disenchantment of the maskilim led ultimately to the closing of *Hamazkir* in 1886. These factors, together with the growth of Zionism at the end of the decade, led to the final disappearance of Agudat Ahim in 1892.[50] In retrospect, the debate over assimilation in 1883 signalled the beginning of the end for that actively polonizing organization.

[49] See Central Archives for the History of the Jewish People, Gelber Collection, P83/C87, letter dated 24 May 1885.

[50] It is interesting to note that the offices of *Ojczyzna*, including all its paraphernalia, became the offices of *Przyszłość*, the first Zionist newspaper in Galicia (in the Polish language). See Dov Sadan, 'First and Foremost—First Because it is Foremost?' (Heb.), in A. Feldman and M. Shtern (eds.), *Elite Groups and Leadership Strata in Jewish and General History* [Kevutsot ilit veshikhvot manhigut betoledot yisra'el uvetoledot ha'amim] (Jerusalem, 1967), 134–5.

# EIGHT

# THE CULTURE OF ETHNO-NATIONALISM AND THE IDENTITY OF JEWS IN INTER-WAR POLAND

## Some Responses to 'The Aces of Purebred Race'

### JOANNA B. MICHLIC

MODERN POLISH national identity manifests itself in two opposing variants: an exclusivist ethno-national strain and an inclusive civic strain. The way in which Polish Jews have fashioned a modern identity in relation to these two varieties of Polish nationalism is an intricate, intellectually fascinating, and still relatively under-researched topic. In his writings Ezra Mendelsohn offers poignant observations about the complexities of the relationship between Polishness and Jewishness in the lives of individuals who belonged to the newly emerging modern Jewish cultural elite in the late nineteenth and early twentieth centuries.[1] His biography of the Polish Jewish painter Maurycy Gottlieb (1856–79) discusses how individuals who hoped to reshape their social identity and to combine love of the Polish state and Polish high culture with loyalty to the Jewish cultural heritage often suffered personal tragedies and experienced a sense of split identity.[2] The strength of exclusivist Polish ethnicity undermined their sense of Polishness and marked them as outsiders. That narrow sense of Polishness, in which there was room only for a single culture and a single faith—ethnic Polish and Roman Catholic—developed in the post-1864 period. This form of ethno-nationalism evolved into the dominant model of national identity in political, social, and cultural realms in the post-independence period, 1918–39.

[1] See Ezra Mendelsohn, 'From Assimilation to Zionism in Lvov: The Case of Alfred Nossig', *Slavonic and East European Review*, 49 (1971), 521–34; id., 'Jewish Assimilation in Lvov: The Case of Wilhelm Feldman', *Slavic Review*, 28 (1969), 577–90.

[2] Ezra Mendelsohn, *Painting a People: Maurycy Gottlieb and Jewish Art* (Hanover, NH, 2002).

In this essay I will discuss the impact of this ideology on two different social groups among inter-war Polish Jewry—the members of the culturally assimilated Polish Jewish intelligentsia and the cultural Jewish nationalists—and examine the responses of both groups to the pressure exerted by militant Polishness. At the centre of my discussion are two protagonists belonging to the same generation with a mere five years between them: Julian Tuwim, one of the most talented modern Polish poets and a translator of Russian poetry into Polish, born in 1894 in Łódź, then a city under Russian rule, and the less well known Polish Jewish writer, Samuel Jacob Imber (Shmuel-Yankev Imber), a cultural Jewish nationalist born in 1889 in Sasów (Sasov) in Austro-Hungarian Galicia. Despite differences in the geography, politics, and culture of the regions in which Tuwim and Imber grew up, both were educated in a Polish gymnasium and were profoundly influenced by Polish Romantic literature.

Although not as prolific as Tuwim, Imber was also highly gifted. He was the rising star of Yiddish poetry in Lwów (Lemberg, now Lviv) in the first decade of the twentieth century and a recognized expert on the Irish playwright Oscar Wilde.[3] In contrast to Tuwim, he vigorously objected to cultural assimilation, and instead advocated and lived by the concept of 'civic assimilation' (*obywatelska asymilacja*). Imber understood by this concept full civil equality combined with a moderate degree of acculturation and an attachment and loyalty to civic values.

By the late 1920s and during the 1930s, Imber had become one of the most outspoken critics and satirists of Polish exclusivist ethno-nationalism. In his passionate polemics with both cultural and political ethno-nationalists, he spoke from the position of a Polish Jew who deeply believed in the civic values of citizenship. In these polemics Imber appears as the unintentional champion of inclusive civic Polishness.

---

[3] See Samuel Jacob Imber, *Pieśń i dusza Oskara Wilde'a* (Warsaw, 1934). Imber made his debut as a Yiddish poet with the volume *What I Sing and Say* [Vos ikh zing un zog] (Lwów, 1909). He is also the author of a long poem in Yiddish, *Esterke*, dedicated to the legendary love-affair between the king of Poland, Casimir the Great, and a Jewish woman. The poem was published in 1911 and enjoyed popularity among Imber's contemporaries. For the literary history of the Esterke story, see the well-known studies by Chone Shmeruk, *The Esterke Story in Yiddish and Polish Literature: A Case Study in the Mutual Relations of Two Cultural Traditions* (Jerusalem, 1985), and *Yiddish Literature in Poland: Research and Historical Debates* [Sifrut yidish bepolin: meḥkarim ve'iyunim historiyim] (Jerusalem, 1981). On the development of Yiddish literature and culture in the first decade of the twentieth century in Galicia, where Imber was born, see Gabriele Kohlbauer-Fritz, 'Yiddish and Jewish Cultural Identity in Galicia and Vienna', *Polin*, 12 (1999), 164–78.

## THE ETHNO-NATIONALISTIC VISION OF A
## POLISH CULTURE AND POLISH JEWS

The defining feature of inter-war Polish ethno-nationalism was the quest to achieve both ethnic and cultural uniformity within the nation. This was the main goal of National Democracy, the core ethno-nationalistic party in inter-war Poland, and its offshoot radical organizations.[4] The Polish Roman Catholic Church, an institution closely linked with National Democracy, was similarly obsessed with the purity of 'the soul' of the Polish Catholic. Both National Democracy and the Roman Catholic Church strove to launch a moral and spiritual revolution that would produce a uniform way of life: conservative, traditional, and Catholic in character. They perceived Jews as the chief obstacle to the realization of this cultural project, as they categorized them as the embodiment and carriers of modernity, liberalism, socialism, and avant-garde ideas, which they defined as alien and a threat to Polishness. They therefore regarded the Jewish influence as the major cause of the imperfections, weaknesses, and shortcomings found among ethnic Poles. In fact, the radical ethno-nationalists argued that the mere presence of the Jewish community in the midst of the ethnic Polish community created a sense of confusion about identity among the latter. They charged the physical proximity of Jews and Poles in cities, towns, and the countryside with 'polluting the mentality and soul of the ethnic Poles'. Poles were, so to speak, prevented from 'breathing in the Polish spirit', and, thus, from becoming 'better Poles'.[5] The 'dejudaization' of culture and society was, therefore, the only viable strategy to help Poles rediscover their 'real identity' and 'collective destiny'.[6]

The project of 'dejudaization' in the realm of culture chiefly targeted the culturally assimilated Polish Jewish intelligentsia and Poles of Jewish origin.[7]

---

[4] The movement was popularly referred to as Endecja in Polish; its followers were called Endeks. On the ethno-nationalists' project of the cultural purification of the nation see Anthony D. Smith, 'Ethnic Nationalism and the Plight of Minorities', *Journal of Refugee Studies*, 7/2–3 (1994), 186–98: 191–2.

[5] See e.g. the Revd Stefan Kaczorowski in *Pro Christo*, no. 7 (1933), 4.

[6] Revd Stanisław Trzeciak, *Pornografia narzędziem obcych agentur* (Warsaw, 1929), 45.

[7] On the subject of the National Democratic treatment of acculturated Polish Jews see Eugenia Prokop-Janiec, *Polish-Jewish Literature in the Interwar Years*, trans. Abe Shenitzer (Syracuse, NY, 2003), 69–82 (first published as *Międzywojenna literatura polsko-żydowska jako zjawisko kulturowe i artystyczne* (Kraków, 1992)), and Małgorzata Domagalska, *Antysemityzm dla inteligencji?* (Warsaw, 2004). See also essays on the situation of Julian Tuwim and Antoni Słonimski written by the controversial literary critic Artur Sandauer, *Pisma*, 4 vols. (Warsaw, 1985), iii. 463–74; Zygmunt Bauman, 'The Literary Afterlife of Polish Jewry', *Polin*, 7 (1992), 273–99; Magnus J. Kryński, 'Politics and Poetry: The Case of Julian Tuwim', *Polish Review*, no. 4 (1974), 11–14; and Antony Polonsky, 'Why Did They Hate Tuwim and Boy So Much? Jews and "Artificial Jews" in the Literary Polemics in the Second Polish Republic', in Robert Blobaum (ed.), *Anti-Semitism and its Opponents in Poland* (Ithaca, NY, 2005), 189–209.

In fact, the ethno-nationalists perceived both of these groups as the most pernicious threat to Polish culture. National Democrats persistently propagated an image in popular culture of the assimilated Jew as the cause of the degeneration or even destruction of cultural institutions such as theatre, cinema, cabaret, and the broadcasting industry. They portrayed Jews as polluting music, the arts, the vernacular Polish language, and Polish literature and history. Ethno-nationalist writers called the Jewish presence in the arts a spiritual disease (*schorzenie duchowe*) and an abomination (*żydowskie paskudztwo*). The Endeks' urge to purify the national language and literature of alien elements closely resembled the trend advocated in late nineteenth-century France by Charles Maurras or in Germany by Richard Wagner.[8] They insisted that Polish Jewish authors who wrote in the Polish language were not creating Polish literature, but were simply exploiting the Polish language as a 'technical medium' for their works. The Endeks categorized works in Polish by Jews as intrinsically alien to Polish spirituality: 'Tuwim does not write Polish poetry; he only uses the Polish language. His poetry does not represent the spirit of Juliusz Słowacki, but that of Heinrich Heine . . . a Jewish poet with the soul of a merchant.'[9]

The more radical ethno-nationalistic Roman Catholic circles also viewed Jewish converts to Catholicism as dangerous because by marriage they could dilute the biological purity of ethnic Poles. They sought to exclude such converts not only from membership in the Polish nation but also from the true Roman Catholic community, and they were assigned a somewhat precarious place in an abstract Catholic Church.[10] The Marian Order monthly *Pro Christo*, the weekly *Kultura*, published by the Central Institute of Catholic Action (Akcja Katolicka), and well-known public figures such as the ultra-conservative journalist and politician Stanisław Mackiewicz-Cat (1896–1966), and the writer Zofia Kossak-Szczucka (1890–1968), a leading member of Catholic Action, were outspoken representatives of this extreme, essentially racist, position.[11] Even moderate influential Catholic papers such

[8] On the importance of language in ethno-nationalistic projects of national self-purification see Elie Kedourie, *Nationalism* (Oxford, 1994), 108–9, and Smith, 'Ethnic Nationalism', 190–1.  [9] See the editorial column in *Kurier Warszawski*, no. 52, 21 Feb. 1921, p. 2.
[10] Anna Landau-Czajka describes cases of denying converted Jews membership of the Polish nation. See Landau-Czajka, 'The Image of the Jew in the Catholic Press during the Second Republic', *Polin*, 8 (1994), 146–75: 152–4.
[11] On cases of well-known conservative intellectuals adopting a negative approach towards converted Jews, see Emanuel Melzer, 'Anti-Semitism', in Yisrael Gutman, Ezra Mendelsohn, Yehuda Reinharz, and Chone Shmeruk (eds.), *The Jews of Poland Between Two World Wars* (Hanover, NH, 1992), 135–6; Szymon Rudnicki, *Obóz Narodowo-Radykalny: Geneza i działalność* (Warsaw, 1993), 307; and Anna Landau-Czajka, *W jednym stali domu . . . Koncepcje rozwiązania kwestii żydowskiej w publicystyce polskiej* (Warsaw, 1998), 251–2. The subject of converted Jews in inter-war Polish society still needs separate scholarly analysis.

as *Przegląd Katolicki* and *Ateneum Kapłańskie* treated converted Jews as an unfortunate group that should have its own separate church.[12]

## THE MILIEU OF THE POLISH JEWISH INTELLIGENTSIA: JULIAN TUWIM'S SENSE OF POLISHNESS AND RESPONSES TO ETHNIC NATIONALISM

In inter-war Poland members of the culturally assimilated, polonized Jewish intelligentsia seem to have been the most disoriented by the various manifestations of the ethno-nationalistic concept of Polishness. Affected on both the professional and existential levels, their reactions ranged from dismissal, mockery, and anger to despair. To grasp fully the anxieties caused by the climate of the times, one has to look at their relationship to Jewishness.

Tuwim, the most famous protagonist of the polonized Jewish intelligentsia and the chief target of the ethno-nationalists' attacks—'the bête noire of the Endeks'—conceived himself primarily as a Polish artist and wanted to be perceived as such. To paraphrase the statement about an attachment and loyalty to France uttered by the French Jewish historian Marc Bloch, Tuwim 'drank of the waters of Polish culture, made Poland's past his own and breathed freely only in her climate'.[13]

Tuwim first expressed his yearning to belong to Polish high culture and to Poland in his poems from the formative period that coincided with the First World War. In these little-known poems, many of which are autobiographical and were never published by the poet himself, Tuwim emerges, to use the lucid though not uncontroversial concept of the scholar Yuri Slezkine, as a universal Mercurian who yearns to become a local Apollonian.[14] Like other Mercurians seeking Apollonian status, young Tuwim embarked on the process of reshaping his identity. On this journey his reactions to Jewishness were personal ambivalence, shame, and embarrassment. He perceived Jewish ethnicity as an unshakeable identity that might hinder his self-transformation.

Tuwim gave passionate expression to all these emotions in the poem 'Pod bodźcem wieków' (Spurred on by Ages Past), which he never attempted to publish. Dedicated to his friend, the poet Witold Wandurski (1891–1937), the poem opens with lines that express the depth of Tuwim's yearning for a total embrace of Polishness; at the same time, he articulates how difficult and tormenting this would be.

---

[12] See Joanna B. Michlic, *Poland's Threatening Other: The Image of the Jew from 1880 to the Present* (Lincoln, Nebr., 2006).

[13] See Marc Bloch, *Strange Defeat: A Statement of Evidence Written in 1940* (New York, 1968), 3, repr. from the first English translation (London, 1949).

[14] See Yuri Slezkine, *The Jewish Century* (Princeton, 2004), esp. 129–37.

Semitic blood flows in me,
Hot blood, passionate blood,
Oh, Aryans, I love you so much,
Oh, Poland—the sun. You are my country.[15]

In this poem Tuwim conveyed his belief in an essentialist notion of Jewish identity that imparted 'a tragic dimension' to his life. This conviction accompanied him throughout the inter-war period and stood in contradiction to his simultaneous insistence on the individual's ability and potential to remodel his or her identity through personal choice and desire, free of any social constraints. In 1924 Tuwim frankly and lucidly spoke about these salient issues in an interview that appeared in *Nasz Przegląd*, the main Polish-language organ of the culturally assimilated Polish Jewish intelligentsia:

For me the 'Jewish Question' exists in my blood; it is a part of my psyche. It is like a wedge that cuts into my world-view and into my deepest and most personal experiences. . . . For me the 'Jewish problem' is a tragedy and I am one of the many anonymous actors in this tragedy. I am unable to foresee the final act or when it will take place.[16]

In the same interview he insisted: 'I am a polonized Jew, "the Jew-Pole", and I do not care what one or the other side [the Poles and the Jews] thinks about this. I have been brought up in Polish culture and my entire soul is unconsciously attached to Polishness.'

Like Tuwim, many others of his generation suffered from an almost 'congenital' nervousness about their Jewish origin that might prevent them from merging with Polishness. For example, the poet Aleksander Wat, born in 1900 to a long-established and distinguished Jewish family, who was attracted to futurism and communism in his youth, would, like Tuwim, have wished to abandon the Jewish world completely if it had only been possible:

You could not call me an antisemite, but at that time I wanted no part of Jewish customs and culture. I was not an assimilationist and had considered myself a cosmopolitan since I was a child. And so this did not come from any desire to be sophisticated: it was not snobbery. I grew up right at the boundary of two worlds, where each was very distinct, condensed, developed: and the point where they met

---

[15] My translation. Alina Kowalczykowa published this excerpt from the poem in 'Jak Tuwim swój młodzieńczy wizerunek korygował', in Ignacy Opacki (ed.), *Skamander*, vol. iii: *Studia o poezji Juliana Tuwima* (Katowice, 1982), 78–85. Eugenia Prokop-Janiec mentions the poem's first two lines in *Polish-Jewish Literature in the Interwar Years*, 281 n. 3.

[16] Interview by S. Leben, in 'Luminarze literatury polskiej o kwestii żydowskiej: Ankieta *Naszego Przeglądu*', *Nasz Przegląd*, no. 6, 6 Jan. 1924, p. 2. This interview can also be found in the collection of interviews with Tuwim from the inter-war, wartime, and post-war periods published by Tadeusz Januszewski, Tuwim's biographer and the leading expert on his poetry: Tadeusz Januszewski, *Rozmowy z Tuwimem* (Warsaw, 1994), 14–15.

was on a high level. I wanted to leave one part entirely behind. And so I moved very far away from Judaism.[17]

Innumerable polonized Jews born on the eve of Poland's regaining independence in 1918 were similarly tormented by a sense of split identity. In his memoirs, the well-known critic and philosopher of theatre Jan Kott, twenty years Tuwim's junior, recalls how he experienced similar dilemmas and torments in his youth. Kott was the great-great-grandson of the nineteenth-century Jewish publisher Hilary Nussbaum. In 1919, when Kott was 5 years old, his father had him converted to Catholicism because he believed that 'otherwise there would be no future for his son among Poles'.[18] The fact that he was raised a Roman Catholic, an identity marker that at the time was commonly understood as the essence of Polishness, did not prevent young Kott from experiencing deep anxieties about the integrity of his Polish identity. He articulated this turmoil in a poem full of Christian imagery:

> To what, Mary, will you turn, where are your brothers and sisters?
> The Star of David always runs after you.
> In vain you wash with water, in vain you try to betray.
> Your mirror shows a forehead furrowed with shades of ancestors.[19]

According to his autobiography, the young Kott found refuge from his distress first in Laski, the Catholic Centre for the Blind near Warsaw, which not only provided a shelter to the sick and needy but also enjoyed the reputation of offering a cultural and spiritual home to Jewish converts to Catholicism in inter-war Poland. In the second half of the 1930s Kott also found a spiritual oasis in Paris during his studies of French literature at the Sorbonne.

The agony over the impossibility of shedding the traces of one's ethnicity was not the Jewish Mercurians' only reaction to their vicissitudes. In fact, they responded in various and contradictory ways, even on occasion opting for a 'retreat into Jewishness'. This points to a fluidity of identity among this group that was manifested not only in changes of identity over time but also in the adoption of different identities by the same person in different political, social, and personal contexts during the same period. Tuwim is a case in point.

Tuwim's poems from his formative period articulate the desire to embrace and reject one's ethnic identity, cultural heritage, and history simultaneously. In 'Tragedia', a poem written approximately at the same time as 'Pod bodźcem wieków', a yearning for union with Poland is accompanied by

---

[17] Wat's comments on his leaving the Jewish world were published in his memoirs, *My Century* (New York, 2003), 152–3 (first published as *Mój wiek* (London, 1977)).

[18] Kott quotes his father in his memoir *Still Alive: An Autobiographical Essay* (New Haven, 1990), 17.    [19] Ibid. 16.

expressions of pride in Jewishness, the 'fruit' of an ancient culture and ancient people. Characteristically, the positive evaluation of Jewishness emerges in the context of the poet's discourse with Polishness in which the latter is criticized, mocked, and ridiculed. It appears that Tuwim's own negative experiences could, at times, trigger the writing of embittered lines about his beloved Poland.

Tuwim, who as a child had witnessed the anti-Jewish riots in Łódź in 1905 and experienced an increasingly anti-Jewish atmosphere in the city during the First World War, was acutely aware that many local Apollonians did not view him as a member of the same community and did not accept the personal interpretation of his identity. This rejection engendered abruptly angry images: suddenly he reverses himself and portrays the Poles as a contemptible people. 'Tragedia' opens with a line expressing anguish over his Jewish ethnic heritage, but it closes on a totally different note with a sharp reversal of the values attached to Polishness and Jewishness:

> My worst tragedy is that I am a Jew
> But I fell in love with the Christian soul of the Aryans.
> Something inside me spurs me sweepingly on
> And reminds me of the ancient racial heritage . . .
> And the Semitic blood fights with another Spirit
> In the aged long storm and in the magnitude of thoughts
> And then I am proud—I, the aristocrat,
> The son of the ancient people—the source of messianism
> And I am ashamed that my blood fraternizes with the nation of slaves
> With the homeless, contemptible cowards.[20]

The acute tension between Jewishness and Polishness expressed here set a pattern for the poet's later literary responses to the intensifying ethno-nationalistic, anti-Tuwim propaganda of the late 1920s and the 1930s. He channelled a lot of his energy into responding to his adversaries. In an important article discussing the National Democrats' hatred of Tuwim, Antony Polonsky provides examples of his poems in which pride in Jewishness is expressed in the context of the poet's mockery of ethno-nationalistic adversaries such as Stanisław Pieńkowski, Jan Rembieliński, and Zygmunt Wasilewski, the principal writers and literary critics of *Myśl Narodowa*, the key theoretical journal of National Democracy.[21]

---

[20] My translation. Alina Kowalczykowa published the poem in 'Jak Tuwim swój młodzieńczy wizerunek korygował'. The poem has various versions that have not been analysed, and I am grateful to Professor Kowalczykowa for discussing these with me.

[21] See e.g. Stanisław Pieńkowski, 'Poezja kryptożydowska', *Myśl Narodowa*, no. 41 (1926), 234–6; Jan Rembieliński, 'Na widowni', *Myśl Narodowa*, no. 45 (1931), 178–9, and no. 47 (1931), 209–10; and Zygmunt Wasilewski, 'Na widowni', *Myśl Narodowa*, no. 10 (1935), 170–1. On the antisemitism of Zygmunt Wasilewski, see Eugenia Prokop-Janiec, *Literatura i nacjonalizm: Twórczość krytyczna Zygmunta Wasilewskiego* (Kraków, 2004), 225–69.

And to think that from all
The fine activity
Of this gentleman—from the spittle
Wheezing, screaming, scribbling,
Spewing, kicking and wailing
On which he has wasted half his life,
From the books and articles,
From the words, sentences and titles,
From the reviews, from the sneering paragraphs
In a word from that whole
Journalistic mess
Will remain . . . one poem
And that will be—mine, not his.
Indeed this very poem . . . O stern revenge
Inspired by a Jewish God.
Here is a phrase, a few words with which I toy
To immortalize my enemy.[22]

From many written records of the inter-war period it is clear that Tuwim, both as an individual and as a poet, suffered tremendously from being labelled an outsider—a Jew and not a Polish poet.[23] Why was one of the most talented Polish poets of the twentieth century so personally affected by third-rate Endek scribblers such as Józef Aleksander Gałuszko? The answer lies in the fact that Tuwim craved recognition from the entire Polish public, even from the Polish world that was driven by a narrow, exclusivist, ethnic sense of Polishness. That world was neither marginal nor lacking influence, even in literary and cultural circles. This fact was driven home to Tuwim when in 1938 his application to become a member of the Polish Academy of Literature, established in 1933, was rejected on the grounds that public opinion was 'not conducive to accepting Tuwim into the Polish literary pantheon and that such acceptance might rebound against the institution itself'.[24] This rebuff was a blow to the poet who so craved recognition from the Polish cultural elite, and fusion with the 'ordinary Polish man'.

Tuwim, of course, found a spiritual oasis—a home—in the poetic group Skamander, to which he belonged, and in the circles of the liberal intelligentsia associated with the *Wiadomości Literackie* that regularly gathered at

---

[22] 'Do St. P' [To St P], trans. in Polonsky, 'Why Did They Hate Tuwim and Boy So Much?', 200–1.　　　　[23] See 'Luminarze literatury polskiej o kwestii żydowskiej', 2.
[24] For insights into this rejection, see the diary of the well-known modern writer Zofia Nałkowska, *Dzienniki*, vol. iv: *1930–1939*, pt. 2 (Warsaw, 1988), 279–80. Nałkowska, who herself was supportive of Tuwim's candidacy, was one of the members of the committee that was responsible for admitting new members. Tuwim was rejected despite the fact that, in the plebiscite organized by *Wiadomości Literackie* in 1934, the paper's readers rated him the most popular poet.

the Café Ziemiańska. His circles of colleagues and friends comprised individuals like himself—members of the culturally assimilated Polish Jewish intelligentsia—Poles of Jewish origin and Christian Poles who viewed Tuwim as a Polish artist and a Pole.[25] This community provided Tuwim with islands of open, civic Polishness. He did not cease, however, to be tormented by the ethno-nationalists' constant baiting. It was the Endek propaganda that prompted the poet's dramatic retreats into Jewishness and his stress on his links to the age-old Jewish people and culture. It was in this context that he emphasized the Hebrew origin of his family name.

Interestingly, when it came to the discussion of Polish antisemitism and its impact on Polish society Tuwim's outlook was gloomy. By the middle of the 1930s, a period that was marked by an alarming increase in antisemitic activities, he had reached the conclusion that anti-Jewish prejudice was poisoning almost the whole of Polish society.[26] He therefore increasingly harboured grave doubts about the cultural assimilation of Polish Jews into the Polish community, even though he himself was a product of this project and had originally seen it as the ideal theoretical solution to the 'Jewish question'. This demonstrates the tragic dimension of his self-awareness: Tuwim saw himself as an individual who could not secure a place in the desirable community that he envisioned.

At the same time, he also thought on occasion that he himself, as well as Jews who maintained a strong moral and cultural code, might be somehow responsible for the persistence of antisemitism.[27] These feelings of guilt suggest that ethno-nationalist claims that the Jews' own behaviour and 'inherent qualities' provoked antisemitic reactions also influenced his views to some degree.

## THE MILIEU OF CULTURAL JEWISH NATIONALISTS: IMBER'S SENSE OF POLISHNESS AND RESPONSES TO ETHNO-NATIONALISTS

Imber did not suffer from the identity crisis that tormented Tuwim. In his writing there is no expression of anxiety over his Jewish cultural identity and heritage. Because of his fervent opposition to cultural assimilation, Imber was a self-defined and self-appointed outsider with regard to a narrowly

[25] Tuwim's attitude to Jewish converts to Catholicism was also ambivalent, verging on condemnation. See Daniel Silberberg's interview with the poet, 'Godzina z Julianem Tuwimem: Rozmowa o Żydach i zagadnieniach literackich', *Nasz Przegląd*, no. 46, 15 Feb. 1935, p. 3.

[26] 'Luminarze literatury polskiej o kwestii żydowskiej', 2.

[27] In an interview in the Polish daily *Dziennik Warszawski*, Tuwim somehow blamed himself and his colleagues from the poetic group Skamander for inflaming Polish–Jewish relations Julian Tuwim, 'Wywiady z pisarzami polskimi pochodzenia żydowskiego', *Dziennik Warszawski* nos. 34 and 35, 6 and 7 Feb. 1927, cited in Januszewski *Rozmowy z Tuwimem*, 25.

defined Polish culture and community. Yet at the same time his polemical and satirical writings indicate that he was steeped in Polish history, politics, and culture. In fact, in the light of his astute understanding of various aspects of Polish life and Polish aesthetics, he could justifiably be labelled 'an inside observer' of the Polish people and culture. Polish Jewry included many such perceptive observers who came from Zionist or other ideological and cultural backgrounds.[28]

Imber regularly wrote critical commentaries on the activities and writings of the Endeks that appeared in two Polish-language Jewish dailies *Chwila*, published in Lwów, and *Nowy Dziennik*, published in Kraków. In 1934 he published a collection of the articles from these newspapers in *Asy czystej rasy* (Aces of Purebred Race),[29] which he dedicated to the memory of his deceased friend Marceli Leonard Krajewski, who had fought for the freedom of Poland and was killed in the battle of Laski on 22 October 1914. The book was an instant success. The entire Jewish press praised it as a masterpiece in the struggle against antisemitism.

From summer 1936 to late 1938 Imber edited the monthly *Oko w oko*, in which he continued to mock antisemitic writers. It was the second monthly he had created and edited: his first, *Nayland*, a Yiddish publication, appeared between 1918 and 1919. In 1939 he published a collection of articles from *Oko w oko* in a book with the witty title *Kąkol na roli* (Weeds in the Fields).[30]

All his polemical works are characterized by the use of an elegant and lucid, yet sharp and passionate, tongue. Ridicule, satire, and irony are Imber's main weapons for voicing indignation at the exclusivist ethnic nationalists, whom he often calls, invoking the traditional Jewish tropes, the representatives of 'the Haman estate' (Hamanistan). His close affinity with Polish culture, combined with a lack of ambivalence regarding Jewishness and its relation to Polishness, give his commentaries qualities that are absent from the writings of the culturally assimilated Polish Jewish intelligentsia.

One of Imber's main strategies in refuting the ethno-nationalistic approach was to draw comparisons between the National Democrats' position on the Jewish minority in Poland and their position on Catholic Polish immigrants in Western countries. For example, in the first issue of *Oko w*

[28] Bernard Singer, the colourful figure of inter-war Polish Jewry and the Warsaw correspondent for the Zionist *Nowy Dziennik*, was one of the sharpest critics and observers of the political scene in inter-war Poland. Like Imber, he vehemently opposed antisemitism in his witty, elegant articles. See Janina Katarzyna Rogozik, 'Bernard Singer, the Forgotten "Most Popular Jewish Reporter of the Interwar Years in Poland"', *Polin*, 12 (1999), 179–97.

[29] Samuel Jacob Imber, *Asy czystej rasy* (Kraków, 1934).

[30] *Kąkol na roli* (Lwów, 1939) includes articles published in *Oko w oko* in July and December 1936, April, May, June, and July 1937, and April and October 1938. The volume is dedicated primarily to Imber's polemics against anti-Jewish positions within the Roman Catholic Church in Poland, particularly the writings of the Revd Stanisław Trzeciak.

*oko*, published in July 1936, he discusses the reactions of the Polish press to Jan Rozwadowski's book about the situation of Polish immigrants in France, in which the author complained about the prejudicial attitudes of the French towards the Poles.[31] Published in 1927 by the Polish Workers' University in France, the book was received with enthusiasm by the Polish press, including moderate papers such as *Kurier Poranny*.[32] In it Rozwadowski asserted that the French treated the Poles as useful cheap labour, but as outsiders: the Poles were treated like the 'Moors', who 'did their deed and therefore must now leave'. Rozwadowski and the Polish press unanimously condemned these attitudes as unjust and prejudicial. Imber points out that, in the debate about the position of the Jewish community in Poland, the Polish nationalists exhibited attitudes towards the Jews that were just like those that they condemned in the case of the French attitudes towards ethnic Poles.

All of those who so unanimously protested against 'the suffering of the Polish "Moor" on French soil' have on their home [ground] nonetheless 'a suffering "Moor"' who does not have spokesmen to express his reaction as freely as do the Poles. It turns out that Jews, who have lived in Poland not for the last nine years but for the last nine hundred years, have suddenly become the 'Moors who long ago did their deed and therefore must now leave' the country. Day after day for many years we have listened to these messages expressed in various ways, starting with almost illiterate slogans posted on the walls and ending with much more fluent, elegant, and stylish calls and brochures produced on every occasion.[33]

Imber is also a master of discussing prejudiced, anti-Jewish attitudes among the Polish Roman Catholic clergy and the impact of anti-Jewish preaching on their parishioners. In a careful analysis of the writings and sermons of the vicious and prolific Reverend Stanisław Trzeciak, Imber points to his endorsement of *The Protocols of the Elders of Zion* as a crucial moment in the development of Trzeciak's radical antisemitism. In his discussion of the attitudes of various European churches towards Jews in the 1930s Imber reveals his expertise in Christian theology and Christian–Jewish relations. He poignantly observes that, among the Christian clergy in Poland who condemned Nazi policies towards Jews, the only Polish voice came from the representative of a religious minority: Grzegorz Chomyszyn, bishop of the Uniate Church of the Stanisławów diocese.[34]

---

[31] Samuel Jacob Imber, 'Melodie murzyńskie', *Oko w oko*, no. 1 (July 1936), 9–13.

[32] Jan Rozwadowski, *Emigracja polska we Francji: europejski ruch wychodźczy* (Lille, 1927).

[33] Imber, 'Melodie murzyńskie', 10–11.

[34] 'Listy, które go nie doszły', *Oko w oko*, no. 3 (1936), 5–12. In this article Imber discusses the responses of the churches published in the small book *Gdy nienawiść szaleje*. On the attitudes of Polish clergy towards the Jews during the inter-war period, see e.g. the standard textbook by Ronald E. Modras, *The Catholic Church and Antisemitism: Poland, 1933–1939* (Chur, Switzerland, 1994), trans. into Polish as *Kościół katolicki i antysemityzm w Polsce w latach 1933–1939* (Kraków, 2004).

What is striking about Imber's polemical exchanges with the ethno-nationalists is his vehement defence of the Polishness of writers and poets such as Julian Tuwim. Imber's approach, unlike that of other Jewish poets and writers with Zionist leanings, is more complex and more sympathetic, even compassionate, towards their predicament.

## IMBER'S POSITION ON ASSIMILATED POLISH JEWISH ARTISTS

Imber and Tuwim belonged to two different Jewish worlds that regarded each other with suspicion, and at times with contempt. The contempt sometimes erupted into outbursts of tension and even hatred. By the second half of the 1930s Jewish nationalists were accusing the culturally assimilated Polish Jewish intelligentsia of disloyalty and betrayal of the Jewish heritage and people, whereas the polonized Jewish intelligentsia charged the cultural Zionists with obscurantism, bigotry, and separatism bordering on Jewish chauvinism. Eugenia Prokop-Janiec and Antony Polonsky discuss many intellectual skirmishes between these two groups in which the categories of 'we' and 'they' are applied to delineate the border between them.[35] This reveals that the increasingly antisemitic climate of the 1930s also contributed to the reinforcement and sharpening of the internal divisions within Polish Jewry, particularly between the Zionists and the culturally assimilated Jews. Ethnic criteria and divisive ethno-nationalistic terms began to be applied in the discourse between them.[36]

Like other cultural Zionist writers, Imber did not approve of Tuwim's choice of self-definition. In his best-known article, 'Co nam i Tobie Tuwimie?', written in December 1929—a year of increasing calls for the dejudaization of Polish culture—he states the reasons for his disapproval.[37] His critical remarks are characteristic of the entire milieu of the Zionist intelligentsia:

What do we and you have in common, Tuwim; what do we and you have in common, Słonimski; what do we and all of you who have denied us or have never known us have in common? You have renounced your affiliation to the Jewish

---

[35] See Prokop-Janiec, *Polish-Jewish Literature in the Interwar Years*, 88–95, and Polonsky, 'Why Did They Hate Tuwim and Boy So Much?', 194–5.

[36] This is a subject that requires a separate analysis.

[37] 'Co nam i Tobie Tuwimie?', in id., *Asy czystej rasy*, 11–42. The article was a direct response to Karol Hubert Rostworowski's lecture, 'O sanację literatury polskiej' [A Call for Moral Cleanliness in Poland]. Its title alludes to the question repeated by the Polish cultural ethno-nationalists in their rejection of culturally assimilated Polish Jewish poets and writers—Tuwim, what have you to do with Poland?'—to stress the lack of an essential connection between the poet and Polish culture. It echoes John's Gospel (2: 4), where Jesus rebukes his mother for urging him to perform a miracle.

nation, you do not know our souls and so frequently treat us like strangers and enemies, your song does not resound with our national language or with the language of our people.[38]

At the same time, Imber was convinced that the culturally assimilated Polish Jewish intellectuals were indifferent to Zionist criticism of them while caring exclusively about the opinions of well-known ethno-nationalistic literary critics such as Karol Hubert Rostworowski and Adolf Nowaczyński. Nonetheless, although he opposed the identity choices of Tuwim and other culturally assimilated Jewish artists, Imber was sympathetic with regard to their tenuous position among the Polish cultural elites and within Polish society as a whole. He astutely assessed their personal and professional struggle:

You have chosen a hard path for yourself, you—dedicated labourers of the Polish word, you vassals of Polish culture. We, the Jewish poets, also do not walk on a bed of roses, but you have chosen a path that resembles the real Way of the Cross. Our audience at worst could reject our inspired words, but anyone from your audience could shout at you: 'Go away! You have no right to speak in our language.'[39]

In defending the Polishness of Tuwim and other like-minded poets, Imber emphasized the criterion of language. As he saw it, language defined the place of the artist in a collectivity and constituted the key criterion of a writer's civic identity.[40] He ridiculed the Endeks' tendency to interpret Tuwim as a non-Polish poet on the grounds that a 'Jewish spirit' contaminated his writings. He mocked the ethno-nationalistic idea that utilitarianism, excess sexuality, sensuality, and revolutionary spirit constituted the essence of Jewish literary endeavour, threatening the 'Polishness' of Polish literature. Imber demonstrated that these allegedly Jewish traits were commonly found among such pure 'Aryan' or ethnic Polish poets and writers of Young Poland as Jan Kasprowicz and Leopold Staff.

Imber's assessment of the artistic and aesthetic role of the polonized Jewish poets closely resembles that of the 'giant' of Polish drama, Witold Gombrowicz, who was a frequent guest at the Café Ziemiańska. Both Imber and Gombrowicz asserted that the culturally assimilated Polish Jewish poets and writers had introduced universal values into Polish literature. According to Gombrowicz, this group of poets and writers 'connects the Poles to the most profound and most difficult problems of the world'.[41]

At the end of 'Co nam i Tobie Tuwimie?' Imber expresses the hope that future generations of Poles will cease to view Tuwim as an outsider and will pay him his well-earned tribute. This stance reveals how much Imber

[38] 'Co nam i Tobie Tuwimie?', 41.  [39] Ibid. 40–1.  [40] Ibid. 21
[41] Witold Gombrowicz, *Polish Memories* (New Haven, 2004), 180 (first published as *Wspomnienia polskie* (Kraków, 2002)).

himself was connected to the Polish world in spite of his chosen position as an outsider, and how much he hoped for the disappearance of the exclusivist, ethno-nationalist way of thinking in Poland.

You, who every day give birth in holy pain to the Polish word and to the free soul of this country, you have to remain intertwined with your creation. The better and more righteous future generations will acknowledge your contribution and will restore to you your deserved place. . . . And no man will say to another 'Why should I have any truck with you?'[42]

In an article published in November 1937, Imber once again vehemently defended the Polishness of Tuwim and other Poles of Jewish origin who belonged to the circle of *Wiadomości Literackie*. He forcefully mocked Karol Irzykowski's claim that the culturally assimilated Jewish intelligentsia and Poles of Jewish origin concentrated in that circle were 'Pole[s] with reservations who could easily cease to be Polish'.[43] Irzykowski, a respected literary critic and writer, had voiced this claim earlier that year in an open letter, published in *Kurier Poranny*, to the cultural Zionist poet Stefan Pomer. Other literary critics, such as Karol Hubert Rostworowski and the popular writer of children's literature Kornel Makuszyński, supported Irzykowski's contention. The young poet Alfred Łaszowski, associated with the radical fascist organization ONR Falanga, followed in Irzykowski's footsteps, and the same year published a similar contention about culturally assimilated Jews in an article entitled 'Prosto z mostu' in the right-wing literary weekly of the same name.[44]

In his letter to Pomer, Irzykowski not only accused Tuwim and Antoni Słonimski of being 'Poles with reservations' but also questioned the Polishness of both Tadeusz Boy Żeleński (one of the best literary critics of inter-war Poland and Irzykowski's competitor) and the acculturated Polish Jew, Wilhem Feldman. A well-known literary critic of the Young Poland period, Feldman had penned an elegant but critical review of Irzykowski's sole, acclaimed, novel, *Pałuba* (The Hag), published in 1903.

Imber's characterization of the author of *Pałuba* as a 'dry, caustic, and colourless writer as well as a jealous and embittered critic' resembles the view of Irzykowski voiced by Czesław Miłosz in his *History of Polish Literature*.[45] According to Imber, Irzykowski's contention that some Jews

[42] 'Co nam i Tobie Tuwimie?', 43.

[43] Imber, 'Smalone duby autora *Pałuby* czyli gdy człowiek robi się starszy', *Oko w oko*, no. 8 (Nov. 1937), 1–16. Imber devoted this entire issue to the discussion of Irzykowski's contention that the culturally assimilated Jew is 'a Pole with reservations who could easily cease to be Polish'.

[44] For interesting observations about Alfred Łaszowki (1914–97) as a radical antisemitic writer, see Ryszard Matuszewski, *Alfabet: Wybór z pamięci 90-latka* (Warsaw, 2004), 280–1.

[45] Czesław Miłosz, *The History of Polish Literature* (London, 1969).

could easily cease to be Polish was an insult not only to present-day assimilated Polish Jews and Poles of Jewish origin but also to many generations of
Polish Jews who had been committed to the Polish state and who had contributed to the development of Polish high culture in the pre-independence
period: 'Many "Jewish Poles"—the politicians and writers, dedicated pub-
lishers, fighters, founders of schools, teachers, artists and scientists—had all
served Poland without reservation and unselfishly, long before voices were
heard from the least worthy political camps speaking in harsh tones about
"the Jewish invasion" and "the unwanted alien elements".'[46]

In retrospect, and especially from a post-1989 vantage point, Imber's
understanding of Polishness resembles the concept that the first post-
communist Polish prime minister Tadeusz Mazowiecki endorsed in his
political manifesto:

The Polish state cannot be an ideological or religious state. It has to be a state in
which no citizen would experience discrimination or would be treated in a privileged way because of his ideological convictions. . . . The government wishes to
co-operate with the Roman Catholic Church and all other denominations in
Poland. . . . Poland is a homeland not of Poles alone. We live on this land together
with representatives of other 'national groups'. The government wishes that they
would see themselves as a part of Poland and would cultivate their languages and
their cultures and thus enrich our common society.[47]

This is the Polishness that many Poles in the past had difficulty envisag-
ing and accepting, as Father Adam Boniecki, editor-in-chief of the liberal
Catholic weekly *Tygodnik Powszechny*, acknowledged during the recent
lengthy debate about Jedwabne.[48] This is also the concept of Polishness that
has been conducive to the revival of institutionalized Jewish life in post-
communist Poland and to the social phenomenon of being 'openly Jewish'
manifested in the positive re-evaluations of their Jewish origins by well-
known intellectuals. A case in point is Michał Głowiński, the distinguished
Polish literary critic and a child Holocaust survivor.[49] Głowiński's public

[46] Imber, 'Smalone duby autora *Pałuby*', 10. On the contribution of Polish Jews to Polish
culture see Aleksander Hertz, *The Jews in Polish Culture* (Evanston, Ill., 1988).

[47] Speech by Tadeusz Mazowiecki delivered in the Polish parliament in August 1989, cited
in M. Czajkowski, 'Chrześcijanin na trudne czasy', *Tygodnik Powszechny*, 28 Aug. 2003, p. 1.

[48] For an analysis of this debate and a selection of the key voices in it see Antony Polonsky
and Joanna B. Michlic (eds.), *The Neighbors Respond: The Controversy over the Jedwabne Massacre
in Poland* (Princeton, 2004).

[49] For Głowiński's account of 'coming out of the closet', see his 'Zapisy Zagłady', *Tygodnik
Powszechny. Kontrapunkt*, 1/2 (special section), 25 Mar. 2001, pp. 14–15. Głowiński is also the
author of a number of recently published personal accounts of his wartime experiences and of his
recent 'rediscovery' of his Jewishness. See e.g. Głowiński, *Czarne sezony* (Warsaw: published by
OPEN, 1999), published in English as *Black Seasons* (Evanston, Ill., 2005), and his interview
with Teresa Torańska, 'Polskie gadanie', *Gazeta Wyborcza*, 23 May 2005, <http://serwisy
gazeta.pl/df/2029020,34471,272112.html>.

endorsement in the new millennium of Jewishness as a positive layer of identity compatible with Polish identity is a new cultural phenomenon that could not develop among the assimilated Polish Jewish intelligentsia of the inter-war period, owing to the climate of exclusivist ethno-nationalism that prevailed at the time.

To conclude: different groups within the community of Polish Jews responded differently to the inter-war culture of ethno-nationalism. Fluidity and contradictory layers of identity were the hallmarks of responses to anti-semitism by members of the culturally assimilated Jewish intelligentsia such as Julian Tuwim. Although Tuwim developed a strong sense of individualist identity that transcended ethnic and national identification, he also sub-scribed to a belief in an essentialist concept of Jewish identity that for him carried a fatalistic, destructive, and—at times—positive, enriching meaning. His occasional retreats into Jewishness in response to dismissive voices from the Polish community were typical in the circles to which he belonged. However, these retreats were complicated and uneasy for those culturally assimilated Jews who yearned to become local Apollonians, and who identi-fied their Jewish legacy as an obstacle to the remodelling of their personal, social, and artistic identity. Thus, in this group ethno-nationalism had the most powerful, complex, and damaging impact in the period called by Ezra Mendelsohn 'a time of hardening ethnic boundaries'.[50]

Conversely, partially acculturated Zionists such as Samuel Imber were the least affected by the culture of ethno-nationalism on the personal and artistic levels. They succeeded in creating an impressive body of polemical writings on extreme Polish nationalism that is well worth revisiting as part of any new assessment of inter-war Poland and of Polish Jewry.

[50] Mendelsohn, *Painting a People*, 181.

# PART III

# INCLUSION/EXCLUSION
## *Society and Politics*

# NINE

# URBAN SOCIETY, POPULAR CULTURE, PARTICIPATORY POLITICS

## On the Culture of Modern Jewish Politics

SCOTT URY

Once, on a Saturday morning, we heard a loud cry coming from the local prayer house. Out of the chaos and confusion, we recognized the cry of a woman that passed back and forth between shouts and tears. All of the neighbors rushed to their windows to see what was happening. . . . Earlier in the morning, the woman had, apparently, snuck inside the prayer house and hid next to the synagogue doors. There, she waited for the morning prayers to begin and for the Torah to be taken out of the ark. At that very moment, she rushed into the synagogue, pounced upon the ark, and clung to the ark's doors so that the Torah couldn't be taken out and read.[1]

With this description of the traditional Jewish practice of prayer protest (*ikuv tefilah*), the journalist and writer Yehiel Hofer summarized the means and methods of politics for many Jews in nineteenth-century eastern Europe. Frustrated at the failure of her husband's employer (a well-known resident of the apartment courtyard where she lived) to take responsibility for her chronically ill and recently unemployed husband, the woman in question apparently felt that she had relatively few means at her disposal to express and act upon her anger and despair. Ultimately, this lone woman's

This essay is part of a larger project on Jewish society and politics in turn-of-the-century Warsaw based on my doctoral dissertation at the Hebrew University under the supervision of Ezra Mendelsohn and the late Jonathan Frankel. My research has been supported, in part, by an East European Studies Doctoral Dissertation Grant from the American Council of Learned Societies (ACLS), and a Doctoral Dissertation Fellowship from the National Foundation for Jewish Culture.

[1] Yehiel Hofer, *A Courtyard on Pokorna Street* [Ḥatser bepokorno], trans. from the Yiddish by Dov Sadan (Jerusalem, 1968), 67. I am grateful to Ephraim Shoham-Steiner for his comments on this issue. For more on the politics of protest in Jewish communities, see Ezra Mendelsohn, *Class Struggle in the Pale: The Formative Years of the Jewish Workers' Movement in Tsarist Russia* (Cambridge, 1970), and id. (ed.), *Essential Papers on Jews and the Left* (New York, 1997).

plea was directed at other members of the Jewish community and staged within the confines of a traditional Jewish communal institution, the local prayer house. Thus, even when acts of protest among Jews took on angry, at times transgressive forms—in this case, the decision of a poverty-stricken woman to enter the sacred male sphere of Torah reading and to challenge the right of local men to carry out their religiously mandated duties threatened both religious and gendered codes of community and communal power—the practice of politics among Jews remained a decidedly internal affair in which grievances were lodged and appeals were almost always made within the context of the Jewish community's traditional institutions.

The politics of Jewish protest had their limits, and in this and countless other cases the social, cultural, geographical, and ideological boundaries of Jewish politics were restricted to institutions and practices that remained under the jurisdiction and, ultimately, control of the Jewish community's traditional, male leadership.[2] These specific limits of Jewish politics were particularly pronounced in the Polish territories that came under Russian control in 1815, where the semi-autonomous communal institution the *gmina* maintained an influential and legal presence in Warsaw and other centres throughout the imperial era.[3] Ironically (or, perhaps, not), the *gmina*'s very existence and legal status helped ensure that the politics of Jewish protest remained a predominantly internal, communal affair.

Despite this and other time-honoured modes of political behaviour and action, the demographic, economic, and structural forces that led to the creation of large urban centres and similarly unwieldy Jewish populations throughout eastern Europe rendered many of these more traditional Jewish institutions and practices increasingly obsolete by the early twentieth century. By the turn of the century, large Jewish centres had begun to arise in cities throughout eastern and central Europe, including approximately 220,000 registered Jewish residents in Warsaw, over 165,000 Jews in Budapest, the capital of Habsburg Hungary, roughly 140,000 Jews in the southern port city of Odessa, and almost 100,000 legal Jewish residents in the new industrial centre of the former Kingdom of Poland,

[2] For more on different efforts throughout this period by the officially recognized Jewish communal bodies—the *kahal* in the Russian empire until its formal abolition in 1844 and, in the Russian empire's Polish lands, the *gmina*—to prevent criticism and critics from going beyond the borders and control of the community, see Jacob Katz, *Tradition and Crisis: Jewish Society at the End of the Middle Ages*, trans. Bernard Dov Cooperman (New York, 1993), 72, and Eli Lederhendler, *The Road to Modern Jewish Politics: Political Tradition and Political Reconstruction in the Jewish Community in Tsarist Russia* (New York, 1989), 38–9, 46–7. See also Scott Ury, 'The *Shtadlan* of the Polish–Lithuanian Commonwealth: Noble Advocate or Unbridled Opportunist?', *Polin*, 15 (2002), 288–91.

[3] On the *gmina* in Polish territories, see e.g. François Guesnet, *Polnische Juden im 19. Jahrhundert* (Cologne, 1998), 338–412.

Łódź.[4] Exponential population increases, breakneck industrialization, and a tremendous amount of internal migration in cities across the European continent created new types of Jewish communities with new types of problems, the scale of which demanded new forms of political organization, expression, and action.[5]

In addition to engendering a growing sense of crisis, these and other urban centres also gave birth to fundamentally new means of communication and collective organization among both Jews and non-Jews.[6] The intersection between the imminent sense of crisis surrounding modernization and urbanization, on the one hand, and, on the other, the transformative role of these new cultural-political institutions will serve as the focal point for this essay. More specifically, I shall concentrate on the role of three fundamentally new cultural-political institutions that combined to transform radically both the form and the content of Jewish politics and community in early twentieth-century eastern Europe.[7] Throughout, I shall examine the impact that the daily press in Yiddish, the Yiddish theatre, and elections to the early Russian State Dumas had on the ways in which Jews in Warsaw (and, by extension, in other locations throughout the Russian empire) envisioned themselves and their communities.[8] Ultimately, I shall argue that

---

[4] Artur Ruppin, *The Sociology of the Jews* [Hasotsiologiyah shel hayehudim] (Berlin, 1931–3), bk. 1, pt. 1, p. 95. Other, 'west European', cities, such as Vienna and Berlin, boasted similarly large concentrations of Jews at the time, with almost 150,000 and over 90,000 Jewish residents respectively. For a discussion of some of the differences between 'western' and 'eastern' Jews in this and related contexts, see Ruppin, *Sociology of the Jews*, bk. 1, pt. 1, pp. 89–94, and bk. 2, pp. 249–50. Also see the classic study by Steven E. Aschheim, *Brothers and Strangers: The East European Jew in German and German Jewish Consciousness, 1800–1923* (Madison, Wis., 1982).

[5] For a discussion of how some of these same issues affected Poles, see Brian Porter, *When Nationalism Began to Hate: Imagining Modern Politics in Nineteenth-Century Poland* (Oxford, 2000). For a view of similar developments and their impact on Jews in the New World, see Tony Michels, *A Fire in their Hearts: Yiddish Socialists in New York* (Cambridge, Mass., 2005).

[6] For more on modes of communication and the construction of modern societies, see Karl W. Deutsch, *Nationalism and Social Communication: An Inquiry into the Foundations of Nationality* (Cambridge, Mass., 1966). On Jewish cities and centres at this time see Dan Miron, *When Loners Come Together: A Portrait of Hebrew Literature at the Turn of the Twentieth Century* [Bodedim bemo'adam: lideyokanah shel harepublikah hasifrutit ha'ivrit bitehilat hame'ah ha'esrim] (Tel Aviv, 1987), 333–81, and Nathan Cohen, *Books, Authors, and Newspapers: The Jewish Cultural Centre in Warsaw, 1918–1942* [Sefer, sofer, ve'iton: merkaz hatarbut hayehudit bevarshah, 1918–1942] (Jerusalem, 2003), 2–4.

[7] On 'the content of the form', see Hayden White, *The Content of the Form: Narrative Discourse and Historical Representation* (Baltimore, 1987)

[8] For more on the different connections between Jewish culture and Jewish politics see Ezra Mendelsohn, *Painting a People: Maurycy Gottlieb and Jewish Art* (Hanover, NH, 2002); Ezra Mendelsohn and Richard I. Cohen (eds.), *Art and its Uses: The Visual Image and Modern Jewish Society* (= *Studies in Contemporary Jewry*, 6) (1990); Ezra Mendelsohn (ed.), *Modern Jews and their Musical Agendas* (= *Studies in Contemporary Jewry*, 9) (1993); id., 'Jews, Communism and Art in Interwar America', in Jonathan Frankel and Dan Diner (eds.), *Dark Times, Dire Decisions: Jews and Communism* (= *Studies in Contemporary Jewry*, 20) (2004), 99–132; and Ezra

these three institutions helped lay the foundations for the construction of a specifically Jewish public sphere and that this Jewish public sphere was an essential condition for the creation of the new modes of political organization, thinking, and action that Ezra Mendelsohn has so eloquently defined under the rubric of 'modern Jewish politics'.[9]

Stemming, in part, from the debates surrounding Hannah Arendt's analysis of the role of 'the Jews' in the course of European history, studies of modern Jewish politics often focus on the wider network of organizations, leaders, and ideas that arose as part of broader efforts to transform 'the Jews' into a modern political community, if not, ultimately, a nation.[10] Modern Jewish politics, according to Mendelsohn, 'refers to the programs formulated by these new movements, that is, the different ways in which they viewed the future of the Jewish people and their proposals for solving, once and for all, the celebrated Jewish Question—and the competition among them for hegemony'.[11]

I will begin my analysis of the culture of modern Jewish politics with a discussion of Jürgen Habermas's now classic term, 'the bourgeois public sphere'. According to Habermas:

> The bourgeois public sphere may be conceived above all as the sphere of private people come together as a public; they soon claimed the public sphere regulated from above against the public authorities themselves, to engage in a debate over the general rules governing relations in the basically privatized but publicly relevant sphere of commodity exchange and social labor. The medium of this political confrontation was peculiar and without historical precedent: the people's use of their reason.[12]

---

Mendelsohn, 'Jewish Universalism: Some Visual Texts and Subtexts', in Jack Kugelmass (ed.), *Key Texts in American Jewish Culture* (New Brunswick, NJ, 2003), 163–84.

[9] For a more encompassing analysis and, essentially, a canonization of the field of 'modern Jewish politics', see Ezra Mendelsohn, *On Modern Jewish Politics* (New York, 1993). Additional studies of 'modern Jewish politics' include Jonathan Frankel, *The Damascus Affair: 'Ritual Murder', Politics and the Jews in 1840* (Cambridge, 1997), and Jonathan Frankel, *Prophecy and Politics: Socialism, Nationalism and the Russian Jews, 1862–1917* (Cambridge, 1981).

[10] For Arendt's comments on 'the Jews', see e.g. her *The Origins of Totalitarianism* (1967; London, 1979), 23. On Arendt as a source of inspiration for other works on modern Jewish politics see Lederhendler, *The Road to Modern Jewish Politics*, 6, 15, 18, and Michael Marrus, 'Hannah Arendt and the Dreyfus Affair', *New German Critique*, 66 (Fall 1995), 147–63: 147. For further discussions of Arendt's reception among Israeli, Jewish, and non-Jewish intellectuals, see Steven E. Aschheim, 'Introduction: Hannah Arendt in Jerusalem', in id. (ed.), *Hannah Arendt in Jerusalem* (Berkeley, 2001), 1–15, and Richard I. Cohen, 'Breaking the Code: Hannah Arendt's *Eichmann in Jerusalem* and the Public Polemic—Myth, Memory and Historical Imagination', *Michael: On the History of the Jews in the Diaspora*, 13 (1993), 29–85, esp. 29–41. See also David Biale, *Power and Powerlessness in Jewish History* (New York, 1987), 5, 98, 142.

[11] Mendelsohn, *On Modern Jewish Politics*, p. viii.

[12] Jürgen Habermas, *The Structural Transformation of the Public Sphere: An Inquiry into a Category of Bourgeois Society*, trans. Thomas Burger (1989; Cambridge, Mass., 1996), 27.

Although Habermas's book has been extremely influential over the years (in particular since its translation into English in 1989), the exact nature of this 'bourgeois public sphere' is somewhat nebulous, if not, at times, self-contradictory. Indeed, throughout the book the 'public sphere' often seems to be at odds with itself as Habermas refers alternately to both physical places and imaginary spaces that enable individual members of a particular body politic to meet and discuss collective affairs. As a result of this dual meaning, some scholars of the public sphere concentrate on the role that imagined spaces play in the creation of new societies while others focus on the role that different institutions play in the construction of actual physical spaces designed to accommodate public assembly and discussion.[13]

Throughout his study, Habermas emphasizes the critical role of newspapers and public theatres in the construction of the bourgeois public sphere.[14] My discussion of the Jewish public sphere begins with an analysis of the transformative role that these and other cultural-political institutions had on the nature, shape, and limits of community among Jews in turn-of-the-century eastern Europe. In line with Habermas's approach, I shall refer to both imaginary and physical sites of community among Jews.

Moreover, whereas other scholars of Jewish history and culture have used the notion of the public sphere and accompanying discussions of public space and civil society to discuss the integration of Jews (primarily as individuals) into surrounding European societies,[15] I shall focus on the transformative role played by those cultural institutions that helped create a specifically Jewish public sphere in turn-of-the-century Warsaw. Ultimately, I shall argue

[13] Literature on the public sphere is vast; the following references to central critiques of the Habermasian model will suffice here. Craig Calhoun, 'Introduction: Habermas and the Public Sphere', in id. (ed.), *Habermas and the Public Sphere* (Cambridge, Mass., 1992), 1–48; Geoff Eley, 'Nations, Publics, and Political Cultures: Placing Habermas in the Nineteenth Century', in Calhoun (ed.), *Habermas and the Public Sphere*, 289–339; and Benjamin Nathans, 'Habermas's "Public Sphere" in the Era of the French Revolution', *French Historical Studies*, 16/3 (Spring 1990), 620–44. See also Marie Fleming, 'Women and the "Public Use of Reason"', in Johanna Meehan (ed.), *Feminists Read Habermas* (New York, 1995), 117–37; Joan B. Landes, *Women and the Public Sphere in the Age of the French Revolution* (Ithaca, NY, 1988); and Harold Mah, 'Phantasies of the Public Sphere: Rethinking the Habermas of Historians', *Journal of Modern History*, 72 (Mar. 2000), 153–82. While Jacob Katz's analysis of the link between the Jewish Enlightenment (Haskalah) and the creation of 'the neutral society' predated Habermas's study of the public sphere by a decade, his work bears many striking parallels to that of Habermas. See Katz, *Tradition and Crisis*, 214–25.

[14] See Habermas, *The Structural Transformation of the Public Sphere*, 16–22, 38–41, 181–95.

[15] See e.g. Richard I. Cohen, 'Urban Visibility and Biblical Visions: Jewish Culture in Western and Central Europe in the Modern Age', in David Biale (ed.), *Cultures of the Jews* (New York, 2002), 731–96, and Michael K. Silber, 'The Entrance of Jews into Hungarian Society in "Vormärz": The Case of the "Casinos"', in Jonathan Frankel and Steven J. Zipperstein (eds.), *Assimilation and Community: The Jews in Nineteenth-Century Europe* (Cambridge, 1992), 284–323.

that this specific set of institutions led to the formation of a space that was simultaneously public and Jewish, and that this newly created—or, at the very least, radically reconstructed—Jewish public sphere subsequently engendered new forms of organization and community that enabled hundreds of thousands of Jews to be both modern and Jewish, insiders and outsiders.

## READ ALL ABOUT IT! OR, PRINT CAPITALISM FOR THE WORLD'S FIRST CAPITALISTS[16]

Following a flurry of cultural and political activity as well as a series of governmental reforms—including, but not limited to, the October Manifesto—Jews throughout the Russian empire witnessed the sudden proliferation between late 1905 and early 1907 of a new wave of newspapers and journals, primarily in Yiddish.[17] Warsaw alone soon became home to five Yiddish dailies (*Idishes tageblat, Di naye tsaytung, Der telegraf, Unzer leben*, and *Der veg*), three dailies in Hebrew (*Hayom, Hatsefirah*, and *Hatsofeh*), one Polish-language daily (*Nowa Gazeta*), and an assortment of Jewish weeklies in Hebrew, Polish, and Yiddish. Although the combined distribution of these Warsaw-based periodicals was close to 100,000, far more women and men read papers that were passed from hand to hand, or, alternatively, had the news read to them in salons, cafés, and other semi-public forums.[18] Just to underscore how revolutionary these changes really were, it is enough to note that until 1903 there was only one Jewish daily published in the Russian

[16] The term print capitalism is often attributed to Benedict Anderson; see his *Imagined Communities: Reflections on the Origins and Spread of Nationalism* (London, 1991), 34–46. For an ostensibly new interpretation of the somewhat old theme of 'the Jews' as the quintessential modern, capitalistic, and in this case, 'Mercurian' people, see the engaging yet problematic study by Yuri Slezkine, *The Jewish Century* (Princeton, 2004).

[17] The impact of these reforms and policies was not limited exclusively to Jews. For more on the popular press and its readers in the Russian empire, see Jeffrey Brooks, *When Russia Learned to Read: Literacy and Popular Literature, 1861–1917* (Princeton, 1985), and Louise McReynolds, *The News under Russia's Old Regime: The Development of a Mass-Circulation Press* (Princeton, 1991). On the Polish periodical press in this period, see Zenon Kmiecik, *Prasa polska w rewolucji 1905–1907* (Warsaw, 1980), and Beth Holmgren, *Rewriting Capitalism: Literature and the Market in Late Tsarist Russia and the Kingdom of Poland* (Pittsburgh, 1998).

[18] For statistics on the distribution of Jewish newspapers at this time, see Marian Fuks, *Prasa żydowska w Warszawie, 1823–1939* (Warsaw, 1979), 298, and Avraham Kirzhnitz, *The Jewish Press in the Former Russian Empire* [Di yidishe prese in der gevezener rusisher imperie, 1823–1916] (Moscow, 1930), 15–36, 72–88. See also Sarah Abrevaya Stein, *Making Jews Modern: The Yiddish and Ladino Press in the Russian and Ottoman Empires* (Bloomington, Ind., 2004), and David Fishman, *The Rise of Modern Yiddish Culture* (Pittsburgh, 2005). On the critical role of women readers at this time see Iris Parush, *Women Readers: On the Benefit of Marginality in Nineteenth-Century Eastern European Jewish Society* [Nashim korot: yitronah shel shuliyut behevrah hayehudit bemizrah eiropah beme'ah hatesha-esreh] (Tel Aviv, 2001), esp. 136–73.

empire, the Hebrew paper *Hatsefirah*, whose distribution rarely went beyond several thousand. Significantly, *Hatsefirah*, the beacon of Zionist thought and propaganda in eastern Europe, closed down in early 1906 after it proved incapable of competing with the onslaught of new Yiddish dailies.[19]

Anecdotal sources further reflect the social and cultural revolution that these statistics represent. Expressing a sense of frustration and a tinge of jealousy over the sudden popularity of the new Yiddish newspapers, the Hebrew writer Hayim Nahman Bialik wrote the following sardonic complaint to the 'grandfather' of Jewish literature, Sholem Yankev Abramovitsh (Mendele Moykher Seforim): 'Ever since the relaxation of censorship restrictions every Tom, Dick and Harry has been given a licence and the Yiddish press has begun to bloom like wild flowers. There are nearly a thousand newspapers. The Bund alone, for example, publishes a dozen papers, including, *Der veker*, *Der leker*, and *Der shmeker*, and many, many more. An endless sea.'[20]

More than any other new cultural institution, the press, in particular the new Yiddish dailies, laid the foundation for the construction of a public sphere that was both public and Jewish.[21] As Habermas has noted, 'the press' was 'the public sphere's pre-eminent institution'.[22] Furthermore, once established, the public sphere would become the central forum for rational public debate between individuals and, in time, a key tool used to disseminate political propaganda and to mobilize the reading public. Elie Kedourie and Benedict Anderson also maintain that increased literacy rates and the advent of a regular press in local vernaculars played a critical role in the transformation of traditional societies into collective polities that were, de facto, 'modern' ones.[23] Furthermore, it was the daily vernacular press that—in the eyes of Anderson and others—would ultimately prove capable of binding complete strangers under the roof of 'the imagined community', a community of hitherto anonymous and disparate individuals that could later

---

[19] For more on Zionism and the Zionist movement in the Polish lands see Ezra Mendelsohn, *Zionism in Poland: The Formative Years, 1915–1926* (New Haven, 1981). On the adventures of Nahum Sokolow, editor of *Hatsefirah*, as a Jewish journalist, politician, and public advocate, see Ela Bauer, *Between Poles and Jews: The Development of Nahum Sokolow's Political Thought* (Jerusalem, 2005).

[20] Bialik to Abramovitsh, Odessa, 3/16 Jan. 1906, in *An Exchange of Letters between Sh. Y. Abramovitsh, H. N. Bialik, and Y. Ravnitzky* [Ḥalifat igerot bein sh.y avramovits uvein ḥ.n bialik vey.ḥ ravnitski], ed. Chone Shmeruk (Jerusalem, 1976), letter no. 2 (p. 33). Unless otherwise noted, all translations from Hebrew and Yiddish sources are my own.

[21] On the gendered nature of reading and the linguistic politics of Jewish society and culture see e.g. Parush, *Women Readers* (Heb.), esp. 136–73, and Naomi Seidman, *A Marriage Made in Heaven: The Sexual Politics of Hebrew and Yiddish* (Berkeley, 1997).

[22] *The Structural Transformation of the Public Sphere*, 181.

[23] Anderson, *Imagined Communities*, 35–46; Elie Kedourie, *Nationalism* (Cambridge, Mass., 1994), 58–68.

be mobilized in support of various political goals, including that of collective self-determination.[24]

Expressing a newfound sense of camaraderie, community, and shared fate with other essentially anonymous readers of the new Jewish press, the young Avraham Gruen from the provincial town of Płońsk used the pages of the Warsaw Yiddish daily *Der veg* and its Hebrew parallel *Hayom* to send Jewish New Year's greetings in the autumn of 1906 'to my parents, my relatives and my friends, and especially to Mr Simha Izaak in Jaffa, in the Holy Land, to Yitzhak Yaakov Estherzon in New York, to all of the Zionists, wherever they may be, and to all of the subscribers to *Der veg* and *Hayom*'.[25] Ironically, Gruen neglected to mention his younger brother, David Joseph Gruen, who later became an almost universal icon of Jewish self-determination in Israel and throughout the world as Israel's first prime minister, David Ben-Gurion. Like their former neighbour and *landsman* Simha Izaak, the young David Gruen had already left eastern Europe for Ottoman Palestine.[26] Simmering sibling rivalries aside, Avraham Gruen's New Year wishes demonstrate how newspapers and the imagined community of fellow readers were already transforming the very nature and limits of Jewish society.

Similarly aware of their newfound role as communal representatives, journalists and newspapers often took conscious steps towards reinforcing the power that came with the advent of a mass-circulation press in Yiddish.[27] Thus, in addition to repeatedly assaulting the established communal leadership, many papers began to fulfil roles previously undertaken by more traditional communal institutions and functionaries. In the era of mass society and constant displacement, it was up to papers like *Hatsofeh* to run the phenomenally popular 'Questions and Answers' column on legal and professional matters; to *Der veg* to inform and educate readers about Jewish

---

[24] On anonymity and nationalism see Anderson, *Imagined Communities*, 6. 'It is imagined because the members of even the smallest nation will never know most of their fellow members, meet them, or even hear of them, yet in the minds of each lives the image of their communion.' I analyse the connection between modernity, anonymity, and nationalism in Scott Ury, 'The Generation of 1905 and the Politics of Despair: Alienation, Friendship, Community', in Stefani Hoffman and Ezra Mendelsohn (eds.), *The Revolution of 1905 and Russia's Jews* (Philadelphia, 2008), 96–110. For Kedourie's discussion of collective self-determination see his *Nationalism*, 56–86.

[25] *Hayom*, 51, 14/27 Sept. 1906, p. 4. For more information on *Der veg* and the activities of its indefatigable editors, the father-and-son team of Tsevi and Noyekh Prilutski, see Keith (Kalman) Ian Weiser, *Jewish People, Yiddish Nation: Noah Prylucki and the Folkists in Poland* (Toronto, forthcoming). I am indebted to the author.

[26] On the Gruen brothers, see Michael Bar-Zohar, *Ben-Gurion*, 3 vols. (Tel Aviv, 1987), i. 4–26, 40–1. See also David Ben-Gurion, *Memoirs* [Zikhronot], vol. i of 6 (Tel Aviv, 1971).

[27] For more on struggles over community and leadership at this time see Mendelsohn, *Class Struggle in the Pale*; id., *Zionism in Poland*; Frankel, *Prophecy and Politics*; Lederhendler, *The Road to Modern Jewish Politics*, and Benjamin Nathans, *Beyond the Pale: The Jewish Encounter with Late Imperial Russia* (Berkeley, 2002).

festivals and their history; and to other papers to raise funds for the impoverished and the disadvantaged.[28]

Not only were papers gradually performing more and more functions formerly reserved for the traditional community but writers had also begun, at times, to replace communal leaders. Hence, the critic and journalist A. Mukdoni (Alexander Kappel) later noted that 'the writer had become a type of rabbi, a new rabbi. Not one who takes requests and payments, not one who gives blessings and advice, but one who teaches. He says something new, something beautiful, something electrifying. And so the young hasid becomes a disciple of the writer.'[29]

Thus, while the press served as the central forum for the newly reconstructed political body, it was the young writer's task to further refine, define, and direct that body, as well as its newly redefined borders of inclusion and exclusion.

## THE THEATRE; OR, IT SOUNDS BETTER IN YIDDISH

Much like the Jewish press, Yiddish theatre experienced a remarkable upsurge during the tumultuous period that would soon come to be known as the revolution of 1905.[30] Here as well, demographic, economic, political, and legal factors led to the rise of Yiddish theatre in Europe's largest and perhaps most important Jewish centre, Warsaw. Moreover, although it is not completely clear how many plays and shows were performed, or how many

[28] Note *Der veg*'s rendition of the Passover story that was designed to encourage Jews in Warsaw to vote in the elections to the First Duma: *Der veg*, no. 73, 27 Mar./9 Apr. 1906, p. 1. See also *Głos Żydowski*, no. 10–11, 6 Apr. 1906, p. 133. For additional examples of papers fulfilling roles traditionally undertaken by communal organizations see e.g. *Der veg*, no. 139, 21 June/4 July 1906, p. 1; *Der telegraf*, no. 121, 4/17 June 1906, p. 1; and *Izraelita*, no. 48, 22 Dec. 1905, p. 561.

[29] A. Mukdoni, *In Warsaw and in Łódź: My Memoirs* [In varshe un in lodzsh: mayne bagegenishn], 2 vols. (Buenos Aires, 1955), i. 35.

[30] The fate of Yiddish theatre in late imperial Russia is a topic of debate among scholars of Jewish history and Yiddish culture. While John Klier contends that the tsarist ban of 1883 on Yiddish theatre was easily evaded and unevenly enforced throughout the period in question, David Fishman and Michael Steinlauf maintain that it was rather effective in suppressing it until the revolution of 1905. See, respectively, John Klier, ' "Exit, Pursued by a Bear": The Ban on Yiddish Theatre in Imperial Russia', in Joel Berkowitz (ed.), *Yiddish Theatre: New Approaches* (London, 2003), 159–74; Fishman, *The Rise of Modern Yiddish Culture*, 18–32, esp. 26–9; and Michael Charles Steinlauf, 'Polish-Jewish Theater. The Case of Mark Arnsteyn: A Study of the Interplay among Yiddish, Polish and Polish-Language Jewish Culture in the Modern Period', Ph.D. diss., Brandeis University, 1987, 139. For more on Yiddish theatre in and out of the Russian empire, see Alyssa Pia Quint, 'The Botched Kiss: Abraham Goldfaden and the Literary Origins of the Yiddish Theatre', Ph.D. diss., Harvard University, 2002; id., 'The Currency of Yiddish: Shlomo Ettinger's *Serkele* and the Reinvention of Shylock', *Prooftexts*, 24 (Winter 2004), 99–115; and Nina Warnke, 'Going East: The Impact of American Jewish Plays and Players on the Yiddish Stage in Czarist Russia, 1890–1914', *American Jewish History*, 92/1 (2004), 1–29.

spectators experienced Jewish theatre in Yiddish, contemporary accounts illustrate that more lenient interpretations of the 1883 government ban on Yiddish theatre led to an unprecedented cultural and political explosion in the spring of 1905.

Reports in the new Jewish dailies, accounts in memoir literature, and other, primarily governmental, sources speak of regular performances in several different theatres—both artistic and popular—in Warsaw. In fact, there were soon no fewer than four commercial theatres in the city dedicated to presenting Yiddish performances: the Bagatela theatre in Mokotów, the Elizeum theatre at 18 Karowa Street, Jardin d'Hiver at 9 Chmielna Street, and the new Muranower theatre.[31] In addition to daily shows, the number of performances often increased markedly during the intermediate days of the Jewish festivals of Passover and Sukkot.

One particularly colourful account of the newfound popularity and untapped potential of Jewish theatre in Warsaw can be found in a letter from Sholem Aleichem to his daughter Ernestina (Tessa) regarding the presentation of his play *Tsezayt un tseshprayt* (Scattered and Dispersed) in Polish several weeks before the ban on Yiddish theatre became more or less obsolete:[32]

What can I tell you about yesterday's victory? While I myself, as a well-loved playwright, have [previously] received applause, I've never seen anything like this, not even in my wildest literary imagination. After the first act, I was covered (literally) with flowers. Afterwards, they took me and put me on the stage several times after every act. During the fourth act, the crowd went crazy and started clapping after every line that was connected to the play's main theme. When it ended, hats began to fly through the air and a powerful, supernatural force overcame me. For a second, I thought that the theatre was going to collapse and I feared that a riot would break out. I don't know how to explain it: Was it due to the popularity of a folk artist? Was the crowd hypnotized by Jewish theatre? Or was it the thrill of being part of an unrestrained mob? A crowd of over a thousand people waited for me at the exit. . . . God in heaven. What would actually happen if it were possible to perform in Yiddish? My fate and their future are intimately bound to the Jewish theatre. Mark this day in your calendar.[33]

Ultimately Jewish theatre, especially when performed in Yiddish, offered spectators an all-encompassing experience, unlike newspapers. Indeed, as

---

[31]  On theatre in Warsaw see Barbara Król-Kaczorowska, *Teatry Warszawy: Budynki i sale w latach 1748–1975* (Warsaw, 1986).

[32]  For more on the Polish production of this play, see Chone Shmeruk, 'Sholem Aleichem's Comedy "Scattered and Dispersed" and the Performances of the Play in Polish in Warsaw in 1905 and 1910', (Heb.), in Ezra Mendelsohn and Chone Shmeruk (eds.), *Studies on Polish Jewry: Paul Glikson Memorial Volume* (Jerusalem, 1987), 79–96.

[33]  Originally written in Russian on 14 Apr. 1905 to Ernestina in Warsaw, this and other letters can be found in Hebrew translation in *Letters of Shalom Aleichem* [Mikhtevei shalom aleikhem, 1882–1916], ed. and trans. into Hebrew by Avraham Yaveen (Tel Aviv, 1998), 23.

Jewish theatre in eastern Europe passed from Polish and quasi-German performances to primarily Yiddish ones the entire experience of Jewish theatre was radically transformed. It was in these theatres that a Jewish spectator could meet, laugh, converse, and simply be in the public presence of hundreds of other Jews, Jews from all different parts of the city and the surrounding area whom he or she did not necessarily know but with whom he or she shared, or, at the very least, imagined that they shared, a variety of economic, cultural, and political interests, causes, and destinies. Moreover, the repeated experience of being in a theatre populated almost exclusively by Jews helped reinforce a specific set of linguistic, cultural, and communal signifiers of belonging and community across early twentieth-century eastern Europe. In this and other ways, theatre in Yiddish helped bring the newly reconfigured Jewish public sphere out of the imaginary realm of reading and imagining other Jews and into the more active realm of seeing Jews, being seen as Jews, and, perhaps most importantly, publicly becoming one of 'the Jews'. Indeed, it was not only the actors who were performing their Jewishness on stage, but, in many senses, also Jewish spectators who suddenly found themselves in new roles as actors in another, parallel drama taking place offstage, the birth of the Yiddish-speaking, and de facto Jewish, *publikum*, as it was regularly referred to in the Yiddish press.

Moreover, in an era of mass migration and social upheaval theatre soon became a key cultural and political tool that helped 'serialize' and standardize Jewish speech, behaviour, and, ultimately, identity.[34] Finally, much like the press, the theatre was not only a cultural forum geared towards entertainment and an economic project aimed at producing revenues, but also an inherently political institution whose very nature mandated that it take part in the larger project designed to reformulate and mobilize the Jewish body politic. From their very inception, urban society, popular culture, and participatory politics were inextricably intertwined.

Theatre critics most notably exemplified this engagement in the combined spheres of entertainment, economics, and politics. Here, as well, the newly self-anointed masters of modern Jewish culture (and politics) immediately took it upon themselves to educate and direct the masses, masses that they simultaneously deified and abhorred.[35] Ultimately it was the critic's responsibility to tell the audience not only what Yiddish theatre was supposed to be but also how it was supposed to understand, appreciate, and

[34] For a discussion of how national identity is reproduced on a mass basis or, in Anderson's language, 'serialized' in the modern age, see Benedict Anderson, 'Nationalism; Identity, and the Logic of Seriality', in id., *The Spectre of Comparisons* (New York, 1998), 29–45.

[35] For more on this critical point see Alyssa Pia Quint, '"Yiddish Literature for the Masses"? A Reconsideration of Who Read What in Jewish Eastern Europe', *AJS Review*, 29/1 (2005), 61–89, and Michael Steinlauf, 'Fear of Purim: Y. L. Peretz and the Canonization of Yiddish Theater', *Jewish Social Studies*, 1/3 (Spring 1995), 44–65.

consume the new phenomenon.[36] At the same time, the critics acknowledged, if at times begrudgingly, that the audience, or *publikum*, remained
the final judge. Ultimately, the *publikum* decided which shows went on and
which folded in shame. Hence, despite his repeated efforts to improve the
apparently low level of Yiddish theatre, the temperamental journalist, publicist, and soon to be leader of the Folkist Party Noyekh Prilutski echoed the
classic dilemma of democratic societies in stating that 'the public wants
funny, happy pieces. And their will is the law.'[37]

If all the world was a stage then there was a distinctly Jewish drama
unfolding, and one that would soon bear the redemptive title of 'The
Revolution of 1905'. However, in order for this political drama to reach its
proper conclusion, both theatres of Jewish politics—the first one on stage
and the second one in the streets—had to be directed with the appropriate
combination of wisdom, vision, and determination.

## THE DUMA ELECTIONS; OR, GOING TO THE PEOPLE

While the press helped construct the Jewish public sphere and the theatre
offered individuals the opportunity to embody that space, it was the experience of participatory politics, and, in particular, the elections to the first
three Russian State Dumas in rapid succession in the spring of 1906 and
twice in 1907 that led to the politicization and mobilization of that entity.
Here, again, the Jewish public sphere underwent a transformative process as
the actual practice of electoral politics forced leaders and activists to define
and mobilize the body politic through a discourse of community and discipline.[38] Urban societies, popular culture, and participatory politics were,
again, inextricably intertwined as east European (Jewish) society bravely
entered the new century with boundless energy and great expectations.

After a slow start, the elections in Warsaw to the First Russian State
Duma in the spring of 1906 quickly turned into angry public confrontations
between two ever more divided political camps—a primarily Polish, patriotic camp led by the increasingly intolerant National Democrats on the one
hand, and a liberal-democratic coalition composed of Polish and Jewish
liberals and various Jewish organizations on the other—over the parliamentary representation and definition of the disputed capital of the former

[36] For more on Yiddish theatre and the role of the theatre critic, see Steinlauf, 'Polish-Jewish
Theater', and id., 'Fear of Purim'. See also Nina Warnke, 'The Child Who Wouldn't Grow
Up: Yiddish Theatre and its Critics', in Berkowitz (ed.), *Yiddish Theatre*, 201–16.

[37] Prilutski, *Yiddish Theatre, 1905–1912* [Yidish teater, 1905–1912], 2 vols. (Bialystok, 1921),
ii. 116.

[38] On the nexus between democracy and discipline in a slightly different context see Porter,
*When Nationalism Began to Hate*, and id., 'Democracy and Discipline in Late Nineteenth-Century
Poland', *Journal of Modern History*, 71/2 (June 1999), 346–93. See also Partha Chatterjee,
*Nationalist Thought and the Colonial World: A Derivative Discourse?* (Minneapolis, 1998).

Congress Kingdom, Warsaw.[39] As a result of these divisions, Jewish activists and political organizations soon turned directly to members of Warsaw's Jewish community as Jews per se in an effort to garner the largest possible number of votes.[40] Warsaw's newly formed Jewish Electoral Committee, for example, repeatedly urged Jews to vote for candidates (either Jewish or liberal Polish) who would defend what they defined as Jewish interests. Furthermore, in an effort to encourage voter registration, many newspapers (both Jewish and Polish) began publishing tables that listed the number of potential voters and electors in different districts by their ethnicity—Poles in one column and Jews in another.[41] Here, in particular, the very nature of participatory politics not only depended upon a public sphere that was specifically Jewish (or, alternatively, effectively Polish), but also led to the further consolidation and mobilization of these bodies through a discourse of community and discipline that repeatedly reinforced the ethno-linguistic lines of belonging and community. Established almost instantaneously in the elections to the First Duma in 1906, these political encampments along ethno-linguistic divides would repeat themselves in all four Duma elections in Warsaw and in many other urban curiae in the former Kingdom of Poland and the rest of the empire's western provinces.[42]

Finally, like journalists and theatre critics, representatives of Jewish electoral organizations repeatedly claimed to lead the very body that would, ultimately, legitimize their own claims to power, 'the people'. Activists regularly took it upon themselves to explain to voters not only how and where to register to vote, but also which electors to choose. Reflecting this didactic approach, an

---

[39] For more on the Duma elections and the somewhat intricate electoral system see Terence Emmons, *The Formation of Political Parties and the First National Elections in Russia* (Cambridge, Mass., 1983); Abraham Ascher, *The Revolution of 1905: Authority Restored* (Stanford, Calif., 1992); and Vladimir Levin, 'Russian Jewry and the Duma Elections, 1906–1907', in W. Moskovich, L. Finberg, and M. Feller (eds.), *Jews and Slavs: Essays on Intercultural Relations*, 7 (Jerusalem, 2000), 233–64. See also Stephen D. Corrsin, 'Polish–Jewish Relations before the First World War: The Case of the State Duma Elections in Warsaw', *Gal-Ed*, 11 (1989), 31–53, and Scott Ury, ' "On the Gallows": The "Politics of Assimilation" in Turn-of-the-Century Warsaw', *Polin*, 20 (2008), 339–54.

[40] On this point see Joshua Shanes, 'Neither Germans nor Poles: Jewish Nationalism in Galicia before Herzl, 1883–1897', *Austrian History Yearbook*, 34 (2003), 191–213. For more on Jewish politics in Galicia, see Rachel Manekin, 'The New Covenant: Orthodox Jews and Polish Catholics in Galicia, 1879–1883' (Heb.), *Tsiyon*, 64 (1999), 157–86, and Manekin, 'Politics, Religion, and National Identity: The Galician Jewish Vote in the 1873 Parliamentary Elections', *Polin*, 12 (1999), 100–19.

[41] See e.g. *Der telegraf*, no. 81, 14/27 Apr. 1906, p. 3; *Der veg*, no. 82, 13/26 Apr. 1906, p. 3, and supplement to this issue, p. 1. See also the following issues of *Kurier Warszawski*: no. 108, 20 Apr. 1906, p. 4; no. 109, 21 Apr. 1906, p. 4; no. 110, 22 Apr. 1906, p. 11; no. 112, 24 Apr. 1906, p. 6; no. 43, 12 Feb. 1907, p. 10; no. 46, 15 Feb. 1907, p. 10; and no. 51, 20 Feb. 1907, pp. 4–6.

[42] A curia was a separate group of voters entitled to elect a given number of Duma representatives.

election flyer from April 1906 calls on 'the Jewish voters in Warsaw' to choose
only those electors listed on the official 'list of the Jewish Electoral Committee
in Warsaw'. The announcement ends with a set of detailed instructions and
warnings: don't write anything on the ballot itself, bring proper voter registration, and do not send a proxy.[43] While 'the people' was acknowledged to be the
final arbiter of political sovereignty, individual voters were not yet entrusted
with the basic responsibility of deciding how that power should be appropriated or exercised. The responsibility again fell upon the self-anointed representatives to lead the noble yet apparently simple masses to their true destiny,
collective self-determination.[44]

*

In his *Class Struggle in the Pale*, *Zionism in Poland*, *Jews of East Central Europe
between the World Wars*, *On Modern Jewish Politics*, and *Painting a People*, and
innumerable volumes, articles, and other contributions, Ezra Mendelsohn
has consistently challenged a community of readers and scholars to take a
new look at the social and cultural praxis of modern politics among Jews
in eastern Europe. Unlike many other studies of Jewish politics that tend
to focus on political leaders, ideological struggles, and party politics,
Mendelsohn emphasizes the daily practices and institutions that made modern Jewish politics such an incredibly new phenomenon for so many Jews in
east European lands. In many of his works, he shows how the actual experience of modern politics redefined the face, tempo, and limits of Jewish—and
non-Jewish—societies and cultures as well as the actual lives of true believers, perennial sceptics, and innocent bystanders in eastern Europe and its
diaspora communities in the New World.

   Throughout this essay I have adopted many aspects of Mendelsohn's
methodological approach and argued that a series of critical institutional and
cultural developments in turn-of-the-century eastern Europe irrevocably
altered the nature of Jewish (and non-Jewish) society in Warsaw and beyond.
The exponential growth of the Jewish press, the renaissance of Yiddish theatre, and the experience of participatory politics helped ensure that Jewish
society in Warsaw of 1907 was far different from that of 1900. Moreover, by
laying the foundations for the construction of a specifically Jewish public
sphere, a public sphere that not only represented but also embodied the
Jewish body politic, these three institutions combined to radically transform
both the form and the content of community and belonging among Jews
in Warsaw. In time, these institutions and practices, both imaginary and

---

[43] *Der telegraf*, no. 77, 10/23 Apr. 1906, p. 1.
[44] See Kedourie, *Nationalism*, 56–8. See also Pheng Cheah, *Spectral Nationality: Passages of
Freedom from Kant to Postcolonial Literatures of Liberation* (New York, 2003).

physical, would help facilitate the politicization and transformation of many Jews in twentieth-century eastern Europe, America, and the Middle East.

Many of these developments were, of course, not limited exclusively to Jews. In many cases, Jews thought, behaved, and acted much like other loyal subjects of the last tsar, be they Catholic, Muslim, Orthodox, Protestant, or Uniate. Like many other residents of the Russian empire's burgeoning new cities, many Jews responded to the curses and blessings of mass society by creating and then embracing modern cultural projects that seemed to flourish in the urban environment. Moreover, when given the chance to participate in popular elections, many Jews—like many Finns, Poles, Russians, Ukrainians, and others—turned to national politics in parallel, yet by their very definition separate, struggles for the same political goal, collective self-determination.[45] On the practical level, the construction, maintenance, and success of many of these cultural, economic, and political projects demanded a detailed knowledge of, if not a near-native familiarity with, the different political institutions, cultural practices, and idiosyncrasies that fuelled and ruled the Russian empire. Ultimately, every legal cultural, social, or political project in turn-of-the-century imperial Russia required that government approval be obtained, that local officials remain sympathetic, and that alliances with representatives of other communities and organizations be created and maintained. Moreover, on the popular level, many Jews—like many other urban residents—began to follow daily news events via newspapers printed in local vernaculars (and oftentimes read aloud to groups of people), attend popular cultural venues such as the theatre, and openly participate in various democratic activities and processes. Lastly, while all this demanded that many Jews change, through either conscious or subconscious acts of mimicry, the way that they thought and behaved to conform with what they believed were the reigning social norms of political behaviour and action, the end result was the construction of a series of cultural and political institutions and an ensuing set of ideas and practices that eventually ensured that Jews would remain simultaneously a part of and apart from other societies, cultures, and peoples—or, in the language of this volume, both insiders and outsiders.[46]

[45] On the path of other nations and nationalisms in this era see John Paul Himka, *Galician Villagers and the Ukrainian National Movement in the Nineteenth Century* (Edmonton, Calif., 1988); Francine Hirsch, *Empire of Nations: Ethnographic Knowledge and the Making of the Soviet Union* (Ithaca, NY, 2005); Porter, *When Nationalism Began to Hate*; Hans Rogger, *Jewish Policies and Right-Wing Politics in Imperial Russia* (Berkeley, 1986); and Theodore R. Weeks, *Nation and State in Late Imperial Russia: Nationalism and Russification on the Western Frontier, 1863–1914* (DeKalb, Ill., 1996).

[46] On Europe's Jews as 'A People Apart' see David Vital, *A People Apart: The Jews in Europe, 1789–1939* (Oxford, 1999), as well as David Engel's review in *Jewish History*, 14/3 (2000), 365–8. For other uses of the insider/outsider motif in the study of Jewish history and culture, see David Biale, Michael Galchinsky, and Susannah Heschel (eds.), *Insider/Outsider: American Jews and Multiculturalism* (Berkeley, 1998).

# TEN

# THE 'NON-JEWISH JEWS'
# REVISITED
## *Solzhenitsyn and the Issue of National Guilt*

### JONATHAN FRANKEL

IN HIS OFTEN-QUOTED essay of almost fifty years ago, 'The Non-Jewish Jew', Isaac Deutscher selected six outstanding examples to illustrate his argument that potentially there were extraordinary intellectual and socio-political advantages in escaping the 'narrow, archaic and conflicting' bounds of Jewry while still not being fully integrated into the wider world beyond— or, in his words, to be in that greater society 'and yet not in it, of it and yet not of it'.[1] Of the six, one was a philosopher, Spinoza; one a writer and poet, Heine; and one a doctor and psychoanalyst, Freud; but the other three were all revolutionaries and deeply committed internationalists: Karl Marx, Lev Davidovich Trotsky, and Rosa Luxemburg.

Given the views of Marx, Trotsky, and Luxemburg with regard to their ethnic roots, the question naturally arises whether they were in any meaningful sense Jews at all and if not, whether they nonetheless do belong within the parameters, as usually understood, of Jewish history. Given a positive answer to that question, in what ways were they, despite everything, not only the 'outsiders' which they proclaimed themselves to be but also 'insiders'?

This conundrum is one of the major issues discussed by Aleksandr Solzhenitsyn in his two-volume work *Dvesti let vmeste* (Two Hundred Years Together).[2] In this book, some thousand pages in length, Solzhenitsyn insists that the 'non-Jewish Jews' (whom he terms 'schismatics') have to be regarded, despite their beliefs and self-perceptions, as 'insiders'.

*Dvesti let vmeste* can be read, inter alia, as a bill of indictment against the Jewish people which, in Solzhenitsyn's estimate, made a major, perhaps a decisive, contribution to the Bolshevik victory in the years 1917–21 and to the consolidation of the Soviet state during the inter-war period. As he describes it, the 'sectarians' of Jewish origin in the upper echelons of the

---

[1] Isaac Deutscher, *The Non-Jewish Jew and Other Essays* (London, 1968), 26–7. 'The Non-Jewish Jew' was based on a lecture delivered by Deutscher in 1958.

[2] *Dvesti let vmeste*, 2 vols. (Moscow, 2001, 2002).

party played a particularly conspicuous role in this development, but in his view the 'Jewish Jews' recruited from below did as much or more to ensure the Bolshevik triumph—a success that steadily transformed them, too, over the following decades into 'non-Jewish Jews'.

Following a relatively lengthy introductory section, this essay will attempt to summarize and scrutinize the case put forward by Solzhenitsyn in his book.

As early as 1903 the young Trotsky, when asked whether he regarded himself as a Russian or a Jew, gave his by now well-known reply: 'Neither! I am a Social Democrat!'[3] Fifteen years later, by then second only to Lenin as a leader of the newborn Soviet Russia, he was reported to have dismissed Jewish delegations that had somehow gained admission to his office with the remarks: 'The Jews do not interest me more than the Bulgars' and 'I am not a Jew, but an internationalist'.[4] And Rosa Luxemburg, in a, today, no less familiar statement, rebuked a close friend in 1917 for choosing to focus on 'special Jewish sorrows'. 'I feel just as sorry for the wretched Indian victims in Putamayo . . . I cannot find a special corner in my heart for the ghetto.'[5]

Lev Trotsky and Rosa Luxemburg represented, of course, only the tip of what was by their time a very large iceberg, some of it clearly visible, much of it submerged in the sea of pseudonyms that hid the ethnic identity of so many revolutionaries in the Russian empire. The sentiments that Trotsky and Luxemburg expressed so vigorously with regard to their internationalist loyalties—and their distance from the Jewish people—were widely shared by innumerable Jews (or one-time Jews) in the Russian and Polish Marxist revolutionary parties: the Bolsheviks, the Mensheviks, and the Social Democratic Party of the Kingdom of Poland and Lithuania, as well as in the anarchist movement.

Seeking to explain this phenomenon, Pavel Akselrod could write in 1882 (he was then not a Marxist but still a revolutionary populist):

as is well known, all [the Russian Jewish socialists]—or, at least, all those who developed under the influence of Russian literature—cast off . . . thoughts regarding the Jewish masses at the first moment that the blinding light of socialist ideas penetrated their minds. I still remember how, reading the book of Lassalle, I felt a kind of shame at my concern for the interests of the Jewish people. What significance could a handful of Jews have in comparison with the universal interests that were the concern of socialism. . . . After all, strictly speaking, the Jewish question does not exist and the only question is the liberation of the working masses of all

---

[3] Quoted in Vladimir Medem, *Towards the Twentieth Anniversary* [Tsum tsvantsigsten yortsayt] (New York, 1943), 10–11 n.

[4] Quoted in Joseph Nedava, *Trotsky and the Jews* (Philadelphia, 1972), 116.

[5] Letter of 16 Feb. 1917, quoted in Robert Wistrich, *Revolutionary Jews from Marx to Trotsky* (London, 1976), 86.

nations, including the Jewish. . . . Would it not be . . . comical to devote one's efforts to the Jewish people, which is no more than a single element in the vast population of the Russian empire?[6]

This passage comes from the pamphlet that Akselrod wrote in order to question whether, in the light of the pogroms of 1881–2, the time had not come to rethink the dismissal of the Jewish people and its problems as too marginal and minuscule to deserve attention. But, significantly enough, under pressure from his revolutionary comrades, he decided to shelve the manuscript and it was published only posthumously, rescued from the archives by Boris Nikolaevsky in the 1920s.

The clash of universalism and particularism, thus brought to the surface by Akselrod for a fleeting moment, found frequent expression in the fictional works produced by the Jewish writers of the period. To take just one example among many, here is a snatch of dialogue—presented by the author ironically but nonetheless with realistic intent—taken from Sholem Aleichem's novel *Der mabl* (The Flood), between Tamara Shostepol, passionately dedicated to what the author terms revolutionary 'cosmopolitanism', and Sasha Rafalovitsh, likewise a student, but in his case a Jewish nationalist:

'What do you want of me?' asks Tamara . . . 'that I should give up the greatest ideal in the world, shut my ears to the cries of hundreds of millions of people shouting for "Bread and Freedom!"—and to do that for the sake of a handful of people who suffer no less and no more than everybody else? For what? Just because they and I belong to one and the same people, share a common history and have the same names?'

'And', interrupts Sasha, 'have the same eyes and are marked by the same noses . . .'
'Now's not the time to look at things like that', fires back Tamara.
'Still', says Sasha, 'people do look at such things and they look very hard . . .'[7]

As a broad generalization, it can be said that, until the fall of communism in Europe in the years 1989–91, scholars paid relatively little attention to the specific role played by Jews—qua Jews—in the internationalist and inter-ethnic revolutionary parties in the Russian empire (or, indeed, elsewhere in eastern and east-central Europe). To be sure, there were a number of detailed studies, by such historians as Eliyahu Tcherikower, Boris Sapir, and Eric Haberer, of those Jews (quite a few in all and of rather marginal importance) who joined the revolutionary Populist parties in the 1870s and 1880s—among the best known being Mark Natanson, Aron Zundelevich, Vladimir Yokhelson, and Isaac Shternberg (the latter two, incidentally,

---

[6] Pavel B. Akselrod, 'O zadachakh evreisko-sotsialisticheskoi intelligentsii', in *Iz arkhiva P. B. Akselroda* (*Materialy po istorii russkogo revolyutsionnogo dvizheniya*), ed. V. S. Voitinsky, B. I. Nikolaevsky, et al., 2 vols. (Berlin, 1924), ii. 217.
[7] Sholem Aleichem, *Der mabl* (Warsaw, 1907), 24–5.

emerging from decades of penal exile in Siberia as among Russia's most famous ethnographers).[8] Then, too, there were the biographical sketches of Jewish revolutionaries in the Russian revolutionary movement ('non-Jewish Jews' included) by Lev Deich and Viktor Chernov, who produced them during the inter-war period in response to requests from the New York Yiddish daily, *Forverts*.[9] All in all, this would appear to leave Leonard Schapiro's perceptive but sketchy and impressionistic article of 1961 something of a lone attempt to provide a more general and theoretical analysis of—in his words—'The Role of the Jews in the Russian Revolutionary Movement'.[10]

A number of factors combined to discourage historians during so much of the twentieth century from turning the spotlight on this particular corner of east European history. In the Soviet Union and its satellite states, the significance of ethnicity in the revolutionary movements generally, and in the Bolshevik Party specifically, was bound to be a taboo subject as far as official historiography was concerned. True, during the comparatively relaxed period of the 1920s the history of the Jewish labour movement in its clandestine years under tsarism became a legitimate object of study as we can see in the books of, for example, Avrom Kirzhnitz and Moyshe Rafes.[11] But they were dealing, after all, with the Jewish Jews, with the revolutionaries who openly proclaimed their national allegiance—a field of historical research lent momentary legitimacy by the Soviet policies of *korenizatsiya* ('indiginization') during the period of the New Economic Policy, and by the partial recognition of the Jewish people as one among the Soviet nationalities.

When, though, it came to the historiography of the Communist Party itself, the emphasis was on iron-clad internal unity and class solidarity, and what was true for all Bolsheviks (even Ukrainians or Georgians, for example) was doubly true for the Jews—defined by Lenin in 1903 as members not of a nation but of a caste destined to undergo a process of rapid and total assimilation and to disappear in the modern period. References to the Jews as an ethnic group within the Communist Party were thus kept furtively behind

---

[8] Eliyahu Tcherikower, *Jewish Revolutionaries in Russia during the Sixties and Eighties* (Yiddish), *Historishe shriftn*, 3 (1939), 60–172; Boris Sapir, 'Jewish Socialists around *Vpered*', *International Review of Social History*, 10 (1965), 365–84; Eric E. Haberer, *Jews and Revolution in Nineteenth Century Russia* (Cambridge, 1995).

[9] Lev Deich, *Rol´ evreev v russkom revolyutsionnom dvizhenii* (Berlin, 1923); Viktor Chernov, *Jewish Activists in the Socialist Revolutionary Party: Biographical Essays* [Yidishe tuer in der partey sotsialistn revolutsyonern: byografishe eseyen] (New York, 1948).

[10] Schapiro's article appeared in *Slavonic and East European Review*, 40 (1961–2), 148–67.

[11] Avrom Kirzhnitz and Moyshe Rafes, *The Jewish Worker: Anthology on the History of the Jewish Worker, Revolutionary and Socialist Movement in Russia* [Der yidisher arbeter: khrestomatye tsu der geshikhte fun der yidisher arbeter, revolutsyoner un sotsyalistisher bavegung in rusland], vols. i and ii: *The Years 1904–1907* [Di yorn 1904–1907] (Moscow, 1925); Moyshe Rafes, *Dva goda revolyutsii v ukraine: evolyutsiya i raskol 'bunda'* (Moscow, 1920); id., *Ocherki po istorii bunda* (Moscow, 1920).

doors, as during the desperate power struggle waged in 1925–6 between Stalin allied to Bukharin on the one hand, and the trio of Trotsky, Zinoviev, and Kamenev (the leaders of the united opposition, all three Jews) on the other. It was all too easy for the Stalinist majority to hint in closed meetings that the opposition marshalled by the minority of malcontents against the slogan of 'Socialism in one country!' was an expression of distrust in the Soviet state and people coming naturally from Jews as deracinated outsiders. Some twenty years later, at the height of the Cold War, such accusations emerged into the open for one brief period with the loudly proclaimed public campaign (doubtless personally engineered by Stalin) against the 'rootless cosmopolitans', with their excessive respect for the West—a campaign that, inter alia, unmasked the Jewish names hidden behind the Russian-sounding pseudonyms of innumerable figures prominent in the world of Soviet culture and the humanities. Stalin's death in 1953 brought an abrupt end to this open display of what was an obviously anti-Leninist line, and the manipulation, by then well established, of ethnic quotas once again reverted to being an issue best kept out of the public eye.

In the West, meanwhile, another set of factors combined to inhibit study of the specifically Jewish ingredient in the history of revolutionary internationalism in eastern Europe. First, above all, there was a widespread reluctance to focus attention on a phenomenon—Jews as internationalist revolutionaries—that had provided the antisemitic movements with a highly effective rallying cry since the beginning of the twentieth century, or even since 1848. The theory that the Bolshevik seizure of power in Russia was part of a plot by the Jewish people methodically to subvert the social system in order then to take control of the entire world constituted from the first a key element in Nazi ideology. It was thus *a*, perhaps *the*, primary justification that, in Nazi thinking and in popular attitudes (in so far as they were involved), made the Holocaust possible.

Western historians thus naturally tended to skirt around a subject so catastrophically exploited by the extreme right in the past and still liable to provide ammunition to antisemitic forces in the present. Moreover, even those historians who were ready, for the sake of historical truth, to ignore this risk could not escape the fact that the Soviet regime, for its own reasons, kept most of the relevant statistical and other key materials securely under lock and key. In addition, the fact that so many Western historians of the revolutionary internationalist left in eastern Europe could themselves perhaps be defined as 'non-Jewish Jews' may have reinforced still further a general reluctance to analyse the issue under discussion here. It is noteworthy, for example, that J. P. Nettl, in his two-volume biography of Rosa Luxemburg,[12]

---

[12] J. P. Nettl, *Rosa Luxemburg*, 2 vols. (Oxford, 1966).

and Isaac Deutscher, in his three volumes on Trotsky,[13] both chose not to discuss their subjects' Jewishness and its possible significance in the formation of their ideological orientation and political behaviour.

The most notable breach in the wall of silence was arguably made by the publication in 1988 of the collection *Ukrainian–Jewish Relations*.[14] Based on papers delivered at a conference held in Canada, it also included extensive extracts from the spirited discussion sessions. Other exceptions that proved the rule were a number of works primarily by Israeli historians—Joseph Nedava, Zeev Ivianski, Binyamin Pinkus, Mordechai Altshuler, and Robert Wistrich.[15]

The period since the collapse of the Soviet bloc has witnessed in this respect a dramatic change, and the reasons are not far to seek. In the post-Soviet galaxy of newly independent states, historians are usually free to research and to write as they choose. Given the depth and breadth of anti-communism, as well as the persistence of antisemitism, in the region, it is inevitable that the issue of the contribution of Jews to the Bolshevik seizure of power and their consequent participation in the Soviet regime should have become the focus of—often highly critical—public attention. This is particularly the case in those countries (the Baltic states, for example, or Ukraine) that find themselves constantly driven onto the defensive by revelations throwing light on the extent to which their nationals collaborated with the German forces in the destruction of their Jewish populations during the war.

In what can easily become a case of tit for tat, it is argued that Jews were heavily over-represented, or even dominant, in the Soviet security forces and secret police which, for example, oversaw the death of millions of Ukrainian peasants during the famine of 1933; that they were responsible in 1939–41 for the deportation of hundreds of thousands of people from the occupied borderlands to Siberia; and that they played a central role in the imposition of the Stalinist dictatorship on eastern Europe in the years 1944–53. It is no wonder, so the line of reasoning goes, that populations—Letts, Lithuanians, Poles, Ukrainians—goaded beyond endurance by Soviet brutality, should, once the tables were turned with the arrival of the Wehrmacht in June and

---

[13] Isaac Deutscher, *The Prophet Armed: Trotsky 1879–1921*; *The Prophet Unarmed: Trotsky 1921–1929*; *The Prophet Outcast: Trotsky 1929–1940* (London, 1954, 1959, 1963).

[14] Peter J. Potichnyj and Howard Aster (eds.), *Ukrainian–Jewish Relations in Historical Perspective* (Edmonton, Alberta, 1988).

[15] Nedava, *Trotsky and the Jews*; Zeev Ivianski, *Personal Terror: The Idea and the Practice* [Hateror ha'ishi: hara'ayon vehama'as] (Tel Aviv, 1977); Binyamin Pinkus, *The Jews of the Soviet Union: The History of a National Minority* (Cambridge, 1988); id. (ed.), *The Soviet Government and the Jews 1948–1967: A Documented History* (Cambridge, 1988); Mordechai Altshuler, *Soviet Jewry on the Eve of the Holocaust: A Social and Demographic Profile* (Jerusalem, 1988); Wistrich, *Revolutionary Jews*.

July 1941, have turned against the Jewish populations that had openly welcomed the invading Soviet forces not so long before.

Given the radically changed circumstances of the post-1991 era, it is not
surprising that a number of books and articles on communism and the Jews
have appeared in Russia in recent years. Historians such as Gennady
Kostyrchenko, Oleg Budnitsky, and Zhores Medvedev[16] (as well as Vladimir
Naumov working in collaboration with Western scholars[17]) have approached
the subject from different angles, but their books are largely based on archival
research and are monographic in form, concentrating on specific themes or
periods. The same holds true of most of the books on Jews and communism
in Russia and eastern Europe that have appeared in the West during the same
period.[18]

There are two works, however, that notably, dramatically even, follow a
different path: Solzhenitsyn's *Dvesti let vmeste* and Yuri Slezkine's *The Jewish
Century*.[19] Both authors set out to produce sweeping syntheses, and both
ascribe extraordinary significance, in the modern history of eastern Europe
or even of the world, to the role played by the Russian Jewish intelligentsia
in general and by the 'non-Jewish Jews', the internationalists, and the Jews as
archetypal Soviet men and women in particular. But whereas Solzhenitsyn
perceives that role in essentially negative and tragic terms, Slezkine interprets it as a natural product of universal modernizing processes and, for all
its costs, essentially progressive. Slezkine opts for the objective, Weberian
stance of the historical sociologist; in contrast, Solzhenitsyn's book, which is
based partly on personal recollections, is marked by its extreme subjectivity
and sense of direct personal involvement. The author does not ask questions
so much as cast down challenges.

The primary issue that lies at the heart of the second volume of *Dvesti
let vmeste* is the extent to which Jews (both 'non-Jewish' and 'Jewish') contributed to the success of the Bolshevik revolution and, subsequently, to the
brutal transformation of society by the communist regime.

[16] Gennady Kostyrchenko, *Tainaya politika Stalina: vlast´ i antisemitizm* (Moscow, 2001); Oleg
V. Budnitsky, *Rossiiskie evrei mezhdu krasnymi i belymi: 1917–1920* (Moscow, 2005); Zhores
Medvedev, *Stalin i evreiskaya problema: novyi analiz* (Moscow, 2003).

[17] Jonathan Brent and Vladimir P. Naumov, *Stalin's Last Crime: The Plot against the Jewish
Doctors 1948–1953* (New York, 2003); Joshua R. Rubinstein and Vladimir P. Naumov (eds.),
*Stalin's Secret Pogrom: The Post-War Inquisition of the Jewish Anti-Fascist Committee*, trans. Laura
Esther Wolfson (New Haven, 2001).

[18] See e.g. Robert Levy, *Ana Pauker: The Rise and Fall of a Jewish Communist* (Berkeley, 2001);
Sonja Margolina, *Das Ende der Lügen: Russland und die Juden im 20. Jahrhundert* (Berlin, 1992);
Jaff Schatz, *The Generation: The Rise and Fall of the Jewish Communists of Poland* (Berkeley,
1991); Claudie Weill, *Les Cosmopolites: Socialisme et judéité* (Paris, 2004). Cf. the articles col-
lected in Jonathan Frankel and Dan Diner (eds.), *Dark Times, Dire Decisions* (= *Studies in
Contemporary Jewry*, 20) (2004).          [19] Slezkine, *The Jewish Century* (Princeton, 2004).

While the question is straightforward enough, any attempt to answer it is bound to be controversial if only because it inevitably forces the historian to make a judgement as to how much weight should be assigned to the roles played respectively by the top leadership in the party; by the middle ranks and (once the party was in power) the bureaucracy; and, finally, by mass support. Thus, if the revolutionary process of 1917 is understood to have been decided ultimately by deep-rooted social forces, by the urban proletariat, the peasantry, and the soldiers (recently recruited peasants themselves, for the main part, in 1917), then the role of the Jewish population was surely minimal. Confined to the western borderlands, which were largely under German occupation in 1917, everywhere a vulnerable minority group, without a peasantry or a large industrial proletariat, and inclined, when given the chance to vote, to support the Jewish and not the inter-ethnic parties, the 'Jewish street' simply could not have significantly influenced the immediate outcome of the 1917 revolutions. (In this context, it is worth noting Jaff Schatz's estimate that even when sympathy for the communists was at its height in the mid-1920s no more than 5 per cent of the Jewish public voted for the Communist Party.[20])

There can be no such straightforward assessment of the part played by intermediate echelons—the middle-ranking party and governmental bureaucracy. Solzhenitsyn is insistent that Jews (at that time still 'Jewish Jews', although soon to become increasingly internationalist) streamed in to man posts in the newly constituted regime from its earliest days in late 1917, a decisive period when the fate of Bolshevik power hung in the balance.

To buttress this thesis, which is of crucial importance to his overall argument, Solzhenitsyn refers, inter alia, to a statement made by Lenin to Shimen Dimanshtein during the Civil War. The latter cited the Bolshevik leader's opinion that it was the early recruitment of a significant number of supporters 'from among the middling strata of the Jewish intelligentsia . . . a reservoir of literate and more or less intelligent and more or less sober new bureaucrats' that made it possible to subvert the strike, 'the sabotage', then being conducted by the previously entrenched civil servants (*chinovniki*).[21]

The chronological framework championed by Solzhenitsyn runs contrary to the viewpoint usually taken for granted in works on Russian Jewish history. In this respect Joseph Nedava can be seen as representative. 'In the first phase of the Bolshevik revolution', he writes,

[20] Jaff Schatz, 'Jews and the Communist Movement in Interwar Poland', in Frankel and Diner (eds.), *Dark Times, Dire Decisions*, 13–37: 21.
[21] Quoted in Solzhenitsyn, *Dvesti let vmeste*, ii. 78–9. For the original see Shimen Dimanshtein, 'Po povodu broshyury "Lenin o evreiskom voprose v Rossii"', in Vladimir Lenin, *O evreiskom voprose v Rossii* (n.p., 1924), 17–18.

the Jews openly expressed their nonconfidence in the usurpers of power in Russia. This is clearly reflected in the election results to both the Jewish Committees in Great Russia [the *kehilot*] and the [Provisional] Jewish National Assembly in the Ukraine (November 1918). . . . The year 1919 has to be seen as the turning point with respect to greater Jewish participation in the Red Army and the Soviet bureaucracy, even in the Cheka.[22]

Whether 1918 or 1919 was the year in which Jews entered the service of the Bolshevik state is an issue that leads naturally to the construction of two contradictory narratives. If the influx took place before the huge wave of pogroms that erupted during the later stages of the Civil War (1919–20), then here was a phenomenon dictated not by necessity but rather by free choice, whether motivated by ideology and a Jewish penchant for utopianism, by the urge to escape the then pervasive hunger and cold, or by personal ambition. And with free choice, Solzhenitsyn maintains, comes responsibility and the risk of moral guilt.

As against that, though, if Jews rallied to the Bolshevik flag only later, in order primarily to contribute to the defeat of the White armies and the many Ukrainian forces perpetrating the pogroms, then it becomes much harder to raise the issue of blame—although, so Solzhenitsyn insists, not impossible. As he puts it, writing of 1919: 'It *seemed* as though not only the Jewish Bolsheviks but, as it were, the Jewish population as a whole had opted in the Civil War for the Reds. Can it be said that there was nothing that drove them to that choice? Certainly not! But can we say that there was no alternative? Once more, the answer is no.'[23] Solzhenitsyn's sympathies here lie with the relatively few Jews, such as Daniel Pasmanik, who opted to cooperate as far as possible with the White administration under the leadership of General Denikin, seeing it, in the last resort, as the lesser evil.

Various contemporary accounts tend to lend a degree of credence to Lenin's opinion as relayed by Dimanshtein. In particular, there are many eyewitness reports of a conspicuously disproportionate participation of Jews in the Cheka (also in the Communist Party *apparat*) in Ukraine following the Bolshevik reconquest of the region in the winter of 1918/19. And Mikhail Beizer has recently drawn attention to articles published in the Zionist journal *Rassvet* early in 1918 describing a substantial flow of Jews into the Bolshevik administration in Petrograd. Although satirical in tone, the following observation, appearing in that periodical in February, was typical:

I do not have statistical evidence, but among my circle of acquaintances, a good half have entered government service: one of my children's teachers has a post with some army department; the assistant *shamesh* [beadle] of our *beis medrash* found with a rifle over his shoulder—he's active in the militia; a reporter whom

---

[22] Nedava, *Trotsky and the Jews*, 154.      [23] *Dvesti let vmeste*, ii. 135.

I have known is a commissar for snow clearance; a shop assistant in a kosher butcher's is in some kind of commission—it's working, it seems, on the formulation of a constitution; my lodger, a first-year student in neuropsychology is employed in supply—of what I don't know exactly; my typist is running some kind of fort or prison.[24]

However, as against this, the available statistics (some long in the public domain, others of recent vintage) tend to underpin the opposite hypothesis that only in 1919 did Jews begin to flow into the institutions of the communist state in large numbers. A most important example is provided by the membership figures of the Bolshevik Party. Early in 1917 there were close to one thousand Jews in the party (less than 5 per cent of the total). During the course of that year, approximately double that number joined the organization, while a similar intake (2,712) was recorded for 1918. On the other hand, in the years 1919–20, at the height of the Civil War, Jewish membership rose by well over 11,000.[25]

Figures that have become available since the fall of the Soviet regime throw a similar light on the ethnic composition of the Cheka during the first year following the October Revolution. Thus, for instance, in September 1918, of 781 middle-ranking employees in the central apparatus of the organization in Moscow, only 29 (3.7 per cent) were Jews, while 278 were Latvians and 49 Poles.[26] Moving up the hierarchy, the percentage of Jews rises significantly, but hardly enough to confirm Leonard Schapiro's statement (approvingly quoted by Solzhenitsyn) that 'anyone who had the misfortune to fall into the hands of the Cheka stood a very good chance of finding himself confronted with and possibly shot by a Jewish investigator'.[27] Of 112 commissars and investigators in the Cheka headquarters, 11 were Jews, 52 Latvians, 35 Russians, and 14 Poles.[28]

That the situation may well have changed sharply, albeit not decisively, during the course of the Civil War is suggested by the fact that, of some 50,000 employees of the Cheka across the entire country in 1920, no fewer than 9.1 per cent were Jews as compared to the Latvians (3.5 per cent), the Ukrainians (3.1 per cent), and the Poles (1.7 per cent).[29] By then,

[24] Mikhail Beizer, *Evrei Leningrada, 1917–1939: Natsional′naya zhizn′ i sovetizatsiya* (Jerusalem, 1999), 77.

[25] Pinkus, *The Jews of the Soviet Union*, 77–9; cf. Budnitsky, *Rossiiskie evrei mezhdu krasnymi i belymi*, 107.

[26] Leonid Krichevsky, 'Evrei v apparate VChK-OGPU v 20-e gody', *Vestnik Evreiskogo universiteta v Moskve*, no. 18 (1995), 104–40: 115.

[27] Schapiro, 'The Role of the Jews in the Russian Revolutionary Movement', 165, quoted in *Dvesti let vmeste*, ii. 211.

[28] Krichevsky, 'Evrei v apparate VChK-OGPU', 116–17; cf. the statistics on the upper ranks of the Cheka in September 1918 to be found in Vadim Abramov, *Evrei v KGB: palachi i zhertvy* (Moscow, 2005), 24.　　　[29] Krichevsky, 'Evrei v apparate VChK-OGPU', 119–20.

though, the Russians made up the overwhelming majority: 77.3 per cent. (Unfortunately, there are no comparable statistics for the initial period of Bolshevik rule, and, pending further research, the question of how many Jews were to be found in the regional branches of the Cheka by the end of 1918 must remain open.)

In the light of the evidence currently available, then, the charge that Jews played a decisive role in assuring the Bolshevik victory in the years 1917–21 has to focus not on the rank and file and not on the middle-level administration but, rather, on the top leadership and elites. It is at this point that the 'non-Jewish Jews', long-time revolutionaries, committed Marxists, and, for the most part, dedicated internationalists—the 'schismatics' or 'renegades' (*otshchepentsy*) in Solzhenitsyn's terminology—become the focus of attention.

Given the extraordinarily narrow line separating victory from defeat during the revolution and the Civil War, it is possible that the role of Jews in the upper echelons of the party and of the post-October regime, although they were far from predominant, might have tipped the scales. In this respect, the number of Jews in the Central Committee of the Bolshevik Party was clearly significant, standing as it did at 6 out of 21 in the summer of 1917, 4 out of 14 in 1918, and 4 out of 19 in the following year.[30] At the famous meeting of the committee held in Nikolay Sukhanov's flat (albeit unbeknown to him) on 10/23 October 1917, which decided in favour of an armed uprising in the immediate future, six of the twelve members present were Jews. (The dramatic significance of this fact, though, is diminished once it is recalled that two out of the six, Kamenev and Zinoviev, the only two dissenters, voted against revolution at that stage.)[31]

In this context, no less importance should, perhaps, be assigned to the statistics relating to the upper levels of the governmental administration. Thus, the percentage of Jews in the executive committees of the ministries in Moscow (the *kollegii* of the People's Commissariats) stood at 21 per cent in April/May 1919 (24 officials out of 114).[32] And of the 25 communists in charge of the party and governmental administration in Petrograd and its environs in 1918, 10 were Jews.[33]

On the other hand, and strikingly—there was a fear of adding fuel to the antisemitic fire—only one of the 15 members of the central government, the Council of People's Commissars (Sovnarkom), appointed in the wake of the October Revolution, was a Jew: Trotsky, at that stage in charge of the People's Commissariat for Foreign Affairs.

In sum, if we resort to counterfactual speculation, it can be argued plausibly enough that without the participation of the veteran Jewish Marxists (the

[30] Pinkus, *The Jews of the Soviet Union*, 78–80.    [31] Solzhenitsyn, *Dvesti let vmeste*, ii. 77
[32] Budnitsky, *Rossiiskie evrei mezhdu krasnymi i belymi*, 103.
[33] Beizer, *Evrei Leningrada*, 78.

non-Jewish Jews) in the October Revolution and in the nascent Bolshevik regime, Lenin's attempt to seize and hold power would have gone down to defeat. But the same conclusion can be drawn even more convincingly with regard to the Latvians and perhaps the Poles. Solzhenitsyn's decision to concentrate attention almost exclusively on the Russian and the Jewish nationalities inevitably serves to obscure this truth.

Of course, with the Bolsheviks' consolidation of their rule and with Stalin's growing ascendancy, the disproportionate presence of the 'non-Jewish Jews' at the very pinnacle of power was much reduced. The defeat in 1925–6 of the 'united opposition', led by Trotsky, Zinoviev, and Kamenev, brought with it the downfall of many lesser figures in the party elite, long-time revolutionaries, very often Jews. Solzhenitsyn recognizes that this seismic tremor carried long-term significance, a first indication of trends that would eventually see the near-total exclusion of Jews from the upper and middle levels of the Soviet political, military, and diplomatic hierarchies. In any case, he writes, from the first, 'The regime was not Jewish, certainly not. It was international. And in its [national] composition, it was to a fair extent actually Russian [*russkaya*]. But for all the variegated nature of its make-up, it acted concertedly as anti-Russian [*antirusskaya*], seeking to destroy the Russian state and the Russian tradition.'[34]

The most reliable source of support for the regime, so it is suggested in *Dvesti let vmeste*, was to be found among the tens and hundreds of thousands of young Jews who so enthusiastically and unreservedly embraced the emergent system during the inter-war decades, or, as he put it:

The Jewish youth, in going over to Bolshevism, found itself thrilled by its new role and by its hold on life. No small number among them even dissociated themselves proudly from their own nationality. But this move to internationalism and unbridled atheism was not *assimilation* in the traditional sense. . . . They left, like all the youth, to create the new Soviet people [*sovetskii narod*].[35]

Solzhenitsyn here anticipates by a couple of years what Yuri Slezkine was to say in *The Jewish Century* about the inter-war generation of Jews dedicated to the construction of the Soviet state and society on radically reoriented foundations: 'No other ethnic group was as good at being Soviet and no other group was as keen on abandoning its language, rituals and traditional areas of settlement. . . . Commendably but also dangerously, the Jews seemed much more Soviet than the Soviet Union.'[36] In other words, in becoming superlative 'insiders' within the new system, they were also ipso facto turning themselves into potential 'outsiders'.

As sketched by Solzhenitsyn, much in the part played by the Jews during the frenetic years of the New Economic Policy (1921–7), the 'Great Turn'

---

[34] *Dvesti let vmeste*, ii. 211.    [35] Ibid. 261.    [36] *The Jewish Century*, 247.

(*velikii perelom*; 1928–33), and the purges (1936–8) was relatively harmless. Sergey Eisenstein doubtless produced brilliant films, but he was too much of a weathervane, shifting with every contrary wind emanating from Stalin's Kremlin. Likewise, Meyerhold was a truly gifted theatre director, but his genuine talent could hardly compensate for his schematic internationalism. Certainly, it was understandable that Jews should have been heavily represented in the field of trade, but could that justify the fact (considered to be a given by Solzhenitsyn) that the overwhelming majority of Soviet trade representatives abroad were Jewish, as were no fewer than 40 per cent of members of the central administration in charge of the People's Commissariat of Internal Trade in the mid-1930s—a ministry 'that actually controlled the entire domestic trade of the USSR (and did so in ways that were hardly disinterested)'?[37]

More significant for the author was the evidence that, during the period of the First Five Year Plan and the collectivization of agriculture, Gosplan— the body primarily responsible for economic planning and direction—was led by a presidium of which half the members were Jews.[38] However, it is when Solzhenitsyn's narrative arrives at the Stalinist penal system, the Gulag, and the security services (situated in the NKVD from 1934), that his stance becomes most openly accusatory.

Dwelling at some length on the ruthless brutality involved in the construction of the White Sea–Baltic Canal, an enterprise that in 1931–2 destroyed 'hundreds of thousands of Russian, Ukrainian and Central Asian peasants',[39] he notes that all eight of the top administrators awarded the Order of Lenin (the highest possible honour) for their part in the project were Jews. Among them was Naftali Frenkel, who is described by Solzhenitsyn as the official assigned overall responsibility for running the entire Gulag system and who is portrayed in *Dvesti let vmeste* in nothing less than satanic terms.[40]

With regard to the NKVD, Solzhenitsyn focuses particular attention on the Central Directorate for State Security (GUGB), a key unit involved in the implementation of the purges, asserting that, in 1936, of its ten most important divisions seven were headed by *chekisty* of Jewish origin.[41] With his characteristic penchant for detail, Solzhenitsyn reels off long lists of Jews appointed to run the NKVD branches across the length and breadth of the USSR. The case that he makes here is powerfully delivered, but it is also selective and impressionistic. Indeed, one of the few statistical facts relevant to the issue of the NKVD personnel to be found in *Dvesti let vmeste* serves, if anything, to subvert his case—the 1,776 Jews employed in the regiona

[37] Solzhenitsyn, *Dvesti let vmeste*, ii. 286.      [38] Ibid.      [39] Ibid. 334
[40] Ibid. 335–6. Solzhenitsyn here terms Frenkel 'the insatiable demon of the Gulag' (p. 335)
[41] Ibid. 292.

offices of the NKVD (excluding the GUGB) represented 7.4 per cent of the total, a disproportionate number, but still only a very small minority.[42]

Ironically, findings that have been published recently in Israel provide a degree of statistical support for Solzhenitsyn's thesis that is missing from *Dvesti let vmeste*. Thus, of the 95 members in the uppermost levels of the NKVD security staff in 1934, no fewer than 37 (nearly 39 per cent) were Jews, and in April 1938 the number was up to 39 (although down in percentage terms to just over 28 per cent). In that four-year period the number of Russians holding such leading positions had leapt from 30 to 75.[43]

Whether or not Jews in the state security organs, as in other key branches of the party and government, had served as an indispensable prop of the regime in the inter-war period—a highly debatable proposition, to say the least—by the 1940s the regime clearly no longer wanted them to play any such role. In 1941, following the ubiquitous purges, only 12 Jews remained in the top security staff of the NKVD out of a total of 187.[44] As already mentioned, throughout the late Stalinist period (that in this context can be dated to the first years of the Second World War), the Jewish presence in the political, military, and diplomatic spheres was being rapidly reduced to levels that were often no more than nominal. While much remains speculative in this context, such facts do cast doubt on the image so widespread in the Baltic states, for example, of the Soviet security forces in 1940–1 as largely, or even predominantly, manned by Jews.

There is nothing easier than to dismiss Solzhenitsyn's *Dvesti let vmeste* as intrinsically, even obsessively, hostile to the Russian Jews, or even to Jews in general. It is possible to accept his assurances to the contrary as sincere and heartfelt and nonetheless note that, throughout much of his book, he does actually sound like an antisemite. There is, after all, something that verges on the grotesque in the very decision to place only two nations in the dock of (tsarist and Soviet) history, subjecting them to relentless quasi-judicial scrutiny when the one people, the Russian (*russkii*), constituted over most periods approximately half the state's population—and the politically dominant nationality—while the other, the Jewish, never represented more than a few per cent. Plucked out of any multinational context, the role played by Jews in the Bolshevik bid for power of 1917–20, in the industrialization, collectivization, and dekulakization, in the forced labour projects, in the Gulag, and in the purges is inevitably placed under a glaringly powerful spotlight, leaving other nationalities—and even at times the Russians— almost entirely in shadow. The result can only be to burden the Jews with an inequitable share of the blame.

---

[42] Ibid. 293.
[43] Arkadii Zeltser, 'Jews in the Upper Ranks of the NKVD, 1934–1941', *Jews in Russia and Eastern Europe*, no. 1(52) (2004), 64–90: 71.     [44] Ibid. 74.

Nonetheless, however flawed *Dvesti let vmeste* is as a work of objective, balanced, and soundly researched history, it still remains of exceptional interest. To follow the author's line of thought is to become familiar with a set of beliefs and assumptions which, when taken together, are profoundly alien to those dominant in the world of Western historiography. Reviving and merging themes from the Slavophile, populist, and statist schools of pre-revolutionary Russian thought, the author still speaks with his own independent voice. There is a passion here that surprisingly manages to breathe life into a thousand-page text replete with innumerable, often dry, quotations. In sum, it is still possible to discern here, albeit through a glass darkly, that quality—a belief in his calling to find the truth, to describe it, and to publicize it—that enabled Aleksandr Solzhenitsyn to write works such as *The First Circle*, *Cancer Ward*, *One Day in the Life of Ivan Denisovich*, and *The Gulag Archipelago*.

The ideological assumptions that underpin *Dvesti let vmeste* can be summarized briefly. Solzhenitsyn was committed to the idea that nations and nationalism had proved themselves to be the predominant factor in shaping the twentieth century and that there was no reason to expect a change in the foreseeable future. Moreover, the ruthless experiment in internationalism imposed by the Bolshevik regime had only served, however paradoxically, to strengthen ethnic divisions, ethnic self-consciousness, and ethnic solidarity

His concept of nations and nationalism would place him, in terms of current scholarly debate, with the 'perennialists' (perhaps at times even with the 'primordialists') as against the 'modernists' who emphasize the radical discontinuities dividing historically rooted identities from the nationalism constructed or invented in the course of the last 200 years. In Solzhenitsyn's eyes, cultural and political traditions shaped over many centuries, or even over millennia, can and usually do exercise a profound impact on the consciousness of national collectivities and hence underpin modern nationalism.

At one point he suggests that what first brought him to this understanding was his realization as an inmate in the Gulag that his fellow prisoners naturally separated into disparate ethnic groups for self-protection: 'Every nation in the Gulag struggled to save itself as best it could. And actually none of them can be blamed for that.'[45] However, continues Solzhenitsyn, he could not but be struck by the fact that while the Jews in general came through the deadly experience comparatively well, thanks in large part to their readiness to lend each other support, the Russians (*russkie*) came out last 'as in the German *Kriegsgefangenenlager*'. He quotes inmates who said contemptuously of themselves: 'We Russians treat each other like wolves.'[46]

---

[45] *Dvesti let vmeste*, ii. 330.     [46] Ibid. 332.

To understand these two nations, 'bound together by fate' but so different in their behaviour, was—as Solzhenitsyn has it—a primary motive in his decision to devote so much time and energy to studying their common history. Potentially, their different qualities could have complemented each other: the Russians as a great state-building people so often ready to recruit talent from other nations; the Jews as potentially an enterprising, innovative and goal-oriented minority eager to be recruited. What, then, went wrong?[47]

The decision to focus attention exclusively on these two peoples cannot, however, be explained in such empirical terms alone. For Solzhenitsyn, the fact that both nations have defined themselves historically as chosen, and hence as especially close to God, must surely have constituted a primary factor in his choice of subject. And, although he does not dwell on the issue, he leaves the reader in little doubt that he, too, sees the hand of God at work in the history of the two (would-be) holy peoples. At one point he states specifically, for instance, that the extraordinary nature of the Jewish fate in the twentieth century (the Holocaust and the creation of the State of Israel) can be explained only in terms of some transcendent mystery 'above the merely human'.[48] In thus seeing the Russians and the Jews as destined potentially to play a unique and positive role in the sacred drama of human history, Solzhenitsyn echoes, among others, Dostoevsky, Vladimir Solovev, and Nikolay Berdyaev.

The sharply judgemental stance adopted by Solzhenitsyn follows logically from his belief that these nations, committed historically and theologically to the quest for holiness, carry a heavy burden of *noblesse oblige*. Whether consciously or not, he adopts the voice in *Dvesti let vmeste* of a biblical prophet holding God's chosen peoples to the highest standards, however unrealistic they might be under the given circumstances. How did it happen, he asks (here quoting a Jewish source from the 1920s), that 'the age-old

---

[47] For a perceptive discussion of Solzhenitsyn's decision to focus his attention on only two nationalities—the Russians and the Jews—see Abram Torpusman, 'Vmeste li? Po stranitsam pervoi chasti knigi A. I. Solzhenitsyna o evreyakh Rossii', *Vremya iskat´*, no. 5 (2001), 82–96, and cf. the thoughtful article of A. Eterman, 'Obernis´ v slezakh', *Vremya iskat´*, no. 6 (2002), 53–76. There was a widespread and extremely divided response to the first volume of *Dvesti let vmeste*, primarily in Russia. For an analysis of the controversy see John D. Klier, 'Sapper in a Minefield: Russians Read Solzhenitsyn's "Two Hundred Years Together"', *Jahrbuch des Simon-Dubnow-Instituts*, 2 (2003), 491–515. The book received less attention in the West, but see e.g. Yohanan Petrovsky-Shtern, 'On Solzhenitsyn's "Middle Path"', *Polin*, 18 (2005), 381–92, and John D. Klier, 'Solzhenitsyn and the Kishinev Pogrom: A Slander against Russia?', *East European Jewish Affairs*, 33/3 (2003), 49–60. For responses to the second volume of Solzhenitsyn's work see e.g. Yuri Tabak, 'Zweifelhafte Empfehlungen auf zweifelhaften Grundlage: Zu Alexander I. Solschenizyns Geschichte der Juden in Russland und der Sowjetunion', *Judaica: Beiträge zum verstehen des Judentums*, 60/3 (2004), 239–50, and Semen Reznik, *Vmeste ili vroz´? Zametki na polyakh knigi A. I. Solzhenitsyna* (Moscow, 2003), 392–24.

[48] *Dvesti let vmeste*, ii. 498.

traditions of this ancient [Jewish] culture proved to be powerless when challenged by . . . the barbaric slogans of the Bolsheviks?'[49] The Russian and Jewish nations, he insists, cannot slough off their responsibility for the many catastrophes produced in both the short and the long run by the Bolshevik revolution. Or, as he puts it:

Jews and Bolsheviks—on this theme too much ink has been spilt already. Whoever feels the need to prove that the revolution was not Russian [*russkii*] . . . points out the Jewish names and pseudonyms in order to clear the Russians of blame for . . . 1917. And as for the Jewish authors—some of whom have tended to deny the intense participation of Jews in the Bolshevik regime, while others do not—they are all unanimous in declaring that they were not Jews *in spirit*. They were *schismatics*.

And we agree with them. People should be judged by their spirit. And they were schismatics.

However, the leading Russian Bolsheviks were likewise not Russian in spirit, often they were actually anti-Russian and hostile to the Orthodox Russian faith. And in their time, Russian culture, which had been so broad, lost its shape, refracted as it now was through the lens of political doctrine and calculation.

Let us pose the question differently. How many random schismatics are needed in order to reach the conclusion that this was no random phenomenon? As for the Russian schismatics we know that there were depressingly, unforgivably, many within the Bolshevik ranks. And how wide-ranging and active was the part played by the Jewish schismatics in the reinforcement of the Bolshevik regime? . . . And we ask: can peoples disavow their schismatics? . . . Should not the peoples remember them, their own progeny? As for that question, there can be absolutely no doubt: *they must remember*. Every people that does not try to hide should remember their schismatics as their own.[50]

That this standpoint is highly debatable goes without saying. In addressing the issue (albeit in another setting and long before the publication of *Dvesti let vmeste*), Shmuel Ettinger firmly rejected the idea that the Bolsheviks of Jewish origin were to be seen as 'insiders'. During the course of a conference on Ukrainian–Jewish relations held in Canada in 1984, he objected fiercely to the decision of the steering committee to include as a topic for debate: 'the Jewish role in the Ukrainian famine [of 1933]'. 'I do not know', he said,

how many Jews were at that time in the GPU, or in other Soviet agencies. . . . [True, Jews] became in some sense overrepresented in the state apparatus after the Revolution. . . . But does that mean that it is the key to Jewish–Ukrainian or Jewish–Russian relations? If a Jewish political party or a Jewish intellectual group had said: 'We should kill all Ukrainians . . .' then I think there would have been a

[49] *Dvesti let vmeste*, ii. 102; quote from I. O. Levin, 'Evrei v revolyutsii', in Iosef M. Bikerman et al. (eds.), *Rossiya i evrei* (first published Berlin, 1923; Paris, 1978), 127.
[50] *Dvesti let vmeste*, ii. 75.

collective responsibility. But it was nothing of the kind. There were people in the state apparatus who . . . I personally don't consider Jews at all. What was Jewish in them? They were born to Jewish mothers and I not being a racist, do not see anything in it. They were not culturally or religiously Jewish. . . . Are we to say that if a Jew, an individual Jew is a criminal, does that mean that all Jews are responsible for his or her actions?[51]

These two theses advanced with such force and cogency by Solzhenitsyn and Ettinger, nationalists and humanists both, are on the face of it irreconcilable. Nonetheless, it can be argued that if the terms of the debate were to be defined with greater precision, their viewpoints would not necessarily stand in contradiction to each other.

I would suggest that it is of key importance in this context to differentiate sharply between the issue of 'guilt' and that of 'shame'. Taking up this theme in the immediate wake of the Second World War, Karl Jaspers concluded, in what has become recognized as an authoritative work on the subject, that the question of German guilt had four separate dimensions: the criminal, the political, the moral, and the metaphysical.[52]

With regard to the first category, he saw it as applying primarily to the outright criminals—the Nazi leaders and key functionaries—who had to be tried and punished, as befitted their monstrous policies and actions. Thus, the Nuremberg trials, however unpopular at the time with much of the public in Germany, were in Jaspers's view fully justified. But, so he reasoned, the German people as a whole, even though not to be confused with the criminals in its midst, could not escape its share in what he termed 'political' guilt, for 'everybody is co-responsible for the way he is governed', and the citizenry of a state has to suffer the consequences engendered by 'the deeds of the state whose powers govern me and under whose order I live'.[53] Jaspers anticipated the fact that Germany would therefore have to pay not only indemnities but also reparations for the crimes of the Nazi state.

In contrast, he described moral and metaphysical guilt as strictly the responsibility of the individual, duty bound to evaluate the particular role that he himself had played during the twelve years of Nazi rule. Here, Jaspers insisted, was the private domain of man's conscience in the face of the ultimate: a region in which 'jurisdiction rests with God alone'.[54]

It should be noted, however, that Jaspers understood all these four categories of guilt to involve only those Germans who had lived in the Hitlerite state. The payment of reparations might stretch into the distant future, but

[51] 'Comments', in Potichny and Aster (eds.), *Ukrainian–Jewish Relations in Historical Perspective*, 481.
[52] Karl Jaspers, *Die Schuldfrage* (first published Heidelberg, 1946; Munich, 1979); trans. into English by E. B. Ashton as *The Question of German Guilt* (New York, 1961).
[53] *The Question of German Guilt*, 31.          [54] Ibid. 32.

the post-war generations could not in any way be considered to share in the national guilt.

Following Jaspers's strict constructionist approach—and it is surely persuasive—it follows that the question of collective guilt simply cannot apply to crimes committed in the first half of the twentieth century. The generations responsible are either dead or close to death. In that sense, it is possible to go beyond Ettinger. Even if the OGPU and the NKVD in the 1930s had been peopled by Jews alone, whether labelled as 'insiders' or 'outsiders', the Jewish people today could not be held to share in their guilt.

However, the question of collective shame is another matter entirely. In so far as members of a nation or an ethnic group regard themselves as in some sense (whether cultural, genetic, or metaphysical) as members of a family-type collectivity, then nothing is more instinctive than for them to feel pride in its heroes and shame with respect to its criminals, be it of the everyday or the political variety. Jaspers, who did not feel comfortable when straying into such hazily defined categories of thought, still felt it necessary to write:

We feel something like a co-responsibility for the acts of members of our families. This co-responsibility cannot be objectivized. We should reject any type of tribal liability. And yet we . . . are inclined to feel concerned whenever wrong is done by someone in the family—and also inclined to make it up to them [the victims] even if we are not morally or legally accountable. . . . It is the concern of one who shares the life of the German spirit and soul—who is of one tongue, one stock, one fate with all the others—which here comes to cause, not as tangible guilt but somehow [as] analogous to co-responsibility.[55]

Solzhenitsyn writes along very similar lines: 'We are answerable just as members of one and the same family are answerable for each other. And if one were to deny this responsibility for one's co-nationals, then the very concept of a *nation* would lose all real meaning.'[56] (One is reminded of Edmund Burke's famous definition of society and state as 'a partnership not only between those who are living, but between those who are living, those who are dead, and those who are to be born'.[57])

In the sixty years since the Second World War, the idea that states should apologize for crimes committed by their nations or nationals in a past long since gone has become part of the political discourse, both internally and internationally. The list of examples is long, involving for example, the Turks and Armenians; the Japanese in confrontation with both Korea and China; the Australian majority and the Aboriginal population; the United

---

[55] *The Question of German Guilt*, 79.         [56] *Dvesti let vmeste*, ii. 120.
[57] Edmund Burke, *Reflections on the French Revolution and Other Essays* (first published 1790; London, 1955), 93.

States and the Native Americans; and the British seeking ways to atone for the slave trade.[58] And in eastern Europe there has been the remarkable example of a Polish president, Aleksander Kwaśniewski, taking part in a memorial meeting at Jedwabne to convey an apology on behalf of the Polish nation for the criminal actions of the villagers in 1941 (even though, acting as a collection of individuals and not as members of a political organization, they did not meet the criteria suggested by Shmuel Ettinger with regard to collective national responsibility).[59]

In the light of these developments, Solzhenitsyn's insistence that the Jewish people cannot simply shrug off the Trotskys, Uritskys, and Yagodas as 'non-Jewish', as outsiders, is certainly persuasive. If Jews take pride in Heinrich Heine, Felix Mendelssohn, Benjamin Disraeli, and Boris Pasternak, who were Jews by birth but were baptized into the Christian faith, can it be logical—as distinct from comfortable—to disown the 'non-Jewish Jews' who as Bolsheviks participated in destroying Russia's emergent democracy in 1917; in establishing a brutal (albeit 'proletarian') dictatorship; and in provoking a ferocious civil war across the length and breadth of that vast country?[60]

---

[58] For a highly perceptive discussion of the issue of national guilt see Ian Buruma, *The Wages of Guilt: Memories of War in Germany and Japan* (New York, 1995).

[59] Kwaśniewski said there, inter alia: 'It is impermissible to speak of collective guilt. . . . Every individual is accountable only for his own actions. Sons do not inherit the guilt of their fathers. But are we permitted to say: that was long ago, these were other people? A nation is a community. A community of individuals, a community of generations. And therefore we must look the truth in the eye. Every truth. Say it was thus, it happened. . . . We are here to perform a collective examination of conscience.' 'Address by President Kwaśniewski at the Ceremonies in Jedwabne Marking the Sixtieth Anniversary of the Jedwabne Tragedy on 10 July 2001', in Antony Polonsky and Joanna B. Michlic (eds.), *The Neighbors Respond: The Controversy over the Jedwabne Massacre in Poland* (Princeton, 2004), 131.

[60] This point was made by Daniil Pasmanik in the early 1920s when he wrote: 'Does the Jewish people [*evreistvo*] bear responsibility for Trotsky? Without a doubt, it does. As a rule, nationally minded Jews choose to include within the fold not only the Einsteins and Ehrlichs, but also Börne and Heine, who opted for baptism. In that case, though, they do not have the right to dissociate themselves from Trotsky and Zinoviev.' ('Chego zhe my dobivaemsya?', in Bikerman et al. (eds.), *Rossiya i evrei*, 212.) Pasmanik's reference is to Paul Ehrlich, a professor at the University of Göttingen, whose research in the field of medicine earned him a Nobel Prize in 1908. In recent books, Yuri Slezkine and Dan Diner both discuss Solzhenitsyn's application of the concept of national guilt to the Jews and Russians in relation to the crimes of the Stalinist era, and they argue that for various reasons this idea will never gain a hold on the collective consciousness of those nations. For example, 'Ultimately nations [in contrast to states] have no way of expiating their guilt. . . . Members of nations might feel ashamed, but nations cannot go to confession, do penance and eventually appear before their creator' (Slezkine, *The Jewish Century*, 185); cf. 'Hitler's crimes are perceived as atrocities committed by Germans *against others*. The Nazi period is considered an integral element of German history; as such it is indelibly engraved in collective memory . . . [But] the crimes . . . of the Communist regime can hardly be conceived as Russian crimes. . . . How can crimes eluding ethnic and hence long-term memory be kept collectively alive?' (Dan Diner, *Cataclysms: A History of the Twentieth Century from Europe's Edge* (Madison, Wis., 2007), 185–6.)

Moreover, it has to be asked how far removed, in reality, from their Jewish roots were those non-Jewish Jews who participated in making the October Revolution. In 1917 the adoption of the Russian language and immersion into Russian culture were relatively new phenomena within the Jewish sub-world that, after all, for the most part was confined to the western and southern (non-Russian) peripheries of the state. Even when children grew up with Russian as their mother tongue, the chances were that the grandparents remained Yiddish-speaking. Trotsky could declare himself to be neither a Russian nor a Jew but an internationalist; yet he came from a home not untypical of the Jewish farming colonies established in the provinces of Kherson and Ekaterinoslav in the first half of the nineteenth century.[61] The Bolsheviks of Jewish origin were rarely far removed from a background that encompassed the Yiddish language, some Jewish customs, and some Jewish ways of thought. Given this fact, it is legitimate to ask, as Solzhenitsyn and others have done, what made it possible for ancient traditions of (relative) quiescence and (relative) non-violence to be cast aside so savagely by so many Jewish communists.

Furthermore, even if the historian were to discount such arguments as of merely marginal significance when set against the evidence that the communist internationalists saw themselves as complete 'outsiders' vis-à-vis the Jewish collectivity and acted accordingly, one still cannot discount the fact that, in the eyes of the population at large, they remained Jews. Given the Judaeophobia that had deep roots within broad strata of society in eastern Europe, it was inevitable that the extent of Jewish participation in the communist leadership would be vastly exaggerated and take on truly demonic proportions in anti-Bolshevik eyes. *The Protocols of the Elders of Zion* dated back to the early years of the twentieth century, but it was only during the Civil War that the work became a handbook for the White armies, an ideological justification for the massive pogroms, and an international bestseller on an astonishing scale.

In sum, however much the non-Jewish Jews dissociated themselves from the Jewish people and however much the Jewish people (in its great majority) might prefer to disown them, the fact is that, in historical and sociological terms, no such exclusion can be justified. To that extent, Solzhenitsyn is right.

Towards the end of *Dvesti let vmeste*, Solzhenitsyn quotes with approval the view of Mikhail Kheifets (a historian who emigrated from the Soviet Union to Israel in the 1970s), who argues that the example set by the German nation in seeking constantly 'to cleanse itself . . . of its horrifying past . . . in the flame of national repentance' should become a model to be followed 'by those peoples that played their part in the crimes of

---

[61] See e.g. the chapter 'The Jewish Background', in Nedava, *Trotsky and the Jews*, 28–47.

Bolshevism'.[62] This idea of national confession and national repentance lies at the very core of Solzhenitsyn's book. But could that idea ever be translated from the realm of theory into that of reality?

Deep into the period of Vladimir Putin as the post-Soviet leader, the Russian state appears to be moving in precisely the opposite direction—towards an under-evaluation of the Stalinist crimes and towards a gradual rehabilitation of the Cheka as an institution that supposedly played an honourable role in a patriotic past. Attempts to keep alive the remembrance of the millions who died at the hands of the regime in the period 1928–53 are left to private and underfunded initiatives associated, for example, with the Memorial organization and groups within the Russian Orthodox Church.

It thus requires a huge leap of the imagination to envisage the day when a major monument is dedicated, in Red Square perhaps, to the innocent victims of the communist regime—and in attendance to express national shame (not national guilt) are, among others, the presidents of Russia, Ukraine, Latvia, Georgia, Korea, and Israel. Here is an image that belongs, or so it would seem today, to the realm of fantasy: unrealistic certainly, but not dishonourable.

[62] *Dvesti let vmeste*, ii. 470, quoted from Mikhail Kheifets, 'Russkii patriot Vladimir Osipov', *Kontinent*, no. 27 (1980), 209.

# ELEVEN

# THE JEWISH INFORMER AS EXTORTIONIST AND IDEALIST

## RUTH R. WISSE

AS PART OF THE GROWING INTEREST in Jewish political history, scholars recently turned the spotlight on the intercessor—the *shtadlan*—who mediates between the Jews and those in power. Lacking a national government and living in conditions of political dependency, the Jews of the diaspora were often in need of a Mordecai and Esther to intercede with the highest local authorities on their behalf. The success of these go-betweens, just as in the story of the ancient city of Shushan, depended on a combination of circumstance, talent, character, and luck. The *shtadlan* rushed in where angels feared to tread.

Yosef Kaplan's illuminating study of court Jews in the Muslim world from the ninth to the sixteenth centuries suggests that typical traits of such lobbyists might include the individualistic spirit that drove them, their claims to leadership or at least their wish to help determine the fate of their communities, and 'their fierce desire to prove that they could surmount the hostility of the surrounding world and approach the summit of power despite their Jewishness'.[1] Kaplan reminds us that Jewish society did not lack power-hungry individuals determined to exert their influence, presumably to the community's benefit.[2] Samuel Zygelboym, representative of the Jewish socialist Bund in the Polish government-in-exile, who in May 1943 tried suicide as a means of persuading the Allies to help the Jews, may be said to have marked both the acme and the nadir of that tradition of intercession in Europe.

In this essay I shall consider another kind of Jewish go-between who mediated between Jews and those in power: the informer, the *moser*, the *malshin*, the denunciator, who is the negative counterpart of the intercessor. No less ubiquitous than the *shtadlan* in Jewish affairs, he manifests some of the same qualities that Kaplan identifies, but utilizes them in working against,

---

[1] Yosef Kaplan, 'Court Jews before the Hofjuden', in Vivian B. Mann and Richard I. Cohen (eds.), *From Court Jews to the Rothschilds: Art, Patronage, and Power, 1600–1800* (Munich, 1996), 25.
[2] Ibid. 21.

rather than for, his community's interests. As a politically dependent minority, Jews were always hostage to their least scrupulous and least satisfied members, as when converts to Christianity testified against the Talmud in Spain or, in examples discussed below, when better-intentioned reformers incited the tsarist regime to legislate against their co-religionists. Regimes unfriendly to the Jews encouraged and rewarded betrayers, who therefore plied their trade under the authority's protection. Hostile conditions stimulated informing, from the time of the Romans to the time of the Nazis. The *malshin* was so prevalent in the period leading up to and during the Inquisition that he gave his name to the Spanish *malsin* and the Portuguese *malsim*.[3] The normal leniency of talmudic law hardened when it came to prescribing their punishment because of the damage they could do, and although Jewish courts in the diaspora did not generally retain their jurisdiction in criminal cases, in the case of informers the death penalty, at least in theory, remained in force.[4]

The tsarist regime was a classic breeding ground for informers, as dictatorial and increasingly paranoid rulers sought information about their minorities and the restive segments of their fast-growing population. The most obvious kind of Jewish informers were those who revealed various secrets in exchange for payment. According to David Assaf, 'They were thus responsible for undesirable government interference in the internal affairs of the Jewish community and endangered both the personal fortunes of individual Jews and the standing of the entire community.'[5] Assaf describes the fate of two such Jews who were put to death in the Ushits case of the late 1830s. Jewish leaders, with the apparent blessing of Rabbi Israel of Ruzhin, sanctioned the killing of these men in the same way that formal governments would have punished acts of treason. The disclosure of the secret executions because of yet another informer's report to the Russian government suggests that by this time Jewish authority was being undermined even as it struggled to protect itself and its constituency.

To be sure, renegades were not the only type of Jewish informer. Ordinary disputes could land up in non-Jewish courts, and denunciation was a tempting form of vengeance. If we took maskilic literature at face value, we might imagine that denunciation to the non-Jewish authorities was the most common form of getting rid of a rebellious member of the community—or of an undesirable suitor: in Sholem Aleichem's otherwise forgettable maiden work of fiction 'Tsvey shteyner' (Two Stones), an irate employer betrays to the tsarist

[3] J.K. [Jacob Klatzkin], 'Informers', *Encyclopaedia Judaica*, vol. viii (Jerusalem, 1971), 1366.

[4] For a summary and discussion of such legislation, see 'Laws of Informers', in Emanuel Quint (ed.), *A Restatement of Rabbinic Civil Law*, vol. x (Jerusalem, 2004), 65–77.

[5] David Assaf, *The Regal Way: The Life and Times of Rabbi Israel of Ruzhin*, trans. David Louvish (Stanford, Calif., 2002), 106.

recruiting board the teacher he had hired for his daughter as a means of breaking up their romantic attachment.[6] And carved deep in the consciousness of
Russian Jewry was the demoralizing historical episode of the professional kid-
nappers or *khapers*, who betrayed poorer Jewish children to the authorities in
order to fill the local conscription quotas for Tsar Nicholas I.

My interest for the moment, however, is not in such private vendettas,
cases of 'frontier justice', or cruel injustice to innocent children, but rather
in acts of 'informing' against the Jewish community as such. While ratting
may be common to all societies, it was an inherent feature of Jewish politics
in ways that sets it apart from the politics of other nations. Moreover, Jews
knew it. The polity that lived on sufferance in other people's lands realized
that it was uniquely susceptible to betrayal by disaffected individuals.
Leaving the rest of the subject for another occasion, I will be considering
only the type of informer who put Jewish communities at risk.

I want to explore some of what east European Jewish culture had to say
about the phenomenon of the informer, stressing the widespread awareness,
acknowledgement, and acceptance of his or her presence. Along with the
rabbi, the *rebbetsin*, the *shohet* (ritual slaughterer) and the *melamed* (*heder*
teacher), there was the Jewish *moser*. 'Since Tomaszow had its *lamedvovnik*
(saintly Jew), it also had to have its *moser*', says Peretz's narrator in his travels
through the region.[7] Yiddish offers as many varieties of the *moser* as French
does of wine: the *rodef*, *oysgeber*, *farkloger*, *tsutroger*, *shantazhist*, *msirnik*,
*bilbulnik*, *farloymter*, *pashkvilant*, *ya'bednik*, *farreter*, *sipak*, *greptser*, and
*donoshtshik*, to name only some.[8] The *moser* appears as a separate category
in the Jewish joke collections of Yehoshua Hana Rawnitzki and Alter
Droyanov, where he is coupled with the *mumar* or convert to Christianity—
who may also turn out to be an informer.

## THE INFORMER AS PRAGMATIST OR EXTORTIONIST

In Yiddish and Hebrew joke books, which are intended for cultural insiders
rather than for a non-Jewish audience, informers and converts appear as
relatively benign categories, undifferentiated as to the damage they may
inflict. Jokes about Jews who quit the community or inform against it tend to
downplay the significance of the defection, as in the famous anecdote about
the Semitic scholar Daniel Chwolson, who, when asked whether he had

---

[6] In *Forgotten Pages* [Fargesene bletlekh], ed. Y. Mitlman and Kh. Nadel (Kiev, 1939), 11–36.
[7] See Isaac Leib Peretz, 'Der moser', in *Collected Works* [Ale verk], 11 vols. in 8 (New York,
1947), ii. 188, trans. Milton Himmelfarb as 'The Informer', in 'Impressions of a Journey
through the Tomaszow Region', *The I. L. Peretz Reader*, ed. Ruth R. Wisse (New York, 1990).
[8] Nahum Stutchkoff, *Thesaurus of the Yiddish Language* [Der oytser fun der yidisher shprakh],
ed. Max Weinreich (New York, 1991), 682. See also the entry on *moser* in Yitskhok Niborski,
*Dictionary of Words of Hebrew and Aramaic Origin in Yiddish* [Verterbukh fun loshn-koydesh
shtamike verter in yidish] (Paris, 1999), 177.

converted to Russian Orthodoxy out of conviction, replied: 'Of course: the conviction that it is better to be a professor in the Academy in St Petersburg than a *ḥeder* teacher in Aisheshok.' The witticism reassures the community that his conversion was merely a ploy to circumvent tsarist restrictions rather than an expression of dissatisfaction with Judaism. Along the same lines is the anecdote about four converts who get drunk together:

The first confesses: 'I converted only because I wanted money, the good life.'

The second says: 'I became a philosophical sceptic. Once everything was equally meaningless, why should I suffer on account of my religion?'

The third divulges that he converted because of a woman.

The fourth says: 'I'm not like the rest of you. I converted out of faith.'

At this, the others laugh: 'Habibi, go tell it to the *goyim!*'[9]

According to this joke, the only *improbable* reason for converting to Christianity is the one that grants it moral and intellectual legitimacy.

This kind of joking diminishes the advantages that Christianity otherwise enjoys. When it was reported to the Lubavitcher Rebbe Menahem Mendel Schneersohn that a certain Jew had converted, he shook his head, and said, 'A *Jew* doesn't convert.'[10] When Rabbi Levi Isaac of Berdichev was told that a Jew of 70 had converted, he sighed and said, 'Lord of the Universe, look down from the heavens and see the great strength of your servant; for seventy years this man remained a Jew!'[11] Each anecdote admits how susceptible Jews have become to the enticements of the surrounding majority yet restores national-religious confidence by boasting how hard it is to bear the yoke of being Jewish.

A second, more complicated, category of joke mocks not the treachery, but the Jewish community that sustains it:

The informer in a certain town had been doing its Jews incalculable damage with his reports to the authorities. One day, he is discovered in a situation that, if it were known to the authorities, could be very damaging to *him*. So the rabbi and community leaders call the squealer in and, very pleased with finally having gained the upper hand, demand that he stop his denunciations or else they will report him to the police. The informer stands there grinning at the elders. Unnerved, they ask him why he is laughing. The *moser* replies serenely, 'I know that none of you is going to want to become an informer.'[12]

Concentrated on the act of informing, our attention is suddenly diverted by the punchline praising Jewish *morality*, demonstrating Freud's theory of displacement whereby the psychical emphasis is diverted to a topic other

---

[9] [Alter] Droyanov, *Book of Wit and Humour* [Sefer habediḥah vehaḥidud], 2nd edn., 3 vols. (Tel Aviv, 1939), ii. 181–2; my translation.      [10] Ibid. 161.      [11] Ibid.

[12] Yehoshua Hana Rawnitzki, *Jewish Humour* [Yidishe vitsn], 2nd edn. (Jerusalem, 1923), 57; my translation.

than the opening one.[13] The compliment to Jewish morality might have been comforting if the person 'praising' the Jews were not intending to exploit them. The community elders assume that if only they can employ their antagonist's weapons, they can prevent the evil he does them. But weapons are useless unless one is prepared to use them. The blackmailer's advantage is not his information but his readiness to use it for his own gain. The Jews of this joke are at risk not only from the government in power, and not even from their would-be betrayers, but also from the moral inhibitions that prevent effective self-defence.[14]

Sholem Aleichem topped off this line of joking in his 1909 story 'Stantsye baranovitsh' (Baranovich Station), situated in the overcrowded third-class carriage of a Russian train. After its Jewish passengers have recited the morning prayers, they eagerly take up such topics as the recent harvest, the war with Japan, the revolution (of 1905), and the Constitution: 'and from the Constitution it was but a short step to the pogroms, the massacres of Jews, the new anti-semitic legislation, the expulsion from the villages, the mass flight to America, and all the other trials and tribulations that you hear about these fine days: bankruptcies, expropriations, military emergencies, executions, starvation, cholera, Purishkevitch, Azeff. . . !'[15] And there the conversation settles. All are abuzz with Azeff, the Jew who has just been outed as an agent of the Russian secret police and is also suspected of being a double agent for the revolutionaries. Although Azeff's tale-bearing was not directed against the Jews, he epitomized both sides of the Jewish nightmare—the accusation that Jews were hostile to the government and that they were untrustworthy by definition.

Yevno Azeff, born Fishelevich to a Jewish family from Grodno, Lithuania, had fled to Germany in 1892 when he faced arrest for alleged revolutionary activities. There he had become a member of the Socialist Revolutionary Party's innermost 'combat group', and in that capacity he had planned the execution of tsarist officials, including Vyacheslav von Plehve, Russia's minister of the interior. At the same time, he supplied information to the

---

[13] Sigmund Freud, *Jokes and their Relation to the Unconscious*, trans. and ed. James Strachey (New York, 1960), 58.

[14] This same aspect of the problem surfaces in I. L. Peretz's depiction of the 'moser' Benish, who is more sinned against than sinner. He has inadvertently told a wealthy relative that he knows the whereabouts of her son who is being hidden from the draft. Benish's wife then discovers that she can use this threat to squeeze the relatives for money. She becomes a successful blackmailer, to her husband's horror, driving him to insanity and death. The principled informer is Peretz's final piece of evidence that far from being exploiters—the Polish charge against Jews that initiated Benish's investigation—his co-religionists are trapped between their self-punishing culture and the punishing outside world. Peretz presents the *moser* as a function of what he elsewhere calls 'the dead town'. See 'Impressions of a Journey through the Tomaszow Region', in *The I. L. Peretz Reader*, 71–5.

[15] Sholem Aleichem, 'Baranovich Station', in *Tevye the Dairyman and the Railroad Stories*, trans. Hillel Halkin (New York, 1987), 152.

Okhrana, the special secret section of the Russian police, leading to the arrest and execution of many fellow radicals. So successful was Azeff in his double role that even after he had been exposed some of his comrades insisted that he had been a sincere terrorist at least part of the time (after all, some of the assassinations he planned had come off successfully), and the tsarist government did not want to advertise the case because it was embarrassed about having failed to stop some of the assassinations, about which it had been warned.

Azeff's notoriety places the story within the context of political unrest. However, because Sholem Aleichem's interest is in Jewish, not Russian, politics, a raconteur in the coach quickly draws the conversation inward with a homespun story about a certain Kivke, and an incident that had occurred in his town of Kaminke during the days of Tsar Nicholas I. For insulting Christianity, this Kivke was sentenced to the crippling punishment of running the gauntlet. The Jews of Kaminke determine to perform the *mitsvah* of *pidyon shevuyim*, the redemption of captives, by bribing the appropriate prison officials. The storyteller's grandfather, one of the town notables, arranges to have Kivke pronounced dead and smuggled out of the prison in a coffin and across the border to Brody. But shortly after Kaminke Jews celebrate their triumph along with the minor officials whom they have bribed, letters begin to arrive from Brody appealing for and then demanding financial rescue. Kivke complains that it would have been better to flog him and get it over with, 'because his wounds would have healed long ago and he wouldn't have been left penniless among Germans with nothing to do but watch his own belly swelling from hunger'.[16] In response to the polite requests for aid, the Kaminke Jews turn out their pockets, but, as Kivke's pleas evolve into blackmail, they grow angry, in an escalating cycle of capitulation and threats. Finally, the grandfather refuses to send more money, Kivke threatens to send the police his correspondence, but, as the story approaches its climax, the conductor calls out the storyteller's destination—*Baranovich!*—and the Jewish listeners are powerless to prevent the storyteller's departure from the train. There are now two betrayers—Kivke the extortionist, and the raconteur who robs his audience of their ending. The listeners' anxieties explode in rage at the Jew who promised to distract them from their anxieties.

Skipping over other angles in this comic tale,[17] we see Sholem Aleichem poking fun at Jews for their *well-meaning* intentions. Tightly squeezed as

---

[16] Ibid. 158.

[17] For narrative strategies see Jonathan Boyarin, 'Sholem Aleichem's "Stantsye Baranovitsh"', in Mark H. Gelber (ed.), *Identity and Ethos: A Festschrift for Sol Liptzin on the Occasion of his 85th Birthday* (New York, 1986), 89–99. Sholem Aleichem's warning not to trust the modern storyteller includes a private in-joke related to the fact that he had suffered a near-fatal collapse in Baranovich while on a speaking tour of Russia. The story can thus be read as a small act of revenge on the city and as a comic reflection on his own mortality that questions what might have happened to Yiddish literature had the author 'got off' at this station.

they are, the Jews on the train press even closer together to make room for the storyteller from Kaminke, just as the politically squeezed Jews in the inner story commit their money and risk their lives to rescue a fellow-Jew. Precisely because they respond to outside pressure with intensified solidarity—*kol yisra'el arevim zeh lazeh* ('all Jews are responsible for one another')— Jews are subject to exploitation by such as Kivke and the storyteller. The cohesion of Jews, which is supposed to be—and often is—their saving grace, leaves them politically vulnerable to those who know how to exploit this virtue.

The Jewish blackmailer had plenty of opportunity in a political system that was hostile to his co-religionists; yet, according to these examples of Jewish humour, the informer as extortionist—someone who defects or betrays for personal gain—does not threaten the Jews' moral security. By the end of the nineteenth century, challenges from Christianity and Christian rulers were an old story, and tsarism, too, was falling on hard times. Jokes are by definition an insider sport that unites in laughter a group that might otherwise be moving apart. All the examples I have cited so far take the edge off the anxieties that they create.

### THE MASKILIC INFORMER

Very different was the attitude towards the fourth Jew in the joke quoted above, who converts out of true conviction—the type who quits or betrays his community *leshem shamayim*—for an allegedly higher purpose. As opposed to the extortionist, this kind of informer professed 'positive' goals and selfless motives. Nineteenth-century maskilim, or enlighteners dedicated to Jewish reform, assumed that they would have to persuade the government to coerce Jews into making the changes traditionalists would otherwise resist. The more idealistic the reformers, the more justified they felt in appealing to the powers that be. Thus Joseph Perl, one of the early masters of Haskalah literature, submitted a memorandum to the authorities in the above-mentioned Ushits case, drawing attention to the personal involvement of Rabbi Israel of Ruzhin in trying to prevent the authorities from discovering the truth. Perl and other radical reformers regarded Jewish abuses much as the Russian revolutionaries did the tsar—considering that nothing short of 'radical' activity, that is, doing away with the system from the roots, would bring about the necessary improvement. The constituted community treated their tale-bearing as an act of treason. Idealistic individuals, who viewed the world in terms of how it could be changed for the better, expected their squealing to be judged according to what it sought to achieve.

In the hands of certain reformers, literature itself became a means of informing to the authorities against the Jewish community. In 1869 Sholem

Yankev Abramovitsh, already known by the pen-name Mendele Moykher Seforim, exposed the corrupt Jewish establishment of Glupsk, recognizably modelled on the city of Berdichev, in his five-act play *Di takse* (The Tax). The play, described by Dan Miron as 'one of the most radical, shrill, and effective exposés of social injustice within the Jewish community to be found in Yiddish literature',[18] shows the 'town benefactors' scheming to get rich at the expense of the poor by raising the tax on meat and otherwise trying to eliminate competition in goods and ideas that would challenge their pitiless rule. Connivers Shinder (Skinner) and Piavkin (Leech) join forces with community leaders to exploit the credulity of the Jewish poor and incite authorities against reformers such as the hero Veker (Waker) and his good friend Pikholts (Woodpecker). When Veker asks why the town doesn't rebel against its exploiters, Pikholts replies that, in the first place, Jews have grown accustomed to suffering, and in the second, whenever they do try to expose the community leaders for misappropriating funds and outright thieving, they are accused of informing: 'a whole town of thousands of ordinary Jews and craftsman is accused of betrayal'.[19]

In a footnote to the work, the fictional editor Mendele Moykher Seforim acknowledges that some Jews refrain from informing against the wicked members of their community 'because they know that the nations of the world [di umes ho'oylem] blame the whole of Israel for its part and attribute the sins of the individual to all the Jews. That is why they are prepared to suffer in silence rather than to complain lest they unintentionally commit a sin [ḥilul hashem—blasphemy]'.[20] Since Abramovitsh was the creator of both the play and of the fictional Mendele-editor, this footnote conveys his ambivalence: he voices Jewish scruples against informing even as he justifies the enlightener who does it.

Here Abramovitsh himself was the culprit in question. He had written the play during a period of Russian reforms, concluding the final act with an impassioned appeal to the downtrodden Jews to put their faith in the Russian government rather than in their Jewish leaders. 'The government is good and kind', Veker assures them; 'it has freed over twenty million peasants, it seeks everyone's well-being . . . and wants to improve our lot. It looks for ways of feeding us Jews, improving our health, and helping us to become worthy human beings.'[21] As confirmation of his own faith in the government, Abramovitsh dedicated the play to his excellency, the governor of Odessa province and mayor of the city, Nikolay Vasilevich Novoselsky, as a

---

[18] Dan Miron, *A Traveler Disguised: The Rise of Modern Yiddish Fiction in the Nineteenth Century* (New York, 1973), 141. Miron was echoing A. Rosentsvayg, *Mendele mokher seforim 1836–1936* (New York, 1936), 16.

[19] Mendele Moykher Sforim, *Di takse*, Act I, scene iii, in *Collected Works* [Ale verk] (Warsaw, 1928), 25–6.     [20] Ibid. 26.     [21] Ibid. 92.

'token of the author's deep esteem and devotion'. He had heard the governor telling a Jewish delegation that they themselves would have to combat the abuses of the meat tax, and these words 'deeply touched the hearts of my co-religionists, who know how to value those who care about the improvement of their condition'.[22] The play asks the Russian authorities to clean up Jewish corruption, and, as if to prove that his reproach hit home, Abramovitsh, like Veker his hero, was rumoured to have left the city under pressure from the town notables whom he had satirized.[23]

However, shortly after writing the play, Abramovitsh underwent one of those conversions that figure so prominently at the crossroads of literature and politics.[24] As the political climate in Russia turned more oppressive, he realized that, in appealing to Russian officials, he had invited the proverbial fox to police the henhouse. The apologia that he wrote for *Di takse*—his allegorical novel *Di kliatshe* (The Mare), or *Susati* in its later Hebrew version—depicts a well-intentioned intellectual who learns humility in the course of trying to improve the condition of his fellow-Jews.[25] The book sympathizes with the predicament of the genuine reformer who wants to bring his people the benefits of enlightenment, but it also widens the lens to reveal the entire political landscape within which he functions. First, the young man comes across the *kliatshe*, the mare, an allegorized, wonderfully intelligent representation of the Jewish people, who reminds him that human rights must be granted and cannot be earned; the right to equal treatment as a human being cannot be made conditional on performance. 'The dance cannot precede the food.' Then he is taken on a 'demonic flight' across Russia and Europe so that he can witness what the Jewish reformer cannot otherwise see, namely, the workings of anti-Jewish politics at the highest levels. In the maskilic

[22] See I. Nusinov, 'From One Book to Another' (Yiddish), *Tsaytshrift*, 2–3 (Minsk, 1928), 431. The dedication in Russian was eliminated from all but the first edition of the play.

[23] This, at any rate, was the rumour in Berdichev as reported to Leo Wiener at the end of the century. See his *History of Yiddish Literature in the Nineteenth Century*, 2nd edn. (New York, 1972), 156.

[24] Applying the later formulation of Irving Kristol, one might say that the liberal Abramovitsh was mugged by reality. Anti-Jewish pogroms in Odessa in 1871 encountered no effective police response. Even assuming that the government to whom he had entrusted the Jews' fate had not colluded in the attacks, it did nothing to quell them. Had he been able to see the whole picture he would have known that the Russian government, which imposed and pocketed the tax on meat, skimmed millions of roubles into its coffers instead of using the money for its assigned purpose to provide services for the Jewish communities. Y.S. [Yehuda Slutsky], 'Korobka', *Encyclopaedia Judaica*, vol. x (Jerusalem, 1971), 1211–12.

[25] I have treated this subject in greater detail in *The Jewish Intellectual and the Jews: The Case of Di Kliatshe by Mendele Mocher Sforim*, Daniel E. Koshland Memorial Lecture of Congregation Emanuel-El (San Francisco, 1992). Shmuel Werses discusses the publication history of the work in 'Demonological Motifs in *Susati*' (Heb.), in *From Mendele to Hazaz: Studies in the Development of the Hebrew Short Story* [Mimendele ad hazaz: sugyot behitpatehut hasiporet ha'ivrit] (Jerusalem, 1987), 70–86.

satire *Di takse*, Abramovitsh showed the Jewish establishment 'riding the Jewish mare'. *Di kliatshe*, its corrective sequel, subsumes those admitted abuses by Jewish authorities under the much greater menace of a hostile Europe. The enlightener is gravely mistaken who thinks the Jews need only clean up their internal corruption to regain their full human potential. Political powers dictate the difference between reformer and betrayer: the well-intentioned Jewish idealist who exposes his fellow-Jews to a hostile regime serves the same ends as the *khaper* who sells Jewish children into tsarist military service.

As it happens, during the last quarter of the nineteenth century maskilic 'informing' went into remission for much the same reasons that Abramovitsh reconsidered his trust in princes. The sharp rise in anti-Jewish politics and anti-Jewish popular sentiment made it harder for reformers who cared about Jewishness as well as Jews to believe that the regime had Jewish welfare in mind. The best of the modern Jewish literary renaissance in both Yiddish and Hebrew developed from the contradictory realizations that, while Jews had to change with the times, they had as much to fear from progressive as from reactionary impulses and from their own reformers as from the tsar. After their initial expectations of the Haskalah, many maskilim realized that they could not ignore the damage that could result from informing to hostile powers. Writers used the themes of madness and suicide to express the conflict that could not otherwise be resolved between their vying impulses of protest and protectiveness.

## THE COMMUNIST INFORMER

No such crisis of self-doubt, however, beset the minority of Jews who embraced the ideals of revolutionary socialism and, after 1917, of communism. At the very time that the Haskalah was re-examining its premises, the revolutionary movement in Russia was focused on overthrowing and replacing the rotten government that oppressed the Jews. Jews who cast their lot with the revolutionary cause were not placing their trust in existing rulers but in a system they expected to help perfect as it came to power. True believers in applied Marxism resembled the early Christians in claiming to be *better* Jews or better *than* Jews by transposing the merely parochial and limited ethical teachings of Judaism into a universal and practical system. 'On the anniversary of our liberation', wrote the Jewish revolutionary Aaron Lieberman in 1875, 'our children will lay flower wreaths on the graves of the heroes who fell in the struggle, water them with tears of gratitude, and commemorate those who are presently hounded and incarcerated for their love of the people.'[26]

---

[26] *Letters of Aaron Lieberman* [Aron liebermans brief], introd. Kalman Marmor (New York, 1951), 37. The original letter was in Hebrew.

The obvious sincerity of those prepared to martyr themselves for their cause added to their moral stature in their own and other Jews' estimation. They could also claim the authority of rational science over that of religion. Marx and Engels argued that because the contradictions of bourgeois society were reaching a crisis it would soon collapse under its own weight, and then a class identified with a mode of production in which those contradictions could be overcome—namely, the proletariat—would take over the political reins. Though we are describing the type rather than its often subtler human exemplars, the Jewish radicals who unmasked the Jewish bourgeoisie considered themselves the driving force of History—which had replaced God as the secular Eternal.

Once Bolshevism came to power in Russia, this ideology gained the authority of the state. Despite Bolshevism's temporary concession to national constituencies as a means of winning broader support from Russia's ethnic minorities, communist doctrine required the dissolution of the Jewish people in particular as a prerequisite for achieving its ends. Jews, who had long ago forfeited their land and whose religion had lately been discredited by Marxism, were expected to serve as the vanguard of the International. Jewish language and culture could be employed as a temporary vehicle for the dissemination of the communist message, but manifestations of Jewish nationalism were considered reactionary by definition. Moreover, since Jews were the most conspicuous merchants, entrepreneurs, and middlemen, they appeared to personify the capitalist menace, and they had to be economically squelched in order to allow a communist economy to emerge. Hence a Bolshevik informer against his fellow-Jews could feel triply justified—by the assurance of historical determinism that he was serving truth, by his moral claim to be pioneering an ideal society, and by the powers granted him by the state.

The communist informer is portrayed in contemporary Jewish literature as a *successful* challenger to Judaism and the Jews. Whether treated positively or negatively, he helps demolish the community from which he emerged. One such positive treatment is Dovid Bergelson's novel *Midas hadin* (The Letter of the Law), written between 1924 and 1927: like Abramovitsh's *Di kliatshe*, it is a work of atonement but moving in the opposite direction, from a world-weary Jewish humanism towards the embrace of communist discipline.[27] The Jewish legal system had generated concepts of *midat hadin* and *midat harahamim*, broadly comparable to severity and leniency in sentencing. The severity invoked by Bergelson's title refers to the requisite imposition of Bolshevik rule on Golikhovke, a largely Jewish town. Bergelson extols the enforced Bolshevik makeover of a Jewish border town several years after the October Revolution. The local administrator Filipov suffers

---

[27] *In shpan* (In Harness) is the name Bergelson gave to the magazine he founded in 1926 in which he set out his rationale for choosing the Soviet Union over Palestine, Europe, or America.

from a serious illness contracted when he worked in the mines; yet he ignores his pain in order to govern the region with the firm hand that the moment requires. *Midas hadin* in this context is the admirable ability to overcome compassion for the sake of progress.

As far as I know, the corpus of modern Yiddish and Hebrew literature contains no positive portrayal of a hard-liner on issues of *Jewish* law to parallel Bergelson's positive use of the term and concept *midat hadin* in reference to communism. The *mahmir*, the strict interpreter of the law, is generally subordinated in modern Jewish culture to the liberal *mekel*, in the way that the imposing rabbi of Brisk defers to the tenderhearted Biale Rebbe in I. L. Peretz's story *Tsvishn tsvey berg* (Between Two Mountains). Even Chaim Grade's post-war portrayals of Lithuanian yeshivas, which try to rehabilitate the traditional religious world of his youth, favour the humanitarian over the judgemental approach, the liberal over the conservative. To be sure, as great writers often appear to have inadvertently joined the Devil's party, the harsh, condemnatory Tsemah Atlas is far more artistically compelling than the sweeter Hazon Ish in their epic clash in Grade's *The Yeshiva*. But neither Grade nor Bergelson leaves the reader in any doubt of his narrative sympathies in the scheme of his novel. Grade exposes the tortured ruin Tsemah Atlas makes of his life. Bergelson exalts Filipov for silencing his humanitarian scruples for the sake of the better society he is determined to build.

The informer is given a cameo but crucial role in *Midas hadin*. Pinke, a young and enthusiastic convert to the Reds, has ridden into Golikhovke to gather information about local smuggling and about a rumoured attack from the still active socialist revolutionary opposition. He knocks at random on a door that is opened by a young Jewish girl with a clever little nose, which surprises Pinke, who has never before seen a cute girl endowed with intelligence. Once the girl realizes that the soldier is a fellow-Jew, she switches from the Russian of her original greeting into a homier Yiddish and reveals how all the Jews of the town profit from those illegally crossing the nearby border:

'Boy, do they ever lick a bone from these services . . . do you understand what I mean? This is Sodom. . . . From what I've already seen in the three weeks I've been here, I'll have enough to tell my children's children. What more do you want? Even my boss the tailor spends more time arranging transport for these "weddings" [smuggling sorties] than he does sewing clothes. There's a certain Yochelson, one of the early communists, they say, who is the go-between for all these deals. And there's a blonde lady, a Christian, who serves as his mistress. Well, don't you think that the man deserves a little pleasure? And there's a road right near the villages Harne and Khutor Belo-kut. For enough money they'll get you across there even in daylight . . .'[28]

---

[28] Dovid Bergelson, *Midas hadin*, in *Collected Works* [Geklibene verk], 9 vols. (Vilna, 1929), ii. 146; my translation.

This clever Jewish girl would put to shame the Soviet boy-hero Comrade Pavlik, or Pavel Morozov, who informed against his parents to the Soviet state. Pinke conveys the girl's information to Filipov, who duly arrests all the miscreants and executes the worst of them. The Jewish idealists who inform against Golikhovke are instrumental in saving the day for Bolshevism in the region.

The previously ironic Bergelson, whose early fiction never introduced a character he did not slightly mock, here idealizes Pinke and his informant. The girl's savoury Yiddish conveys her trustworthy character, and her clever little nose sniffs out the ostensible corruption. She and Pinke enjoy the only genuine romance in the book, as opposed to its other liaisons, which are mutually exploitative or merely dutiful. Only in the book's closing pages do we learn the dear girl's name—Basye—uttered with sacral wonderment as Pinke takes her hand for the first time. Until then she has been for him the selfless, anonymous communist: the two heroic informers wait to secure Golikhovke for the Reds before expressing their love for one another. At the end, they gather up red flags to encircle the commander Filipov, who has been killed in battle.

Bergelson was not alone in depicting the communist informer as a woman—a gender choice that heightens the character's appeal or menace, depending on the point of view. The stereotypical female communist is like Rosa Luxemburg, ideologically indifferent to the Jews and their 'particular Jewish sorrows'. Because Jewish women of the pre-modern age were presumed to be family nurturers, the absence of such inclinations draws attention to itself in fictional females, whether the female revolutionary gives herself over completely to her cause (in positive portrayals), or, like Lady Macbeth, is ruthlessly 'unsexed'.

The same type of character whom Bergelson praises is deplored by his Hebrew contemporary Hayim Hazaz in his *Pirkei mahapekhah* (Revolutionary Chapters; 1924) and the larger novel *Daltot neḥoshet* (Gates of Bronze) that grew from that novella. According to Hazaz's anonymous narrator, Henya Horowitz 'had an infernal spirit, [she was] a rotten pest, not a maiden, an angel of destruction!'[29] During the chaotic struggle among the various Jewish and anti-Jewish, democratic and anti-democratic forces, she evolves into a pitiless Bolshevik commissar. It is Henya's signature that seals the doom of the hasidic Jew who refuses to join the Bolsheviks, and it is she who informs on her father for concealing textile merchandise under the floorboards of his home.

The female informer also figures in my final example, Moyshe Kulbak's novel, *Zelmenyaner* (1929–35), one of the comic masterworks of modern

[29] Hayim Hazaz, 'Revolutionary Chapters', trans. Jeffrey M. Green, in David G. Roskie (ed.), *The Literature of Destruction: Jewish Responses to Catastrophe* (Philadelphia, 1989), 299.

Jewish fiction. *Zelmenyaner* describes three generations of a Jewish family in a city modelled on Minsk that is undergoing the enforced process of sovietization—voluntarily or otherwise. Kulbak uses the progeny of Reb Zelmele—the Zelmenyaner who inhabit the *rebzehoyf*, the courtyard of Reb Zelmele—as a microcosm of Russian Jewry, situating 'himself', the implied author, among the youngest generation either as or alongside Tsalke the poet and family chronicler. Tsalke is vainly in love with his cousin Tonke, the family's most committed communist. Some of the book's inter-generational conflict is common to the genre of the family saga, and some of it parodies the imposed innovations of Soviet rule.

Kulbak wrote this novel after having crossed the closed border from Poland into the Soviet Union in 1927, either to join his extended family, or out of ideological preference, or a combination of motives that remain tanta-lizingly unclear. His immediate artistic profit from the move was this rollick-ing fiction, the first volume of which shows hardly a trace of inhibition in spoofing both sides of the cultural struggle. Deaf granny persists in asking her Young Pioneer grandson whether he has said his morning prayers, and a second grandson defies the family by naming his uncircumcised son Marat. Technological and ideological innovations such as the advent of electricity or the ideal of intermarriage are satirized in one episode after another, as is the Yiddish poet Tsalke, who makes a speciality of unsuccessfully trying to commit suicide. But, keeping pace with sovietization, the mood of the novel steadily spirals into a grim and grizzlier mode. The pressure of conformism that was being exerted on the author becomes manifest by the end, when the hapless Tsalke finally succeeds in hanging himself.

At the book's conclusion, the informer takes centre-stage. The Zelmenyaner sit tightly squeezed together, just like the Jews in Sholem Aleichem's third-class railway car, gathered this time to witness the trial of Folye, one of four Zelmenyaner uncles, a tanner employed in a leather factory, who has tried to sell on the black market the hide of a horse he skinned. He is on trial before 700 workers. Among them, the Zelmenyaner occupying the front rows feel that they, not Folye, are the defendants, but as they listen nervously to the proceedings, their shame switches sides.

Tonke, the fiercest ideologue among the Zelmenyaner, eagerly takes the stand for the prosecution. 'Unbelievable that one's own blood could carry such hatred for the family. She spoke Russian, so they didn't understand everything, but the words they didn't understand also hit their mark.'[30] Hers are the typical anti-Jewish accusations against a population that is bourgeois in its instincts and reactionary in its orientation. She says the family tried to hush up Folye's theft because all of them function as small-time thieves. One

---

[30] Moyshe Kulbak, *Zelmenyaner* (Moscow, 1971), 245; my translations.

woman in the family owns a single silver spoon that is enough to make her feel superior to the proletariat.

'Di zelmenyaner klaybn fun doyres a shtrikele tsu a shtrikele un af dem boyen zey di velt'—generations of Zelmenyaner have constructed their world from bits of string—a bit of pride, a bit of mendacity, a bit of theft, a bit of bribery. They never owned the banks or large estates, so instead they collected slop pails and copper pans. They live off the leavings of others: remnants of religion, superstition, naive and twisted versions of various fields of knowledge. There are even those who try to cobble together from these bits and pieces a culture of the *rebzehoyf*.

The character in the novel who has been 'cobbling together' this new culture of Soviet Jewry is none other than the author's stand-in, Tonke's lovesick cousin, Tsalke the poet. Exemplar of the false Jewish national consciousness, Tsalke has been a running joke for most of the novel, making many suicide attempts out of unrequited love for this woman whose passion is reserved for her political ideal. Far from softening Tonke's contempt for him, his successful suicide makes her despise him all the more. According to her, this native of the place studied the habits of the Zelmenyaner for so long 'that their spiritual decrepitude finally made him hang himself'. Through this merciless denunciation, Kulbak registers communism's scorn for the author and its posthumous verdict on his work.

As opposed to Bergelson's treatment of denunciation, this book represents it as perfidy, pure and simple. When they exit from the hall, the Zelmenyaner give Tonke the cold shoulder: 'Antisemitke, avek fun unzer orntlekher mishpokhe' ('Antisemite, stay away from our decent family'). Moreover, the high-ranking Soviet official who is present at the trial shows his solidarity with the family rather than with their accuser, appreciating that they are decent, if only ordinary, people. (In this way, Kulbak limits his censure to the *Jewish* commissars, insulating the Soviet state from his condemnation.) In repudiating the informer's attack on the Jews, the book remains loyal to its Yiddish roots, but it cannot deny Tonke her political victory. In the final pages of the book, the *rebzehoyf* is being torn down to make way for a Soviet-style urban development. The Jewish informer merely feeds the appetite of a system that would have crushed her Jewish family with or without her help.

Knowing that both writers met a similar fate, readers may argue over which is the more heart-wrenching—Bergelson's endorsement of Soviet repression or Kulbak's awareness of the trap being set for him. Kulbak was one of the first of the Yiddish writers to be sentenced and to die in the Gulag. Bergelson was spared until 12 August 1952, when he faced the firing squad with his co-defendants of the Jewish Anti-Fascist Committee. Both writers were themselves denounced by informers within a system that no longer distinguished between extortionists and idealists, encouraging the former as a species of the latter. Yet Kulbak managed a victory from beyond the grave, for the Zelmenyaners' repudiation of Tonke is his way of passing judgement on the treason that did him in. Over time, the artistic fate of fiction differs from that of its authors, who have no recourse when they are condemned to death. Bergelson outlived Kulbak by many years by following the party line, but not without damage to his later work and posthumous reputation. The life that Kulbak forfeited for writing this comic novel remained—for whatever it's worth—free of compromising stain.

Clearly, Jewish culture had much to say about informers, who came into their own under communism with greater self-confidence than they had ever before enjoyed. In trying to achieve hegemonic rule, the Soviet Union institutionalized betrayal as the Inquisition had done, but whereas the Catholic Inquisition was overtly anti-Jewish, the Soviet Union professed to be working for the interests of Jews against their would-be persecutors. Despite their different treatments of the phenomenon, Bergelson, Hazaz, and Kulbak all show how self-assuredly the Jewish informer turned in those whom he (or, in all these cases, she) considered in the wrong. Informing in the Soviet context was obviously not specific to the Jews, yet the *moser* also had a function in Jewish politics that adapted neatly to the Soviet system. As compared with those who sought personal gain—those whom I have labelled extortionists—the idealists were certain of their 'selfless' aims. The extortionist exposes only as much as it profits him to uncover, while the idealist exposes as much as possible in order to inflict the greatest damage.

## POSTSCRIPT

I am mindful of several risks in treating this subject. In the course of preparing this essay, I punched into Google the keywords 'Jewish informer' and was instantly rewarded with information about Mordechai Zalkin's research on the Jewish underworld in Poland as it had been reported in the Israeli daily *Haaretz*. This material was featured on the website of David Irving, the Holocaust denier, who writes that he makes no apologies for reproducing this article. 'Once again', he writes, '*Haaretz* excels itself in its objectivity and evenhandedness: it is a credit to journalism. Imagine the outcry if a non-Jewish historian had produced this piece of reporting.'[31] (I leave it to the editors to confront the implications of praise and gratitude from this source.) Irving conscripts both Zalkin and *Haaretz* to vilify critics who dispute his hateful claims. Descriptions of the Jewish underworld obviously satisfy Irving's idea about the Jews' corrupting effects on civilization, and so he gleefully disseminates them among like-minded readers. Given the way

[31] <www.the7thfire.com/politics_and_society/new_world_order/zionism/world_of_the_ewish_Mafia.html>. The website reproduces the article in question: Kobi Ben Simhon, World of the Jewish Mafia'.

negative revelations about the Jews are increasingly exploited by their opponents, one knows that any discussion of Jewish misconduct may likewise be twisted into anti-Jewish defamation. Scholars—and newspapers—are obliged to pursue truth but also to refute the hateful uses to which such studies are put.

This essay runs a different kind of risk in having the *moshl* (*mashal*; fable) mistaken for the *nimshal* (the moral lesson it conveys). My subject is not communist informers as such, though I deplore the paucity of serious study about their lingering influence on Jewish politics. I focus on them here as part of an extended enquiry into Jewish political behaviour, which I consider not only different from but, in crucial ways, opposite to the norms of other nations.[32] There have been many warnings against the corruptions of power, fewer about the corruptions of powerlessness, to which Jews are more susceptible. Protracted political dependency created among Jews the need for intercessors between them and those in power; some of them worked heroically for the benefit of the community, and others sought advantage through defection in greater proportion than was usual among other peoples, or even among other minorities. This situation has not changed with the creation of Israel, which is not only besieged by enemies but also subjected to the kind of delegitimization that Christianity and Marxism, in their time, applied to Judaism and the Jewish people. The contemporary pressure against Israel on many fronts encourages Jewish defection and 'tale-bearing', which will probably rise in proportion to the vehemence of the attacks.

Israel's democratic system exacerbates the problem because democracy requires vigorous debate among parties, each of which seeks power through its ability to 'expose' the flaws of the other side. Absent enemies at the gate, such debate is seldom a liability. A democratic polity may even get to the point of civil war without endangering its unity. The United States is a prime example of a democracy that, paradoxically, grew stronger as a result of the civil war that was waged over the South. The situation is different when enemies exploit divisions for their own hostile ends, by conscripting allies from within the polity to help destroy its democratic unity. The Jews and Israel have never been without enemies at the gate, enemies many times their political and demographic strength. The latitude enjoyed by Israelis in blaming their government and one another is subject to exploitation for anti-Jewish ends.

Though it always was and still remains painful to identify as informing the kind of behaviour that I have called idealistic, political action is judged by its effects rather than by its declared intentions. While every new political situation presents a new set of co-ordinates, I hope that examples from the past may help to form present judgements. East European Jews joked about their informers. They ought also to be studied seriously.

---

[32] See Ruth R. Wisse, *Jews and Power* (New York, 2007).

# PART IV

## TWO CITIES AND TALES OF BELONGING

# TWELVE

# A JEWISH EL DORADO?
## Myth and Politics in Habsburg Czernowitz

### DAVID RECHTER

A VENERABLE READING of the course of post-Enlightenment European Jewish history proceeds along the related axes of emancipation, acculturation, and antisemitism, following a loosely demarcated East/West divide that separates pre-modern from modern, unemancipated from emancipated, unassimilated from assimilated. As modernity made ever greater claims, national, religious, and cultural diversity loosened the bonds of a once relatively stable and homogenous Jewish society. The instability of Jewish status and identity in post-Enlightenment Europe, as perceived by Jews or others, was proverbial, a cause and consequence of the extended and convoluted process of Jewish acculturation: the Jews' often successful efforts to become insiders, part of the natural flora and fauna of their local society, alongside the many and varied rebuffs they experienced. The persistence of the 'Jewish question', the problem of the Jews' place in modern European society, testifies to the more than residual outsider status that stubbornly adhered to them. The give and take of a century and a half of this unfinished project of integration rendered Jews at one and the same time insiders and outsiders in many European societies, making them an archetypal European minority—everywhere a minority, nowhere a majority.

To move from the domain of generalities to a particular instance, we can turn to the Jews of Czernowitz (and Bukovina). The myth of a Jewish El Dorado in this far eastern corner of Habsburg Austria is a case study in modern Jewish success and failure. More the former than the latter, and it is only stating the obvious to observe that local experience is embedded in any number of extra-local contexts. The history of the Jews of Czernowitz is partly Bukovinian, partly Galician, partly imperial Austrian, partly Romanian, partly Ukrainian, and partly Soviet. And for eastern and central Europe such an example is quite typical. The case of Czernowitz (and this is even more true of Bukovina as a whole) is of particular import in terms of the east/west divide. Resorting again to broad generalization, west European Jews were ostensibly insiders, at least in their own eyes, and to some extent to society at large, arguably the exact opposite of the situation in most parts of eastern Europe.

In Czernowitz and Bukovina, however, these geopolitical and conceptual boundaries were blurred, demonstrating the difficulties of Jewish definition. In revealing both sides of the coin, this is an example that makes clear that there is no 'European Jewry' but rather many European Jewries, and that the pan-European dimension of the history of the Jewish minority grows out of the multitude of local circumstances. Even if we take diversity as a given, we can nonetheless find threads that connect the experience of Jews across political and cultural borders: in, for example, the drive towards integration into the surrounding society and the encounter with antisemitism. Or, in other words, in their experience as insiders and outsiders, which should perhaps be conceived not so much as a dualism but as the shifting poles of a continuum that helped to define and shape European Jews and their history.

*

Czernowitz does not lack for commentary and literature. Quite the contrary. The city, its people, and its culture have been the subject of countless descriptions. Most often they have been examined from the vantage point of literary criticism and cultural studies, but there are also numerous historical, imaginative, and nostalgic accounts. Casting a large shadow over all of these interpretations is the tragic version of the city's post-Habsburg decline and fall, from the inter-war Romanian years through the Second World War and the Soviet era (when Czernowitz becomes first Cernăuţi and then Chernovtsy). Running like a thread through virtually all depictions of the city is, in one form or another, the Czernowitz myth, part of a larger Bukovina myth of considerable longevity, wherein both the city and the region stand as exemplars of national and inter-ethnic co-operation, political moderation, and cultural efflorescence. On the one hand, this is a function of nostalgia for the supposedly better and more peaceful times prior to the First World War; on the other, it is a perspective favoured in particular by writers and historians who find nationalism to be disturbingly aggressive and predatory. Accordingly, they are intent on finding here an instance of nationalism reined in for the sake of a greater good—harmony between otherwise combatant nationalities.

Here was 'tolerance and the coexistence of diverse cultures', a veritable 'Babylon on the river Pruth', a region infused with what Otto von Habsburg (son of the last Habsburg emperor) called 'a synthesis of national consciousness with a higher . . . European outlook'. In a similar vein, writer Gregor von Rezzori imagined Czernowitz as 'the melting pot for dozens of ethnic groups, languages, creeds, temperaments, and customs'.[1] In this stylized

---

[1] Gregor von Rezzori, *The Snows of Yesteryear* (London, 1990), 277; see also ibid. 275–90. For the other quotations, see Ihor Czechowskyj, 'Das "Czernowitzer Schiff": Unter dem Segel der Toleranz in ein vereintes Europa', in Cécile Gordon and Helmut Kusdat (eds.), *An der Zeiten Ränder: Czernowitz und die Bukowina* (Vienna, 2002), 363, 375.

vision of Czernowitz, the Jewish element is indispensable as both the principal beneficiary of this outbreak of harmony and tolerance and as crucial to the creation of the reigning ethos and cultural elan of the city. If the idea of a German–Jewish symbiosis has fallen into disrepute elsewhere, this is one field in which it is alive and well, with Paul Celan its most eminent son.[2]

Just as the Jews played a significant role for Czernowitz, it is equally true that Czernowitz played a notable role for the Jews. The Jewish version of this myth lauds the Habsburg state for its protective and even-handed approach towards the Jews that shielded them from the excesses of antisemitism and the belligerent nationalism that grew apace among many of the empire's peoples in the second half of the nineteenth century. That the Jews were the Austrian *Staatsvolk* par excellence has been much commented upon, and this is as true of the Jews in Czernowitz as it is of those in Vienna, Prague, or the towns and cities of Galicia. As far as the myth is concerned, the distorting mirror of the often unhappy post-Habsburg era is at work for émigrés and historians alike, merging nostalgia with a touch of tunnel vision. Czernowitz was an 'Austrian Jerusalem', a Jewish success story made possible by 150 years of 'relative peace and quiet' under Habsburg rule; both the city and the province as a whole had been a 'paradise' for Jews.[3] The First World War, according to one recent account, 'put an end to the unbroken tranquility and prosperity that characterized the second half of Austrian rule in Bukovina'. Another, emphasizing that Czernowitz and Bukovina were 'different' from neighbouring regions, called the local Jews the 'most fortunate Jews in Eastern and East Central Europe'.[4] It

[2] On this myth see Harald Heppner, 'Eine Stadt wird ein Begriff: Czernowitz', in id. (ed.), *Czernowitz: Die Geschichte einer ungewöhnlichen Stadt* (Cologne, 2000), 167–78, esp. 177. For examples of this approach see Emanuel Turczynski, *Geschichte der Bukowina in der Neuzeit* (Wiesbaden, 1993); Robert A. Kann, *The Multinational Empire: Nationalism and National Reform in the Habsburg Monarchy, 1848–1918*, 2 vols. (New York, 1977), i. 330–2; Fred Stambrook, 'National and Other Identities in Bukovina in Late Austrian Times', *Austrian History Yearbook*, 35 (2004), 185–203; Wilhelm Kosch, 'Juden und Deutsche in der Bukowina', *Neue Jüdische Monatshefte*, 1/6 (1916), 143–52: 143; Richard Wenedikter, 'Die Karpathenländer', in Karl Gottfried Hugelmann (ed.), *Das Nationalitätenrecht des alten Österreich* (Vienna, 1934), 724–37.

[3] See Markus Krämer, *Die Stimme* (Dec. 1949), 3–5; Arieh Zahavi-Goldhammer, 'Tshernovits', in Judah Leib Maimon (ed.), *Great Jewish Cities* [Arim ve'imahot beyisra'el] (Jerusalem, 1950), 89–90; Avraham Kavish, *Stations* [Taḥanot] (Tel Aviv, 1960), 11, 43.

[4] For the first quotation, see David Sha'ari, 'The Jewish Community of Czernowitz under Habsburg and Romanian Rule', *Shvut*, 6/22 (1997), 178. For the second, see Fred Stambrook, *The Golden Age of the Jews of Bukovina, 1880–1914*, Working Paper 03–2, Center for Austrian Studies at the University of Minnesota (Minneapolis, 2003), 14. This approach has a long pedigree. The Austrian folklorist Ludwig Adolf Simiginowicz-Staufe described Bukovina as a second Canaan' in his *Die Völkergruppen der Bukowina: Ethnographische Culturhistorische Skizzen* (Czernowitz, 1884), 183. See also Yosef Kisman, 'The Jewish Social Democratic Movement in Galicia and Bukovina' (Yiddish), in G. Aronson et al. (eds.), *The History of the Bund* [Di geshikhte fun bund], vol. iii (New York, 1966), esp. 447–9. More generally, see the impressionistic account by Hermann Sternberg, 'Zur Geschichte der Juden in Czernowitz', in Hugo Gold (ed.), *Geschichte der Juden in der Bukowina*, 2 vols. (Tel Aviv, 1958, 1962), ii. 27–47.

should be noted that this perception of Czernowitz and Bukovina as sites of unusual national or ethnic significance was not unique to Jewish memory and historiography but was shared—*mutatis mutandis*—by Romanians, Ukrainians, Germans, and Poles, the other major population groups.[5]

As is true of most historical myths, this idealized reading of Czernowitz and Bukovina involves much wishful thinking. Nonetheless, a dispassionate observer can still recognize a core of historical truth in this vision of virtuous harmony. The historian Raphael Mahler referred, rather more neutrally than those cited above, to the 'marked individual characteristics which made [Bukovinian Jewry] conspicuous amongst the other Jewish communities of Eastern Europe during the nineteenth and twentieth centuries',[6] a quality noted also by contemporaries. In 1907, for example, a Zionist correspondent commented that Jews enjoyed such a degree of independence and political respect in Bukovina that the province was sometimes called 'Palestine'. Formally represented at all levels of public administration and governance, the Jews were a 'decisive factor' in local politics.[7] Jewish 'influence' was 'dominant in all spheres of public life', observed a prominent Czernowitz journalist; this was, he proclaimed, the 'El-Dorado of diaspora Jewry', a sentiment echoed—using precisely the same phrase—by the writer and folklorist S. An-ski.[8] 'Peaceful coexistence and tranquil development' were the norm in 'this much-celebrated paradise of the Jews',[9] and 'in no other large city in Austria, in Europe, or even across the Atlantic, do the Jews enjoy anything like the same social, economic, and political status'.[10]

While there is no doubt a great deal of hyperbole in these descriptions, and while parallels can be found in other places and times, the image they convey was not entirely a fiction. Needless to say, there was also a darker

---

[5] See the articles in Heppner (ed.), *Czernowitz*, esp. Ștefan Purici, 'Die Geschichte der Bukowina' (pp. 179–82). More generally, see also Emil Biedrzycki, *Historia Polaków na Bukowinie* (Warsaw, 1973); Ion I. Nistor, *Der nationale Kampf in der Bukowina: Mit besonderer berücksichtigung der Rumänen und Ruthenen* (Bucharest, 1918); Ivan M. Nowosiwsky, *Bukovinian Ukrainians* (New York, 1970); and Franz Lang (ed.), *Buchenland: Hundertfünfzig Jahre Deutschtum in der Bukowina* (Munich, 1961).

[6] Raphael Mahler, *A History of Modern Jewry 1780–1815* (London, 1971), 340.

[7] *Jüdische Zeitung*, 8 Nov. 1907, p. 2.

[8] *Die Welt*, 11 Oct. 1901, p. 5; S[olomon] An-ski [Shloyme Zanvl Rappoport], *Collected Writings* [Gezamlte shriftn], 15 vols. (New York, 1921), vi. 115.

[9] *Jüdische Zeitung*, 18 Dec. 1908, p. 4; 8 Jan. 1909, p. 2.

[10] *Die Welt*, 11 Oct. 1901, p. 5. See also *Jüdisches Volksblatt*, 24 Oct. 1902, p. 3: 'Bukovina has often been called the Jewish El Dorado, and rightly so'; Salomon Kassner, *Die Juden in der Bukowina* (Vienna, 1917), 46, who notes that the phrases 'Jerusalem am Pruth' and 'Jewish El Dorado' were also part of the antisemitic lexicon. In a memorandum of 1909 to the minister of the interior, a Jewish nationalist organization claimed that it was in large part due to the moderating role played by Jews in the nationalities conflict that the various groups in 'idyllic' Bukovina lived in serene and enduring peace with one another. See *Jüdische Zeitung*, 8 Oct. 1909, p. 3.

side, especially towards the end of the nineteenth century, when the area experienced an array of ills typical of most of the Habsburg lands—widespread poverty and unemployment, economic stagnation, national conflicts, and a rising tide of antisemitism of various stripes: Christian Social, German nationalist, and a combination of religious, national, and economic resentments from Romanians and Ukrainians. All this notwithstanding, the Jewish popular imagination perceived and experienced it as a place that offered Jews an unusual, if not unique, sense of security and comfort.

A significant contributory factor to the myth of Czernowitz and Bukovina is that it has proved difficult to define either city with any degree of precision or consensus. Any number of geographical and cultural markers have been proposed for this northern Moldavian territory ceded by the Ottoman empire to Austria in 1774/5.[11] It has been described, for example, as the 'northern border zone of south-eastern Europe',[12] or, and this is a description that neatly incorporates both the city and its hinterland, a 'Black Forest village, a Podolian ghetto, a small Viennese suburb, part deepest Russia and part modern America'.[13] One of the best-known nineteenth-century chroniclers of life in this area, Karl Emil Franzos, rather notoriously conceived of the surrounding area as 'semi-Asiatic', but he described Bukovina as a 'flourishing little piece of Europe' and as akin to Switzerland in its tolerant atmosphere of 'peace and harmony' between peoples.[14] This latter image was subsequently echoed and expanded by many others over the next century— the region as a miniature Austria, the city of Czernowitz as its correspondingly miniature Vienna. Finally, Czernowitz has been seen as exemplifying the kind of urban milieu found at the eastern edge of the Carpathian mountains, a conduit for transmitting all manner of ideas, goods, and people between central and eastern Europe, eastern and south-eastern Europe, and even between Europe and Asia.[15]

[11] At the time, much of it was occupied by Russian troops following the Turkish–Russian war of 1768–74. The Austrians took partial possession in August 1774, but a formal treaty was not signed until May 1775. See Hamish M. Scott, *The Emergence of the Eastern Powers, 1756–1775* (Cambridge, 2001), 242–8; Michael Hochedlinger, *Austria's Wars of Emergence: War, State and Society in the Habsburg Monarchy, 1683–1797* (London, 2003), 356–8.

[12] Trude Maurer, 'National oder Supranational? Prag und Czernowitz: Zwei deutsche Universitäten in Ostmitteleuropa (1875/1882–1914)', *Zeitschrift für Ostmitteleuropa-Forschung*, 49/3 (2000), 341–82: 343 n. 14.

[13] Erich Beck, *Bukowina: Land zwischen Orient und Okzident* (Freilassing, 1963), 22, cited in Klaus Werner, 'Czernowitz: Zur deutschen Lyrik der Bukowina im 20. Jahrhundert', in Andrei Corbea and Michael Astner (eds.), *Kulturlandschaft Bukowina: Studien zur deutschsprachigen Literatur des Buchenlandes nach 1918* (Iaşi, 1990), 46. This would appear to be a condensed paraphrase of the depictions in Karl Emil Franzos, *Aus Halb-Asien: Culturbilder aus Galizien, Südrussland, der Bukowina und Rumänien*, 2 vols. (Leipzig, 1876), i. 160–4.

[14] Franzos, *Aus Halb-Asien*, i. 113, 185–6. See also ibid. 158–65 on Czernowitz.

[15] For the Carpathian perspective, see Harald Heppner, 'Czernowitz im städtegeschichtlichen Vergleich', in id. (ed.), *Czernowitz*, 1–9, esp. 1–2. On Bukovina as the Austrian Switzerland and a

These endeavours to reach all points of the compass are reflected, once more, in Jewish perspectives. The Jews of the province, commented Philipp Menczel, a notable journalist and writer, in 1901, were an almost indefinable mixture of Galician, Polish, Romanian, and Russian Jewries, with a thin veneer of German Jewry. And all this in a city that he described as part-European, semi-Asiatic, and partly Transcaucasian![16] Living in this border-land enclave between east and west, Jews here were neither east nor west European, wrote a Czernowitz Jewish activist and publicist, but were in fact 'sui generis'.[17] Such difficulties of definition emerge from the intimate coexistence of different types of Jewish society, the long-standing convenient labels for which are 'east' and 'west' European Jewries. If there is a central European counterpart to east and west, or perhaps a central European amalgam of the two, then Habsburg Jewry in general has a claim to be just this, while in the Habsburg context Bukovina has a strong claim to be regarded as Habsburg Jewry writ small.[18]

In less abstract terms, Jewish society here was characterized by an uncommonly intense relationship between east and west, a familiarity born of proximity: small physical distances mitigated the effects of vast cultural differences. Emblematic of this proximity, the hasidic kingdom of Sadagora (the Jewish Vatican, as it has been called[19]) was to all intents and purposes a suburb of Czernowitz. To use Ezra Mendelsohn's terms: the blend of, on the one hand, a modernizing east European Jewry rooted in traditional Jewish society with, on the other, a highly acculturated west European Jewry, in a multinational context with no dominant nationality led to the development of what was described by one Czernowitz Jewish insider as 'a singular type of Austrian Jewry'.[20] The qualifier 'Austrian' is crucial. Czernowitz and Bukovina Jewry can properly be understood only when viewed against the background of Austrian Jewry.

These somewhat grand claims and perceptions can be supported by some impressive demographic facts: Bukovina had the highest proportion of Jewish population of any Austrian Crownland—almost 13 per cent, numbering a little over 100,000 just prior to the First World War. At the same time,

miniature Austria and for Czernowitz as a miniature Vienna, see also Gerald Stourzh, 'Der nationale Ausgleich in der Bukowina 1909/10', in Ilona Slawinski and Joseph P. Strelka (eds.), *Die Bukowina: Vergangenheit und Gegenwart* (Bern, 1995), 42; Kassner, *Die Juden in der Bukowina*, 11 n. 7, 49, 57–8.

[16] *Die Welt*, 11 Oct. 1901, p. 5.                    [17] Kassner, *Die Juden in der Bukowina*, 45
[18] For the models of east and west European Jewries, see Ezra Mendelsohn, *The Jews of East Central Europe between the World Wars* (Bloomington, Ind., 1983), 6–7. See also Nathanie Katzburg, 'Central European Jewry Between East and West', in Yehuda Don and Victo Karady (eds.), *A Social and Economic History of Central European Jewry* (New Brunswick, NJ 1990), 33–46.
[19] Mordechai Rubinstein [Ben-Saar] (ed.), *Die jüdische Vatikan in Sadagora 1850–1950*, vols. (Tel Aviv, 1954–8).                    [20] Kassner, *Die Juden in der Bukowina*, 4

Czernowitz had the highest proportion of Jewish population of any of the larger Austrian cities, with its nearly 30,000 Jews making up approximately 33 per cent of the city's residents; this made it the fourth-largest Jewish city in Austria, after Vienna, Lemberg (Lviv), and Kraków. This was not, though, merely a matter of numbers; Jews were indispensable to the city in numerous ways. Their role, whether in the professional and commercial classes, the structures of political power, civic society, or the cultural sphere, was undeniably critical to the emergence and development of Czernowitz as an urban success story in the second half of the nineteenth century.[21]

Part of what allowed the Jews to play such an important role was the fact that Czernowitz as a city of any consequence was of very recent provenance. In effect, both the city and its Jews were starting from scratch and their development took place in tandem. Prior to the Austrian takeover in 1774/5, Czernowitz amounted to little more than a few hundred modest wooden houses. Although a handful of Jews had established a presence there by the early eighteenth century, engaged for the most part in trade, the Jewish population began to grow consistently only in the Austrian period and increased by leaps and bounds in the latter half of the nineteenth century, as is true of the city's population in general.[22] Notwithstanding this rapid growth, Czernowitz was long regarded as a provincial outpost, a pale reflection of the splendour of Vienna and a remote outlier of German culture. In 1808 the area was described in the Austrian press as 'terra incognita', while the popular German author Johann Georg Kohl wrote in the early 1840s that Czernowitz was merely a 'suburb' of the imperial capital. Even in 1845, Bukovina (probably unfairly by this point) was referred to as an Austrian Siberia.[23]

Such perceptions are not surprising, given its recent origins. Czernowitz as a metropolis was a product of the region's economic expansion in the late

[21] For relevant statistics, see Albert Lichtblau and Michael John, 'Jewries in Galicia and Bukovina, in Lemberg and Czernowitz: Two Divergent Examples of Jewish Communities in the Far East of the Austro-Hungarian Monarchy', in Sander L. Gilman and Milton Shain (eds.), *Jewries at the Frontier: Accommodation, Identity, Conflict* (Urbana, Ill., 1999), 46–50; Nathan M. Gelber, 'Geschichte der Juden in der Bukowina (1774–1914)', in Gold (ed.), *Geschichte der Juden in der Bukowina*, i. 11–66: 45–8, 63–4 n. 10; *Die Welt*, 12 June 1914, pp. 579–80; Kassner, *Die Juden in der Bukowina*, 42–3.

[22] See Oleksandr Masan, 'Czernowitz in Vergangenheit und Gegenwart', in Heppner (ed.), *Czernowitz*, 11–44: 19, 23. Bukovina was granted the status of an autonomous Crownland in February 1861, with its own parliament and administration. Between 1786 and 1848 it was formally an administrative district of neighbouring Galicia. See Mihai-Ştefan Ceauşu, 'Der Landtag der Bukowina', in Helmut Rumpler and Peter Urbanitsch (eds.), *Die Habsburgermonarchie 1848–1918*, vol. vii, pt. 2: *Die regionalen Repräsentativkörperschaften* (Vienna, 2000), 2171–98.

[23] Johann Georg Kohl, *Reisen im Inneren von Rußland und Polen*, pt. 3: *Die Bukowina, Galizien, Krakau und Mähren* (Dresden, 1841), 17; Andrei Corbea-Hoişie, *Czernowitzer Geschichten: Über eine städtische Kultur in Mittelosteuropa* (Vienna, 2003), 15, 20.

nineteenth century, involving gradual industrialization, the construction of a railroad network (although here that generally reliable engine of economic progress was slower than elsewhere to produce results), an influx of capital, a shift away from agriculture, and a rate of growth that in most sectors outstripped that of Austria as a whole. (Agriculture was still, however, the dominant sector, employing some 80 per cent of the labour force in the eastern part of the empire in the early twentieth century.) The state propelled the development of the city in other ways, too, most notably by populating it with a German-language civil service and *Bürgertum*. The administration encouraged the settlement of 'productive' elements in order to stimulate growth in what was perceived to be, along with Galicia, the empire's most backward region, both economically and culturally.[24] For quite some time, though, Jews occupied 'least favoured nation' status in this regard. Especially in the initial decades of Austrian rule, government policy was to limit—and even reduce—the Jewish population, in order to minimize the economic and moral damage it purportedly caused.[25]

Provincial or otherwise, the image of Czernowitz as an 'eastern Vienna' is a commonplace of both contemporary and historical literature about the city.[26] From the point of view of Jewish cities, however, Czernowitz might be considered a counterpart not so much of its distant westerly capital Vienna as of its closer neighbour Odessa, some 250 miles to the south-east. As new cities whose success and growth owed much to Jews, both had something of the frontier atmosphere about them due to their near-border location; both were decidedly cosmopolitan and multinational; both were of economic and strategic importance; and in both we find strong and distinctive forms of Jewish politics, most evident in its modernist and nationalist streams. Common, too, was the decisive influence of Galician immigration, which helped shape Jewish society in both cities.[27]

A recurring refrain in the Habsburg-era Czernowitz Jewish myth sings the praises of the city's unique Jewish political culture and holds that Jewish political achievements in both city and province ought to be considered an

---

[24] See Josef Buszko, *Zum Wandel der Gesellschaftsstruktur in Galizien und in der Bukowina* (Vienna, 1978), 31–9; David F. Good, *The Economic Rise of the Habsburg Empire, 1750–1914* (Berkeley, 1984), 146–8.

[25] See e.g. N. M. Gelber, 'On the History of the Jews of Bukovina from 1776–1786' (Heb.), *Tsiyon*, 7 (1941/2), 94–103; Samuel Josef Schulsohn, 'Die Vertreibung der Juden aus der Bukowina', *Jeschurun*, 15 (1928), 33–49, 153–79; id., 'Geschichte der Juden in der Bukowina von 1789–1792', *Monatsschrift für Geschichte und Wissenschaft des Judentums*, 72 (1928), 274–86.

[26] Not a characterization unique to Czernowitz, of course. It was true also, for example, of Lemberg. See Anna Veronika Wendland, 'Post-Austrian Lemberg: War Commemoration, Interethnic Relations, and Urban Identity in L'viv, 1918–1939', *Austrian History Yearbook*, 34 (2003), 83–102: 84.

[27] On Odessa see Steven J. Zipperstein, *The Jews of Odessa: A Cultural History, 1794–188* (Stanford, Calif., 1986).

exceptional triumph. Once more, there is an element of truth in this. What distinguished the politics of Jewish Czernowitz (true of Bukovina too) was first, as already noted, its hybrid character—in other words, the intense east-meets-west relationship—and, second, its remarkably strong autonomous streak—that is, a broad cross section of local society accepted that the Jews were a separate group with their own political interests and needs. As ever, consensus as to what sort of a group the Jews were remained elusive, but few doubted that Jewish politics was much more than a marginal subset of a larger and more important political scene, as was the case in many other cities; here, it was on the political map in its own right. Context was decisive in an environment where the Austrian occupation imported new political and cultural norms and elites. To reiterate, Czernowitz was the eastern out-post of a multinational empire and the unchallenged urban centre of a strik-ingly multinational province. The lack of a dominant nationality changed the ground rules of politics here, enabling and sustaining the development of a separate Jewish political sphere alongside those of the Ukrainians, Romanians, Germans, and Poles.

This autonomous sphere was formidable, particularly from the 1880s. It can be divided along what might (with apologies) be called standard Mendelsohnian lines, in that we have nationalists of all stripes; integra-tionists, who from the 1890s overlapped with autonomous ethnic politics more than was the case elsewhere; and a powerful Orthodoxy in the form of the hasidic movement.[28] The 'Jewish street' was always a prominent pres-ence in the political discourse of Czernowitz; its substantial weight as a power broker derived in the first instance from Jewish electoral success at all levels, from chambers of commerce through municipal councils to regional and imperial parliaments. This was the sole province of the empire where Jews received formal recognition as a nationality (in the context of negotia-tions for reform of the regional parliament's electoral rules); the only major city that elected a Jewish nationalist mayor; the only regional parliament in the empire with a Jewish Club, or bloc; and the only regional executive with Jewish nationalist representation. Jews were also well represented in the Great Landowners' electoral curia (the Großgrundbesitzer). One should note, too, the classic situation of Jewish prominence in mainstream liberal politics; Bukovina has been described as a 'remote eastern bastion' of Austrian liberalism, and Czernowitz was the key to this development, thanks in particular to its Jews and Germans.[29] From the 1880s, much of this Jewish

---

[28] Ezra Mendelsohn, *On Modern Jewish Politics* (Oxford, 1993), ch. 1.

[29] Martin Broszat, 'Von der Kulturnation zur Volksgruppe: Die nationale Stellung der Juden in der Bukowina im 19. und 20. Jahrhundert', *Historische Zeitschrift*, 200 (1965), 575. More generally, see Peter Pulzer, *Jews and the German State* (Oxford, 1992), 85–96, 121–47, 324–37, and Gary B. Cohen, 'Jews in German Liberal Politics: Prague', *Jewish History*, 1/1 (1986), 55–74.

support for liberalism, like that of other groups, was redirected into a more particularist assertion of ethnic and national rights. This autonomist, or nationalist, sphere gathered strength from the early 1890s, making the city and the region appear, in the words of a sympathetic Galician observer, as a kind of 'Piedmont of the Jewish national movement in Austria', where assimilation rapidly became an 'obsolete farce'.[30]

A feature of the nationalist/autonomist camp was what contemporaries liked to call Jewish *Realpolitik*, the local version of *Landespolitik*. Because Jews wielded unusual political and economic clout in the city and the region, and because no single national group could dominate the others, their active engagement in local politics was the order of the day. Rehearsing familiar arguments from the wider Zionist context, *Realpolitik* advocates issued a call to arms, particularly resonant in the context of a political scene that they perceived as without limit in its potential for Jewish achievement. With a Latin exhortation, *Do ut des* (literally, 'I give that you may give'—i.e. do unto others as you would have them do unto you), they extolled the benefits of exploiting to the full Jewish influence where—as in Bukovina, Galicia, or Moravia—Jews potentially held the balance of power. Participation at all levels of political life, therefore, was essential.[31] Even in such a favourable environment, or perhaps precisely because of it, this engagement evoked controversy. Indeed, the issue of *Landespolitik* was a core element of the rift that divided the loyalties of Czernowitz Jewry and split it into two bitterly opposed camps for many years. On one level, this was an ideological conflict between competing versions of Jewish nationalism—Palestine-centred work or involvement in diaspora politics—that constituted a perennial source of tension within the Zionist movement.[32] On another level, it was personal: a vicious and endlessly escalating feud between apparently irreconcilable factions, which has been described, only partially in jest, as a 'thirty-year war'.[33] This feud remained unresolved; it undermined the Zionist movement in Czernowitz throughout this period by draining away enormous reserves of energy and sapping its power and influence both on the Jewish street and more generally.

The war revolved around one of the most extraordinary and successful Jewish diaspora politicians of this or any other era, Benno Straucher, the

---

[30] *Neue National-Zeitung*, 4 July 1913, p. 105.

[31] See e.g. *Die Welt*, 25 Jan. 1901, pp. 3–5; 8 Feb. 1901, pp. 5–7; 22 Feb. 1901, pp. 6–7; *Jüdische Zeitung*, 8 Nov. 1907, p. 2; *Jüdisches Volksblatt*, 3 Apr. 1903, p. 4; Manfred Reifer, *Dr. Mayer Ebner: Ein juedisches Leben* (Tel Aviv, n.d.), 39; Adolf Gaisbauer, *Davidstern und Doppeladler: Zionismus und jüdischer Nationalismus in Österreich 1882–1918* (Vienna, 1988), 185–6.

[32] Generally, see Mendelsohn, *On Modern Jewish Politics*, 57–8. On the situation in Austria see Gaisbauer, *Davidstern und Doppeladler*, 451–523.

[33] Reifer, *Dr. Mayer Ebner*, 51; *Die Stimme* (Dec. 1965), 4.

embodiment of Czernowitz's unique form of ethnic politics. An unashamed populist and a nationalist of liberal-democratic bent, Straucher was the pivotal public figure of Jewish Czernowitz, equally at home in the coffee-houses and wine cellars where he famously held court; in local associational life and the municipal administration (he was a city councillor and served on the council executive); in the Kultusgemeinde, of which he was president for many years; in the regional parliament (both as a representative and an executive member); and in the imperial parliament in Vienna, where he represented Czernowitz from 1897 to 1918. Initially elected to the Reichsrat on an independent democratic ticket, he gradually donned the mantle of a Jewish *Volkstribun*, a worthy successor to Joseph Samuel Bloch, the publicist and activist rabbi who had represented an east Galician constituency in the Reichsrat from 1883 to 1895 and similarly made his name as a vocal advocate of Jewish causes and defender of Jewish rights.[34] Unlike Bloch, Straucher showed little inclination for the niceties of ideology; rather, he adhered with great single-mindedness to an uncomplicated set of ideas about the existence of a Jewish *Volk* and its collective rights.

Straucher's rapid rise on the local scene beginning in the mid-1880s was widely interpreted as a reflection of popular resentment against the germanized notables who to that point controlled much of the infrastructure of Jewish Czernowitz. With his catchphrase 'Jewry is in danger', Straucher rode the rising nationalist and democratic tide and enjoyed a glittering career; his opponents observed with alacrity that he was in some respects a Jewish version of the charismatic Christian Social leader Karl Lueger. Like Lueger, the mayor of Vienna from 1897 to 1910 and no great friend of the Jews, Straucher was something of a demagogue, a self-proclaimed champion of the proverbial 'little man' and the voice of the Jewish masses.[35]

Given that Straucher was instrumental in virtually every political accomplishment of Czernowitz Jewry, it should come as no surprise that the magnitude of his dominance was matched only by the volume and intensity of the vitriol that he attracted. To his rivals, he was a megalomaniac (how else to explain the bronze statue of Straucher outside one of the Jewish community's most important buildings?), a dictator devoid of authentic ideological beliefs, a corrupt and unscrupulous master of political intrigue. The contempt was mutual, each side hurling abuse at the other and trading insults at every opportunity. The battle was noteworthy not so much for

[34] Ian Reifowitz, *Imagining an Austrian Nation: Joseph Samuel Bloch and the Search for a Multiethnic Austrian Identity, 1846–1919* (Boulder, Colo., 2003); Robert Wistrich, *The Jews of Vienna in the Age of Franz Joseph* (London, 1989), ch. 9.

[35] See Gelber, 'Geschichte der Juden', 60; *Die Stimme* (Dec. 1949), 3–5; (Nov. 1960), 3, 8; Gaisbauer, *Davidstern und Doppeladler*, 511–15. Examples of his rhetoric can be found in Benno Straucher, *Die Lage der Juden: Reden des Abg. Dr. Straucher in den österr. Delegationen und im österr. Abgeordnetenhause* (Czernowitz, 1907).

what was said, which—although on occasion tasteless and scurrilous—was on a par with the generally overheated tenor of contemporary Jewish political rhetoric, but rather for the astounding longevity and pervasiveness of the conflict.[36] It assumed institutional forms, too, perhaps the most notable example of which was the Jewish Volksrat (People's Council). Created in early 1911 with the express purpose of building a power base to counter Straucher's influence, the Volksrat was a merger of pure Herzlian Zionists, *Landespolitik* devotees, and synthetic Zionists, united by what can only be called their all-consuming hatred of Straucher and his works. At its helm stood Leon Kellner, a moderate Herzlian in his views and a professor of English literature at the University of Czernowitz. The Volksrat was the centrepiece of a concerted Zionist effort, spearheaded by Kellner, to outflank Straucher by purging the local Zionist leadership of his followers, establishing a weekly newspaper to campaign against him, setting up a Toynbee Hall (later described as the 'Zionist temple') as a counterweight to Straucher's Jewish National House (itself analogous to the German and Polish Houses in Czernowitz), and in general promoting active opposition to him in each and every area of the Jewish public sphere. Volksrat candidates were elected both to the regional parliament and the Czernowitz municipal council, and the Volksrat drew the regional government directly into its fight with what it referred to as Straucher's 'despicable mafia'. While it evidently made inroads into Straucher's support, the Volksrat fell short of achieving its goals, and Straucher's primacy remained intact.[37]

The ripple effects of this rancour spread far beyond Czernowitz. To take perhaps the most important case, it bears a large measure of responsibility

[36] See Reifer, *Dr. Mayer Ebner*, 51–62. On the bronze bust of Straucher in the lobby of the Jewish House, see ibid. 57 and *Der Jüdische Volksrat*, 3 Feb. 1911, p. 4; for an example of tarring him with the Lueger brush, see Reifer, *Dr. Mayer Ebner*, 53. Mayer Ebner was one of Straucher's principal opponents. Many years later scores were still being settled. Besides Reifer's hagiographical volume on Ebner, see Leon Arie Schmelzer, 'Geschichte des Zionismus in der Bukowina', in Gold (ed.), *Geschichte der Juden in Bukowina*, i. 91–112: 97–9, and Sternberg, 'Zur Geschichte der Juden in Czernowitz', 32–4. See also *Der Jüdische Volksrat*, 20 Jan. 1911, pp. 4–7; *Neue National-Zeitung*, 4 July 1913, pp. 105–6 and 1 Aug. 1913, pp. 121–2; Gaisbauer, *Davidstern und Doppeladler*, 518–20.

[37] The Volksrat was set up in direct opposition to one of Straucher's power bases, the Jewish National Party (Jüdische Nationalpartei), a semi-functional organization that had for some years led an on-off existence. See Gaisbauer, *Davidstern und Doppeladler*, 515–16; *Jüdische Zeitung*, 7 Feb. 1908, p. 5; 15 Apr. 1910, p. 4. On the establishment of the Volksrat see *Der Jüdische Volksrat*, 20 Jan. 1911, pp. 1–3, and the October 1910 announcement 'An di yidn di bukovine', in the Central Zionist Archives (Jerusalem), Z2/390. See also the characteristically anti-Straucher pamphlet, *Appeal of the Jewish Council to All the Jews in Bukovina* [Oyfruf tsu ale yidn in der bukovine fun dem yidishe folksrat] (Czernowitz, 1911). For Toynbee Hall as the 'Zionist temple', see Schmelzer, 'Geschichte des Zionismus in der Bukowina', 99. See *Jüdische Zeitung*, 22 Jan. 1909, p. 4, on the opening of the Jewish House. On elections, see *Der Jüdische Volksrat*, 28 Apr. 1911, pp. 1–4; 7 Mar. 1913, pp. 1–2; on government intervention, see ibid., 30 May 1913, pp. 1–6. For mafia descriptions, see ibid., 13 June 1913, pp. 3–4.

for crippling one of Austrian Jewry's most ambitious political projects: the first and only Jewish Club (Der Jüdische Klub) (that is, a Jewish bloc) in the Reichsrat. The Club, of which Straucher was the elected leader, stood at the apex of the Jewish nationalist movement in the empire between 1907 and 1911; it offered an unprecedented forum for the advancement of Jewish political interests, with potential benefits for Jewish politics across Europe. At most, it can be said that the Club only partially fulfilled these great expectations. Its four members proved adept at exploiting the many opportunities their status afforded them—in parliamentary debates, in committee work, and in innumerable meetings and consultations with government representatives. In all these areas, the thread holding their work together was their conviction that it was incumbent upon them to act explicitly and overtly as representatives of the entirety of Austrian Jewry. While their record was mixed, they certainly succeeded in one of their prime goals—making Jewish issues and politics a familiar and regular part of the state's political discourse at the highest levels. Unfortunately, before long the Straucher effect began to poison the Club's work, too. Relations between its members reportedly deteriorated to the point where co-operation became impossible, and the Club slowly and painfully dissolved in a welter of recrimination and abuse. Such was the animosity that two Club members resorted, so it was reported, to the challenge of a duel in order to resolve their differences.[38]

*

How, then, can we square this particular circle? On the one hand, an El Dorado for the Jews and their politics, a remarkable success story with few parallels. On the other, a site of bitter division that seeped into every corner of Jewish life, a conflict played out in local associations and clubs; in public meetings and coffee-houses; in the Zionist movement; in the wider ranks of the Jewish nationalist/autonomist movement; in the Jewish and general press; and at every level of public administration. If the success was singular, the conflict and division were almost axiomatic in the context of Jewish political culture. In fact, there is no need to square the circle, to reconcile such signal success with such dismal failure, because there is no necessary contradiction. The great strength and the terminal weakness were two sides of the same coin—that is to say, the unusual politics of this unusual city and region, where the tremendous strength of *Landespolitik* constituted the fatal

---

[38] On the challenge of a duel, reportedly between Arthur Mahler and Heinrich Gabel, see *Neue National-Zeitung*, 4 Mar. 1910, pp. 1–2. See also ibid., 10 June 1910, pp. 3–4, for a sample of the heated rhetoric. More generally on the Club, see Harald Binder, *Galizien in Wien: Parteien, Wahlen, Fraktionen und Abgeordnete im Übergang zur Massenpolitik* (Vienna, 2005), 48–54; Gaisbauer, *Davidstern und Doppeladler*, 479–88; Leon Wechsler and Heinrich Gabel, *The Jewish Club* [Der yidisher klub] (Buczacz, 1908); and *Jüdische Zeitung*, 20 June 1907, p. 1–2; 19 July 1907, pp. 1–2.

weakness of the Zionist movement. For Czernowitz Jewry, allegiance to a particularist, corporate form of politics worked hand in glove with devotion to Austria. The Jewish condition in Czernowitz and Bukovina was made possible by Habsburg state and society, and it compared favourably to that prevailing elsewhere in Europe, especially when viewed from the post-Habsburg perspective. As the ur-Zionist Nathan Birnbaum expressed it, noting in 1907 that Jewish nationality was 'acknowledged in public life in Bukovina as nowhere else in Austria', a 'separate Jewish nationality in Bukovina is anchored to such an extent in the consciousness of all peoples and parties, and in governing circles, that it is impossible to imagine a breach of this now stable notion'.[39]

For Birnbaum and many others, the Jews were one group among others, and if not *primus inter pares* then something close to it. Or, to express it in a folk idiom: Jews were just like other people, only more so. Here, then, the insider/outsider dualism proves to be something of a false dichotomy, perhaps better conceived, as noted at the outset, as two shifting poles of a continuum. An insider/outsider framework implies an at least somewhat stable centre around which an individual or a collective situates itself. Czernowitz and Bukovina—a new provincial capital in a new imperial borderland—were, however, less than stable referents. The post-1848 years saw a breakneck pace of economic growth, variegated social and cultural development, and an unsettled political dynamism, creating a unique multi-ethnic agglomerate that lacked an obviously dominant majority. In such a fissiparous society the binding force of the Habsburg idea could not always effectively constrain the powerful centrifugal currents, although it was surprisingly effective in the circumstances. But if the centre itself shifts, how to fix its boundaries? As a consequence, determining the relative status and meaning of insider/outsider is fraught with difficulty, and these sometimes useful terms should be applied selectively and with due caution here. At most, we can say that both are true: the successful Jewish bourgeoisie of Czernowitz was constitutive of local society, while the hasidim of Sadagora were an exotic supplement. Yet exotic supplements were themselves famously a constituent of the Czernowitz and Bukovina landscape. Neither one nor the other category—insider or outsider—will suffice; in combination, though, they are not entirely inappropriate. And what is true of the Jews is true also of other groups in the city and region.

Whether as insiders or outsiders, the Jews of Czernowitz, to return to the myth with which we began, clearly felt that they had much for which to be grateful, and while, naturally, we need to be critical and sceptical, we should not entirely gainsay their view. A myth of this nature cannot serve as the basis of a viable historical account; it can, though, offer a valuable point of entry.

[39] *Neue Zeitung*, 20 Sept. 1907, p. 2.

# THIRTEEN

# WILNO/VILNIUS/VILNE
## *Whose City Is It Anyway?*

### M O R D E C H A I   Z A L K I N

Dear Tomas. Two poets, one Lithuanian, the other Polish, were raised in the same city. Surely that is reason enough for them to discuss their city even in public. True, the city I knew belonged to Poland, was called Wilno, and its schools and university used the Polish language. Your city was the capital of the Lithuanian Socialist Republic, was called Vilnius . . . nevertheless, it is the same city; its architecture, its surrounding terrain, and its sky shaped us both. . . . I have the impression that cities possess their own spirit or aura, and at times, walking the streets of Wilno, it seemed to me, that I became physically aware of that aura.

This paragraph, written in 1979 by the famous Polish poet Czesław Miłosz to his younger colleague, the Lithuanian poet and dissident Tomas Venclova, is taken from the opening remark of what is known as 'A Dialogue about Wilno'.[1] At the basic level, this dialogue, or in fact this city, situated on the banks of the Neris river, serves both the Polish and the Lithuanian poets as a platform for an examination of their own personal and national identity. It is the same city and yet not the same city. At times, indeed, the reader may even think that they are talking about two totally different places. Admitting that, for the Poles, 'Wilno was a provincial city rather than a capital',[2] Miłosz still considered it an important centre of Polish life, primarily because of its unique cultural heritage. For him, the famous opening line of Adam Mickiewicz's poem *Pan Tadeusz*—'Litwo! Ojczyzno moja!' (Lithuania! My homeland!)—is more than anything else a cultural statement or, as he defined it, 'Wilno cannot be excluded from the history of Polish culture, if only because of Mickiewicz, the Philomaths, Słowacki and Piłsudski'.[3] In fact, Adam Mickiewicz and Juliusz Słowacki were part and parcel of the self-image of only a handful of Polish residents, mainly the intellectual circles connected to the local Stefan Batory University. The rest of the 'Polish' inhabitants were, according to Miłosz, just 'Polish-speaking Lithuanians'. In

---

[1] Czesław Miłosz and Tomas Venclova, 'A Dialogue about Wilno', in Tomas Venclova, *Forms of Hope* (New York, 1999), 5–31: 5. On Venclova, see Donata Mitaitė, *Tomas Venclova: Speaking through Signs* (Vilnius, 2002).     [2] 'Dialogue', 7, 27.     [3] Ibid. 6.

other words, the entire concept of a Polish Wilno was based on religious and cultural perceptions, on an unrealistic image, a dream. Discount the Stefan Batory University and the Matka Boska Ostrobramska (the church of Our Lady of the Gate of the Dawn, one of the most popular Marian shrines of eastern Europe) and there is no longer a Polish Wilno.

For Tomas Venclova, less famous than Miłosz but still an important figure in the process of defining a modern collective Lithuanian identity, Vilnius is the one and only city.[4] He acknowledges the peculiar paradox of Vilnius as both the historical capital of Lithuania and a frontier town, a capital city that, at its finest, 'reminds one of a palimpsest—an ancient manuscript in which the text reveals traces of an earlier text'. Yet for him, as for most Lithuanians, Vilnius is 'a symbol of continuity as well as of historical identity. . . . Lithuania without Vilnius is an ephemeral nation but with Vilnius, its past and its historical responsibility are secured.'[5] However, in the Lithuanian case the gap between symbol and reality is much wider than that pertaining to the Polish vision of the city. In fact, Vilnius has hardly ever been Lithuanian in the demographic sense. Thus, for instance, in the late nineteenth century ethnic Lithuanians constituted only 2.1 per cent of the city's population.[6] Well aware of this problematic situation, Venclova illustrates it with an anecdote taken from his own childhood. Lost in the city's unfamiliar alleys while trying to make his way home from school, he suddenly realized that hardly anyone understood him because he was speaking Lithuanian, or, as he put it, thousands of Lithuanians considered Vilnius to be their historical capital, but in reality the town was alien to them.[7] In many ways the city's role is reminiscent of that played by Jerusalem for the Jews over the centuries; as Venclova put it, 'For the Lithuanians [Vilnius] is a symbol of continuity as well as historical identity—somewhat like Jerusalem.'[8] But though the city fuelled and ignited the ethnic and national dreams of Lithuanians they did little to turn myth into reality.

Despite the importance of the city's cultural dimension for the Poles and of its historical associations for the Lithuanians, both Miłosz and Venclova felt that their dualistic concept of Wilno/Vilnius was unsatisfactory. 'Something' was missing. This feeling led Miłosz to conclude that 'Wilno is an enclave. It was neither Polish nor not-Polish, neither Lithuanian nor not-Lithuanian, neither a provincial nor a capital city. And, really, Wilno was an oddity, a city of mixed-up, overlapping regions.'[9]

---

[4] See Tomas Venclova, *Vilnius* (Vilnius, 2001).                              [5] Ibid. 27
[6] Kevin O'Connor, *The History of the Baltic States* (Westport, 2003), 66; Šarūnas Liekis *A State within a State? Jewish Autonomy in Lithuania 1918–1925* (Vilnius, 2003), 55.
[7] Venclova, *Forms of Hope*, 18.                                             [8] Ibid. 27
[9] Cited ibid. 7. See also Czesław Miłosz, 'Vilnius, Lithuania: An Ethnic Agglomerate', i George de Vos and Lola Romanucci-Ross (eds.), *Ethnic Identities: Cultural Continuities an Change* (Palo Alto, Calif., 1974), 339–52.

One might assume that the background to Miłosz's attempt to depict the city in such indeterminate colours was the wider unresolved historical dispute between Poles and Lithuanians over the ethnic and political identity of the 'Polish–Lithuanian Commonwealth' (Rzeczpospolita), and of the 'polonized Lithuanians'.[10] But it seems more likely that the missing part of the puzzle is the massive Jewish presence in Vilna before the Second World War. It is not that Miłosz or Venclova tried in any way to ignore or to underestimate the significance and importance of this presence. For both writers, the local Jewish quarter signified much more than an old residential area in which tens of thousands of Litvaks dwelled. 'In talking of Wilno', writes Miłosz, 'it is important to mention that it was an appreciably Jewish city.'[11] He saw this Jewishness, first and foremost, in such phenomena as the Jewish socialist organization, the Bund; the YIVO Institute for Jewish Research (Yidisher visnshaftlekher institut), founded in Vilna in 1925 and dedicated to the study of east European Jewish life; and the contribution of local Jews to the rebirth of Hebraism in Israel. Venclova, in turn, focused on the 'Jewish character' of Vilna by emphasizing the importance of the various Jewish cultural activities and institutions located there, such as the Romm printing house and the Strashun library. Such reflections are hardly surprising, considering the fact that in the inter-war period roughly a third of the local population was Jewish.[12] It is worth mentioning here that as early as 1975 Venclova published an essay entitled 'Jews and Lithuanians', which was nothing less than revolutionary in the Lithuanian and Soviet context of the time.[13]

While dreaming about their own Wilno or Vilnius, both writers willingly admitted, directly or indirectly, that the inter-war city had a triple identity: Wilno/Vilnius/Vilne.[14] Its skyline was dominated by a virtual 'sacred triangle', composed of three huge monumental sites: the Matka Boska Ostrobramska church, surrounded every Sunday by thousands of Polish

[10] See Saulius Kaubrys, *National Minorities in Lithuania* (Vilnius, 2002), 11–16, 79–85.

[11] Quoted in Venclova, *Forms of Hope*, 13. See also Alfonsas Tamulynas, 'The Demographic and Social-Professional Structure of the Jewish Community in Vilnius (Based on the Census of 1784)', in Izraelis Lempertas (ed.), *The Gaon of Vilnius and the Annals of Jewish Culture* (Vilnius, 1998), 331–53; David A. Frick, 'Jews and Others in Seventeenth-Century Wilno: Life in the Neighborhood', *Jewish Studies Quarterly*, 12/1 (2005), 8–42.

[12] Israel Klausner, *Vilna, 'Jerusalem of Lithuania': From 1881 to 1939* [Vilna: yerushalayim delita, dorot aharonim 1881–1939] (Tel Aviv, 1983), 250.

[13] On this essay see Mordechai Zalkin, 'Tomas Venclova: Jews and Lithuanians' (Heb.), *Iyunim betkumat yisra'el*, 14 (2004), 461–78.

[14] The long period of the repressive Russian occupation left hardly any significant imprint on the city's character. For a 'Russian portrait' of Vilnius see e.g. A. Janikas (ed.), *Vilnius: Architektūra iki XX amžiaus pradžios* (Vilnius, 1955); Juozas Jurginis and Vladislavas Mikučianis, *Vilnius: Tarybų Lietuvos sostinė* (Vilnius, 1956). See also Remigijus Civinskas, Disputes between Jews and Townspeople in Lithuania and Russia's Policies Concerning Jews', in Jurgita Šiaučiūnaitė-Verbickienė and Larisa Lempertienė (eds.), *Central and East European Jews at the Crossroads of Tradition and Modernity* (Vilnius, 2006), 332–60.

pilgrims; the Lithuanian Gedimino Pilis (the castle of Gediminas, grand duke of Lithuania and founder of the city); and the Jewish Shulhoyf—the synagogue courtyard, the complex of the old main synagogue, and the various adjacent social and religious institutions. The symbolism of this 'sacred triangle' and, in fact, of the entire city was far-reaching. For the hundreds of thousands of Polish pilgrims who thronged every year to this 'Civitas Dei' to seek indulgences and absolution from the Baltic equivalent of the Polish Matka Boska Częstochowska (the Black Madonna of Częstochowa); for the Lithuanian peasant in a remote village in the northern region of Žemaitija who always dreamed about 'Castle Hill' as the symbol of Lithuanian statehood and independence but never saw it with his own eyes; and for the shtetl's Jewish water-carrier, who envisioned the 'Jerusalem of Lithuania' as the world capital of Torah study and of elite scholarship, the city was a capital regardless of its formal status. It was the home of the Polish poet Adam Mickiewicz, of the patriarch of the Lithuanian National movement Jonas Basanavičius, and of Rabbi Elijah ben Solomon Zalman, the Vilna Gaon. These various perceptions of the city inevitably influenced the attitude of its inhabitants towards the 'other', their known/unknown neighbours. To a significant extent the members of each of the three ethnic groups considered themselves not just as residents but also as having been 'chosen' by their co-religionists to guard the city from falling into the hands of these 'others'; in other words, to serve as the guardians of the religious/national/scholarly treasure.

The multidimensional reality of Vilna was—and still is—deeply rooted in historical, literary, and artistic perceptions of the city.[15] Thus, almost every book about it, whether it contains lithographs, paintings, or photographs, is dominated by the ethnic, religious, and national orientation of the artist or editor. This perception of separate cities characterizes, for instance, the works of Vladas Drėma, Piotr Popiński and Robert Hirsch, and Leyzer Ran.[16] Predictably, each of these editors focuses almost solely on his own 'imagined city' while barely mentioning the city's other quarters, or simply pushing them to the periphery.[17] Another quite fascinating example of this

---

[15] For a 'Jewish history' of the city see e.g. Ephim Jeshurin, *Wilno* (New York, 1935); Israel Cohen, *Vilna* (Philadelphia, 1943); and Israel Klausner, *Vilna, 'Jerusalem of Lithuania': From 1495 to 1881* [Vilna: yerushalayim delita, dorot rishonim 1495–1881] (Tel Aviv, 1983–88). For a literary treatment see e.g. Abraham Karpinovitch, *Tales of Vilna* [Sipurei vilna] (Tel Aviv, 1995).

[16] See Vladas Drėma, *Dingęs Vilnius* (Vilnius 1991); Piotr Popiński and Robert Hirsch, *Dawne Wilno na pocztówce* (Gdańsk, 1998); and Leyzer Ran, *Jerusalem of Lithuania: Illustrated and Documented* (New York, 1974). See also Moses Raviv (ed.), *A Jewish Street in Vilna* [Yidishe gass in vilne] (Zurich, 1931); Geinrikh Agranovsky, *Litovskii Ierusalim* (Vilnius, 1992); and Izraelis Lempertas, *Mūsų Vilne* (Vilnius, 2003).

[17] See e.g. Vytautas Lisauskas, *Vilnius: Vokiečių gatvė* (Vilnius, 2003); Valentina Brio, 'The Space of the Jewish Town in Zalman Shneur's Poem *Vilna*', in Jurgita Šiaučiūnaitė-Verbickienė and Larisa Lempertienė (eds.), *Jewish Space in Central and Eastern Europe, Day-to-Day History* (Newcastle upon Tyne, 2007), 254.

tendency is Jonas Kazimieras Vilčinskis's famous collection *Vilniaus albumas*, in which all the lithographs are by well-known nineteenth-century painters, such as Vasily Sadovnikov, Isador Laurent Deroy, Jan Chrucki, Konstantinas Kukevičius, and Victor Adam.[18] Like Czesław Miłosz and Tomas Venclova, all these artists were well aware of the strong Jewish presence in Vilna. However, despite the visibility of Jewish life, it is barely represented in most of these colourful works, or, at best, is pushed to the shadowy margins of the scene.[19]

## JERUSALEM IN LITHUANIA?

Symbolically, the virtual centre of the 'sacred triangle' was the main intersection of the Jewish quarter, at the meeting point of Gaon Street (Gaono gv.) and Glaziers Street (Stiklių gv.). Here, among the crowded bustle of female pedlars looking for potential customers, young children rushing to the *ḥeder* or to school, and stooped artisans sitting on footstools in their dimly lit workshops, a Jew could feel, more than anywhere else in the city, the beating heart of the 'Jerusalem of Lithuania'. Yet they only needed to raise their eyes from the surrounding tumult for this illusion of a fully Jewish environment to vanish: they were constantly being 'watched' by the Matka Boska cross and the Lithuanian flag on the tower of Gedimino Pilis.

What, then, did the words 'Jerusalem of Lithuania' actually mean for Vilne's Jewish population? Did the Jews consider themselves sons and daughters of the city in the broadest sense? Or, to be more precise, did they relate to Vilne as did the Poles and the Lithuanians, in terms of 'ownership'? After all, they constituted the city's largest and most stable ethnic group. (Even when the idea of emigration to Palestine or elsewhere crossed their minds, it was, for most of them, as likely as not nothing more than a passing thought.)

An insight into how they saw themselves is provided by the comments of Hillel Noah Maggid-Steinschneider, very much a 'Vilner Yid', who dedicated his life to writing the history of the local Jewish community:

I have seen, and it is engraved upon my heart, that our city of Vilna is a magnificent city, and in it Torah and wisdom have combined from time immemorial. Within it, are yeshivas for Torah, *batei midrash* for wisdom, houses of prayer for worship, and many different charitable organizations. All people, from one end to

---

[18] Jonas Kazimieras Vilčinskis, *Vilniaus albumas* (Vilnius, 1987); see nos. 5, 9, 19, 22, 12 respectively.
[19] For the changing image of Jewish Vilnius in Lithuanian historiography, see Jurgita Šiaučiūnaitė-Verbickienė, 'Żydų Vilnius Lietuvos istoriografijoje: vaizdinių kaita', in Larisa Lempertienė et al. (eds.), *Jewish Intellectual Life in Pre-War Vilna* (Vilnius, 2004), 25–34.

the other, this one hither and that one thither, work as one, to increase and enhance Torah, so that the name of Israel shall not be forgotten.[20]

Indeed, Maggid-Steinschneider perceived himself as a son of the city, a true Vilner, as well as its historian. His Vilne, however, was solely Jewish. Anything beyond the boundaries of the Jewish ethnic and cultural area, whether geographical or social, was irrelevant to him, and his works reflect the perception of the traditional Vilner Jew, for whom the boundaries of the world were identical with those of the local Jewish community. An expression of this awareness is to be found, for example, in a scene from the novel of the Vilne-born author Chaim Grade, *The Agunah*:

In order to get to the Jewish communal courtroom from Glazers Street [Stiklių gv.], Reb Shmuel-Munye had to pass German Street [Vokiečių gv.] and Vilna Street [Vilniaus gv.]. But he turned into Gaon Street [Gaono gv.], passed along gardens and churches, until he arrived at Mickiewicz Street [Gedimino gv.], where no Jew dares to show his face among those gentiles wearing curly mustaches. They were looking at his long black coat in contempt, as if he contaminated the air of their neighborhood. This so frightened him, his sarcastic smile disappeared into his beard like a sunray in a thicket. As there was no choice, he had to walk around three quarters of the city. Only when he finally disentangled himself from the camp of the uncircumcised and found his way to the Jewish communal offices, did the sarcastic smile return.[21]

Likewise for Joseph Buloff, the famous Yiddish actor, the boundaries of Jewish Vilne were identical to those of the old marketplace in Breite Gass (Didžioji gv.), the natural territory of orphans and abandoned children, stealing an apple or a piece of bread out of hunger.[22] With Maggid-Steinschneider and Reb Shmuel-Munye, Buloff was acutely aware of the existence of his Lithuanian, Polish, Russian, and German neighbours, but they served merely as a background, at times vague and at times vivid and colourful, to the *real* world—the Jewish one. The points of communication and contact with life beyond that world were derived from the basic needs of daily life and not from a sense of neighbourly brotherhood. Indifference to the existence of the 'other' is one thing; but in the Jewish consciousness it went further: it was the elimination of the 'others' from the 'local narrative' that defined the way in which many Jews related to their native city.[23] Wilno/Vilnius/Vilne 'belonged' to everybody, but at the same time it

[20] Steinschneider, *The City Vilna* [Ir vilna] (Vilna, 1900), p. ix. On Steinschneider see Mordechai Zalkin, 'Community—City—History: Hillel Noah Maggid and the Emergence of the Jewish "Vilner" Historiography', in Lempertienė et al. (eds.), *Jewish Intellectual Life in Pre-War Vilna*, 7–24.

[21] Chaim Grade, *The Agunah*, trans. Curt Leviant (New York, 1974), 119.

[22] Joseph Buloff, *Tales from the Old Marketplace* [Mikikar hashuk hayashan] (Tel Aviv, 1986), 9.

[23] See Chaimas Nachmanas Šapira, *Vilnius naujojoj žydų poezijoj* (Kaunas, 1935).

'belonged' to nobody. All its inhabitants, regardless of their ethnic origins, were simultaneously insiders and outsiders—or, as Laimonas Briedis defined it recently, a city of strangers.[24] Thus the question of loyalty in this case has to be addressed in a more complex context. Even the local Jews who were culturally polonized did not identify as Poles, although they shared the same language, dialect, terminology, and, to a significant extent, even some cultural values, with their Polish neighbours. Anyone who is familiar with the local patriotic literature will be aware of the analogy between Mickiewicz's 'Litwo! Ojczyzno moja!' and Abraham Kariv's best-known essay, 'Lite mayne heymland'.[25]

In terms of identity, however, most local Jews did not consider themselves citizens of Wilno but 'Vilner Yidn', sons and daughters of Vilne. 'Vilne' was not just the Jewish name for 'Wilno' or 'Vilnius'. It was a unique and specific entity. For the Jews, as for Miłosz, Vilne was an enclave in which the individual was entitled to define his or her own allegiance: their fidelity to their native city was loyalty to their *Jewish* city. And this loyalty was total, all-embracing, and unlimited, regardless of ideological, religious, or economic differences. Even the socialist, ideologically secular, and anti-clerical spirit that swept the streets of Jewish Vilne at the end of the nineteenth century did not undermine this deep sense of a common fate. Thus, when the poor young socialist Jewish shoemaker Hirsh Leckert was taken to the scaffold for the attempted assassination of the governor general of Vilna, Victor von Wahl, who had ordered the flogging of twenty-two Jewish and six Polish demonstrators and strikers, he was considered a martyr by all the city's Jews.

However, this loyalty was not just an expression of identification with the local community. Besides being members of the virtual fraternity of the 'Jerusalem of Lithuania', many of the city's Jews developed a deep sense of belonging to the 'earthly' Vilne, even a certain type of local patriotism.[26] This unique sense of 'joint belonging' that weaves amorphous feelings into the city's physical reality is admirably expressed in Moyshe Kulbak's famous poem 'Vilne':

> You are a Psalm spelled in clay and iron,
> A prayer in every stone, a chant, a melody in every wall,
> You are an amulet darkly mounted in Lithuania,
> A book is every stone, a scroll, a parchment is every wall.[27]

[24] *Vilnius: City of Strangers* (Vilnius, 2008).

[25] Kariv's title also translates as 'Lithuania My Homeland'; published in his *Lithuania My Homeland* [Lita mekhorati] (Haifa, 1960).

[26] This tendency is very noticeable in Zalman Šik's book *A Thousand Years of Vilne* [1000 yor vilne] (Wilno, 1939).

[27] Cited in Arcadius Kahan, 'Vilna—the Sociocultural Anatomy of a Jewish Community in Interwar Poland', in id., *Essays in Jewish Social and Economic History*, ed. Roger Weiss (Chicago, 1986), 149–60: 149. See also Justin D. Cammy, 'The Politics of Home, the Culture of Place:

To borrow Tomas Venclova's words, 'The city merges with its setting.'[28] Surprisingly enough, these two seemingly contradictory environments coexisted peacefully. On the one hand, the reference to the city as the 'Jerusalem of Lithuania' was not just a phrase. Vilne Jews dreamed of Jerusalem and longed for it. For them, however, Vilne was, first and foremost, 'the promised land', a locally realized version of the ancient, eternal Jerusalem, earthly as well as heavenly. This image of Vilne crossed the boundaries of the local Jewish community, spreading throughout the Jewish Lithuanian cultural region. This was, for instance, the context of the poet Zalman Shneour's most famous expression: 'Vilne—my magnificent grandmother.'[29] On the other hand, however, this longing was transferred from the remote heavenly sphere to the immediate, mundane city. The Vilija river, the 'Hill of the Three Crosses', the green bridge ('der griner brik')—all these famous 'non-Jewish' symbols of the city gradually became part and parcel of their childhood scenery, of their very existence as sons and daughters of the 'real' city.

In the first half of the twentieth century the ongoing process of secularization among Jewish youth, combined with the almost irresistible attractiveness of contemporary Polish and Russian culture, led many young Jews to develop a new attitude towards their 'citizenship' of this multinational city. This process was characterized, first and foremost, by a strong ambition to 'leave' Vilne behind and to become citizens of 'The City'—of a non-religious entity. This desired destination could be reached via involvement in various 'neutral zones', that is to say, social areas that were considered open to everyone, regardless of their religious or ethnic identity.[30] One of the most attractive of these allegedly 'neutral' zones was the university. In fact, local Jews had attended the lecture halls of this institution as early as the first quarter of the nineteenth century. Most of these early students were adherents of the Haskalah (the Jewish Enlightenment) and thus numbered only a few dozen.[31] Now, some eighty years after these harbingers of the Haskalah 'introduced' the importance of secular higher education to the local ultra-conservative Jewish society, it seemed as if their dream was finally close to

The "Yung-Vilne" Miscellany of Literature and Art', in Marina Dmitrieva and Heidemarie Petersen (eds.), *Jüdische Kultur im Neuen Europa* (Wiesbaden, 2004), 117–33. For a different attitude see Samuel D. Kassow, 'The Uniqueness of Jewish Vilna', in Lempertienė et al. (eds.), *Jewish Intellectual Life in Pre-War Vilna*, 147–61: 150.

[28]  Venclova, *Forms of Hope*, 16.
[29]  Zalman Shneour, *Collected Writings* [Ketavim] (Tel Aviv, 1960), 240.
[30]  A typical example of such a 'neutral' zone was the realm of popular sport. On the intensive activity of young Vilna Jews in this field in the inter-war period see Jack Jacobs, 'Jews and Sport in Interwar Vilna', in Šiaučiūnaitė-Verbickienė and Lempertienė (eds.), *Jewish Space in Central and Eastern Europe*, 165–73.
[31]  Pinhas Kon, 'Jewish Students in the Former University of Vilna' (Yiddish), *Vilner Tog*, 6 Aug. 1923; Jacob Shatzky, *Cultural History of the Haskalah in Lithuania* [Kultur-geshikhte fun der haskole in lite] (Buenos Aires, 1950), 58–63.

realization. Thus, as a natural continuation of the mass participation of Jewish youth in the modern, to a certain extent secular, local school system,[32] in the inter-war period Yiddish became as popular as Polish in the courtyards of the University of Vilnius. About a thousand local Jewish students (25 per cent of the total enrolment) turned their backs on the local traditional Jewish educational and vocational institutions in favour of the faculties of medicine, the sciences, and the humanities.

In this context the attendance of a large number of Jewish students at Stefan Batory University represents much more than just a new trend of professional preference. To a significant extent their decision to mingle, day in day out, with multicultural and multinational groups of non-Jewish students in a non-Jewish environment testifies to their weakened traditional and religious sense of belonging. These Jewish students needed to cross the unseen local boundaries and become true 'insiders'. The impact of this phenomenon on the texture of Jewish society was so profound that many considered it to be a sign of the possible disintegration of that society. This process, described by the poet Hayim Nahman Bialik as one in which 'They were all swept by a foreign spirit; they were all taken away by the light',[33] in fact reflected a realistic analysis of contemporary social developments. Like their Jewish counterparts who made every possible effort to become members of the Russian socialist movements, they longed for a new 'neutral' urban society that welcomed every caring and involved citizen regardless of his or her ethnic or religious identity.

On the surface, and in the spirit of the years following the First World War, these widespread hopes for a new social order, at least in the local context, were not baseless. By the early 1920s the currents of socialism and cosmopolitanism, so prevalent in contemporary eastern Europe, were perceived by many—Jews and non-Jews alike—as the way towards establishing an equal and humane society. Such beliefs were very popular among the circles of young Jews in Vilnius, the birthplace of the Bund, and naturally, in particular, among these students.[34] And yet, according to historian Arcadius Kahan, 'Hope for a positive response to this historic opportunity for a multinational cultural coexistence and cross-fertilization, at least in the area of the humanities and cultural studies, was short-lived.'[35] Following the emotion-laden

[32] Kaubrys, *National Minorities in Lithuania*, 140–71.

[33] Hayim Nahman Bialik, *Collected Poems 1899–1934* [Shirim 1899–1934] (Tel Aviv, 1990), 131.

[34] See Vladimir Levin, 'Jewish Politics in the Russian Empire during the Period of Reaction 1907–1914' [Hapolitika hayehudit ba'imperyah harusit be'idan hare'aktseyah 1907–1914], Ph.D. diss., Hebrew University of Jerusalem, 2007; Isaac Broides, *Zionist Vilna and its Functionaries* [Vilna hatsiyonit ve'askaneiha] (Tel Aviv, 1939), 295.

[35] Arcadius Kahan, 'The University of Vilna', in id., *Essays in Jewish Social and Economic History*, 165–9: 165.

Polish–Lithuanian struggle for Vilnius, in the nationalistic atmosphere of inter-war Polish Wilno, the idea of a 'neutral' urban society was no more than a mirage. Moreover, relationships between different ethnic groups deteriorated rapidly, and, as Tomas Venclova wrote, 'all ethnic groups except the Poles were increasingly isolated and ousted to the fringes of society'.[36] Thus the struggle over the nature of the city became a constant point of contention. During the 1930s the fragile threads of the local social web gradually disintegrated, and the citizens of this 'Civitas Dei'—the Poles, the Lithuanians, the Belorussians, the Russians, and the Jews—all constituted their own old-new Vilnius/Wilno/Vilne/Vilna.

[36] Venclova, *Vilnius*, 59.

# Notes on Contributors

STEVEN E. ASCHHEIM holds the Vigevani Chair of European Studies at the Hebrew University of Jerusalem, and is presently director of the Franz Rosenzweig Research Centre for German-Jewish Literature and Cultural History. He is the author of several books, most recently *Culture and Catastrophe: German and Jewish Confrontations with National Socialism and Other Crises* (1996); *In Times of Crisis: Essays on European Culture, Germans and Jews* (2001); *Scholem, Arendt, Klemperer: Intimate Chronicles in Turbulent Times* (2001; also translated into Italian); and *Beyond the Border: The German-Jewish Legacy Abroad* (2007).

KAREN AUERBACH is an Applied Research Scholar in the Center for Advanced Holocaust Studies at the US Holocaust Memorial Museum in Washington, DC. She holds a doctorate in modern Jewish history from Brandeis University.

RICHARD I. COHEN holds the Paulette and Claude Kelman Chair in French Jewry Studies at the Hebrew University of Jerusalem. He is the author of *The Burden of Conscience: French Jewish Leadership during the Holocaust* (1987) and *Jewish Icons: Art and Society in Modern Europe* (1998). He has recently edited and introduced Raymond-Raoul Lambert, *Diary of a Witness, 1940–1943: The Ordeal of French Jews during the Holocaust* (2007) and *Image and Sound: Art, Music and History* (Hebrew; 2007); and, with Jeremy Cohen, he has co-edited *The Jewish Contribution to Civilization: Reassessing an Idea* (2008).

JONATHAN FRANKEL was the Saveli and Tamara Grinberg Professor of Modern Jewish History (Emeritus) in the Department of Russian and Slavic Studies and the Harman Institute of Contemporary Jewry at the Hebrew University of Jerusalem. His *Prophecy and Politics: Socialism, Nationalism, and the Russian Jews, 1862–1917* (1981) marked a turning point in modern Jewish historiography and was awarded a number of prestigious prizes. He is the author of *The Damascus Affair: 'Ritual Murder', Politics, and the Jews in 1840* (1997), and the editor of many books, including several volumes of *Studies in Contemporary Jewry*. He also published numerous works on modern Jewish politics, with an emphasis on the emergence of Jewish nationalism, the history of the Jews in tsarist and Soviet Russia, and Jewish historiography. An edition of his essays, *Crisis, Revolution, and Russian Jews*, was published by Cambridge University Press in 2009.

STEFANI HOFFMAN is the former director of the Mayrock Center for Russian, Eurasian, and East European Research at the Hebrew University of Jerusalem. She is currently involved in freelance research, editing, and translation on topics related to Russian Jewish history and society. She is co-editor, with Ezra Mendelsohn, of *The Revolution of 1905 and Russia's Jews* (2007) and, with Yitzhak Brudny and Jonathan Frankel, of *Restructuring Post-Communist Russia* (2004).

ZVI JAGENDORF is Professor Emeritus of English and Theatre at the Hebrew University of Jerusalem. He has written widely on Renaissance and modern drama, comedy, and modern European literature. His translations of Hebrew poetry have appeared in many journals, and his novel *Wolfy and the Strudelbakers* (2001) won the British Society of Authors Sagittarius Prize.

HILLEL J. KIEVAL is the Gloria M. Goldstein Professor of Jewish History and Thought and Chair of the Department of History at Washington University in St Louis. His research interests lie in the social and cultural history of the Jews in east-central Europe since the Enlightenment and in Jewish–non-Jewish inter-action and conflict. Among his publications are *The Making of Czech Jewry: National Conflict and Jewish Society in Bohemia, 1870–1918* (1988); *Languages of Community: The Jewish Experience in the Czech Lands* (2000); and *Blood Inscriptions: The 'Ritual Murder' Trial in Modern Europe* (forthcoming).

RACHEL MANEKIN is an assistant professor of Jewish history at the University of Maryland. She has written many articles on the social, political, and cultural history of Galician Jewry, and served as division editor on 'Galicia' for the *YIVO Encyclopedia of Jews in Eastern Europe*. She received her Ph.D. in Jewish history from the Hebrew University of Jerusalem and has been a fellow of the Herbert D. Katz Center for Advanced Judaic Studies at the University of Pennsylvania and a visiting scholar at the Institute for Advanced Studies at the Hebrew University.

AMITAI MENDELSOHN holds an MA in art history from the Hebrew University of Jerusalem, and is a doctoral student in art history at the Ben-Gurion University of the Negev. He is curator of Israeli art at the Israel Museum, Jerusalem. Exhibitions he has curated at the museum include 'Prophets and Visionaries: Reuven Rubin's Early Years, 1914–23' (2006), 'Landscapes of Longing: Avraham Ofek's Early and Late Works' (2007), and 'Real Time, Art in Israel: 1998–2008' (2008, in conjunction with celebrations for Israel's sixtieth anniversary).

JOANNA B. MICHLIC is director of the Project on Families, Children and the Holocaust at Hadassah-Brandeis Institute, Brandeis University. Until December 2008 she was an associate professor at the Department of History and Chair in Holocaust Studies and Ethical Values at Lehigh University, Bethlehem, Pennsylvania. Her major publications include *The Neighbors Respond: The Controversy over the Jedwabne Massacre in Poland* (2003; co-edited with Antony Polonsky) and *Poland's Threatening Other: The Image of the Jew from 1880 to the Present* (2006). She is currently working on two monographs, *The Social History of Jewish Children in Poland: Survival and Identity, 1945–1949* and *Bringing the Dark to Light: The Memory of the Holocaust in Postcommunist Europe* (the latter co-edited with John-Paul Himka).

ANTONY POLONSKY is Albert Abramson Professor of Holocaust Studies at Brandeis University and the United States Holocaust Memorial Museum. Until 1991 he was Professor of International History at the London School of Economics and Political Science. He is chair of the editorial board of *Polin: Studies in Polish Jewry*, author of *Politics in Independent Poland* (1972), *The Little Dictators* (1975), *The Great Powers and the Polish Question* (1976), and co-author of *A History of Modern*

*Poland* (1980) and *The Beginnings of Communist Rule in Poland* (1981). His most recent work is the three-volume *The Jews in Poland and Russia*, the first volume of which, covering the period 1350 to 1881, is due to appear in 2009.

DAVID RECHTER is University Research Lecturer in Oriental Studies at the University of Oxford, and Research Fellow in Modern Jewish History at St Antony's College, Oxford. He is the author of *The Jews of Vienna and the First World War* (2001) and is currently at work on a history of the Jews of Habsburg Bukovina.

SCOTT URY is a postdoctoral fellow in Tel Aviv University's Department of Jewish History. A book based on his dissertation, written at the Hebrew University and with the tentative title *Red Banner, Blue Star: The Revolution of 1905 and the Transformation of Warsaw Jewry*, is due to be published by Stanford University Press. He is also co-editing two volumes: *Jews and their Neighbors: Isolation, Confrontation, and Influence in Eastern Europe* (to be published as volume 24 of *Polin: Studies in Polish Jewry*) and *Cosmopolitanism, Nationalism, and the Jews of East Central Europe* (to be published as a double issue of the *European Review of History* in 2010). He has also published pieces in *Jewish Social Studies*, *Polin*, the *YIVO Encyclopedia of Jews in Eastern Europe*, and other academic forums.

LEON VOLOVICI received his Ph.D. from Jassy University, Romania. Settling in Israel in 1984, he worked between 1984 and 1990 in the Yad Vashem Archives, Jerusalem. Until his retirement in 2008 he was head of research and a board member at the Vidal Sassoon International Center for the Study of Antisemitism, at the Hebrew University of Jerusalem, and one of the series editors of ACTA (Analysis of Current Trends in Antisemitism), published by the Center. He has published *Nationalist Ideology and Antisemitism: The Case of Romanian Intellectuals in the 1930s* (1991), and many studies and essays on antisemitism in eastern Europe and on Jewish intellectual life in Romania. He has also edited the works of Romanian Jewish writers, among them the original Romanian version of Mihail Sebastian's *Journal*. He is the editor of Romanian Jewish history for the *YIVO Encyclopedia of Jews in Eastern Europe* (2008).

RUTH R. WISSE has taught Yiddish and comparative literature at Harvard University since 1993, and before that at McGill University. Her books include *A Little Love in Big Manhattan* (1988), *The Modern Jewish Canon: A Journey through Language and Culture* (2000), and *Jews and Power* (2007).

MORDECHAI ZALKIN is an associate professor at the Department of Jewish History at the Ben-Gurion University of the Negev. His research concentrates on social and cultural aspects of nineteenth-century east European Jewry, mainly in Lithuania. He is the author of *From Heder to School: Modernization Processes in Nineteenth-Century East European Jewish Education* (Hebrew; 2008) and *A New Dawn: The Jewish Enlightenment in the Russian Empire* (Hebrew; 2000), and editor of *The City of Vilna* (Hebrew; 2002).

# Index

# Index